BEGINNER'S GUIDE TO CHARACTER CREATION IN MAYA®

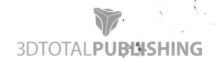

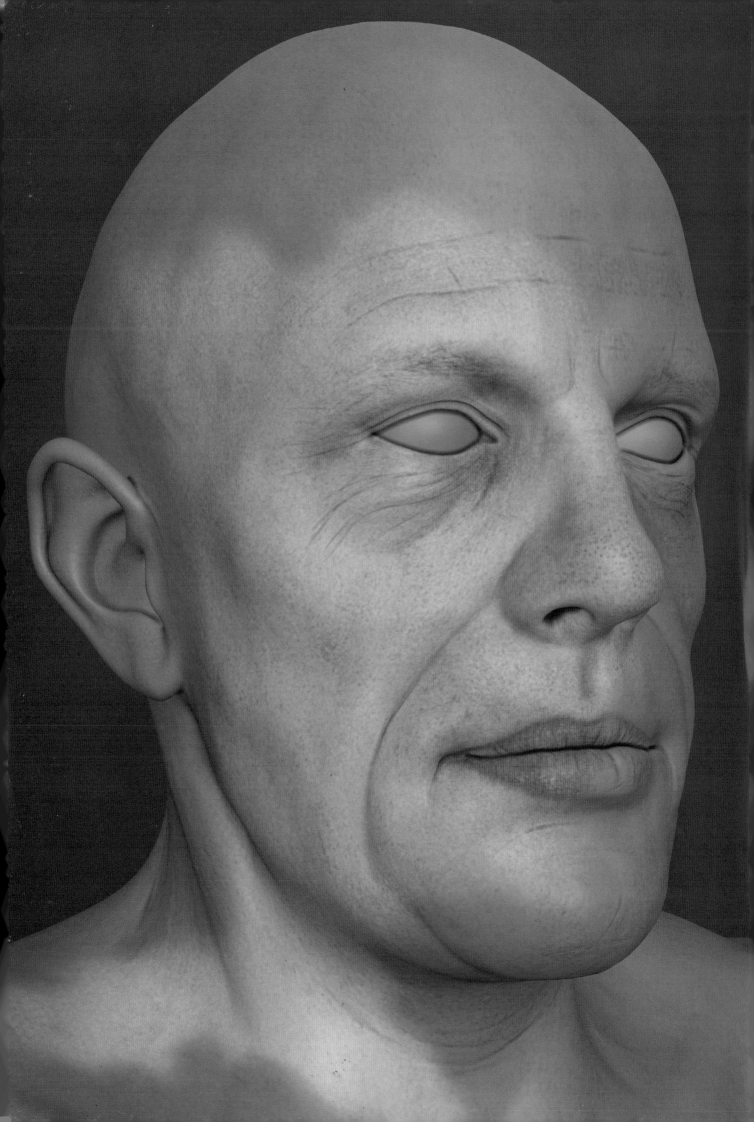

3DTOTAL PUBLISHING

Correspondence: publishing@3dtotal.com

Website: www.3dtotal.com

First published in the United Kingdom, 2015, by 3dtotal Publishing. 3dtotal.com Ltd, 29 Foregate Street, Worcester WR1 1DS, United Kingdom.

Soft cover ISBN: 978-1909414204

Printing and binding: Everbest Printing (China)

www.everbest.com

Visit **www.3dtotalpublishing.com** for a complete list of available book titles.

Junior editor: Marisa Lewis

Proofreader: Melanie Smith

Lead designer: Imogen Williams

Cover design: Matthew Lewis

Template designer: Aryan Pishneshin

Designers: Aryan Pishneshin, Cameron Dallimore

Managing editor: Lynette Clee

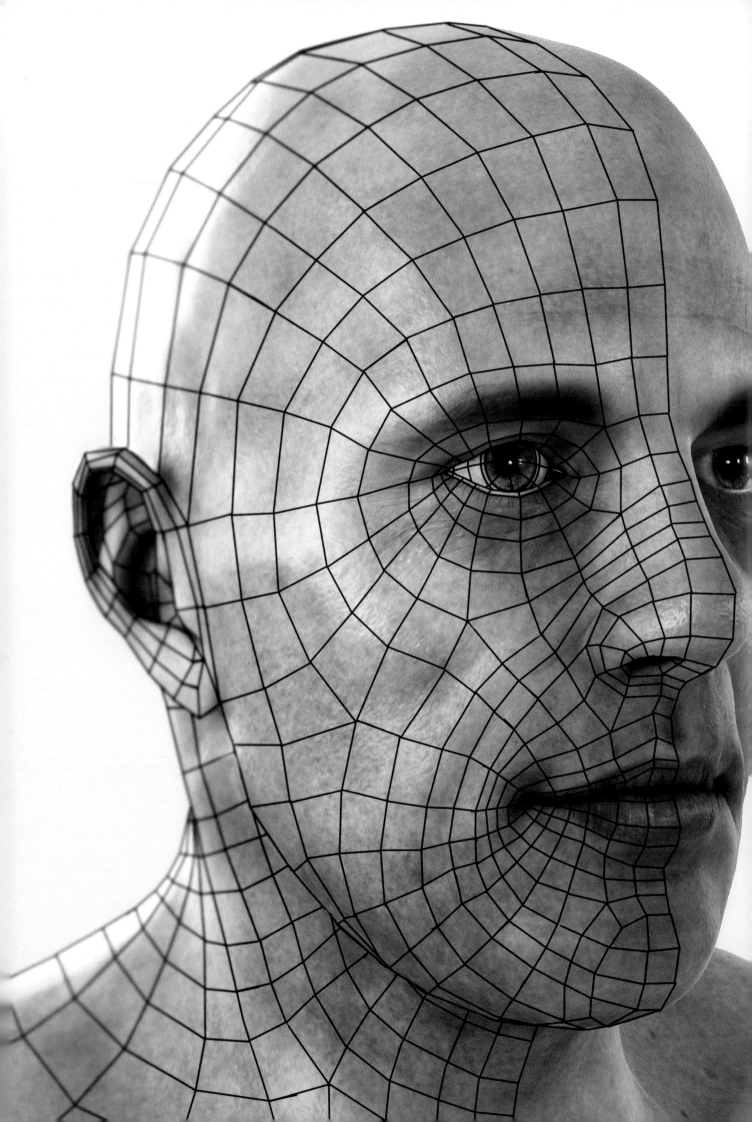

Contents

Introduction

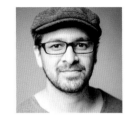

Hello and welcome to the book. If you're reading this as a beginner to CG animation, then hopefully you'll be excited to get started. However, the little geek in your head might be too hungry to hit the keyboard, press buttons, create something, make it move and, hey, maybe even get to blow it up! Please try to calm that little geek for a short while, as our approach in this book is a bit different.

What I want to do is take a small but essential step back before we even open Maya or your preferred package. Computer animation, whether it is hyperrealistic or totally fantastical, must be believable; the audience must be held or the illusion has not worked and we haven't done our job.

The key to this believability is the real-world basis for the work we do. At every stage of the CG pipeline, be it modeling, rigging, or animation, there's some study which needs to be done of the real-world background that should feed and inform your work. This is why the tech-hungry geek must be held at bay for just a while.

I'd like to explain this by considering the example of character creation. Say you're looking to create a CG human, much like the guy we're going to have made by the end of this book. What must precede key-hitting is some very keen observation of the human body: how light affects the skin; how we move; what we can see happening at skin-level when muscles contract and joints articulate.

We hope that this book will encourage you to start looking at people and at your environment in general with a new level of awareness. A CG torso must move in such a way that there is evidence of a rib cage lying beneath the skin, or the illusion is broken. What we need, therefore,

is an understanding of human anatomy and kinesiology, however rudimentary.

This is where the little geek in your head breathes a sigh of relief: he wanted to make a sewer-dwelling mutant anyway, so who needs human anatomy? Let's hit the keyboard! Sorry, but the same rules apply to fantastical characters. The general rule of thumb is that character work which is based on something known, either consciously or unconsciously, is far more likely to be accepted by an audience.

Let's take the example of Leatherback from *Pacific Rim*: its movement was informed by a study of gorillas. Similarly, the movement of Toothless from *How to Train Your Dragon* took ideas from a study of the motion of cats and bats. The forest vegetation from *Avatar* was inspired by marine life such as Christmas tree worms. There are countless examples which you, the audience, will have taken in either consciously or unconsciously.

Regardless of context, believability in CG depends on previous observation of the real, and this premise provides the foundations for this book. We will work together on one continuous project, creating a human male asset from start to finish, from a primitive shape in Maya to a fully lit and rendered animated character.

Each section concerning the CG pipeline will be divided into two parts. The

first (signified by a light bulb icon) will be an exploration of the real-world examples that will inform the technical creation to follow second (signified by a mouse icon). For example: section 02, which deals with modeling, will be prefaced by an overview of human anatomy, and section 04, which focuses on rigging, will look firstly at the mechanics of motion.

This does not mean there will be any less attention paid to developing technical expertise in the 3D package of your choice. Quite the contrary: the videos accompanying the book are to be used alongside the steps in each section, as they add essential technical information as well as tips and tricks you wouldn't be without. Readers will gain core skills which will remain strong regardless of the package they choose.

In this book we will use predominantly Maya and Mudbox, but the skills gained, because they are the true fundamentals of CG, will be transferable, and all the more useful for being so. Through this, we'll endeavor to keep the geek on your one shoulder and the artist on your other in enduring, contented balance.

Jahirul Amin

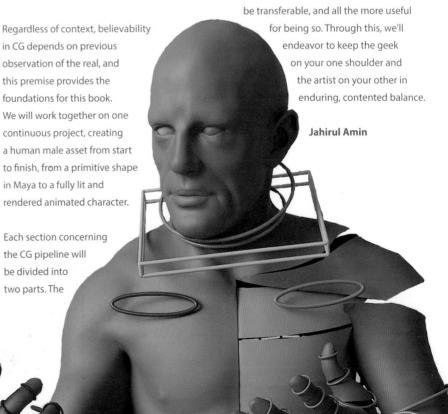

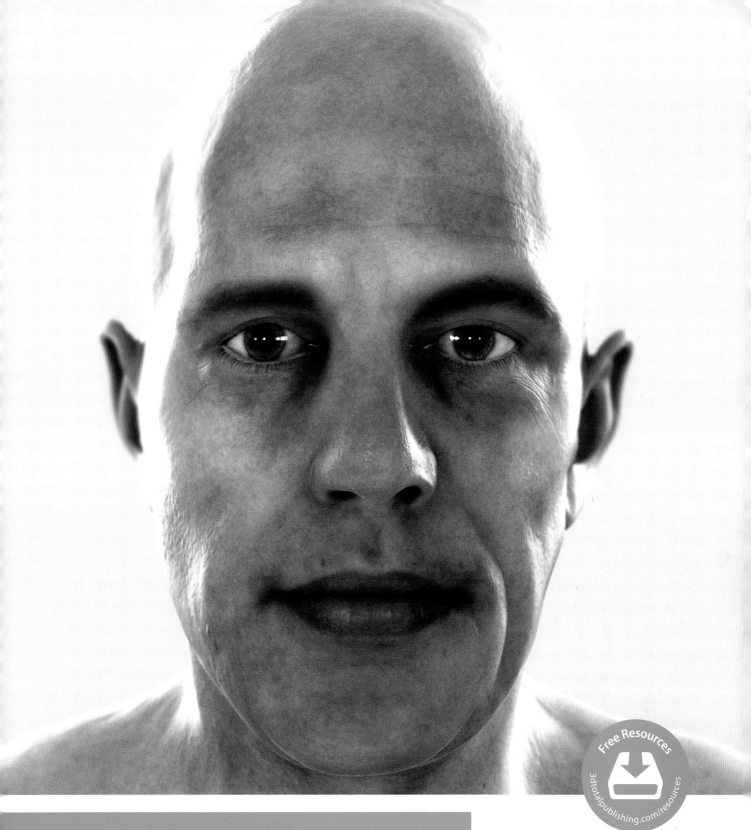

Free Resources

3dtotalpublishing.com/resources

Meet the artist

Jahirul Amin is a 3D Trainer at Double Negative in London, UK. Prior to this, he was an Associate Lecturer at the prestigious National Centre for Computer Animation at Bournemouth University, where he was responsible for the Maya input on both the bachelor's and master's degree courses for several years.

Having taught Maya to students and professionals alike for a number of years, he is perfectly placed to lead an in-depth book for beginners dedicated to character creation. His lessons are always thoughtfully written, with helpful tips and video guides that ensure a quality learning experience for every student.

Free resources

To show the software in action and help you get the most out this book, Jahirul has provided videos, documents, and files to accompany many of the practical sections.

Chapters with a companion video are marked with a blue download icon. Visit the book's resource page at **www.3dtotalpublishing.com/ resources** to download your extra content!

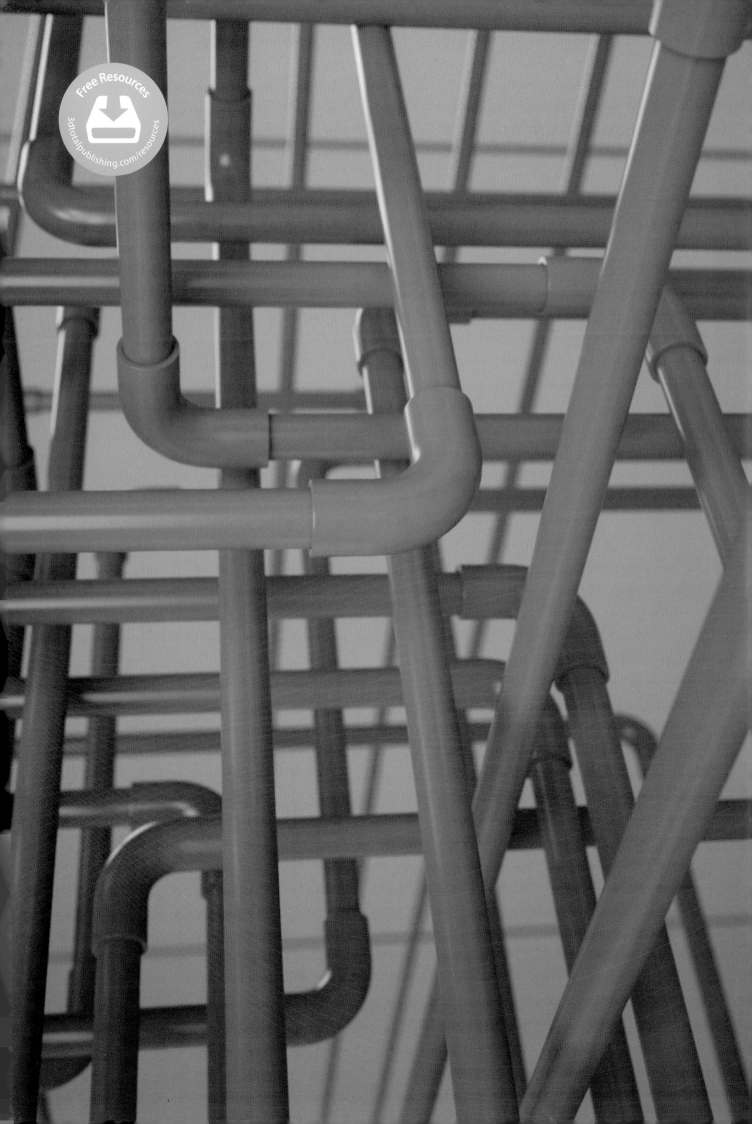

Pipeline and interface

Planning a workflow and getting to know your tools

In the opening section of this book, we'll be laying the important groundwork for your Maya project. Whether you're working by yourself or as part of a team, knowing how to plan ahead is invaluable: it's good professional practice and will also save you from tearing your hair out later! We'll be breaking tasks down into a simple pipeline that will help you streamline your work and use your time wisely. This section will also walk you through the fundamentals of Maya and Mudbox, covering the essential menus, tools, and shortcuts you need to get your project off the ground.

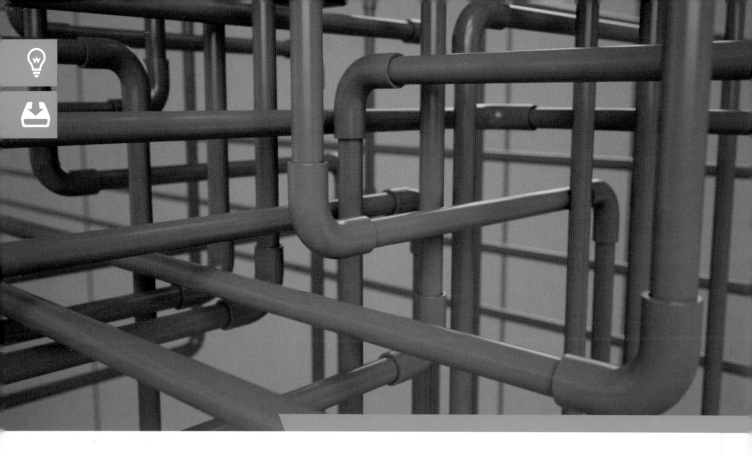

Introduction to the digital pipeline

Pipeline example and workflow diagram

This first section will lay the digital groundwork for our work ahead. We'll begin with an overview of a digital pipeline and see how it can be used to our advantage. There will be introductions to the interfaces of Maya and Mudbox. Then we'll see how the pipeline works in Maya, using a simplified example to demonstrate how an asset can be taken from start to finish. Finally, we'll create a new Maya Project to set ourselves up for the task ahead.

"There is no one-pipeline-fits-all scenario"

Before we jump in and start creating models, rigs, textures and so on, we should spend time setting up a system that allows us to keep track of all this digital data, maintain the upstream and downstream of assets from modeling to rendering, and – most importantly – make sure that we're working

with the most up-to-date files. We'll refer to this as the digital pipeline (**Fig.01**).

Although this pipeline will be pretty generic and transferable to other projects, we want to make it customizable so it doesn't restrict our work. I've broken it down into sections, which I'll refer to from now on as "departments". They are Concept, Modeling and Sculpting, UVs, Texturing, Rigging, Animation, Look Development, Lighting, Rendering, Sound and Edit, and then Print (image or sequence).

It's important to emphasize that there is no one-pipeline-fits-all scenario, and that the breakdown of the departments doesn't have to be as segmented as my flowchart suggests. A modeling artist may also create the UVs, and also be responsible for creating the textures and the high-resolution sculpt. A lighter may also be responsible for rendering out the passes used for compositing, and so on.

Getting as many departments as possible up and running simultaneously is more important than working in a linear fashion. This may not be so pressing when working as an individual, but it becomes vital when working in a group. You don't want to be a lighter and be told you'll have just two days to light a scene because the assets won't be ready on time. What you want is the most up-to-date file; this may not be the final file, but it'll allow you to get started. This is what having a working pipeline allows.

Although for this project I will be taking the asset from start to finish as an individual, I'll be instilling the workings of a pipeline, allowing me to have flexibility as I carry the asset through. For example, I may find during the rigging phase that the model needs updating, or I may be animating and need to add an extra feature to the rig. Using the workings of a pipeline, I can go back and forth between the departments more easily without losing any of my current work. Another positive of the pipeline is ensuring that the work you do is fit for purpose. Early on in the rigging process, for example, your work to date can be checked over by the animators, who can feed back to you with potential changes. This kind of communication allows for problems to be solved early, with the minimum loss of time and energy. Individuals also get a greater sense of their role within the team, and the adage that "the whole is greater than the sum of its parts" becomes very much the case.

How this all works is a process known as Publishing and Referencing. "Publishing" is the release of the most up-to-date asset, which is overwritten constantly as progress is made. This asset is called in by another department, a process which is termed "Referencing". As the Published file is constantly overwritten, the department(s) that Reference the file will be assured that they are working with the most recent asset. I'll give an example of this towards the end of the section before we start our project.

Next, I want to talk about one of the most important but often ignored factors that will help to streamline your (or your team's) work: consistency. What I mean by consistency in

this context is very simple: before we start, we need to lay down some ground rules and conventions, allowing the assets that we carry through the pipeline to be easily recognizable and in the correct working order.

"Don't be lazy, don't tell yourself you'll do it later – do it now"

Here are some of the ground rules I apply to my work and will be following throughout this project. Firstly, and very importantly, is naming: every model, texture, joint, locator, and so on will have a name. As a trainer, one thing I absolutely cannot stand is being asked to problem-solve someone else's file and opening it up to find that they have 50-plus nameless locators. You ask them what this does, or what that is, and they have no clue. Usually, I send them off to rename everything and then come back, and during this process they fix the problem by themselves. So don't be lazy, don't tell yourself you'll do it later – do it now. You create something, you name it. Job done.

Secondly, still related to naming, is establishing a naming convention. Again, this is to add clarity to our scene files and make it easier for others to help if we need them to. Using a naming convention also

allows us to quickly spot a joint from a light, a locator from an IK handle, and so on.

Finally, setting and working to a scale will play a huge role if we are to light and shade our scenes with realism in mind. Energy-conserving materials and plausible lighting all work best when working with real-world units, but that's not to say we can't bend or even break this format, especially when working with a more stylized look in mind. By default, Maya is set to work in centimeters, although there some attributes are set to inches or meters. Where these occur, I'll point them out. We can take advantage of the Measure tool in Maya and Caliper tool in Mudbox to keep everything lined up. Later on, I'll present some measurements taken from the photo-shoot and model that should help in the process of setting up our reference images in Maya, and aiding the sculpting process in Mudbox.

In terms of software, I'll be using Maya 2015 (Service Pack 2), Mudbox 2015, Photoshop CS6, and NUKE, but there's no reason why you can't replace these with your preferred package. One of the main objectives in this book is to provide you, the reader, with transferable skills.

Alright, I have now stepped down from my soapbox and we are ready to rock and roll.

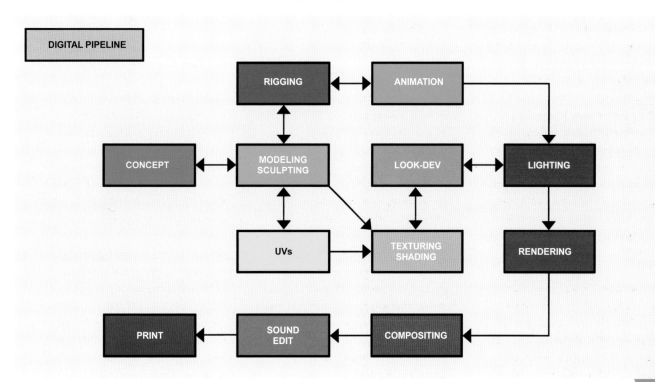

The departments of our digital pipeline, and how they interact

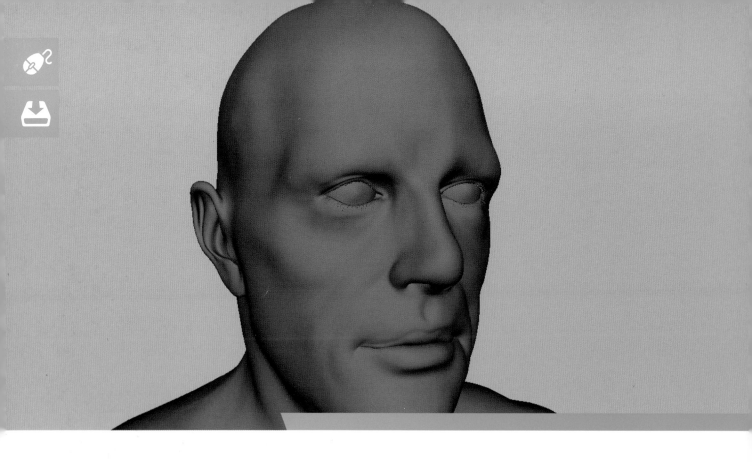

Introduction to the Maya interface

Getting to know the Maya user interface

When you first open Maya, things can feel a little overwhelming. To help calm your nerves, we are going to break the user interface (UI) down into manageable chunks.

There's just one proviso before we start, though: throughout this project I will be showing you my preferred techniques. I can't stress highly enough, however, that it is always possible to approach any one task in a number of ways. Please don't be afraid to press a few buttons and find your own way to navigate around the software.

01: The Maya interface

When first opening Maya, you will see what has been reproduced in **Fig.01**. Here's a quick breakdown of the highlighted regions, as marked out in the image:

A: Main menu bar
B: Status bar
C: Shelf (Shelves) bar
D: Viewport panel bar
E: Toolbox
F: Window configuration options
G: Timeline and Playback controls
H: Time Range and Character Sets
I: Command line and Script Editor
J: Channel Box
K: Layer Editor

The majority of the menus have dotted lines running alongside them, enabling you to tear off the menu and reposition it as you like, or leave it free-floating.

As the Qt framework (a framework used for developing applications) is the basis for Maya's interface, it is very easily customized. If you find that you want to take your menus that step further, you can use the Qt designer to create your own custom UI. We won't go into that here, however.

> "To get comfortable in any 3D software, you will need to learn how to navigate around the program's 2D and 3D spaces"

02: Navigation and viewport layout

To get comfortable in any 3D software, you will need to learn how to navigate around the program's 2D and 3D spaces. In Maya, it's all about using the Alt key with a combination of one of the three mouse keys, as described below (see also **Fig.02a**):

- To rotate the camera, use Alt+left mouse button (LMB).

- To track the camera, use Alt+middle mouse button (MMB).

- To zoom in and out, hold Alt+right mouse button (RMB).

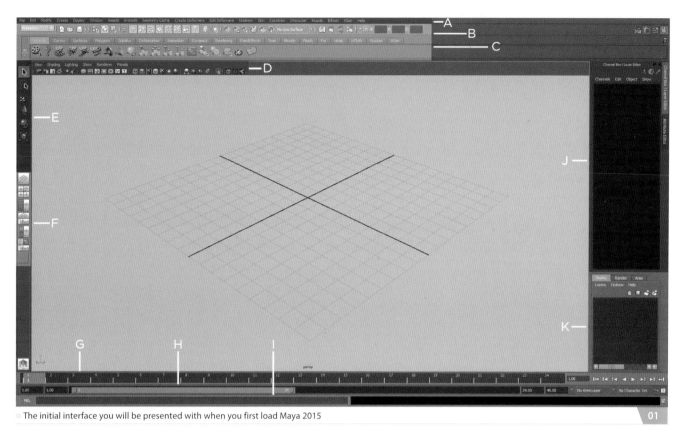

○ The initial interface you will be presented with when you first load Maya 2015 `01`

You can also scroll the MMB up and down to zoom in and out. You'll notice that in Perspective view, you are able to use all three types of movement, while in the Orthographic views (top, side and front), you are restricted to just track and zoom.

Another couple of useful keyboard shortcuts are the bracket keys ([and]), which allow you to undo and redo camera moves in Maya. When navigating in windows such as the Graph Editor or Hypershade, these same settings will also apply.

In addition, you can maximize and minimize the viewports by tapping the keyboard spacebar in any of them (see **Fig.02b** on the next page), allowing you to jump quickly from a maximized viewport to a four-pane viewport.

You can also use any of the predefined layout settings from the Window configuration menu set to suit the task in hand.

03: The menu bar, status bar, and hotbox

Back to the interface: the menu bar at the top of the UI will have all your general tools, such as Save and Save As under File, and Undo and

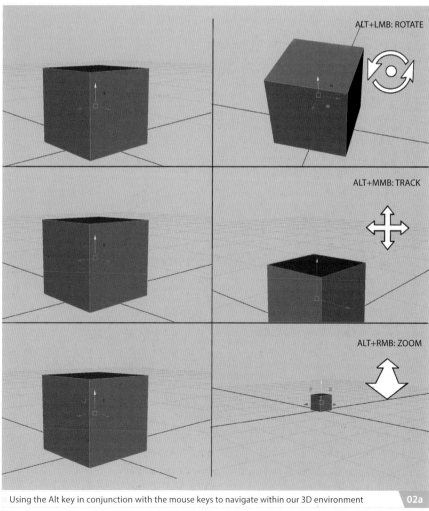

○ Using the Alt key in conjunction with the mouse keys to navigate within our 3D environment `02a`

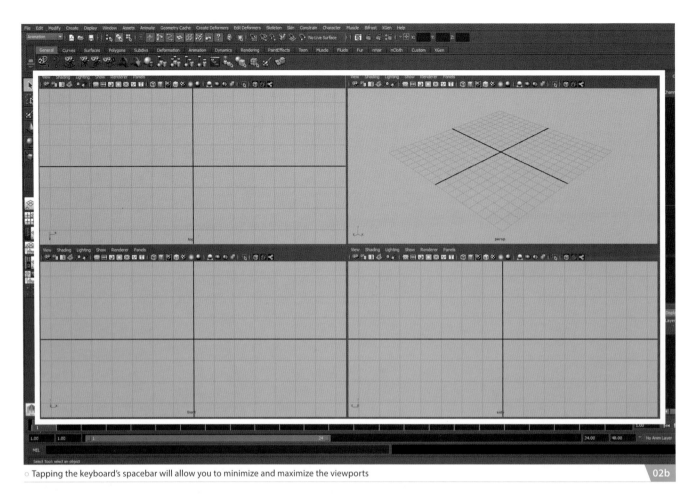

o Tapping the keyboard's spacebar will allow you to minimize and maximize the viewports

02b

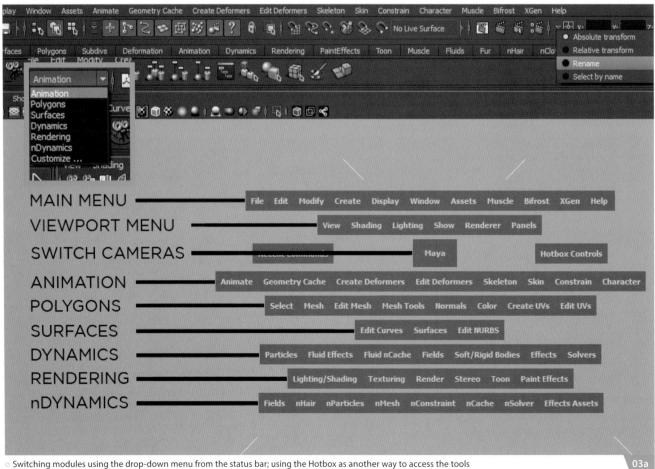

MAIN MENU ——————— File Edit Modify Create Display Window Assets Muscle Bifrost XGen Help

VIEWPORT MENU ——————— View Shading Lighting Show Renderer Panels

SWITCH CAMERAS ——————— Maya Hotbox Controls

ANIMATION ——————— Animate Geometry Cache Create Deformers Edit Deformers Skeleton Skin Constrain Character

POLYGONS ——————— Select Mesh Edit Mesh Mesh Tools Normals Color Create UVs Edit UVs

SURFACES ——————— Edit Curves Surfaces Edit NURBS

DYNAMICS ——————— Particles Fluid Effects Fluid nCache Fields Soft/Rigid Bodies Effects Solvers

RENDERING ——————— Lighting/Shading Texturing Render Stereo Toon Paint Effects

nDYNAMICS ——————— Fields nHair nParticles nMesh nConstraint nCache nSolver Effects Assets

o Switching modules using the drop-down menu from the status bar; using the Hotbox as another way to access the tools

03a

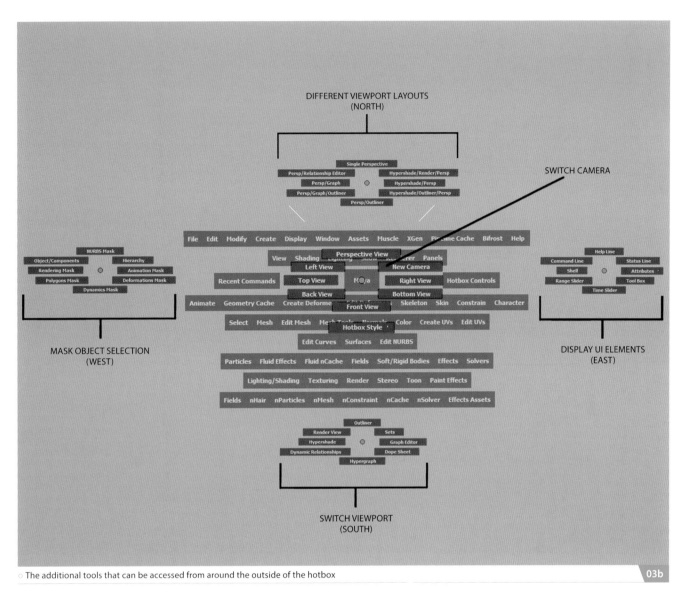

○ The additional tools that can be accessed from around the outside of the hotbox   03b

Redo under Edit. Just underneath the menu bar you will see a drop-down menu (Fig.03a) where you can change to working in a different module within Maya. The modules are:

• Animation
• Polygons
• Surfaces
• Dynamics
• Rendering
• nDynamics
• Customize

As you work, you will find that you switch constantly between the above modules in accordance with the task you are working on. (You can use the keyboard's F2 to F6 keys to switch between the modules.) The menu bar will automatically alter as you switch between modules in order to provide you with the tools you require.

"There are many ways to get to the same tool in Maya, so I won't preach about which is best"

The hotbox is another way to access menus, providing you with all the tools from every module at once. To select the desired tool, hover over one of the menus and hold down any one of the mouse buttons.

If you click and hold down the LMB in the center of the hotbox, you will be able to change the view of the current viewport without having to jump into a four-pane view and back again.

Holding down the LMB around the hotbox will also reveal four further sets of tools, which we'll refer to as North, East, South, and West (Fig.03b). To the North of the hotbox, you'll find a selection of different viewport layouts

to pick from. On the East side, you can show and hide parts of the UI. The South side will switch your current view to the selected view mode. Finally, to the West, you can mask what object types can and cannot be selected.

As you can see, there are many ways to get to the same tool in Maya, so I won't preach about which is best. Simply work in the manner that suits you.

If I had to share my preferred method, it would be to use the main menu bar in combination with marking menus (pop-up menus that allow for quick access to specific tools).

04: Toolbox, tool settings, and manipulator
The basic tools that you will be using are the selection tools and transformation tools. In the top half of the Toolbox, you have the

17

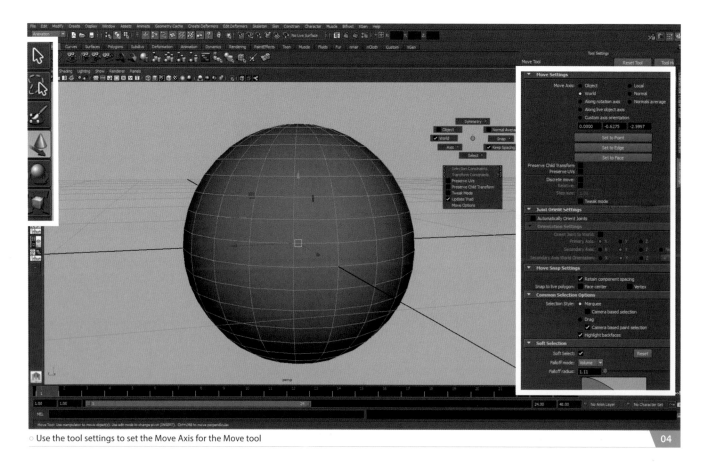

○ Use the tool settings to set the Move Axis for the Move tool   04

general Select tool (keyboard shortcut: Q) and, working downwards, you have the Lasso tool and Paint Selection tool (refer to the left-hand side of **Fig.04**). Below them, you have the Move, Rotate, and Scale tools (keyboard shortcuts: W, E, and R, respectively).

You can double-click any of the tools to bring up the settings for that tool, which is useful for many reasons, such as switching between working in world or local mode.

A useful shortcut is to hold down the keyboard shortcut button and LMB to bring up a small marking menu to edit the tool's settings. For example holding down W+LMB will allow you to edit the Move tool settings.

As you work, you might find that the manipulator (the yellow box with axis arrows you can see in **Fig.04**, used to help orient objects) is either too large or too small. To adjust this, use the keyboard's + and – keys to increase and decrease its size.

"It's very important to keep your scenes clean, and the Outliner is one of the quickest places to do so"

05: Outliner, Channel Box, and Attribute Editor

You will be spending a lot of time in these three windows so this is a quick breakdown of where to find them and what they do.

To access the Attribute Editor or the Channel Box, hit Ctrl+A. This will switch between the two menus unless you customize your scene and have both in view.

The Channel Box will allow you to edit parameters for a selected object, such as its position, orientation, and scale. If you add any custom parameters to an object, they will also pop up here.

The Attribute Editor is similar, but reveals many more parameters as well as the object's material properties.

The Outliner can be found in the Window configuration tool set (third icon down; refer to back to **Fig.01**) or in the menu bar under Window > Outliner. It reveals what's in your Maya scene file and is one of many places from which you can organize your scene, as well as perform parenting, renaming, and selection tasks. It's very important to

keep your scenes clean, and the Outliner is one of the quickest places to do so.

Other windows that we will be delving in and out of on a regular basis include Hypershade, the Node Editor, and Hypergraph: Hierarchy. You'll find all these windows under Window. Like the many ways in which you can access the tools, the same goes for making connections.

"This is the time to get to know your new best friend: play around a little and familiarize yourself with it before trying to embark on too serious an undertaking"

For now though, try opening up a few of the windows and creating a few primitive objects. Have a closer look at how things are connected and the attributes that these objects start off with.

This is the time to get to know your new best friend: play around a little and familiarize yourself with it before trying to embark on too serious an undertaking. We will deal with the more specific tools in their corresponding chapters.

🔍 PRO TIP

Press all the buttons

Before you dive in and begin to work on the main project, I strongly suggest that you get into Maya and Mudbox and start pressing the buttons to see what happens. Don't read any manuals yet, just press each button and let things happen. I find it's a good way to loosen up and let the software know that you are in charge of it, and not the other way around. If things start to explode and get angry, we can simply recreate the default settings.

To recreate the default settings on a Windows machine, pop into your My Documents folder (C:\Users\name\Documents\) and go to Maya > 2015-x64. In here you will find the prefs directory. By re-creating this directory we can restore Maya to its default settings. Rather than deleting

this file, I simply rename it to back it up; then reload Maya and you'll notice that a new prefs directory is automatically re-created.

Sometimes you'll find Maya can be a little temperamental. One way to help relieve this is to delete the userPrefs.mel file, found in the prefs folder. Again, Maya will rebuild this when you restart the package. You can also do the same for Mudbox by renaming the data and settings directories in My Documents and reloading Mudbox to rebuild a fresh environment.

If you are using a Mac, you will need to navigate to the following location to make the changes:
/Users/name/Library/Preferences/Autodesk/maya/2015-x64/prefs/

On Linux, you will need to navigate to the following location to make the changes:
/home/name/maya/2015-x64/prefs/

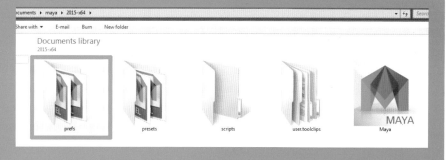

○ If things go a little awry, rebuild the default settings by recreating the preferences ("prefs") folder

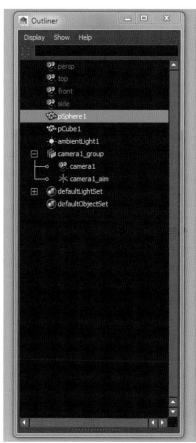
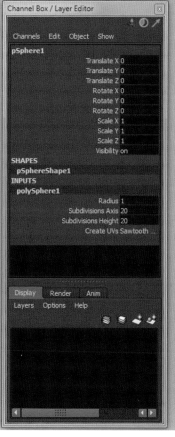
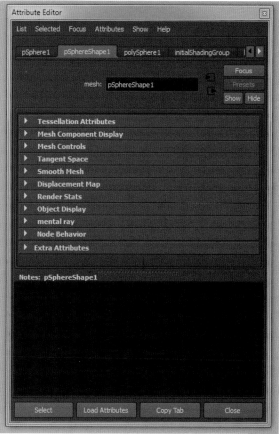

○ The Outliner, Channel Box, and Attribute Editor

05

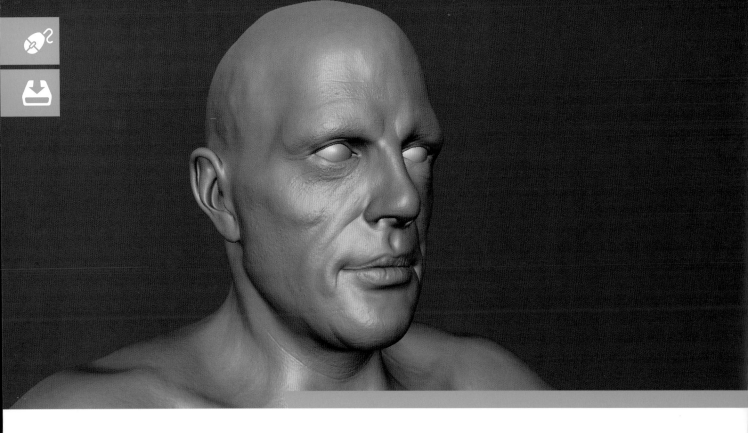

Introduction to the Mudbox interface

Getting to know the Mudbox UI

In comparison with the oh-so-many windows of Maya, Mudbox is very stripped down. Let's take some time to familiarize ourselves with the Mudbox environment.

01: The Mudbox interface
When you load Mudbox, you'll be asked to start a new sculpture or open a file. Once you have a model loaded, you should see a graphical user interface (GUI) as in **Fig.01**. Here's a breakdown of the regions highlighted in the image:

A: Main menu bar
B: Viewport tabs
C: Sculpt, Paint, Curve, Pose, and
   Select/Move tools
D: Stamp, Stencil, Material, and Lighting Presets
E: Layers, Object List, and Viewport Filters
F: Tool properties

You'll find the usual Save, Load, and Export tools as you would in most packages

in the main menu bar, along with a heap of tools that we'll come back to as we progress through the project.

> "Once you're familiar with navigating in one package, you should find it a breeze to navigate in the other"

One thing I recommend you do now is go to Windows > Preferences and open up the Render tab. Now change Render Selected to By Face as opposed to By Vertex. You will find that this will make it easier to select parts of the mesh later on.

Like Maya, you can also customize the Mudbox environment by dragging the menu windows from the dotted lines and dropping them somewhere else. By default, this ability is locked in Mudbox 2015, so go to Windows and disable Lock Layout.

02: Navigating in Mudbox
One of the benefits of using a combination of Maya and Mudbox is that navigation is handled exactly the same way in both packages. Therefore once you're familiar with navigating in one package, you should find it a breeze to navigate in the other.

In both packages, you can also use the keyboard shortcut A to frame all the objects in the scene, and F to frame the selected object in the scene.

03: Sculpt, Paint, and
Select/Move tools
The Sculpt and Paint tools will be our primary tools while in Mudbox. Here you'll find a range of brushes that are easily customizable to create an infinite amount of different effects, from building up major forms to adding finer details.

A useful shortcut to switch between the different tools is to use the keyboard number

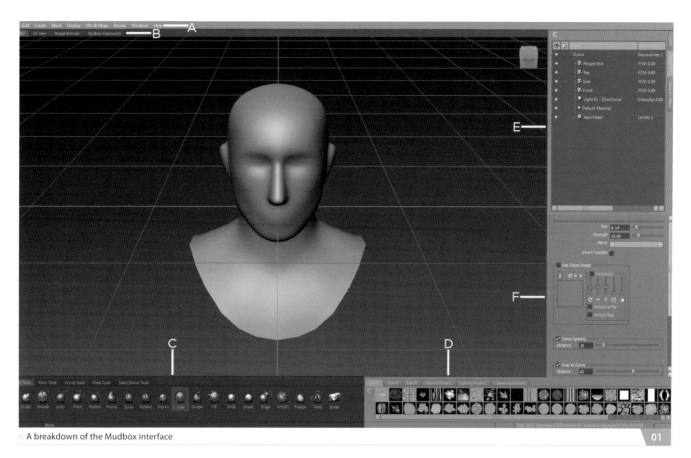

A breakdown of the Mudbox interface

01

"The Caliper tool allows you to make quick measurements on the model. It's really useful if you are trying to match your geometry with a real-world asset"

pad. Using the keys from 1–9, you can switch between the tools. You can also re-adjust the position of the tools by using the MMB to drag and drop within the menu.

A new tool added to the 2015 version of Mudbox is the Caliper tool, which you'll find under the Select/Move Tools tab. This allows you to make quick measurements on the model. It's really useful if you are trying to match your geometry with a real-world asset.

04: Stamps and stencils

To add texture to your brushes, you can use the Stamps tab. In a way, this attaches an image to the end of your brush.

Stencils, on the other hand, allow you to project detail through an image onto the model. This is a great way to add finer

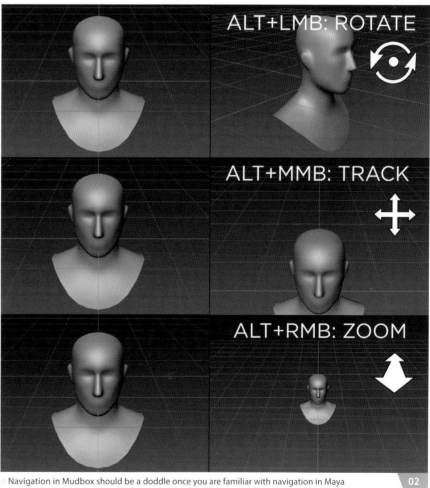

Navigation in Mudbox should be a doddle once you are familiar with navigation in Maya

02

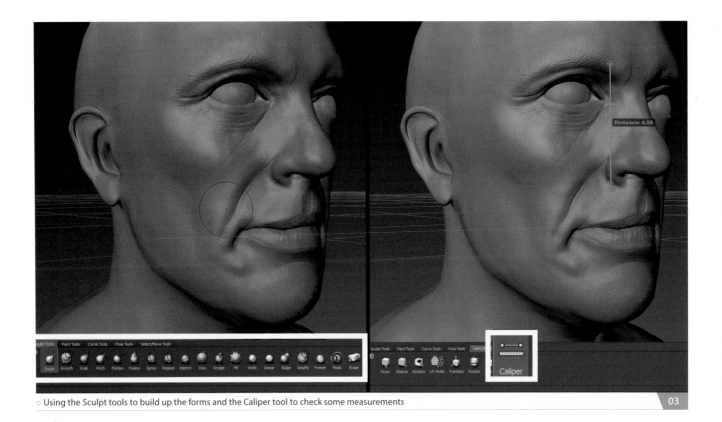

○ Using the Sculpt tools to build up the forms and the Caliper tool to check some measurements

03

details such as skin pores onto a mesh, You can also easily add your own Stamps or Stencils to help refine your models.

Note that as you select different tools in Mudbox and when you sculpt on different meshes in the scene, the tool

properties and Layers menus will provide you with the parameters and information for the selected object or tool.

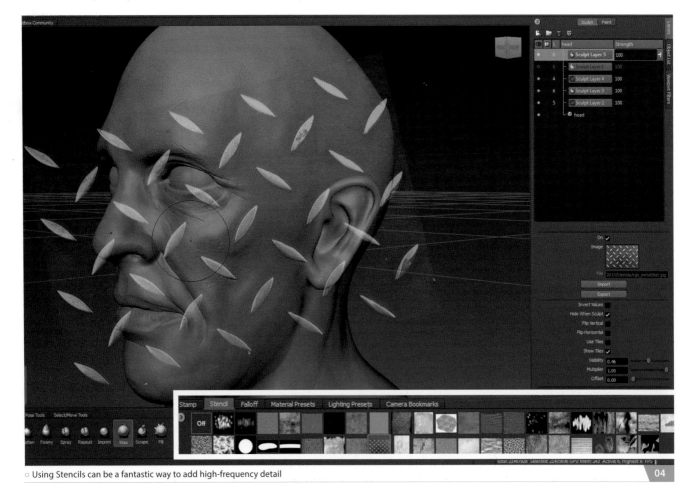

○ Using Stencils can be a fantastic way to add high-frequency detail

04

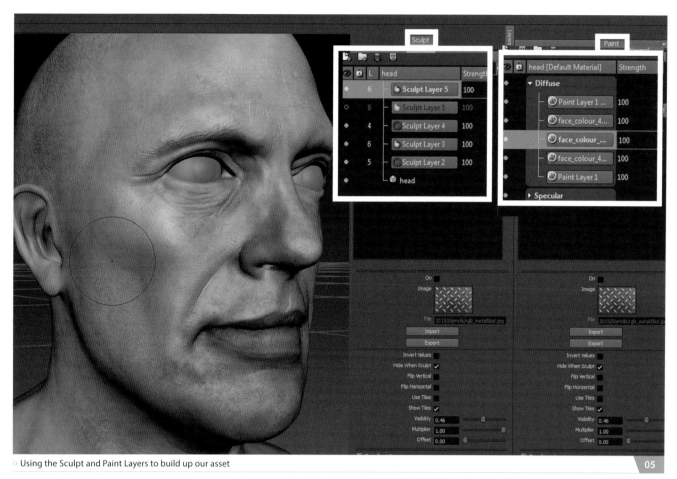

○ Using the Sculpt and Paint Layers to build up our asset

05

Alongside the Stamp and Stencils tabs, you also have the Falloff tab. The Falloff determines the behavior of your stroke, allowing you to create strokes that are very soft or strokes that are very hard and sharp.

"I urge you to load up one of the default Mudbox meshes and have a good play with all the tools"

Then you have the Material and the Lighting Presets, followed by the Camera Bookmarks. We'll use these once we start modeling, but feel free to have a little play with them now. In fact, I urge you to load up one of the default Mudbox meshes and have a good play with all the tools to better familiarize yourself with what can be achieved.

05: Sculpt and Paint Layers
Using the Sculpt and Paint Layers in Mudbox allows you to manage your process in the same way you would build up an image in a package like Photoshop. For example you could sculpt the major primary forms on one layer and then the high-frequency details on another layer.

By working in this manner, you can very easily decrease the amount of influence that a layer has over the overall sculpt, or conversely crank it up. It's a great way to work because it's non-destructive and allows you to be more flexible in your approach, as opposed to using a standard undo/redo workflow.

Paint Layers in Mudbox is also akin to the layers system in Photoshop in that you have a range of blending modes to aid in the creation of your textures.

06: Switching camera views
Mudbox also allows you to switch between a Perspective camera and the usual Orthographic cameras. You can find a list of these cameras in the Object List window.

If you select any of the cameras, you can set the field of view (FOV), the Near Plane, Far Plane, and so on, to your liking. This is very useful when trying to line up a photograph to a sculpt. Later on, we'll be handling this in Maya, but if we need to update any cameras, we can also do so here without having to go back and forth between the packages.

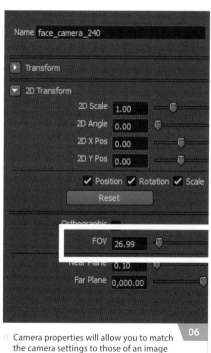

○ Camera properties will allow you to match the camera settings to those of an image

06

We'll leave Mudbox here for now, as we'll be delving deeper in the relevant chapters, but I really do recommend that you spend a bit of time just playing with the tools and settings.

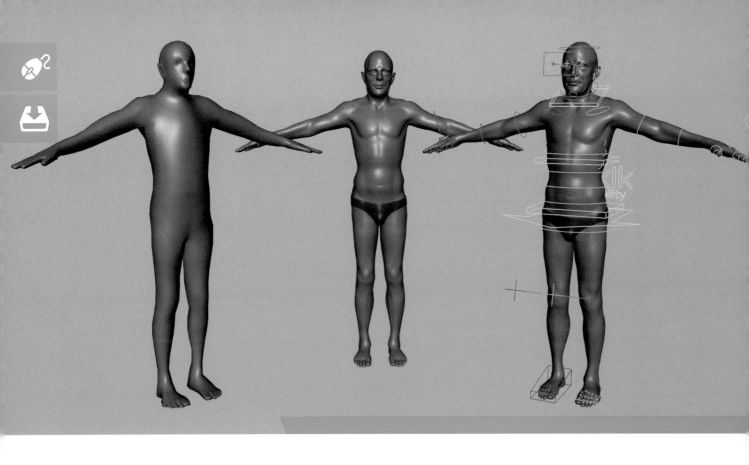

How the pipeline works

Publishing and Referencing an asset as part of the digital pipeline

Now I'd like to demonstrate how we'll be approaching our project using a pipeline workflow, getting the modeling and rigging departments up and running at the same time. This will implement the publishing and Referencing system we explored previously, keeping an asset updated so we don't end up working with old files. The files used for this example have been supplied for you in a Maya directory called "pipeline_demo".

01: Modeling and publishing the asset

We'll start by popping on our modeling hat. The first thing we need is a model. In this case, I've roughly blocked out the proportions of what would become the final mesh using very primitive shapes.

With the proportions of the character locked down, we can actually pass this asset on to the rigging department to start blocking out joint placements for the rig. It's important to remember that this is just a work-in-progress asset model that will be constantly updated.

First, I go to File > Save Scene As to save a local copy (mod_wip1.ma) so I can refer back to it and continue to develop the model. Then I will save the same file in a PUBLISHED directory (**mod_PUBLISHED.ma**), ready for other departments to use. This will be the single file that we'll constantly overwrite as

the model is updated, so all departments are calling in the most up-to-date asset.

02: Referencing the asset

Now let's presume we're in the rigging department and we've been informed that a model has been prepared and is available for

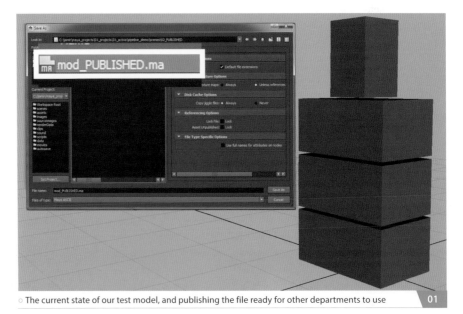

○ The current state of our test model, and publishing the file ready for other departments to use **01**

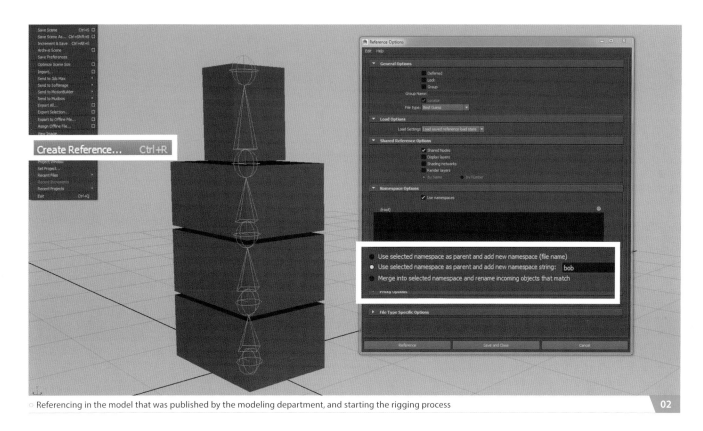

○ Referencing in the model that was published by the modeling department, and starting the rigging process 　　02

us to start working on. In a new Maya scene file (Ctrl+N), I go to File > Create Reference (Options – the square box) to bring up the Reference Options box. I like to give a custom namespace to the scene file we're calling in so that it doesn't clash with other assets in the scene. Usually this will be the asset's name; in this case, I've called it 'bob'.

If you now open up the Outliner (Window > Outliner), you'll notice some blue diamonds by the objects we've called in, indicating that they are Referenced objects. You'll also notice that you can't delete the objects using the keyboard's Delete key. To remove the Referenced file, you will need to go to File > Reference Editor and do so within this window.

Although the model is at a very primitive stage, the rigger can get a good idea of the proportions and start to create a skeleton for the rig. It's important to note that should the proportions of the model change drastically (for example if the length of the torso is increased), this will have major consequences for the rigger.

Therefore, it is very important that the scale and proportions of the character are determined early on. Working within a pipeline, especially when part of a team, requires everyone to

sing from the same hymn sheet, and the only way to do that is to communicate.

Now save this scene file locally (**rig_wip1. ma**). Let's pop back into the modeling department. We know that this is not the final model, so by referencing this file, any changes that are made to the model will automatically update the rig scene file.

03: Making modeling updates

Pop your modeling cap back on and load the scene file, **mod_wip1.ma**. We continue

to develop the model by creating a single unified mesh using the modeling tools in Maya. I've performed some simple extrudes and introduced some edge loops, both of which we'll examine in the next section (pages 58–59). I've also renamed the mesh **bob_geo**. You'll notice that I've kept the same proportions as I did during the blocking phase (**Fig.03**).

With the next iteration of the still-incomplete model ready to go, I again save a local copy (**mod_wip2.ma**) and then overwrite the Published file (**mod_PUBLISHED.ma**) with

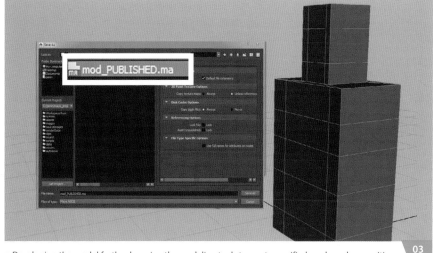

○ Developing the model further by using the modeling tools to create a unified mesh, and overwriting the published model file 　　03

PRO TIP
Creating assets

Another way to control the upstream and downstream of your assets in Maya is to actually use the Assets tools. This gives you a wider range of tools to organize your models, rigs, and so on, which will then be contained within an asset node. Through the asset node, you can use encapsulation to hide information and attributes you don't wish others to see. It's a great way to minimize the chances of your asset being accidentally tampered with because it progresses through the pipeline. It's overkill for this particular project, as I'll be handling the asset from start to finish as an individual, but it's something to bear in mind for future reference if you become part of a team.

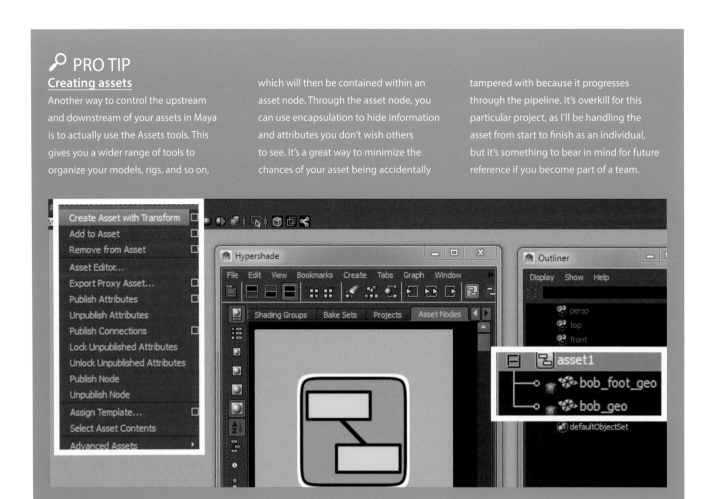

○ Using the Asset tools to prepare assets before publishing

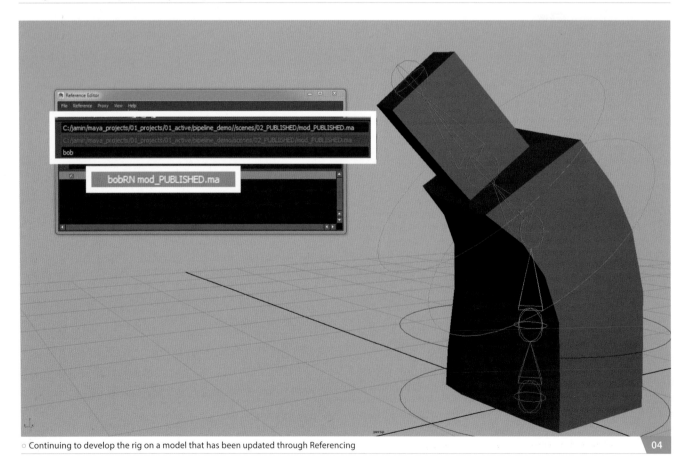

○ Continuing to develop the rig on a model that has been updated through Referencing

"As the proportions of the model weren't altered, our joints still line up nicely"

this updated model. Let's leave the model here for now and pop on our rigging cap.

04: Updating the Referenced asset
Open up **rig_wip1.ma** and you'll notice that the model has been automatically updated to the new unified mesh and our work has been left intact. As the proportions of the model weren't altered, our joints still line up nicely.

Let's now presume that this mesh is close to being final and continue to develop the rig by adding controls and also skinning the mesh to the joints. This will allow us to deform the mesh for animation.

Other great features of Referencing are that we can very easily switch the file that

we are calling in in the Reference Editor and we can also create Proxy versions to lighten the size of our scene files.

Although we've just focused on two departments here, this workflow can be continued throughout the digital pipeline. It's important to note that it's a good idea to sometimes break a Reference file and actually import it into the scene as you deliver assets towards the end of the pipeline.

05: Referencing dos and don'ts
Using the process of publishing and Referencing is a great way to work but, like everything else, there are limits. We'll discover some of these as we go along and then discuss how we can work around them. Here are two quick examples of changes that you can make: one successful and one that will result in a digital nightmare, as shown in **Fig.05**. So far in the rigging department we have

skinned the mesh to the joint chain, allowing us to deform the mesh. Now, if the modeler makes any modeling updates by pushing and pulling the existing vertices to change the silhouette, the model can be published with little to no consequence to the rigger, other than having to add some extra weight painting.

However, if the modeler decides to introduce additional vertices by adding extra edge loops to the model and then publishing the file, well, you can see the results in **Fig.05** below.

This is possibly not the look you were going for, caused by the number of vertices being different to the original number that had been skinned to the joint chain. If you need to make changes to the model by adding extra detail, you would have to either re-skin the updated model or copy the weights over from one model to another. Nothing is foolproof, so test out the pipeline early on to minimize problems.

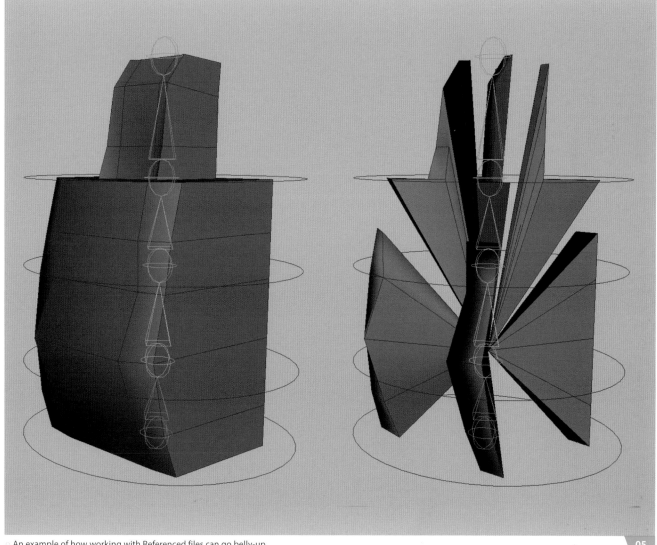

An example of how working with Referenced files can go belly-up

05

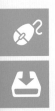

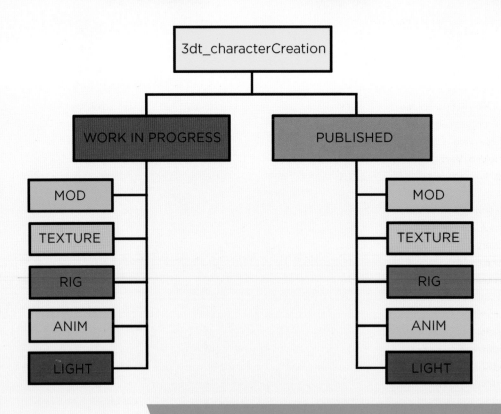

Creating a new project

Getting everything prepared

**So now we are ready to begin a new
project. The first thing we need to do is
create a new project directory in Maya.**

01: Project Window

Go to File > Project Window, click on the
New button to the right of the Current
Project input box, and then give your
new project a name. I've decided to call
my project **3dt_characterCreation**.

Also make sure you check the location that
the project directory will be saved to, as we'll
be using these folders on a regular basis.

With everything else in its default state, hit
Accept. If you go to File > Open, you will notice
that it automatically sends you to the scenes
folder of the **3dt_characterCreation** directory.

By working within a Maya Project directory,
you can very easily carry the entire project
to a new workstation, and Maya will be able
to source where all the images, textures,
scripts, and so on, should be called in from.

02: What will be saved where

Before modifying the project directory,
I just want to give a quick overview
of what files will be going where.

Firstly, all our Maya and Mudbox scene
files will be going into the **scenes** folder.
All the reference images, videos, and

texture files we create and use will be
dropped into the **sourceimages** folder.

Images that we render in Maya will go into
the **images** folder and any scripts that we use
will go into the **scripts** folder. We'll use some
of the other folders when required, but these
few will be where we spend most of our time.

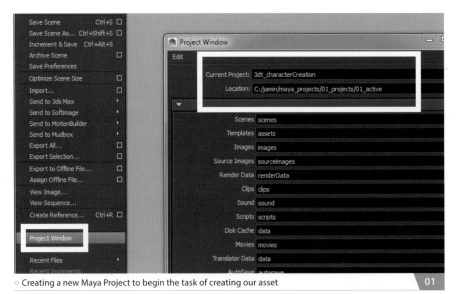

○ Creating a new Maya Project to begin the task of creating our asset   01

If you're working on numerous projects at once, you can go to File > Set Project and select a project directory to make that the active project. Again, as long as the files are in the relevant folders, Maya should be able to hook everything up correctly.

03: Add a document directory

I've added an extra folder called **documents** to our project directory, into which I can drop any extra information about the project, for example information about the group members if you're part of a team (names, emails, telephone numbers, and so on). It could also contain information specific to the project, such as the company you are working for, the details of the project, the resolution size, the frame rate, and so on.

Having a folder of documents like this makes it easier to get new members settled in and have them conform to the working style of the team. For now, I've created a document that lays out some of the naming conventions I will be using throughout the project. I've added a local copy and a published copy so I can keep track of when the changes were made and by whom.

04: Create some default directories (A)

Now let's add some additional folders to get this project up and running. Start by popping into the scenes folder and creating a new folder. Call this folder **01_WIP**. This folder will house all the work-in-progress files (the local files) that we will create throughout the project.

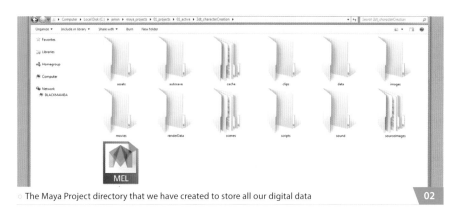

○ The Maya Project directory that we have created to store all our digital data　02

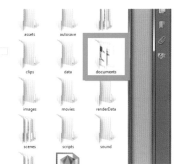

○ Adding a documents folder to house any information about the project　03

In the **01_WIP** directory, create five new folders called **01_MODELLING_SCULPTING**, **02_TEXTURING_SHADING**, **03_RIGGING**, **04_ANIMATION**, and **05_LIGHTING**. We'll add plenty of other folders as we progress but this should be enough to get us started.

05: Create some default directories (B)

Pop back up a couple of levels to the scenes directory and create a new folder called **02_PUBLISHED**. This is where we will house all the assets that we Publish. Within this

directory, create the same five folders that we set up for the **01_WIP** directory. Unlike the **01_WIP** directory, where we will house many iterations of our work, the **02_PUBLISHED** directory will only house one file (or on the odd occasion, two files) per folder.

At this point the preparatory work has been completed and we are now ready to commence modeling.

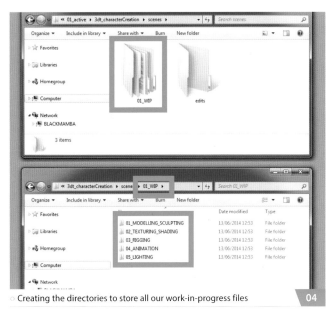

○ Creating the directories to store all our work-in-progress files　04

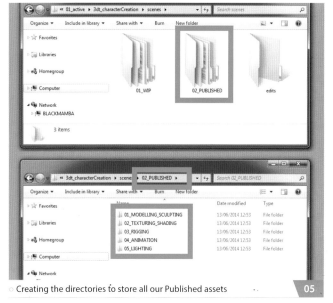

○ Creating the directories to store all our Published assets　05

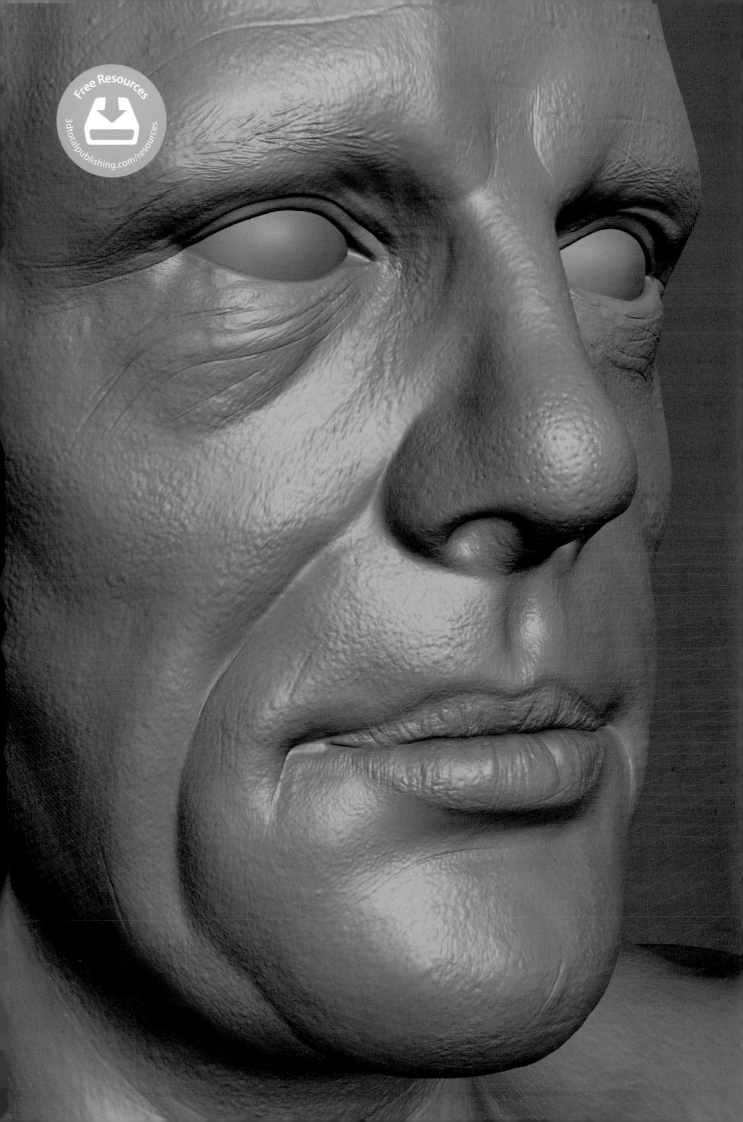

Anatomy, modeling, and sculpting

Learning about the human body and creating your model in Maya

If you want to make a realistic character, you can't jump straight into Maya without understanding what you're trying to create. Whatever tools you're using or character you're creating, it's important to have a solid foundation in reality and how things work. This section will give a walk-through of the human body's skeleton and muscles, covering all the major details a 3D artist should bear in mind, from bony landmarks to prominent muscle groups, all labeled and color-coded for easy reference. After that, we'll set up some useful reference cameras and move on to blocking in, sculpting, and retopologizing your model, taking him from a simple cube to a detailed human likeness.

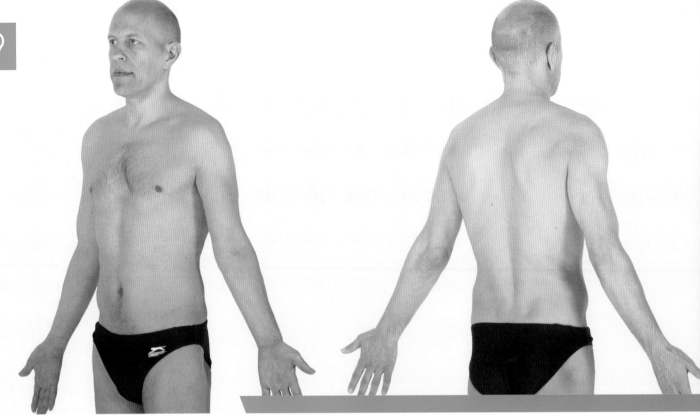

The anatomical position

Learning about the anatomical planes

This chapter will be devoted to providing an overview of human anatomy. Volumes could be filled about this fascinating, complex and surprisingly controversial subject. However, as our objective in this book is to recreate the human form in CG, we will primarily focus on the bones and muscles that affect the surface.

When creating a digital model, there is a danger of focusing too narrowly on the exterior. Yet if this exterior fails to convey a sense of the forms beneath it, the illusion of reality we are trying to convey will immediately be broken.

For example, consider the face, the lines of which reflect the skull beneath. Think also of the hand, which contains 27 bones; without giving a sense of this underlying structure, the hand would be reduced to a rubbery mass. Therefore it is vital, when modeling a character, to pay attention to the anatomy, without which our digital character could not sit, stand, or move.

This chapter will provide an overview of the bones and muscles that can be "seen" at skin level. Occasionally we will also take in deeper muscles that are seen when the body is in extreme poses.

As you work, remember that you are your own totally 3D, living, breathing reference. Examine your own body: clench and unclench your fist while looking at your forearm to see the flexor and extensor muscle groups at work. Feel your face and head to trace the lines of the skull.

Reference is key to creating digital believability, but don't let yourself be ruled by it: develop an understanding and use it to guide and inform your work.

I mentioned that the subject of anatomy is a controversial one: many anatomists disagree on key areas of their field, such as the numbers of true and floating ribs. As frustrating as this can sometimes be, it helps us remember that the human

form is not from a mold on a factory line; it is unique to everyone and therefore grants us much freedom of expression.

Jumping in and exploring bones, muscles, tendons, and so on can feel rather daunting, especially when the language of anatomy is unfamiliar. So before we go any further, let's take a look at the anatomical position. This will allow you to develop an understanding of the vocabulary used when describing the position and orientation of different parts of the body. It will also give you a common language enabling you to communicate with other artists, rather than having to describe a part of the body as "that hard bit under there and to the left".

The anatomical position places the subject in a pose in which the forms can be clearly examined and described. The body stands erect with the face and eyes looking forward. The feet stand around 6–8 inches apart, with the toes forward. The arms are down to the side, palms facing forwards and thumbs pointing outwards. This is called the supine anatomical position.

We can then use anatomical planes to describe and separate the different locations of structures and see how they relate to other structures of the body. We can also use the anatomical planes to give clarity to movement. The three main anatomical planes are:

• the horizontal (or transverse) plane, which divides the body into the superior (upper) and inferior (lower) portions;

• the median (or midsagittal) plane, which divides the body from the left to the right portion and creates the midline;

• the frontal (or coronal) plane, which divides the body into the anterior (front) and the posterior (back) portions.

The terminology used to describe the relationship of one structure to another can appear complicated, so the following table gives a quick breakdown of some key terms used in regards to position and orientation, which I'll be using further on in the book.

Take a look at **Fig.02**, **03**, **04**, and **05** to see how these labels are applied in different aspects and to different orientations.

Term	Description
Superior/Cranial	Closer to the head
Inferior/ Caudal	Closer to the feet
Medial	Towards to the midline
Lateral	Away from the midline
Posterior/Dorsal	Towards the back
Anterior/Ventral	Towards the front
Proximal	Closest to
Distal	Farthest away
Supine	Palm up
Prone	Palm down

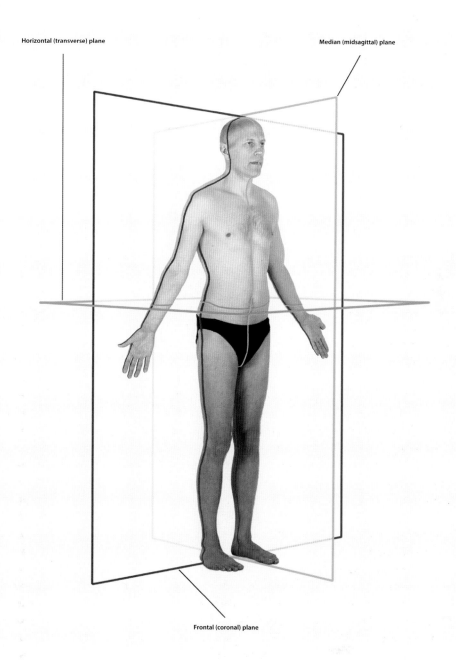

Horizontal (transverse) plane

Median (midsagittal) plane

Frontal (coronal) plane

○ The supine anatomical position

01

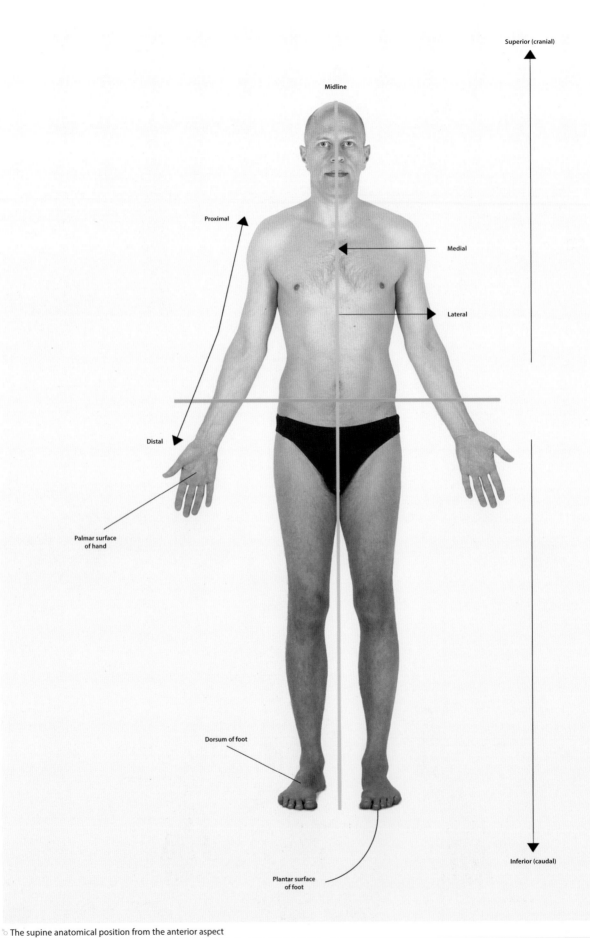

The supine anatomical position from the anterior aspect

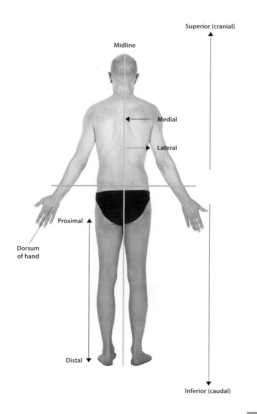

Superior (cranial)

Midline

Medial

Lateral

Proximal

Dorsum
of hand

Distal

Inferior (caudal)

○ The supine anatomical position from the posterior aspect   **03**

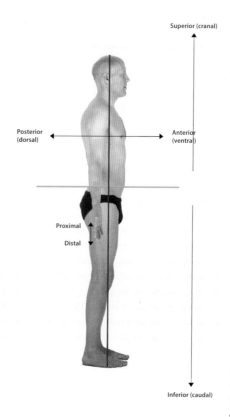

Superior (cranal)

Posterior
(dorsal)

Anterior
(ventral)

Proximal

Distal

Inferior (caudal)

○ The supine anatomical position from the right lateral aspect   **04**

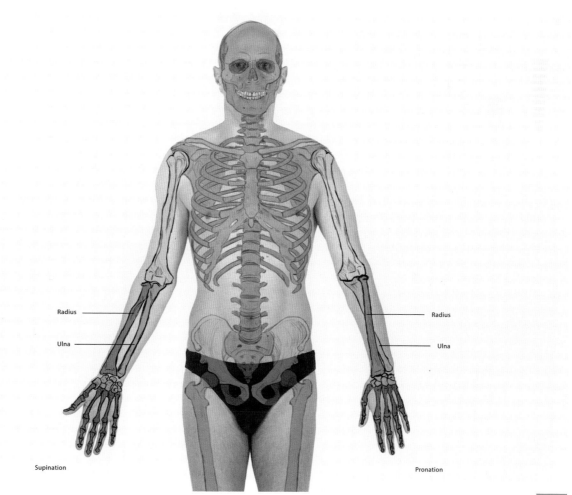

Radius

Ulna

Radius

Ulna

Supination

Pronation

○ Supination and pronation of the forearms   **05**

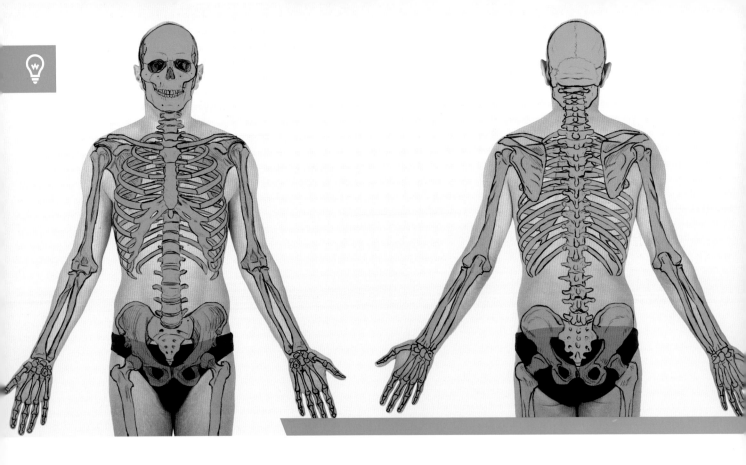

Overview of the skeleton

Learning about the axial and appendicular skeleton

Now that we have a common language to describe the structures of the body, let's take a look at the scaffolding that supports our flesh: the skeleton.

At birth, the skeleton consists of 300 or so bones. By the time we hit adulthood, many bones have fused together, such as those of the sternum and the cranium, taking that total down to around 206. If you are interested in finding out about each and every bone, I suggest you grab a copy of Henry Gray's *Gray's Anatomy*.

For this, we need only focus on the bones that are visible on the surface of the skin, or the so-called "bony landmarks". These landmarks, regardless of a person's physical attributes, are pretty uniform from one person to another and are so prominent that they can often be detected through clothes.

The skeleton can be used as a primary source to lay out the proportions of a character, as the size of a person's bones correlates directly to their overall size. For example, the

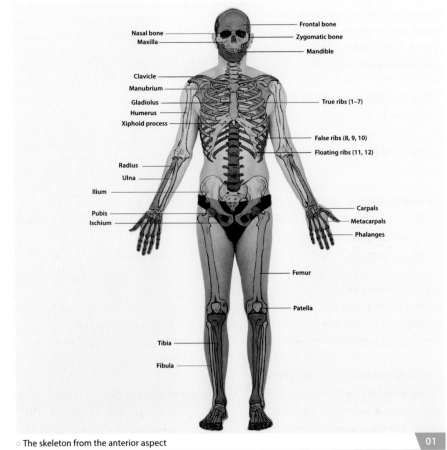

Nasal bone
Maxilla
Frontal bone
Zygomatic bone
Mandible

Clavicle
Manubrium
Gladiolus
Humerus
Xiphoid process
True ribs (1–7)

False ribs (8, 9, 10)
Floating ribs (11, 12)

Radius
Ulna
Ilium

Pubis
Ischium

Carpals
Metacarpals
Phalanges

Femur

Patella

Tibia

Fibula

○ The skeleton from the anterior aspect

01

36

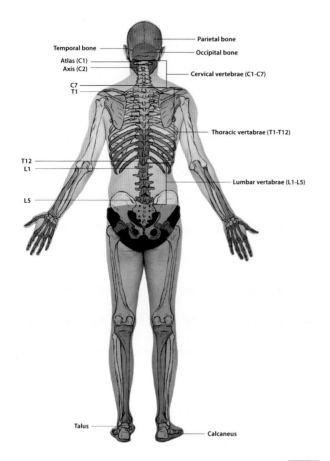

Parietal bone
Temporal bone
Occipital bone
Atlas (C1)
Axis (C2)
Cervical vertebrae (C1-C7)
C7
T1
Thoracic vertabrae (T1-T12)
T12
L1
Lumbar vertabrae (L1-L5)
L5
Talus
Calcaneus

The skeleton from the posterior aspect **02**

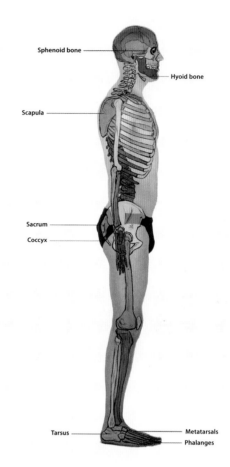

Sphenoid bone
Hyoid bone
Scapula
Sacrum
Coccyx
Tarsus
Metatarsals
Phalanges

The skeleton from the right lateral aspect **03**

humerus is approximately 80 percent of the length of the femur in everybody. In contrast, relying on the flesh can be hazardous, as age and weight play a major part.

Before we take a closer look at the bony landmarks, however, let's divide the skeleton into two major structures: the axial skeleton and the appendicular skeleton.

The axial skeleton

The axial skeleton consists of 80 bones, and for simplicity, let's categorize them into three main groups: the skull, the vertebral column, and the thoracic cage.

The skull is made up of the cranial, facial, and auditory bones. The vertebral column (spine) consists of the cervical, thoracic, and lumbar vertebrae, the sacrum, and the coccyx.

You should take note of how the vertebral column affects the back in the lateral view (Fig.03). It forces the shape of the neck as it curves to support the head. It then curves again to support the rib cage,

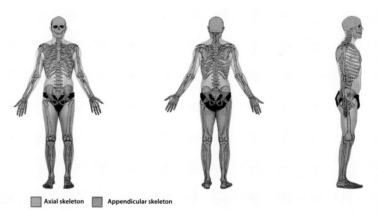

Axial skeleton   Appendicular skeleton

Dividing the skeleton into two major structures: the axial and appendicular skeletons **04**

forcing the belly to come forward before curving once more to support the pelvis.

Lastly, we have the thoracic cage, which is composed of the 12 pairs of ribs and the sternum.

The appendicular skeleton

The appendicular skeleton consists of 126 bones and, again for simplicity, let's categorize them into four main groups: the shoulder girdle, the pelvic girdle, the upper extremity, and the lower

extremity. The shoulder girdle (also referred to as the pectoral girdle) consists of the clavicles and the scapulae. The pelvic girdle (also referred to as the bony pelvis) consists of two mirrored bones (hip bones). Each hip bone is made up of three sections: the ilium, ischium, and pubis.

We then have the upper extremity, which is composed of the humerus, ulna, radius, carpals, metacarpals, and phalanges. Lastly, we have the lower extremity, consisting of the femur, patella, fibula, tibia, tarsals, metatarsals, and phalanges.

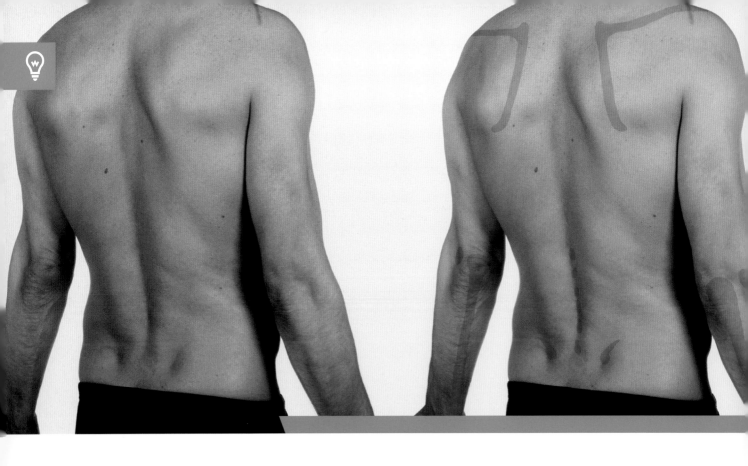

The bony landmarks

Bony landmarks of the axial and appendicular skeletons

Now that we're familiar with the axial and appendicular skeletons, let's focus on the bony landmarks (Fig.01, 02a, 02b, 02c). By introducing them to our mesh, we can create the illusion that our digital character has an underlying skeleton.

Bony landmarks of the axial skeleton

Let's start with the landmarks of the axial skeleton, beginning at the skull and working our way down the vertebral column. The skull can be divided into two sections: the bones of the cranium and the bones of the face, totaling 22 bones. The shape of the head is forced by the shape of the cranium, encasing the brain like a protective helmet and providing attachment for the muscles of expression.

The main bones that affect the surface of the skin are the frontal bone, the parietal bones, the occipital bone, the zygomatic bones, and the body of the mandible (take a look at Fig.02a, 02b, 03). If you place your fingers against your forehead, or against your

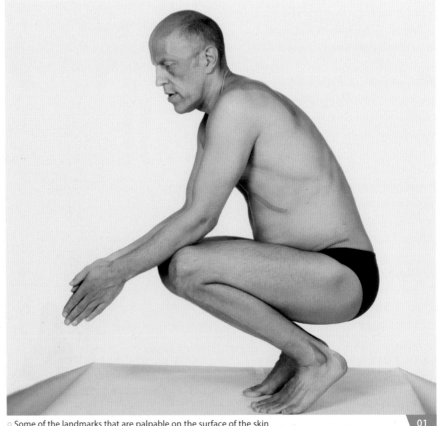

○ Some of the landmarks that are palpable on the surface of the skin

01

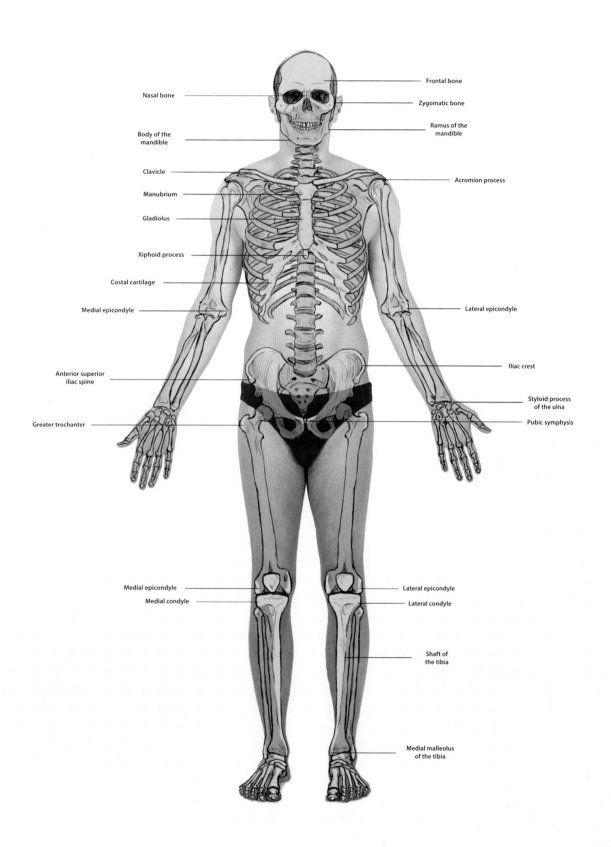

Nasal bone

Frontal bone

Zygomatic bone

Body of the mandible

Ramus of the mandible

Clavicle

Acromion process

Manubrium

Gladiolus

Xiphoid process

Costal cartilage

Medial epicondyle

Lateral epicondyle

Anterior superior iliac spine

Iliac crest

Greater trochanter

Styloid process of the ulna

Pubic symphysis

Medial epicondyle

Lateral epicondyle

Medial condyle

Lateral condyle

Shaft of the tibia

Medial malleolus of the tibia

Bony landmarks of the skeleton from the anterior aspect

02a

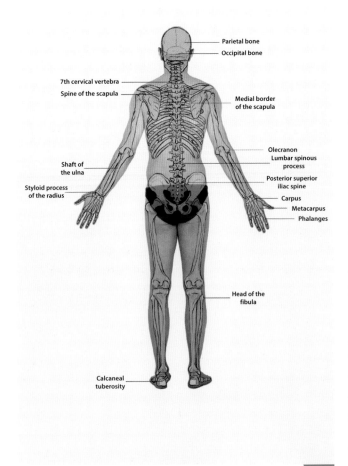

○ Bony landmarks of the skeleton from the posterior aspect   **02b**

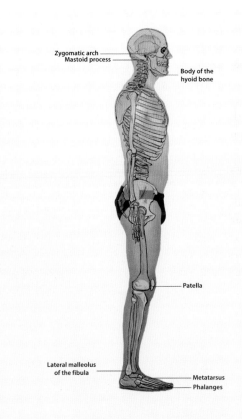

○ Bony landmarks of the skeleton from the right lateral aspect   **02c**

cheek, you will discover that you can very easily feel the structures of the frontal bone and the zygomatic bone. Put your hand to your chin as if in a thinking pose and you'll press against the body of the mandible.

If you look at different people from different races and genders, of varying age and weight, irrespective of these differences you can still see or feel this underlying structure coming through.

Even with fantasy characters, such as the alien that features in *Predator* or a cave troll from *The Lord of the Rings*, you will still be able to see evidence of the skull pushing through and forcing the form.

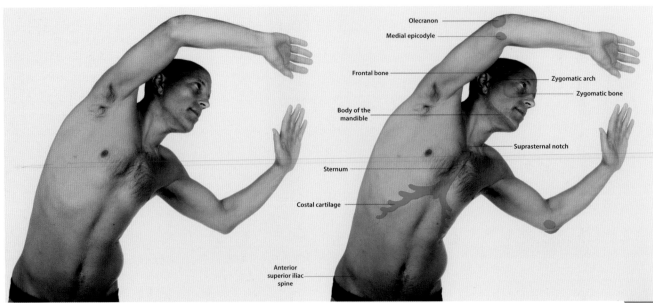

○ The landmarks of the cranium, mandible, and anterior aspect of the torso   **03**

Of the cervical portion of the spine, a key landmark to bring to your attention is the 7th cervical vertebra (C7). The most caudal of the cervical vertebrae, the spinous process of the C7 sits close to the skin, creating a very visible landmark (as shown in Fig.04).

It's for this reason that the C7 is also referred to as vertebra prominens. If you bring your chin towards the pit of your neck and place your hand at the back of your neck, you should easily feel this landmark.

At the front of the chest, we then have the sternum (breastbone; Fig.05), which in adults is composed of three fused bones: the manubrium (handle), the gladiolus (blade), and the xiphoid process (sword)

"The xiphoid process often has little influence on the surface, but is sometimes notable in its position just above the pit of the stomach, especially in young children"

(Fig.02a). Just above the manubrium, we have the suprasternal notch (the pit of the neck; Fig.05). This is a large visible dip at the base of the neck between the clavicles.

The manubrium and the gladiolus are entirely subcutaneous on the anterior surface. A noticeable plane change can also be evident where the two meet. This plane change is referred to as the sternal

angle. The xiphoid process often has little influence on the surface, but is sometimes notable in its position just above the pit of the stomach, especially in young children.

The ribs attach to either side of the sternum through costal cartilage, as shown in Fig.05. The costal cartilage is made from a hyaline material that gives elasticity to the thorax; hence you can give someone cardiopulmonary resuscitation (CPR) without busting through their chest. The true ribs (1–7), attach by way of cartilage directly to the sternum, while the cartilage of the false ribs (8, 9, and 10) each attaches to the cartilage of the rib above.

The inferior rim of the costal cartilage creates the costal (or thoracic) arch, and it is this

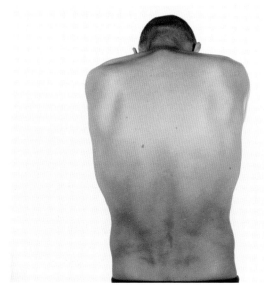

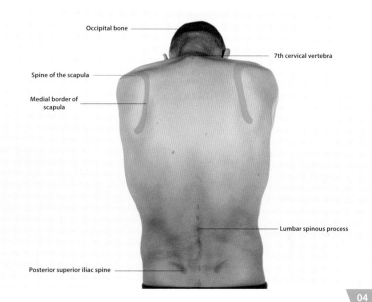

Occipital bone
7th cervical vertebra
Spine of the scapula
Medial border of scapula
Lumbar spinous process
Posterior superior iliac spine

○ The landmarks on the posterior aspect of the torso

04

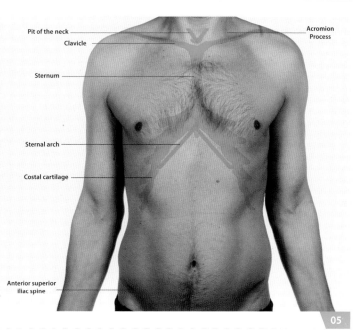

Pit of the neck
Clavicle
Acromion Process
Sternum
Sternal arch
Costal cartilage
Anterior superior iliac spine

○ Highlighting the pit of the neck and the sternal arch

05

arch that we want to pay attention to. In the anatomical pose, the evidence of this arch may be subtle on some, but when the torso is pushed to more extreme poses (**Fig.06**) it can be very obvious. In males the costal arch forms an angle of 90°, while in females it's closer to 60°.

The floating ribs (11 and 12) have no cartilage and, unlike ribs 1–10, do not meet the sternum. As the trunk moves, the superficial muscles of the back are thinned and the floating ribs are sometimes revealed (as are the spinous processes of the lumbar vertebrae).

Our final landmark of the axial skeleton is the sacral triangle. In actuality, the hip bones also play a part in this landmark. The sacral triangle is created by the sacrum, which is wedged between the iliac bones of the hip. The posterior superior iliac spines create two indentations (the "dimples of Venus") lateral to the midsagittal plane. When a line is drawn between these two indentations and then to the gluteal cleft, the sacral triangle is formed.

Bony landmarks of the appendicular skeleton

Now we'll move on to the landmarks of the appendicular skeleton and look firstly at the upper extremity, as shown in **Fig.06**.

The clavicle (also known as the collarbone) is the only link between the upper extremity and the axial skeleton. It is an S-shaped bone and can be easily seen and felt under the skin,

especially on those with less fat. Notice how the medial end of the clavicle is rounded, while the lateral end is flattened at the point at which it connects to the next landmark of interest: the acromion process of the scapula. The acromion process is a subcutaneous, rectangular, flat, bony process that forms the highest point of the shoulder and is most noticeable when the arm is raised because a depression is created.

As we move around to the posterior aspect of the shoulder girdle from the acromion process, we follow another major landmark – the spine of the scapula – which then meets the medial border of the scapula (**Fig.04**). Both the spine of the scapula and medial border of the scapula are superficial and of great significance when considering the attachment points of the muscles of the scapula and back.

Working our way to the inferior extremity of the humerus, we have two very important landmarks: the medial epicondyle and the lateral epicondyle.

With your arm extended and hanging by your side, the medial epicondyle is the more visually prominent, while the lateral epicondyle (**Fig.02a**) can be felt in the dimple at the back of the arm. During flexion of the elbow, however, both the medial and the lateral epicondyles will be palpable.

In between the medial and lateral epicondyles we have the very prominent olecranon of the ulna (the elbow; **Fig.03**). The

beak-like olecranon bites onto the spool-shaped trochlea of the humerus, allowing flexion and extension of the forearm.

Examine your own elbow and take note of the line created by these three landmarks when your arm is extended, and the triangle created by the three landmarks during flexion.

The shaft of the ulna (**Fig.02b**), also known as the ulna furrow, is another point of interest. This landmark also helps to break up the flexor from the extensor muscles of the forearm.

At the distal end of the ulna, we come to the styloid process of the ulna (**Fig.02a, 06**), which you can easily feel as you press against the pinky side of your wrist. On the thumb side of the wrist, you have the styloid process of the radius (**Fig.02b**). Depending on the individual and the pose of the hand, the prominence of this landmark is more or less obvious at a surface level.

Our final points of consideration in the upper extremity are the hands and the fingers: the carpals, the metacarpals, and the phalanges (**Fig.02b**).

We are primarily interested in the dorsum of the hand, where we can see and feel the bony protrusions of the bones affecting the surface of the skin.

When the wrist is extended, the trapezium and the pisiform of the carpals can be prominent. On

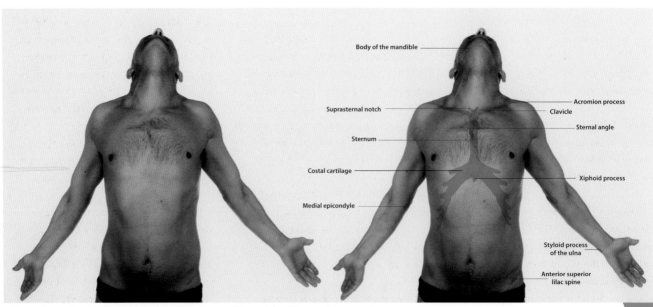

○ Depending on the articulation of the torso, the presence of the costal cartilage can be more or less apparent

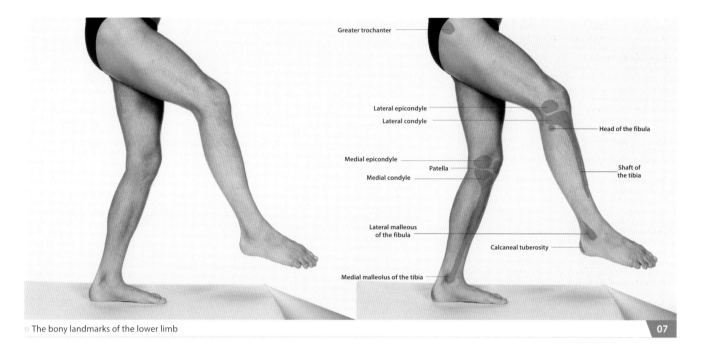

Greater trochanter

Lateral epicondyle
Lateral condyle
Head of the fibula

Medial epicondyle
Patella
Shaft of
the tibia
Medial condyle

Lateral malleous
of the fibula

Calcaneal tuberosity

Medial malleolus of the tibia

○ The bony landmarks of the lower limb

07

the one hand (no pun intended), the distal ends of the metacarpals are spherical, creating small knuckles, as are the distal ends of the proximal and medial phalanges. The distal phalanges, on the other hand, are shaped like arrowheads, allowing a surface for the nail to sit on.

Let's move on to the landmarks of the lower extremity now, shown in **Fig.07**, starting with the pelvic girdle. We first come to a landmark that is regarded as one of the most important of the body: the anterior superior iliac spine (ASIS; **Fig.02a, 06**).

The ASIS is a bony protrusion that sits in the anterior end of the iliac crest and can be used to divide the upper body from the lower. Running your fingers from the ASIS along the exposed portion of the iliac crest will bring you to the posterior superior iliac spine (PSIS; **Fig.04**), where the sacral triangle can be drawn, as mentioned earlier.

Like the sacral triangle, you can also create a triangle at the front of the pelvis by creating a line from ASIS to ASIS and then down to the pubic symphysis (**Fig.02a**).

We now come to the longest bone in the human body: the femur. On the superior lateral end of the femur, sitting in between the head and the neck of the bone, we have the greater trochanter (**Fig.07**). This bony protrusion affects the surface on the lateral side of the hip, and depending of the articulation

"Bony landmarks can be compared to a physical map of the world: both provide a sense of what lies beneath the surface"

of the leg, can more or less be easily spotted. If you place your fingers against the lateral side of your hip, however, it can almost always be felt. Moving to the distal portion of the femur, we come to the medial and lateral epicondyles, just as we saw with the humerus.

Alongside the epicondyles, the patella creates plenty of interesting surface change. In the straightened leg, for example, notice the two dimples either side of this flat, triangular bone.

From the femur, we come to the second and third largest bones in the body: the tibia and fibula. The tibia, a weight-bearing bone, also referred to as the shinbone, is the larger of the two, and it alone makes contact with the epicondyles of the femur. Its superior extremity creates two bony landmarks on either side of the knee: the medial and lateral condyles.

Like the ulna crest, a sharp ridge can be felt on the anterior side of the tibia. This is known as the crest of the tibia. This portion of the bone is extremely superficial and can easily be felt pressing against the surface of the skin.

On the distal end of the tibia, we also have the medial malleolus (the inner ankle bone).

Again, this is a very prominent protrusion that affects the silhouette of the ankle.

Sitting slightly behind the tibia is the fibula (a stabilizer bone), which presents two further landmarks for the lower leg. On the proximal end, we first have the head of the fibula; on the distal end, we have the lateral malleolus (the outer ankle bone). Take note of how the lateral malleolus sits slightly below the medial malleolus.

Like the hand and the fingers, the foot and the toes display similar patterns and can be broken down into three portions of interest: tarsals, metatarsals, and phalanges (**Fig.02c**).

Of the tarsals, the calcaneus (the heel) is the largest and most prominent of the seven bones. Like the bones of the fingers, the metatarsals and phalanges of the toes are most noticeable on the dorsum of the foot, whilst the underside (or palmar) of the foot is cushioned to allow for shock absorption when the foot makes contact with the ground. Take note of the tuberosity of the 5th metatarsal, which creates the widest part of the outside of the foot.

In their entirety, bony landmarks can be compared to a physical map of the world: both provide a sense of what lies beneath the surface. An animation of a character who lacks bony landmarks will therefore beg the question from its audience: "How did it move without a skeleton?"

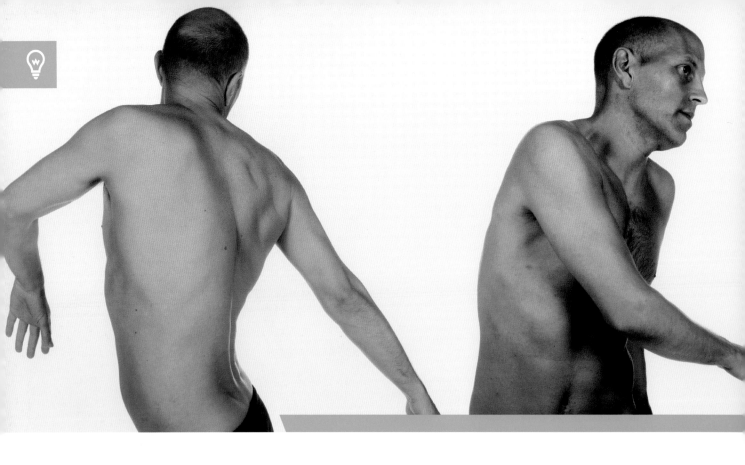

Muscles and tendons

Understanding human musculature

Now we'll examine the muscles and tendons. There are three types of muscle in the body: skeletal, cardiac, and smooth. Cardiac muscles relate to the heart; smooth muscles are found in the walls of the organs. We have no voluntary control over them and they usually don't affect the surface forms, so we'll leave them be.

Our attention will be on the skeletal (striated) muscles. To put a number on how many striated muscles are in the human body would probably raise a few eyebrows. As with many aspects of anatomy, doctors, physicians, artists, and so on, tend to bicker about what is and isn't a muscle. To offend none of these groups, let's say there are 640 to 850 skeletal muscles, all of which are under our control (even if we don't know it).

That's too many muscles for our needs here, so we'll focus on the core muscles that affect the surface of the skin and see how we can group muscles together to make their study more manageable.

Muscles and tendons

A muscle is a fibrous band of tissue with two main portions: the red contractile portion (the belly) and the tendon either side that connects the muscle to the bones. The shape of the muscle belly can change (for example with exercise), while tendons tend to stay as they are. If you examine overly muscular people, such as bodybuilders, you'll notice depressions where the tendons have remained the same while the muscle bellies have developed around them.

The muscles that drive the skeleton need to pass over a joint to be able to do their job. All muscles have to start and end at a fixed

position, too, known as origin and insertion points, respectively. If they didn't, you simply wouldn't move in the way you do.

Issues of most importance to us are the direction in which the muscle fibers run, how the muscles are layered on top of each other, and the origin and the insertion points. By focusing on these aspects, we can very easily run lines from A to B to build up the forms (Fig.01, 02, and 03). We'll take a closer look at the functions of the muscles later, when we start rigging the character, but for now I want to share a few terms that will help demystify their names:

Term	Description
Flexor	A muscle which decreases the angle between the bones of a limb or digit
Extensor	A muscle which increases the angle between the bones of a limb or digit
Abductor	A muscle which moves a part of the body away from the midline of the body
Adductor	A muscle which moves a part of the body towards the midline of the body
Pronator	Rotation of the forearm and the hands towards the midline of the body
Supinator	Rotation of the forearm and the hands away from the midline of the body
Longus	Refers to a long muscle. Where you see a longus, expect a brevis as well
Brevis	Refers to a short muscle. Where you see a brevis, expect a longus as well

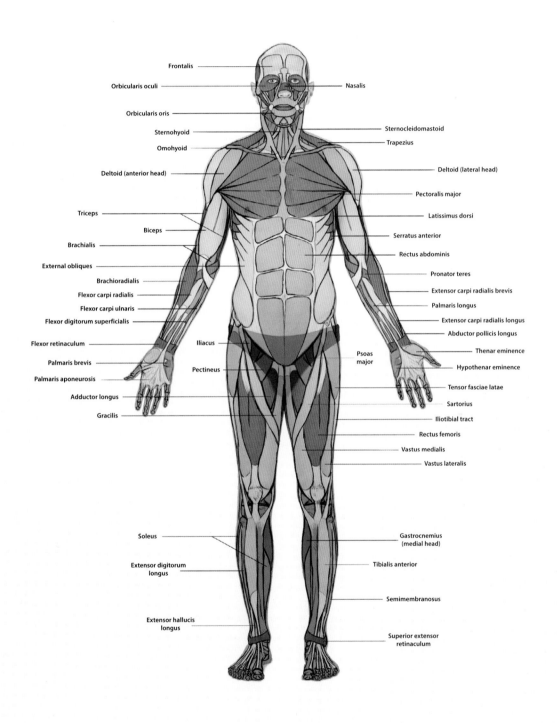

Frontalis

Orbicularis oculi

Nasalis

Orbicularis oris

Sternohyoid

Sternocleidomastoid

Omohyoid

Trapezius

Deltoid (anterior head)

Deltoid (lateral head)

Pectoralis major

Triceps

Latissimus dorsi

Biceps

Serratus anterior

Brachialis

Rectus abdominis

External obliques

Brachioradialis

Pronator teres

Flexor carpi radialis

Extensor carpi radialis brevis

Flexor carpi ulnaris

Palmaris longus

Flexor digitorum superficialis

Extensor carpi radialis longus

Abductor pollicis longus

Flexor retinaculum

Iliacus

Thenar eminence

Palmaris brevis

Psoas major

Hypothenar eminence

Pectineus

Palmaris aponeurosis

Tensor fasciae latae

Adductor longus

Sartorius

Gracilis

Iliotibial tract

Rectus femoris

Vastus medialis

Vastus lateralis

Soleus

Gastrocnemius (medial head)

Extensor digitorum longus

Tibialis anterior

Semimembranosus

Extensor hallucis longus

Superior extensor retinaculum

The muscles of the body from the anterior aspect

01

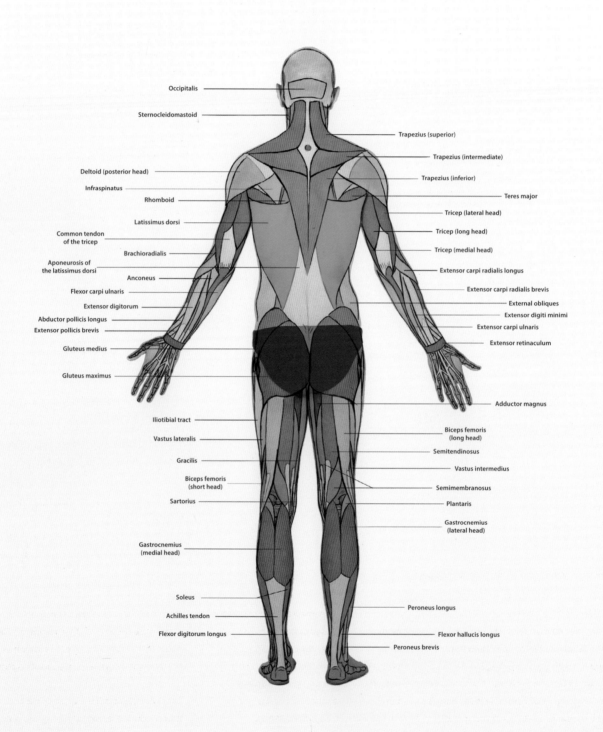

Occipitalis

Sternocleidomastoid

Trapezius (superior)

Trapezius (intermediate)

Deltoid (posterior head)

Trapezius (inferior)

Infraspinatus

Teres major

Rhomboid

Tricep (lateral head)

Latissimus dorsi

Tricep (long head)

Common tendon
of the tricep

Tricep (medial head)

Brachioradialis

Extensor carpi radialis longus

Aponeurosis of
the latissimus dorsi

Extensor carpi radialis brevis

Anconeus

External obliques

Flexor carpi ulnaris

Extensor digiti minimi

Extensor digitorum

Abductor pollicis longus

Extensor carpi ulnaris

Extensor pollicis brevis

Extensor retinaculum

Gluteus medius

Gluteus maximus

Adductor magnus

Iliotibial tract

Biceps femoris
(long head)

Vastus lateralis

Semitendinosus

Gracilis

Vastus intermedius

Biceps femoris
(short head)

Semimembranosus

Sartorius

Plantaris

Gastrocnemius
(lateral head)

Gastrocnemius
(medial head)

Soleus

Peroneus longus

Achilles tendon

Flexor digitorum longus

Flexor hallucis longus

Peroneus brevis

○ The muscles of the body from the posterior aspect

02

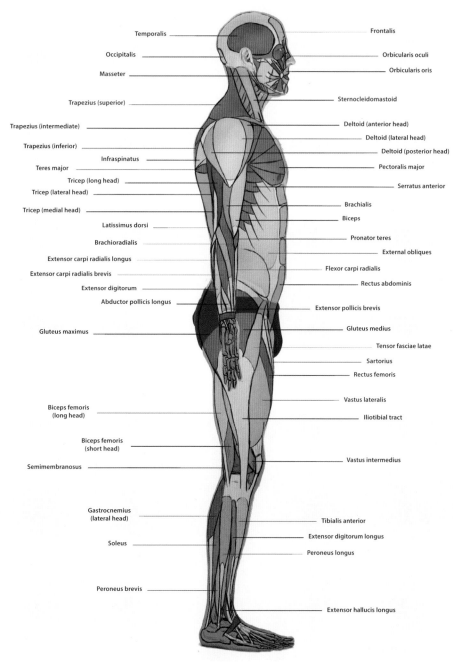

Temporalis

Occipitalis

Masseter

Trapezius (superior)

Trapezius (intermediate)

Trapezius (inferior)

Infraspinatus

Teres major

Tricep (long head)

Tricep (lateral head)

Tricep (medial head)

Latissimus dorsi

Brachioradialis

Extensor carpi radialis longus

Extensor carpi radialis brevis

Extensor digitorum

Abductor pollicis longus

Gluteus maximus

Biceps femoris
(long head)

Biceps femoris
(short head)

Semimembranosus

Gastrocnemius
(lateral head)

Soleus

Peroneus brevis

Frontalis

Orbicularis oculi

Orbicularis oris

Sternocleidomastoid

Deltoid (anterior head)

Deltoid (lateral head)

Deltoid (posterior head)

Pectoralis major

Serratus anterior

Brachialis

Biceps

Pronator teres

External obliques

Flexor carpi radialis

Rectus abdominis

Extensor pollicis brevis

Gluteus medius

Tensor fasciae latae

Sartorius

Rectus femoris

Vastus lateralis

Iliotibial tract

Vastus intermedius

Tibialis anterior

Extensor digitorum longus

Peroneus longus

Extensor hallucis longus

○ The muscles of the body from the right lateral aspect   **03**

Muscles of the head and neck

There are over 40 muscles in the head and face. The facial muscles are small and thin, intertwining with each other to allow for the complexity of facial expressions. If you created a full facial rig, you would examine these muscles in detail. For our project, it's not these muscles that concern us, but the fat covering the face and the superficial evidence of the skull.

The skull is hard, rigid, and palpable, taking care of the superior region of our face. In contrast, the inferior portions of our faces are soft, malleable, and fleshy. The nose,

ears, and chin are particularly flexible as they are mainly composed of fat and cartilage. Some muscles that affect the face's surface forms are the temporalis muscle and the masseter, as shown in **Fig.04**. Both are muscles of mastication (chewing); you can see them at work while eating.

The temporalis muscle originates from the temporal fossa, passes through the zygomatic arch, and grabs onto the coronoid process of the mandible and ramus of the mandible, letting you close your mouth against the force of gravity. The masseter originates from the

inferior border of the zygomatic arch and inserts into the lateral surface of the ramus and the angle of the mandible. Like the temporalis, the masseter helps keep your mouth closed.

Other muscles that I use to block out the forms include the orbicularis oris, orbicularis oculi, and frontalis muscles. I'll refer to some of these muscles when creating the final retopologized mesh later on (see pages 76–89).

Coming to the neck, we have a favorite muscle of mine: the sternocleidomastoid (**Fig.04**). It sounds like a mouthful, but like many muscles,

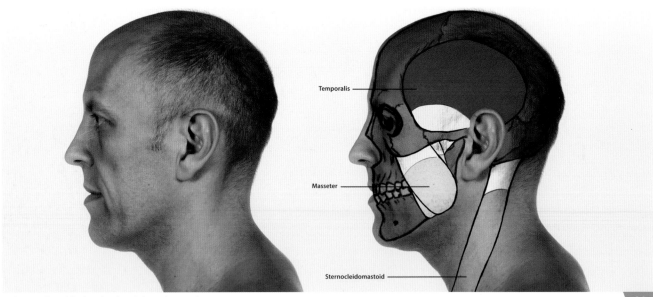

Temporalis

Masseter

Sternocleidomastoid

○ The muscles of the head and neck from the anterior aspect

04

we can break the name down to understand it. The sternal head originates at the sternum and the clavicular head originates at the clavicle; then the muscle inserts into the mastoid process and nuchal line of the occipital bone. So we have *sterno-cleido-mastoid*.

As we turn our heads from side to side, you can see and feel the sternocleidomastoid in action. It's worth taking a look at the platsyma too. This is a thin, broad muscle that originates from the fascia of the deltoid and the pectoralis and inserts into the mandible and the lower face.

Muscles of the torso

We now come to the torso muscles (**Fig.05** and **06**), starting with the pectoralis major and minor. The pectoralis major creates the majority of the surface form. This muscle originates at the medial half of the clavicle, the sternum (excluding the xiphoid process), and the abdominals, and inserts into the greater tubercle of the humerus. See how the pectoralis major sits on top of the bicep, and the deltoids lie on top of the pectoralis muscles (**Fig.03**).

Sticking with the anterior aspect of the torso, we then have the rectus abdominus. This straight abdominal muscle originates at the pubis and pubic symphysis, and inserts into the costal cartilage of ribs 5, 6, and 7 and the anterior portion of the xiphoid process. The two halves of the rectus abdominus show some asymmetry, and are separated by the linea alba; the muscle itself sits within a layer of aponeurosis (the rectus sheath). Attached

to the rectus sheath, and on the lateral and anterior portion of the trunk, are the external obliques. These originate on the outer surface of ribs 5–12 and also insert into the ASIS, the iliac crest, and the pubic tubercle. The flanks of the external obliques create the "love handles" on the lateral aspect of the torso.

The fibers of the external obliques also interdigitate with the fibers of the serratus anterior. The serratus anterior originates from the anterior border of ribs 1–8 (sometimes 9) and inserts into the medial border of the scapula. Sausage-like in shape, the digits from ribs 1–5 are covered by the pectoralis muscle, so only the remaining digits are usually on display. As the torso articulates and the latissimus dorsi muscle is thinned, the serratus anterior becomes more prominent (**Fig.05**). Most people think they're looking at the ribs, when in fact it's the flared-out digits of the serratus anterior that affect the surface forms.

Now on to the latissimus dorsi, the largest muscle of the back. The origin of this muscle runs from the spinous processes of T7 down to the sacrum, the posterior aspect of the crest of ilium, and from ribs 9–12. It then inserts into the intertubercular groove at the front of the humerus. There's a notable line, known as the "line of the fibers", as the fibers of the muscle belly of the latissimus dorsi meet the tendon.

The superior border of the latissimus dorsi is covered by the tail of the next muscle of interest: the trapezius. This large diamond-

shaped muscle can be broken down into three main sets of fibers: superior, intermediate, and inferior. Starting with the superior set of fibers, this portion originates from the external occipital protuberance, the ligamentum nuchae, and the spinous process of the C1–C7 vertebrae, and then inserts into the lateral third of the posterior border of the clavicle.

Originating from the spineous process of the 7th cervical vertebrae, and between the 1st and 3rd thoracic vertebrae, is the intermediate set of fibers. These fibers then insert into the superior border of the scapula and acromion process. The inferior set of fibers originates from the spineous processes of the thoracic vertebrae between T4 and T12, then inserts into the inferior medial border of the scapula.

Coming off the scapula are the supraspinatus, infraspinatus, teres minor, and teres major. We're just going to focus on the teres major here, but do observe how the infraspinatus can help to create the bulge that we associate with the scapula. The teres major originates just below the teres minor muscle from the inferior angle of the scapula, and inserts into the crest of the lesser tubercle of the humerus. This tube-like muscle, along with the latissimus dorsi, helps to create the silhouette on the lateral portion of the torso. Another muscle of interest is the rhomboid (**Fig.02**), which creates a noticeable bulge as the scapula is pulled towards the spine.

Lastly, let's look at the strong cord muscles that lie either side of the spine. The erector spinae

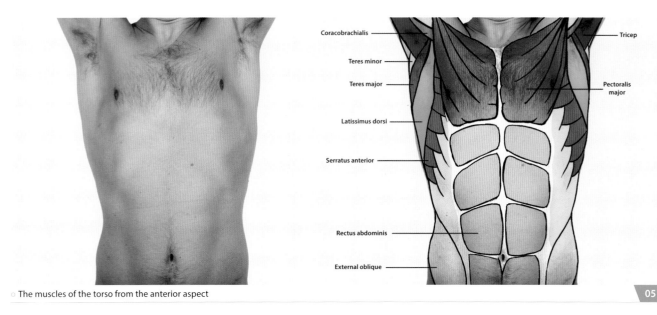

Coracobrachialis

Teres minor

Teres major

Latissimus dorsi

Serratus anterior

Rectus abdominis

External oblique

Tricep

Pectoralis major

The muscles of the torso from the anterior aspect

05

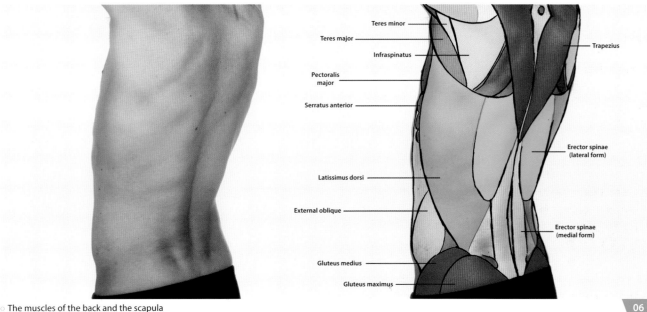

Teres minor

Teres major

Infraspinatus

Pectoralis major

Serratus anterior

Latissimus dorsi

External oblique

Gluteus medius

Gluteus maximus

Trapezius

Erector spinae (lateral form)

Erector spinae (medial form)

The muscles of the back and the scapula

06

(or sacrospinalis) is a deep set of three muscles: the illiocostalis, longissimus, and spinalis. The muscles originate from many points on the posterior aspect of the trunk, including the sacrum and the vertebral column, and then insert through many muscular slips to various points of the vertebral column, the ribs, and the mastoid process of the skull. The three sets of muscle create two major forms: the medial form and the lateral form. You'll see the medial form as tubular mass that runs either side of the lumbar vertebrae. The lateral mass sits laterally and superiorly to the medial mass and is more bulbous in its shape (take a look at Fig.06).

Muscles of the upper limb

We now move on to the muscles of the arm, shown in Fig.07 and 08, beginning with

the deltoid. This muscle has three heads: anterior, lateral, and posterior. The anterior head originates from the anterior lateral third of the clavicle, the lateral head from the acromion process, and the posterior head from the spine of the scapula. All three heads share an insertion point, around halfway down the humerus at the deltoid tuberosity. As you block in the deltoid and pectoralis muscles, take note of the small depression (the infraclavicular fossa) evident on the anterior aspect of the torso between the two muscles.

Next we have the tricep on the posterior aspect of the arm. As the name suggests, this is another three-headed muscle, having a lateral, long, and medial head. The lateral head originates on the superior third of the

humerus, the long head from the infraglenoid tubercle of the scapula, and the medial head from the lower third of the humerus. All three heads insert into a common tendon, which then attaches itself on to the olecranon of the ulna, allowing you to extend your forearm. There's a noticeable line where the fibers of the lateral and long head of the muscle belly meet the tendon, creating a V-shaped notch.

For the anterior aspect of the upper arm, three muscles of interest are the coracobrachialis (Fig.05), brachialis, and biceps brachii (Fig.08). The small, sausage-like coracobrachialis helps to fill the underarm, originating from the coracoid process of the scapula and inserting into the upper third of the medial surface of the humerus. You may just about make out

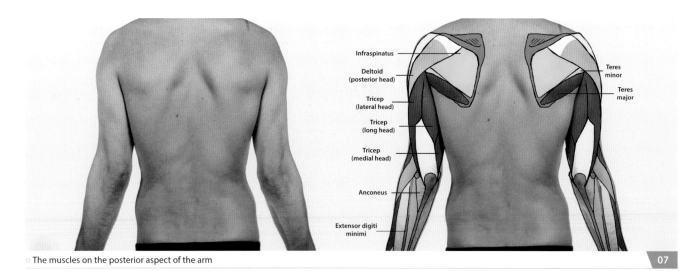

Infraspinatus

Deltoid (posterior head)

Tricep (lateral head)

Tricep (long head)

Tricep (medial head)

Anconeus

Extensor digiti minimi

Teres minor

Teres major

○ The muscles on the posterior aspect of the arm

07

Brachialis

Brachioradialis

Bicep

Abductor pollicis longus

Extensor carpi radialis longus

Extensor carpi ulnaris

Extensor pollicis brevis

Extensor digitorum

○ The muscles of the upper limb

08

this muscle on the raised arm of an average person, but it creates a very noticeable surface effect on a more developed individual.

Sitting beneath the bicep is the pillow-like brachialis. It originates from the anterior surface of the humerus, close to where the deltoid terminates, and inserts at the coronoid process of the ulna. This muscle helps to fill out the anterior aspect of the upper arm.

Now we come to the bicep: a two-headed muscle with a long head and a short head. The long head originates from the supraglenoid tubercle of the scapula, inserting into the radial tuberosity of the radius. The short head originates from the coracoid process of the scapula, inserting into the bicipital aponeurosis (deep fascia of the forearm). You may think of the bicep as a flexor muscle, but it's also a pronator muscle, helping to carry the radius over the ulna.

Most people have a whopping 27 muscles in their forearm – though around 14% of the population is missing the palmaris longus (believed to no longer have a practical purpose). Getting acquainted with that many muscles may seem onerous so let's break them down into their two functional groups: flexors and extensors. Flexor muscles lie primarily on the anterior aspect of the forearm, and extensors primarily on the posterior aspect, but both groups do tend to spill over.

Before we look at the flexors and extensors, let's look at the ridge muscles. The brachioradialis originates from the distal lateral supracondylar ridge of the humerus and the lateral intermuscular septum, inserting into the lateral side of the styloid process of the radius. The extensor carpi radialis longus originates from the lateral supracondylar ridge of the distal humerus and the lateral intermuscular septum, passes under the muscles of the thumb, and

inserts into the base of metacarpal 2 (the index finger). Together, the two muscles create a unified form that appears as a bulge just above the lateral epicondyle of the humerus. This is most noticeable on the extended arm.

Moving on to the flexor muscles of the forearm, the four of interest are the: flexor carpi ulnaris, flexor carpi radialis, palmaris longus, and flexor digitorum superficialis (**Fig.01**). All four originate from a common tendon attached to the medial epicondyle of the humerus. For the flexor carpi ulnaris, we want to keep an eye out for its tendon, as it inserts into the pisiform and the base of the 5th metatarsal bone.

The flexor carpi radialis inserts into the base of the 2nd and 3rd metacarpal bones; as well as creating surface change as the wrist is flexed, its tendon is also prominent, and can be seen up to the point where it passes beneath the flexor retinaculum. The palmaris longus inserts into the palmar aponeurosis and its tendon passes over the flexor retinaculum, making it very visible, especially during flexion of the wrist.

The flexor digitorum superficialis sits between the palmaris longus and the flexor carpi ulnaris. The tendon of this muscle passes beneath the flexor retinaculum and inserts into the middle phalanges of fingers 2–5 (thumb is referred to as 1), allowing for flexion of the fingers. You've probably seen that all four muscles originate as a fleshy mass before turning into very visible tendons.

Now let's look at the extensors. The superficial muscles of interest here are the extensor digitorum and extensor carpi ulnaris. Both originate from a common tendon of the lateral epicondyle of the humerus and pass under the extensor retinaculum before hitting their insertion points.

Unlike the tendons of the flexors that are more noticeable at the wrist, the tendons of the extensors reveal themselves on the dorsum of the hand, past the wrist. The muscle

belly of the extensor digitorum is large and tubular, and the tendon itself divides and inserts into the 2nd, 3rd, and 4th metacarpals. The extensor carpi ulnaris lies along the ulna furrow, and then inserts into the base of the 5th metacarpal bone. Between these two muscles sits the extensor digiti minimi (Fig.07), which is more noticeable on developed bodies, so you may want to take it into consideration.

Before moving on to the hand, I just want to bring to your attention a few more muscles

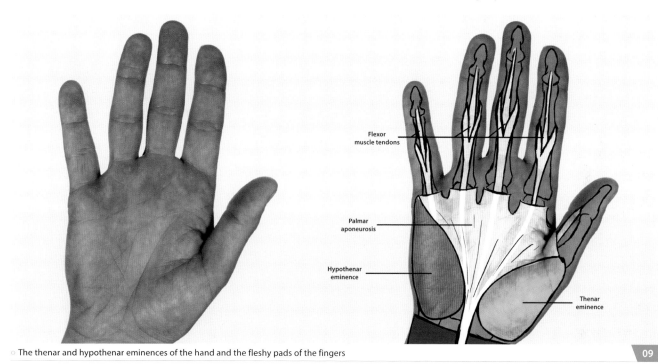

The thenar and hypothenar eminences of the hand and the fleshy pads of the fingers

09

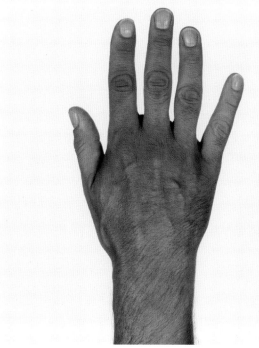

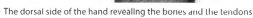
The dorsal side of the hand revealing the bones and the tendons

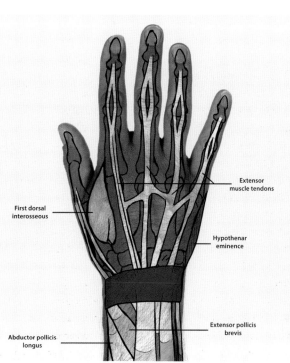

10

that are of interest. Firstly, we will consider the abductor pollicis longus and extensor pollicis brevis. These two muscles of the thumb pass over the extensor carpi radialis brevis and the extensor carpi radialis longus, creating surface change on the radial side of the forearm. You may also want to look into the anconeus and the pronator teres, both of which can create surface change depending on the articulation of the arm.

Our final area of interest in the upper limb is the hands (**Fig.09 and 10**). Like the face, it's mainly the relationship between bone, fat, and tendon that we want to pay attention to. The dorsal side is the bony region with the tendons of the forearm muscles visible, while the palmar side is fleshy. On the palmar side, two masses of muscle stand out and are of interest to us: the thenar eminence (on the thumb side) and the hypothenar eminence (on the pinky side).

Sitting between the metacarpals of each finger, and between the index finger and thumb, are also interosseous muscles, which help to fill the spaces between the bones. The first interosseous muscle (sitting between the thumb and index; **Fig.10**) creates the most surface change as the thumb is brought in to lie against the index finger. There are no other muscles in the fingers and thumbs as, interestingly enough, they're all tendon-driven.

Muscles of the lower limb

Now let's hit the muscles of the leg, as illustrated in **Fig.11** and **12**, starting off with the gluteal

muscles. There are three in number but only two are of interest to us: the gluteus maximus and gluteus medius. First we'll look at the former, which creates the majority of the form. This muscle originates from the posterior iliac crest, the posterior surface of the sacrum and the coccyx, and from the fascia of the gluteus medius. The upper fibers of this muscle meet the iliotibial tract while the lower fibers travel deep and insert into the gluteal tuberosity of the femur – a rough surface of the bone.

The gluteus medius originates from the lateral surface of the ilium and inserts into the lateral surface of the greater trochanter of the femur. The separation between these two muscles is evident as you stand up straight and tense up, creating a butterfly-like shape. I'm also going to include the tensor fasciae latae here, which originates from the ASIS and inserts into the iliotibial tract. Together, these three muscles create the mass that runs along the iliac crest from the ASIS to the PSIS. All the muscles interact with the iliotibial tract, a strong fibrous band that helps to shape the lateral aspect of the thigh. As the name suggests, the tract runs from the crest of the ilium to the lateral condyle of the tibia.

We'll now move on to the sartorius (**Fig.11**), which is the body's longest muscle. It originates from the ASIS and then inserts into the medial surface of the tibia. As it makes its way from origin to insertion like an S-shaped ribbon, it separates the adductor muscles from the quadriceps.

The quadriceps sit between the sartorius and the tensor fasciae latae. As the name suggests, four muscles make up this mass, but only three will be important to us: the vastus medialis, the vastus lateralis, and the rectus femoris. The rectus femoris originates at the anterior inferior iliac spine, with the other heads originating from the medial, anterior, and lateral surface of the femur. We could go into further detail about the origin of the vastus medialis and the lateralis but I don't think it's necessary here. The muscles all come together and meet a common tendon that passes over the patella to become the patella ligament.

The tear-shaped vastus medialis, which creates a noticeable bulge just above the knee, borders the sartorius and lies closest to the patella. The fibers of the rectus femoris are worth noting. As this is a bipennate muscle, its fibers radiate to either side and create a furrow; this muscle belly then grabs on to the common tendon at the highest point. The vastus lateralis may seem small from the anterior aspect, but truly reveals its size when viewed from the lateral aspect, where it creates a visible bulge just above the patella.

I'll briefly mention the band of Richer. This is a strap of fibrous tissue that comes off the iliotibial tract and runs over the quadriceps muscles, playing a part in creating the bulge of the medial lateralis. Next, we'll take a look at the adductor muscles of the thigh, which include the adductor longus, brevis, and magnus, iliacus, psoas major, gracilis, and

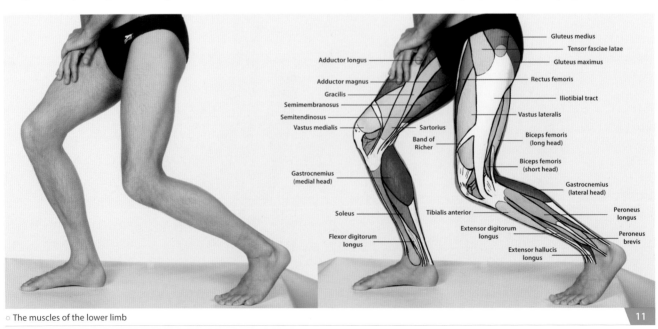

○ The muscles of the lower limb

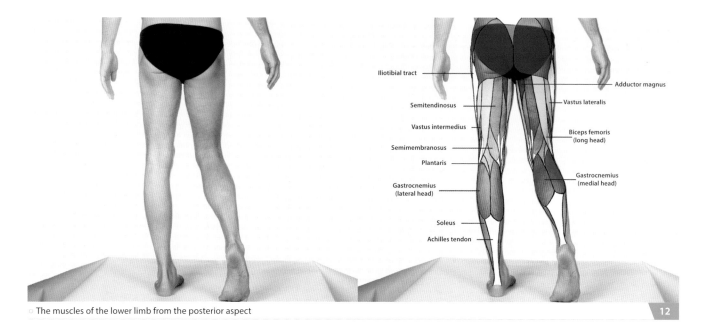

○ The muscles of the lower limb from the posterior aspect

12

pectineus. I'm not going to go into the detail of the insertion and origin points of every muscle from this group as they pretty much create a common form on the average person. Put simply, the origin of the muscles is the pubic bone and they insert into the femur. Most importantly, they create a noticeable change of plane when there is transition from the adductors to the quadriceps.

On the posterior aspect of the thigh, we have the hamstrings. This group is made up of three muscles which again create a common form, although the separation of the muscles can be more noticeable on some than others. These muscles are the biceps femoris, the semitendinosus, and the semimembranosus.

The bicep femoris, as the name suggests, is a two-headed muscle with a long head and a short head, the long head being the more dominant of the two. This head originates from the ischial tuberosity (a bony bump at the back of the pelvis that you can feel when sitting) and inserts into the head of the fibula. The tendon of this muscle is very exposed and can be seen clearly on the straight leg. The short head originates from the linea aspersions of the femur and inserts into the head of the femur, and is usually hidden behind the long head. Both the semitendinosus and the semimembranosus originate from the ischial tuberosity. The former inserts into the tuberosity of the tibia, and the latter inserts into the medial condyle of the tibia. The semitendinosus pretty much sits on top of the semimembranosus,

but you should notice a bubble-like form behind the knee created solely by the latter.

We now come to the calf muscles, which lie on the posterior aspect of the lower leg. Here we have the gastrocnemius and the soleus muscles, accompanied by the Achilles (or calcaneal) tendon. The gastrocnemius muscle has two heads, the medial head originating from the medial epicondyle of the femur and the lateral head originating from the lateral epicondyle of the femur. Both heads meet at the Achilles tendon, which then meets the calcaneus bone. Take note of how the medial head sits slightly lower than the lateral head and can also be seen from the anterior aspect.

Sitting beneath the gastrocnemius is the soleus muscle. A flat muscle which can also be seen from the anterior aspect, it originates from the head of the fibula and the posterior surface of the fibula and the tibia, and also grabs on to the Achilles tendon, adding further volume to the region.

Looking at the lateral aspect (**Fig.11**), we have the poroneus longus and the poroneus brevis. Both lie on the fibula, with the poroneus longus sitting on top of the brevis. We'll treat these muscles as one form, but note that during plantar flexion of the foot, a noticeable dimple can be seen, created by the poroneus longus. The tendon of the poroneus brevis can be visible as it runs over the lateral malleolus (using it as a pulley) and then inserts into the tuberosity of the 5th metatarsal.

On the anterior aspect of the lower leg, we then have the tibialis anterior muscle. This muscle originates from the lateral border of the tibia, running medially and inferiorly to then insert into the base of the 1st metatarsal (big toe). This muscle sits alongside the shaft of the tibia and creates noticeable surface change during dorsiflexion of the foot. The tendon of this muscle is also visible as it runs over the anterior aspect of the ankle.

We come now to the foot, though I'm not going to go into much detail as it's very similar in makeup to the hand. Like the hand, the dorsal side of the foot is very bony, with tendons on display, while the plantar side is thick and fleshy. The tendon of the poroneus brevis (as mentioned before) creates surface change, as does the tendon of the extensor digitorum longus. The tendon of the latter muscle splits into four and inserts into the middle and distal phalanges of toes two to five.

We also have the tendon of the extensor hallucis longus muscle, which inserts into the distal phalanx of the big toe, and which can affect the surface form. There are other muscles in the foot, but I find the modeling process is better informed when focusing on the relationship between the bones, tendons, and fat.

Now that we have an understanding of the structure of the human form, let's look at some aspects which are very different from person to person: fat and wrinkles.

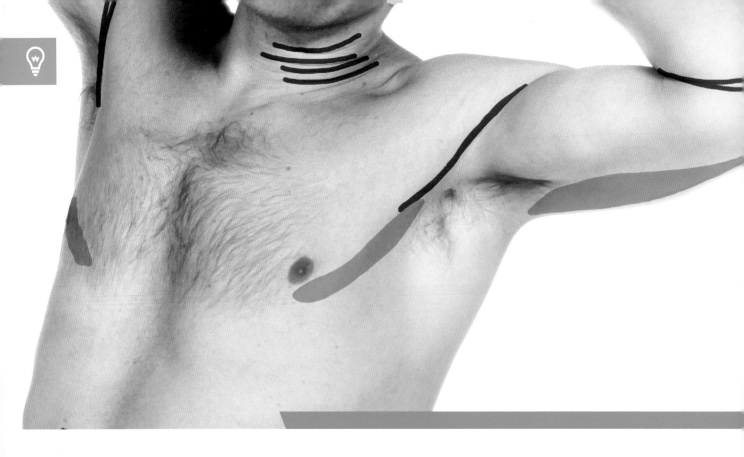

Body fat and proportions

Other anatomical details: fat, wrinkles, and symmetry

Although we've primarily been studying the skeleton, muscles, and tendons of the human body, it's important to remember that sitting on top of all of this like a draped cloth is the largest organ of all: the skin. And with skin comes fat and wrinkles. (See Fig.01a and 01b, marked in blue and red respectively.)

Fat and wrinkles

Fatty deposits can be found throughout the body, even on the leanest of individuals. We've already mentioned the fatty deposits on the face, hips, hands, and feet, but you should also take into consideration areas such as gluteal fat and the backs of the knees.

The back of the knee is an interesting area: a depression known as the popliteal fossa is actually present where the muscles of the hamstrings interlock with the calf muscles. Therefore, if you were to purely focus on the muscles and ignore the fat, your model may look slightly less believable. Adding fat is a good thing and will ultimately add further life to your model.

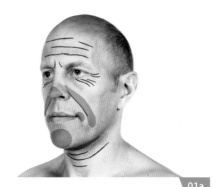

○ Some areas of the face where fatty deposits and wrinkles commonly occur **01a**

We also need to pay attention to wrinkles – their direction in particular. You'll notice that throughout the body, wrinkles tend to flow perpendicular to the muscles. Flexing your wrist will clearly demonstrate this.

Also look at the wrinkles and folds created by your clothing as you move around. You should notice that the position of the wrinkles will tend to be in the same place as on your skin. This will be an important consideration later on, as it will help us to lay out the joints for rigging.

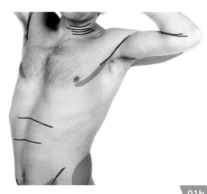

○ More areas of the body where fat gathers and wrinkles form **01b**

Proportions and measurements

I'm not going to go into too much detail regarding proportions as they're really beyond the scope of this book. However, I want to share some of the data I captured of the model, Paul, to aid in the process of creating the asset.

When it comes to proportions, I like to use a combination of two units of measurement: head height and "five-eyes wide", as shown in Fig.02a. I generally use the head height as my main unit of measurement for blocking

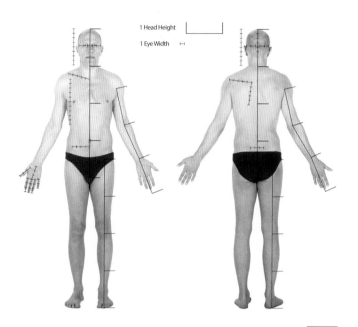

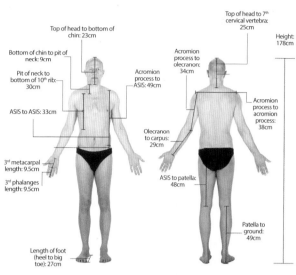

○ Measuring Paul with the head height and "five-eyes wide" methods **02a**

○ Preparing for the task ahead by breaking down the reference images **02b**

out the larger forms, and then use the unit of five-eyes wide for the smaller forms, or anything that goes either side of a head height.

I don't want to dictate how you should assess the proportions of your models, but I thought I'd share how I usually break down my references before hitting the computer. In **Fig.02b**, you'll find the measurements that I captured from Paul with my trusty tape measure (no calipers to hand, unfortunately).

Symmetry

In CG, it's always good to come up with methods and techniques to reduce the amount of repetitive work you'll need to do. One of the most frequent methods is to create a symmetrical mesh. By doing so, you only need to focus on one half, which can then be mirrored over.

By having a symmetrical mesh, you can also very easily create symmetrical UVs, mirror joints over, mirror skin weights, and so on. Without a doubt, working with a symmetrical mesh is a huge time-saver.

However, when creating a realistic model, especially a human being, a purely symmetrical mesh screams "CG!" to me. Therefore, I prefer to add very realistic touches of asymmetry to my models, particularly in the face. We could of course add asymmetry later on

– for example, with a blend shape – and if I was to make multiple assets I would probably look at taking that route.

However, as we're only creating one asset, I've decided to add asymmetry at the first hurdle. That way I can capture the likeness of the model at the earliest stage.

> ## "When creating a realistic model, especially a human being, a purely symmetrical mesh screams "CG!" to me"

To get an idea of why I like to add asymmetry, please take a good look at the following images, shown in **Fig.03**. The first one is Paul's head without any mirroring. For the second, I've simply mirrored the left side of Paul's face over his right side, and for the last image I've done the reverse.

You can see by doing this how the face can become thinner or wider as one side is clearly wider than the other. Interestingly, in right-handed people, the right side of the face (and body) is often slightly larger, and the same in reverse for those who are left-handed.

These differences are not as noticeable in the rest of the body as they are in the face, so I'll be keeping the bulk of the body symmetrical. But that's enough talk – let's start modeling!

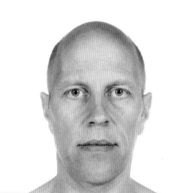

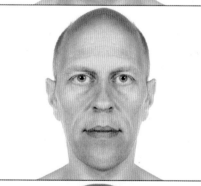

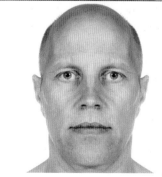

○ The model Paul's face with and without symmetry **03**

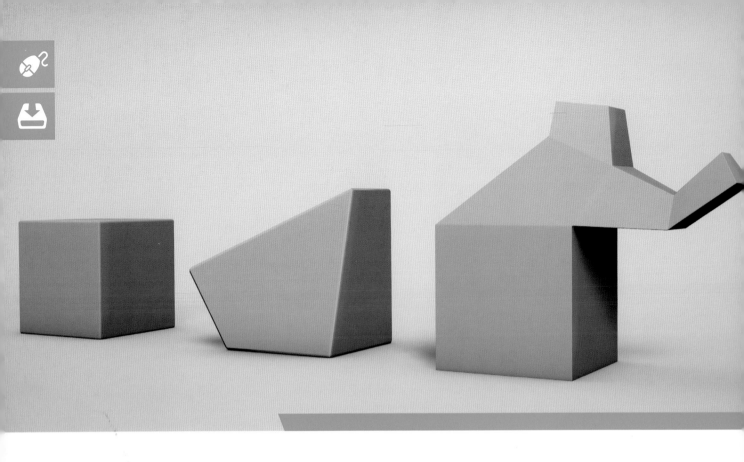

Introduction to the Maya modeling tools

Component modes and modeling tools

This chapter will open with a look at how we can manipulate an object on a component level. This will be followed by an introduction to a few of the key modeling tools we will be using in Maya to create the base mesh for our sculpt. Later on in this section, we'll meet Maya's Modeling Toolkit, which also has a few nice tricks up its sleeve.

01: Object and sub-component modes

Start by switching to the modeling module by either using the drop-down menu on the Status Bar or hitting F3 on the keyboard. From this menu, the three main sets of tools we will be using are the Mesh, Edit Mesh, and Mesh Tools (**Fig.01a**). Now create a cube by going to Create > Polygon Primitive > Cube. If we activate the Move (W), Rotate (E), or Scale (R) tools, we will be manipulating the cube in object mode. This affects the transform node associated with the object.

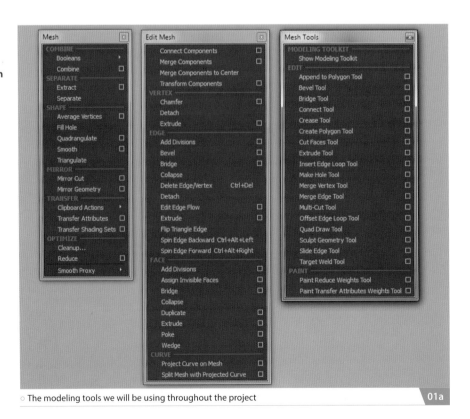

○ The modeling tools we will be using throughout the project

01a

If you open up the Outliner (Window > Outliner) and go to Display and enable Shapes, you will be able to view the associated shape node. If you pop into the Attribute Editor (Ctrl+A), you will also find a tab for the transform node and shape node for the cube (Fig.01b). To edit the shape itself, we need to switch to one of the three component modes: vertex, edge, or face.

To switch to any of the component modes, hold down the RMB over the cube and a marking menu should be revealed. You'll see Vertex, Edge, and Face towards the top half of the marking menu (Fig.01c). Drop the cursor over Vertex and release the RMB to step into that mode. You should now be able

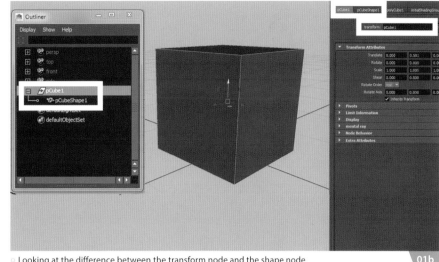

○ Looking at the difference between the transform node and the shape node   **01b**

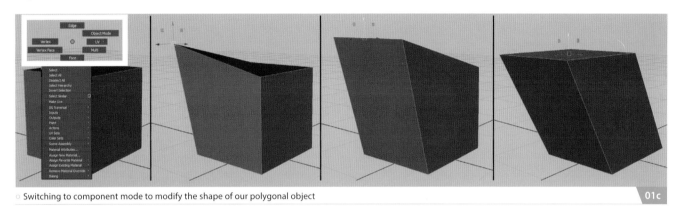

○ Switching to component mode to modify the shape of our polygonal object   **01c**

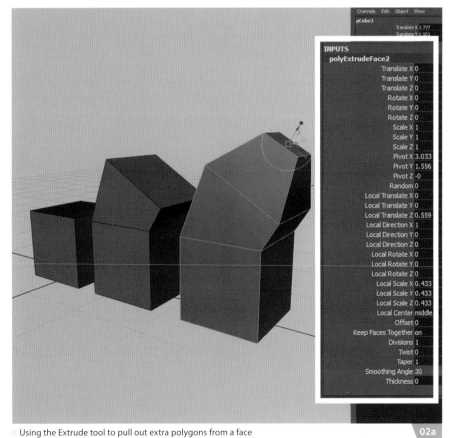

○ Using the Extrude tool to pull out extra polygons from a face   **02a**

to select an individual vertex or selection of vertices to manipulate the shape.

Once you've had a little play in vertex mode, do the same in the edge and face modes to get accustomed to pushing and pulling the sub-components. To come out of sub-component mode, hold down the RMB to bring up the marking menu, and drop the cursor over Object. Another quick way to jump between object mode and one of the component modes is to use the keyboard shortcuts: F8 (Object), F9 (Vertex), F10 (Edge), F11 (Face), and F12 (UV).

02: The Extrude tool

Let's look at the Extrude tool next. This tool allows you to add extra polygons by pulling the selected vertex, edge(s), or face(s) outwards or inwards. Select a single face and go to Edit Mesh > Extrude, which is found under the Face section. The Extrude manipulator will now be present, allowing you to pull out the face in any direction of your choosing. You can also rotate or scale the selected components using the Extrude manipulator (Fig.02a).

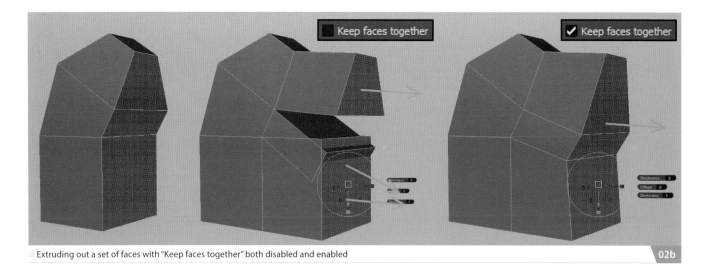

○ Extruding out a set of faces with "Keep faces together" both disabled and enabled   **02b**

To the upper-right side of the Extrude manipulator, you will also find a little blue icon. Clicking on this icon allows you to extrude locally or in world mode. I switch between the two often, depending on the direction I want the extrusion to occur. Now try selecting and extruding a couple of the cube's faces with Edit Mesh > Extrude.

Use the manipulator to pull the faces out. You'll probably notice that the Extrude tool has extruded out each face individually. Sometimes this is a good thing, but for the majority, I like my extrudes to treat all the selected components as one mass.

You can enable this feature by popping into the Channel Box, and under INPUTS you will find the Extrude node (polyExtrudeFace1). Open the node up by clicking on it and then enable "Keep faces together" (located towards the bottom) (**Fig.02b**).

To set this as the default behavior, go to Window > Settings/Preferences > Preferences. Now Under Settings, find the Modeling category. Under the Polygons tab, enable "Keep faces together" (**Fig.02c**).

Rather than coming into the Edit Mesh tools to use the Extrude tool, I usually use the marking menu shortcut. Simply select a component and hold down Shift+RMB.

03: The Insert Edge Loop tool
In a new Maya scene, create a new polygon cube. With the cube selected, go to Mesh Tools > Insert Edge Loop Tool. With the tools activated, you can now click and hold

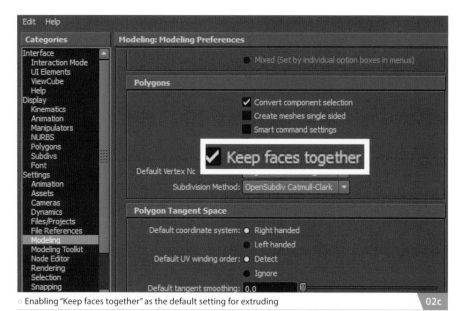

○ Enabling "Keep faces together" as the default setting for extruding   **02c**

🔍 PRO TIP
Object display quality

A quick way to assess your mesh for any errors or anomalies to is smooth the model. We could use Mesh > Smooth Tool, but this will also subdivide the mesh, adding more geometry. Instead, I hit the 3 key on the keyboard to activate Smooth Mesh Preview. The benefits of this are that I can easily step back to the original mesh by hitting 1 on the keyboard, and no additional geometry is created. If you use the 2 key, you can also view the Smooth Mesh Preview as well as the cage of the original mesh.

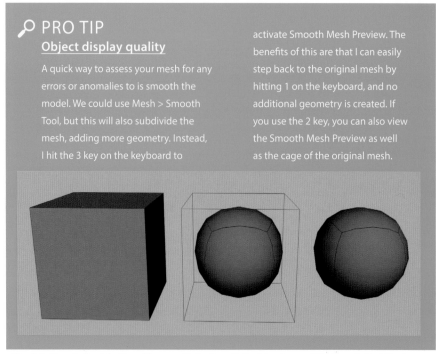

○ The default mesh, the default mesh's cage with the Smooth Mesh Preview, and the Smooth Mesh Preview

the LMB over an edge to create a loop of edges that will cut around the mesh.

If the mesh is made from quadrangles (quads), then the loop will happily cut all the way around the mesh, back to its starting point. However, if the mesh is a combination of triangles (three edges), quads (four edges), or n-gons (more than four edges), the tool may create some unwanted artifacts.

By opening up the options for the tool (the little square icon by its name), you can also change the tool's behavior. For example, you can create multiple edge loops at a time, or insert a new edge loop evenly between two existing edge loops.

To activate this tool using a keyboard shortcut, hold down Shift+MMB with the cube in object mode (F8). A marking menu should pop up, allowing you to easily access the tool.

"The Cut Faces tool can come in handy when you're looking to chop up a model quickly"

04: The Cut Faces and Multi-Cut tools

Once again, open a new Maya scene and create a new polygon cube. With the cube in object mode, go to Mesh Tools > Cut Faces Tool. You can now hold down the LMB in the viewport to angle where the cut will occur. If you release the LMB, you will notice a cut has been made through the entire mesh.

While in this tool, if you hold down the Shift key, you can also angle the cut line in 45° increments. We won't be using this tool much, but it can come in handy when you're looking to chop up a model quickly.

A more useful tool is the Multi-Cut tool (in Maya 2014, this is the Interactive Split tool), which allows you to manually cut into the selected geometry. This tool is part of the Modeling Toolkit (more on that later – see page 77) and when activated, you can LMB-click on an edge or vertex to create additional vertices.

Clicking between two vertices will create an edge, and pressing the RMB will create the cut but leave the tool active so you can add

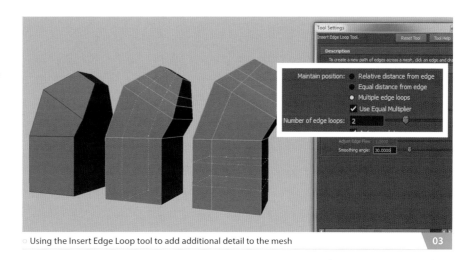
○ Using the Insert Edge Loop tool to add additional detail to the mesh   03

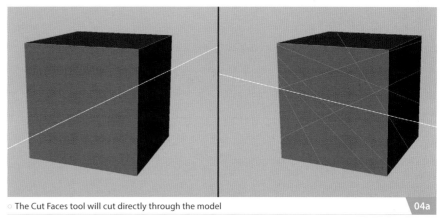
○ The Cut Faces tool will cut directly through the model   04a

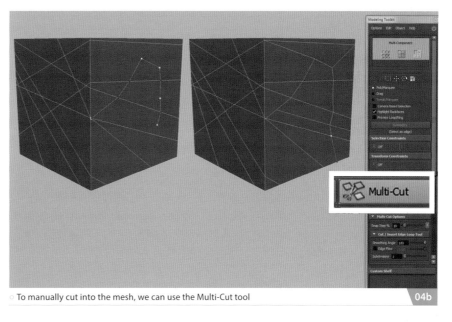
○ To manually cut into the mesh, we can use the Multi-Cut tool   04b

extra detail in other areas. It's important to note that even though you can drop vertices anywhere on a face, your initial and exit cut must occur on a vertex or an edge. The Multi-Cut tool also has a snapping behavior that will try to help you as you make your cuts.

To activate this tool using a keyboard shortcut, with the cube in object mode (F8), hold down

Shift+MMB. A marking menu should pop up allowing you to easily access the tool.

The tools just mentioned will be the main tools used to create the base mesh for our sculpt, so if you are new to modeling, do spend a bit of time getting used to them.

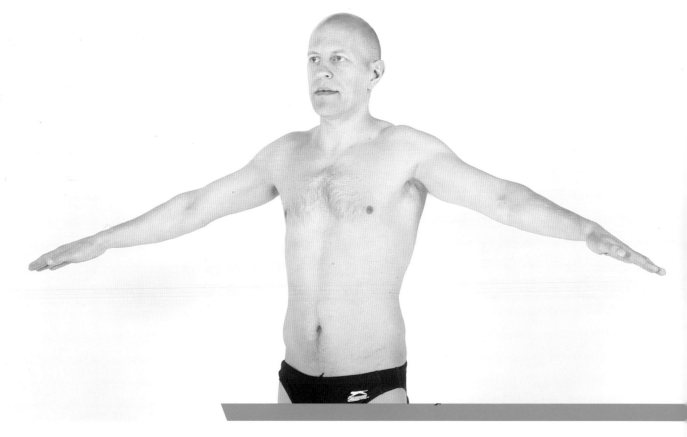

Using reference images in Maya and Mudbox

Setting up images and cameras to use for modeling reference

In this chapter we will take the images from the first photoshoot and resize them, using Adobe Bridge in Photoshop (https://creative.adobe.com/products/bridge) and Camera Raw 8.1 (http://helpx.adobe.com/photoshop/camera-raw.html), in order to make them more suitable for being used as reference planes in Maya.

We will then move into Maya to create the cameras that we will be modeling to. We are also going to create a few custom Maya Embedded Language (MEL) buttons to make our workflow more efficient.

I will not be using the Orthographic front or side cameras to attach my reference images to because these cameras have no perspective and are completely flat. Therefore, if we were to try to match our 3D model (which would be flattened in these viewports) to our reference images

(that have some perspective to them), we could get into a bit of bother.

The difference between working with the Orthographic cameras and the perspective cameras may be subtle at times, but it's enough to keep me away from using the former, especially if I have plenty of camera information to run with.

However, if you were planning to use technical drawings (for example of buildings, tables, cars, and so on), then slotting your reference images into the front and side camera views would do the trick perfectly.

01: Preparing the reference images

Starting off in Photoshop, you need to go to File > Browse in Bridge and navigate to the folder containing the full body RAW images (\sourceimages\01_WIP\02_modelingReference\00_RAW\01_FULL_BODY).

If you select any of the images here, you will be able to see plenty of information about the type of camera used, the lens, and so on.

To select all of the images, select the first image of the sequence, then hold Shift while selecting the last image. Click the RMB and select Open in Camera Raw.

Once the images have loaded in Camera Raw, first make sure you turn on Select All in the top-left corner so that we can affect all the images at once. Now switch to the Lens Corrections tab and turn on Enable Lens Profile Corrections. The images were taken with a 50mm lens, so the distortion is minimal, but I prefer to get rid of it.

Click on the Workflow Options button so we can reduce the size and bit depth of the image. Set the depth to 8 Bits/Channel and enable Resize to Fit. Set the width to 1500 and the height to 1000, then hit OK.

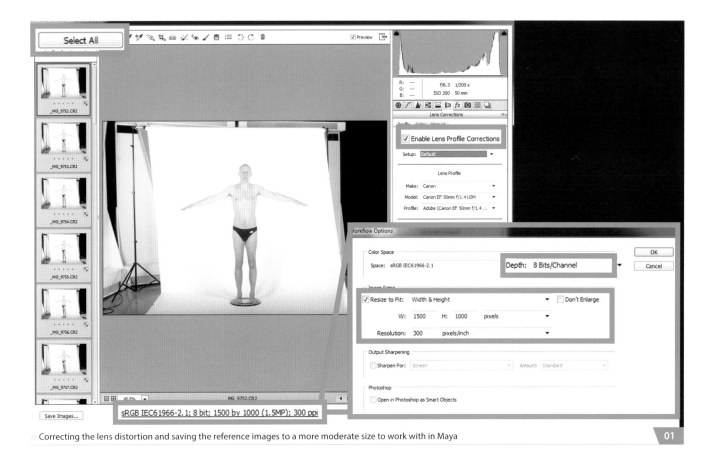

○ Correcting the lens distortion and saving the reference images to a more moderate size to work with in Maya

01

"Rename the files so that they are more easily understandable when it comes to attaching them to the Maya cameras"

02: Saving the reference images
We now want to save our files out to a file type that Maya will be happy with, and also rename the files so that they are more easily understandable when it comes to attaching them to the Maya cameras.

Still in Camera Raw, hit the Save Image button on the bottom-left corner. When the window pops up, select a location for the images to be saved into.

I create a folder labeled 01_PRIMARY, located in: \sourceimages\01_WIP\02_ modelingReference\01_IMAGES. Set the name to **fullBody_mod_ref** with a 2 Digit Serial Number. Add 0 into the Begin Numbering box. Change the file extension to .TIF and save. Give it a minute or two to save out the image files.

Once you have finished the full body reference images, do the same for the head shots.

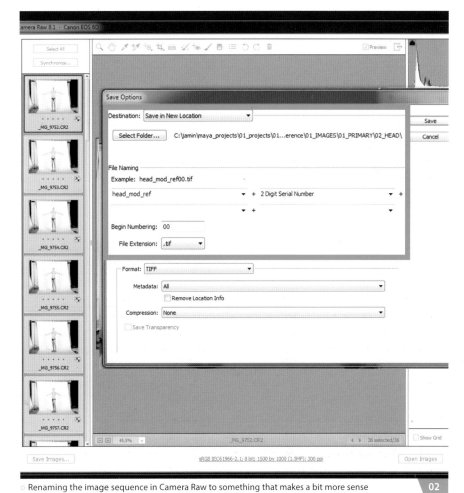

○ Renaming the image sequence in Camera Raw to something that makes a bit more sense

02

03: Working to scale

To ensure we're working to the correct scale, let's create some dummy geometry and use the Measure tools to line things up. We have the measurements of the turntable used during the shoot, so let's create a digital version of it.

Start by going to Create > Polygons Primitives > Cylinder, and under INPUTS in the Channel Box, change the height to 1.8 and the radius to 20.25. In the side view, translate the cylinder up slightly to sit on the grid. You may find it easier to turn on wireframe mode to do this (keyboard shortcut 4).

Still in side view, go to Create > Measure Tools > Distance Tool. Make a first click at the top of the cylinder (the turntable). Then hold down the X key on the keyboard to activate Snap to Grid and make a second click somewhere above.

You should now have two locators and a value giving you the distance between them. Select the second locator and translate it up in the Y-axis until the measurement is 178 (the height of our model in cm).

Lastly, create a cube and scale it up to match the height of the second locator from the top of the turntable. Now we have something to use as a guide when we introduce the reference cameras.

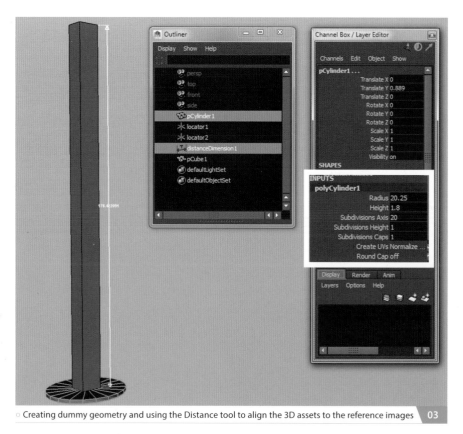

○ Creating dummy geometry and using the Distance tool to align the 3D assets to the reference images **03**

04: The first reference camera

To create a new camera, go to Create > Camera > Camera and rename this camera **fullBody_camera_0**. To look through the camera, in the Viewport menu, go to Panels > Look Through Selected. With the new camera now active, in the Viewport menu, go to View > Camera Attribute Editor. Now start by setting the Focal Length to 50 (the same as the lens used during the shoot) and make sure Film Gate is set to 35mm Film SLR. To position the camera, make sure you have **fullBody_camera_0** selected, and in the Channel Box, set Translate Y to 107 and Translate Z to 512.

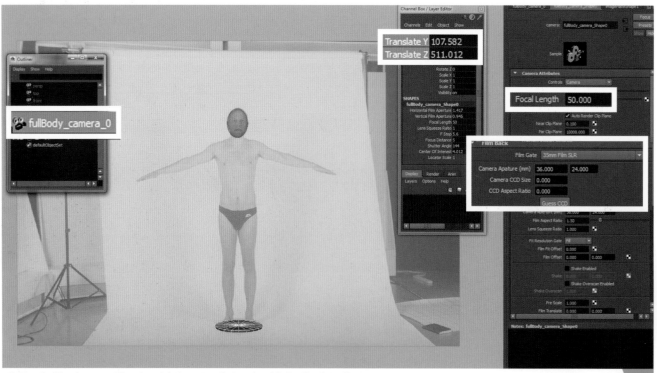

○ Setting the Maya camera settings to match the camera that was used during the photoshoot **04**

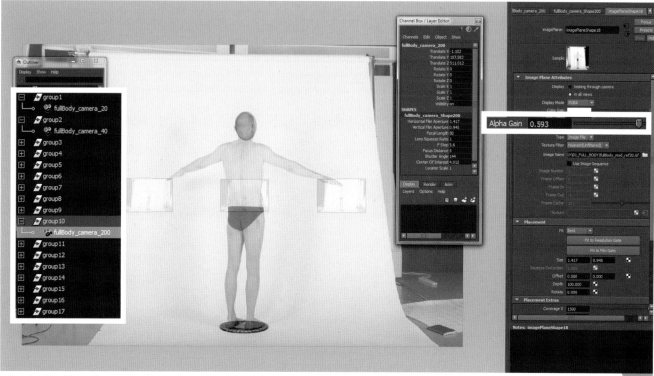

Creating the additional cameras and lowering the Alpha Gain to add transparency to the reference images

05

We can now add the image to see if everything lines up. Make sure you are still looking through the camera and, in the Viewport menu, go to View > Image Plane > Import Image. When the dialog box pops up, navigate to \sourceimages\01_WIP\02_ modelingReference\01_IMAGES\01_ PRIMARY\01_FULL_BODY and select **fullBody_mod_ref00.tif** (00 being 0°).

05: Adjusting the first camera and creating the additional cameras

With the image loaded and **fullBody_camera_0** still selected, look for the ImagePlaneShape1 tab in the Attribute Editor. In this tab, reduce Alpha Gain down to somewhere around 0.5 so we can see through the image.

Now let's frame the image so it's not cropped in the viewport. With the camera selected, drop down to the Display Options in the Attribute Editor and set Overscan to 1.3.

When you are happy with the position of your camera, do not move it. Later on we'll lock the ability to do so, but for now if you need to move around the 3D environment, do so using the Perspective camera. If you want to switch between the Perspective and the new camera, in the Viewport menu, go to Panels > Perspective > fullBody_camera_0.

This will be one way to switch between all the additional cameras we will create.

Delete the cube we have at the moment and create a polygon primitive sphere. With the sphere selected, scale and position it to roughly match the size of the model's head and then delete the distance node and the two locators used to determine the height. We'll use the sphere as a loose guide for adding the extra cameras.

Now select **fullBody_camera_0** and hit Ctrl+D to duplicate it, renaming the camera **fullBody_camera_20**. With the duplicated camera selected, hit Ctrl+G to group it to itself.

With that group node now selected (it should be easy to find it in the Outliner), pop a value of 20 into the Rotate Y channel to position and orient the camera in the correct location.

06: Additional cameras continued

Select **fullBody_camera_20** and, in the Viewport menu, go to Panels > Look Through Selected. Then go to View > Image Plane > Import Image and select **fullBody_mod_ref02. tif** (02 being 20°). Again, take down the Alpha Gain for the ImagePlaneShape2 node and look to see if the sphere lines up. Be aware that some images may be slightly off, but this is due to the fact that the model may have moved during the photoshoot.

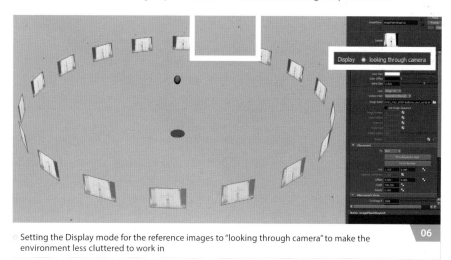

Setting the Display mode for the reference images to "looking through camera" to make the environment less cluttered to work in

06

Now take the **group1** node in the Outliner, duplicate it again (Ctrl+D), and this time pop a value of 40 into the Rotate Y channel. Within that group node, you will find a camera that has also been duplicated. Rename this camera **fullBody_mod_ref40** and attach the image **fullBody_mod_ref04. tif** (04 being 40°). Lower the Alpha Gain.

"With so many cameras in the scene now, and group nodes aplenty, let's do a bit of housework to keep our scenes neat"

Repeat this step in increments of 20° all the way around. Also add a camera at 90° and 270°, allowing us to have both lateral views while we model. As you do this, remember to rotate the group nodes, not the cameras.

Once you have all the cameras in place, go to each ImagePlaneShape node one by one and change the Display to "looking through camera" to make for a cleaner area to work in when in Perspective mode.

07: Cleaning up the scene

With so many cameras in the scene now, and group nodes aplenty, let's do a bit of housework to keep our scenes neat. Start by selecting all the group nodes in the Outliner and, on the Status Bar, change the input line menu of operations to Rename. Now type in **camera_grp** and hit Enter. Select **camera_grp** in the Outliner now and rename it to **camera_grp0**.

Now select all the current camera group nodes that we have and hit Ctrl+G to pop them under a new group node. Rename this new group node **camera_grp**.

Next select all the cameras in the scene and in the Channel Box highlight all the transform attributes (Translate, Rotate, and Scale) and the attributes under the SHAPES node. Hold down the RMB and choose Lock Selected. Then select all the group nodes that we have in the scene, highlight all the transform attributes, and do the same again.

Select all the cameras via the Outliner and, in the Layers Editor, go to Layers > Create

Layer from Selected and then rename that layer to **reference_cam_layer**. Also, set the middle box on that layer to R (reference) by clicking it twice, so we can no longer select the cameras within the scene. Finally, select the cylinder and the sphere that we have in our scene and hit Ctrl+G to group them together. Rename this group node to **temp_geo_grp**.

08: 2D Pan and Zoom

We've now locked all the cameras off so we do not accidentally move them in 3D space or change the focal length. A negative of this, however, is that we cannot get close to the reference.

To allow for this, we can use the 2D Pan and Zoom tools that are available in the Attribute Editor for each camera and in the View menu. It takes a few clicks to get them going but we can make the process a little snappier. As mentioned in section 01's introduction to the Maya interface, the Maya UI is highly customizable, so let's create some buttons using MEL.

Start by creating a new shelf by clicking on the small arrow to the left of the Shelves bar and going to New Shelf. Rename this shelf **modelingCamera** or something that makes sense to you.

Now open up the Script Editor, make sure you are in a MEL window, and type in the following three lines:

```
setToolTo $gPanZoomCtx;
panZoomCtx -e -panMode PanZoomContext;
panZoomCtx -e -zoomMode PanZoomContext;
```

Highlight the first line and use the MMB to drag and drop it onto your new shelf. Then highlight the second line and drop it onto the shelf, and then again for the last line. If you click on these buttons now, the first will turn on the 2D Pan/Zoom tool, the second will pop you into Pan mode, and the third will take you into Zoom mode.

If you open up the Shelf Editor (click on the tiny arrow to the left of the Shelves bar) you can rename the contents to make them more easy to understand as you work. I renamed the commands (in order) to **panZoom, pan**, and **zoom**. Under Options, I also set the mode to Icon/Text Beside to simplify what each tool does.

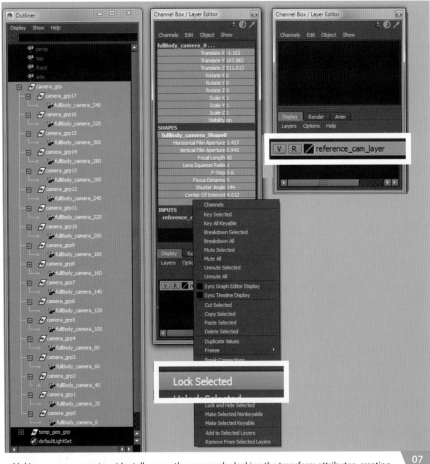

○ Making sure we cannot accidentally move the cameras by locking the transform attributes; creating a layer allowing us to easily show and hide the cameras

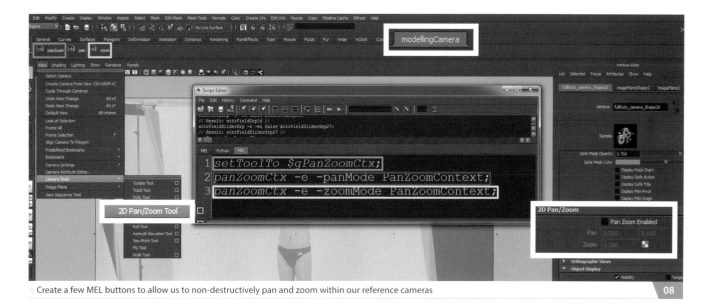

○ Create a few MEL buttons to allow us to non-destructively pan and zoom within our reference cameras **08**

"Like we did for the 2D Pan and Zoom, let's create a few custom MEL buttons to speed up the process"

09: Switching reference cameras

To currently switch between the reference cameras, you need to go to Panels > Perspective > and then select the camera you want. This is also a few too many clicks for my liking. Like we did for the 2D Pan and Zoom, let's create a few custom MEL buttons to speed up the process. Back in the Script Editor, type the following line:

lookThroughModelPanel fullBody_camera_0 modelPanel4;

In your viewport, switch to the Perspective camera, then highlight the line of code in the Script Editor and hit Enter on the numpad on your keyboard (or go to Command > Execute).

You should notice that the viewport camera has now switched to **fullBody_camera_0**. Use the MMB to drag and drop this line of code onto the modelingCamera shelf. Re-write the line to read the following for the second camera:

lookThroughModelPanel fullBody_camera_20 modelPanel4;

Again, use the MMB to drop that line onto the shelf. Do the same for all the cameras and you will have a line of buttons allowing you to easily switch between one camera and another. Remember to go into the Shelf Editor and rename what each button does.

The scene should now be ready for us to start building the base mesh, which we will do in the next chapter.

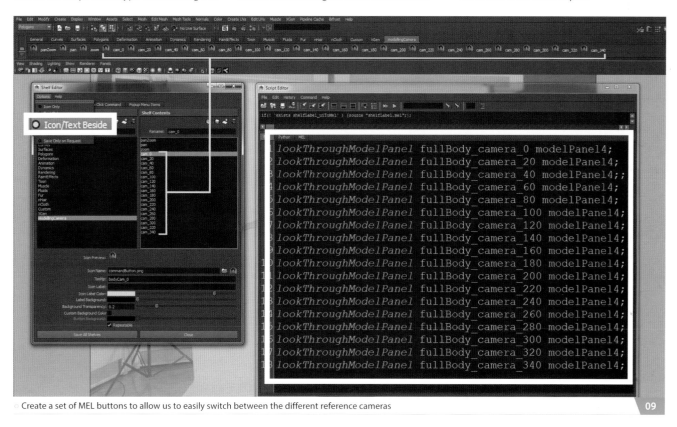

○ Create a set of MEL buttons to allow us to easily switch between the different reference cameras **09**

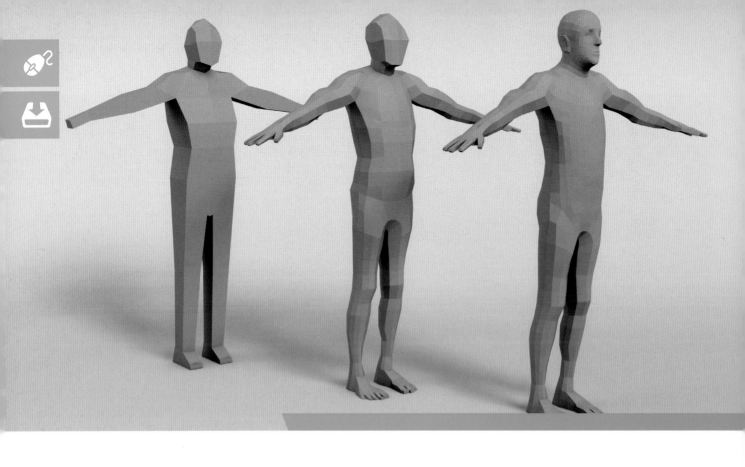

Creating a base mesh in Maya and Mudbox

Building up a base mesh in Maya and testing it in Mudbox

We are now officially ready to create the base mesh in Maya. We will later take this mesh into Mudbox to sculpt the forms and add the fine detail. We'll be using a technique known as box modeling, and employing the tools that were introduced earlier in this section. To get an overall idea of how we'll be creating the asset from modeling to texturing and shading, look at the diagram on the right. As with everything in CG, there'll be some back-and-forth, but this should give you the bigger picture.

01: The trusty cube and Duplicate Special

If you still have the sphere from the previous chapter in the scene, simply select it and hit Delete on the keyboard to get rid of it. Then select the **pCylinder1** object, rename it **turntable_geo**, and pop it into a new display layer. Rename this new layer **temp_geo_layer** and then set it to Reference so you cannot select the cylinder.

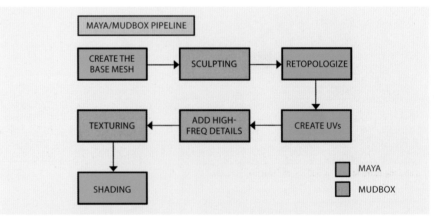

○ The planned route to create our character from a base mesh to a final shaded asset

Create a polygon primitive cube and, under INPUTS, set the Subdivisions Width to 2 (**Fig.01a**). Now switch to face mode, select all the faces on the left-hand side of the cube, and delete them. Switch back to object mode and go to Edit > Duplicate Special (Options). When the dialog box pops up, set the Geometry type to Instance and the Scale to -1, 1, 1. Hit

Duplicate Special and you should have a full cube once more (**Fig.01b**). If one side of the cube is black, simply go to the viewport menu and enable Two Sided Lighting under Lighting. We'll fix this properly later on.

If you manipulate one side of the cube now when in component mode, your actions will be

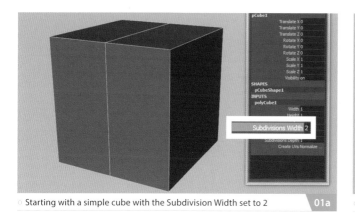

○ Starting with a simple cube with the Subdivision Width set to 2   01a

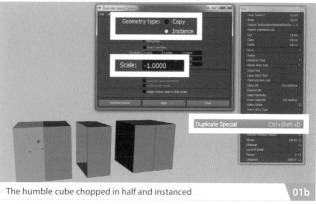

○ The humble cube chopped in half and instanced   01b

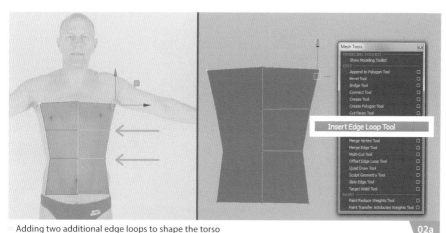

○ Adding two additional edge loops to shape the torso   02a

mirrored to the opposite half. By doing this, we only have to do half the work. Note, however, that later on I will be adding asymmetry to the model to maintain believability.

As we model, we'll want to keep both halves of the cubes together, so try not to pull the vertices that run down the middle away from the center line in the X-axis, as this will create an open seam. Also be aware that when we transform one half of the object when in object mode, these transforms will not be mirrored over to the other half.

02: Block out the torso

Jump into vertex mode, select all the vertices, and scale the cube to match the length of the torso.

Use the Insert Edge Loop tool to add two additional edge loops to further refine the shape (Fig.02a). Remember to check in multiple views to see how things are lining up.

Select the bottom face of your modified cube and use the Extrude tool to pull it downwards and create the mass for the pelvis (Fig.02b). To create a clean downward extrusion, I enabled world mode on the Extrude manipulator.

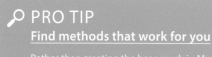

○ Using the Extrude tool to pull out the mass of the pelvis   02b

🔑 PRO TIP
Find methods that work for you

Rather than creating the base mesh in Maya using box modeling techniques, why not try using ZSpheres or DynaMesh in ZBrush? Otherwise, you can start with a simple primitive and push and pull the forms in Mudbox, using the retopology tools to reduce any artifacts as you build up the forms. There are invariably numerous ways to tackle a problem, so work the way that suits you best.

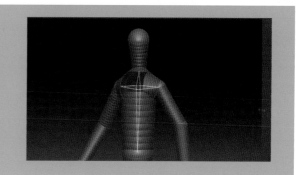

○ Using ZSpheres to block out the overall mesh can be a great way to get things going

03: Internal faces and pulling out the leg

If you hit the 3 key on your keyboard now, with the object selected, you'll notice that an internal face is present where we just created the pelvis. Select this face and delete it so we do not run into any bother later on (Fig.03a).

Next, take the outer edge of the pelvic mass and translate it towards the center line to create a line that runs from the ASIS to the spine of the pubis (inguinal ligament). When you tuck this edge in, make sure you leave him some room for his manly bits. Then take the face on the outside and extrude it downwards to introduce the start of the upper leg (Fig.03b).

Again, I set the Extrude manipulator to world mode, to pull it down cleanly, and then scale the selected face on the Y-axis to flatten it out.

04: The shoulder and arm

Jump up to the top of the torso now, select the upper-most face, and extrude it up (in world mode) to create the chest region. Again, an internal face will be present, so do make sure you delete it. Tweak the vertices so the highest point at the center sits at the pit of the neck and the outside edge sits at the acromion process.

Take the top face on the lateral side of the mesh and extrude it out to create the shoulder mass. Now take the top-outer edge from the newly created mass and tuck it inwards, towards the acromion process, to form the highest part of the shoulder (Fig.04a).

Now take the outer-lower edge from the shoulder mass and pull it upwards and outwards to where the deltoid muscle would insert into the humerus.

Next take the face below the shoulder mass and scale it in slightly so we can pull out an arm that is of a reasonable size for the figure. With that face still selected, extrude it outwards in order to create the geometry for the upper arm (Fig.04b).

Remember to check your work in other camera angles as you progress. Some things will not line up 100% as the model will have moved slightly, so pick a few reference cameras as your primary source and the other cameras as a secondary source.

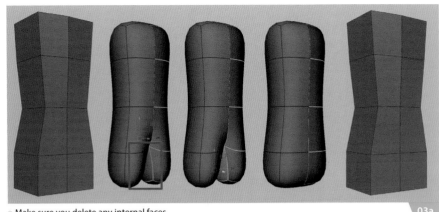

○ Make sure you delete any internal faces   03a

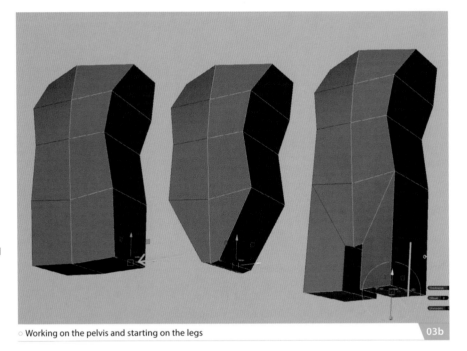

○ Working on the pelvis and starting on the legs   03b

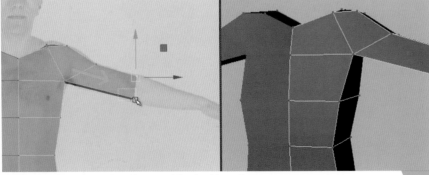

a   b   c   d

○ Forming the shoulder mass by pushing and pulling a couple of the edges   04a

○ Pulling out the upper arm from the mass of the shoulder region   04b

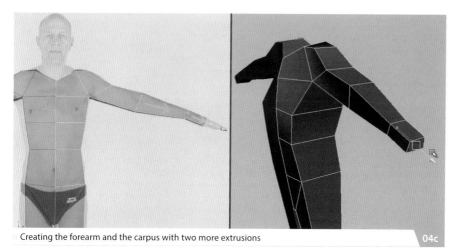

Creating the forearm and the carpus with two more extrusions 04c

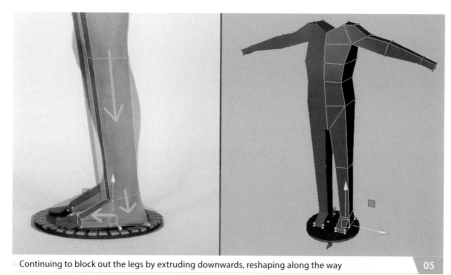

Continuing to block out the legs by extruding downwards, reshaping along the way 05

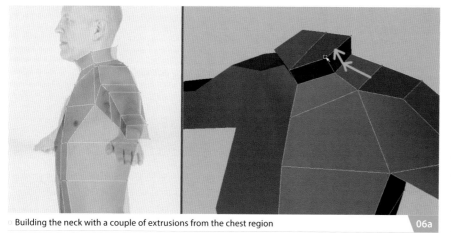

Building the neck with a couple of extrusions from the chest region 06a

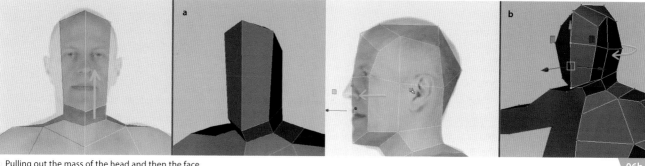

Pulling out the mass of the head and then the face 06b

Finish off the arm with two more extrudes to create the mass for the forearm and the carpus (Fig.04c). As you work your way down the arm, also scale the faces in slightly. This is because you'll find that throughout the body, as we move from root (proximal) to tip (distal), the forms start to taper.

05: Blocking out the rest of the leg

Back to the leg now. As we did for the arm, perform an extrusion to pull out the mass for the lower leg, and then another extrusion to create the mass for the ankle.

At this stage you should have reached the turntable. Now take the bottom-front face of the leg (from the ankle mass) and do one more extrusion to create the form that will later be refined into the dorsum of the foot.

As well as using the images provided as a source of reference, remember to look at your own body. As mentioned at the start of this section, you are a living, breathing, 3D primary reference source, which is the best kind there is.

06: Blocking the neck and head

Move back up to the chest region now so we can pull out the neck and the head. As we create the following extrusions, remember to delete the internal faces that will be present.

Select the upper-most face, extruding it upwards and scaling it in to form the base of the neck, meeting the pit of the neck at the front and the 7th cervical vertebra at the back. Take the upper-most face again and extrude it once more to create the mass of the neck (Fig.06a).

To create the geometry that will later become the face, first take the face at the top of the neck and extrude it upwards to the top of the skull. Then select the front-most face and perform another extrusion to create the front

69

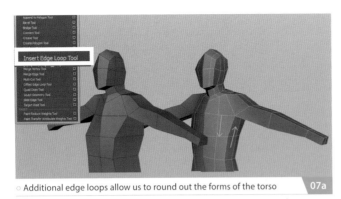

○ Additional edge loops allow us to round out the forms of the torso 07a

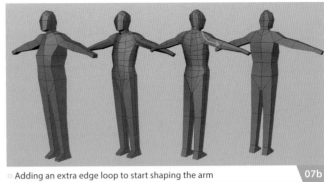

○ Adding an extra edge loop to start shaping the arm 07b

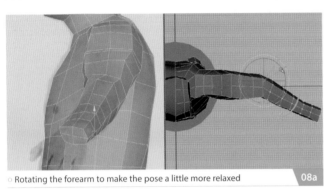

○ Rotating the forearm to make the pose a little more relaxed 08a

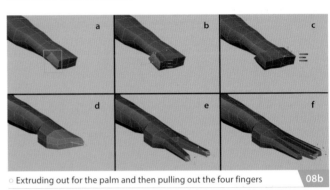

○ Extruding out for the palm and then pulling out the four fingers 08b

of the face (Fig.06b). To help refine the current shape, insert an edge loop to cut around the head mass and then push and pull the vertices to create a more pleasing result.

07: Rounding out the current forms

To round out some of the forms of the arm and the shoulder, I introduce another edge loop. At this stage, we should be ready to round out the legs, push the arms further, and introduce the hands and feet.

08: Refining the arm and adding the hand

To add more shape to the arm, add a couple more edge loops to the upper arm region and three more edge loops to the forearm. To break up the very rigid, straight arm, select the vertices of the forearm, switch to the Rotate tool, and hit Insert on the keyboard so we can edit the position of the manipulator (Fig.08a).

Move the manipulator to the elbow region, hit Insert once more, and then rotate the lower arm to a more relaxed pose. Now push and pull the vertices to refine the shape of the arm with the extra edge loop detail present.

Moving on to the hand, we require a bit more geometry to allow us to pull out the four fingers and the thumb. Start by selecting the two outside faces on the end of the carpal

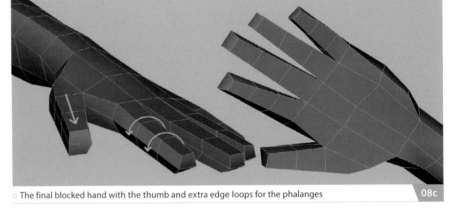

○ The final blocked hand with the thumb and extra edge loops for the phalanges 08c

region and extrude them out. Then do the same for the faces on the opposite side. Then select all the front faces and extrude them forwards to create the box-like palm region.

Now select the two faces that will become the index finger, and the two faces that will become the ring finger, and extrude them out. Then go back and select the remaining four faces (two for the middle finger and two for the pinky finger) and extrude them out as well (Fig.08b).

Select two faces on the inside of the palm and extrude them out a few times to create the thumb. Once you have all the fingers and the thumb blocked out, add additional edge loops to divide the fingers and thumbs into the phalanges. Remember that the thumb has only two phalanges (proximal

and distal) while each finger has three phalanges (proximal, middle, and distal).

09: Adding the toes

We'll block out the toes in the same manner that we did with the fingers. Select the outside face of the foot and extrude it out. To make sure we have enough detail to pull out each toe, we'll need to insert an extra edge loop running down the foot. Make sure you clean up the leg as this cut runs through the mesh. Then take the face on the inside of the foot and extrude it out.

You should now have five front-facing faces that you can extrude the toes out from. If you do this as one extrusion, ensure you disable Keep Faces Together under the INPUTS stack, so as to create individual toes. Otherwise you can extrude them out in twos, as we did for the fingers.

Now continue to refine the toes by adding extra edge loops to break up the phalanges. Toes 2–5 are "stepped" downwards in shape, as opposed to toe 1, which tends to round up, so try to mimic this feature as you block them out. Like the thumb, remember that the big toe has only two phalanges: the proximal and the distal.

10: Blocking out the eye sockets

We'll use the Multi-Cut tool to start laying out the geometry of the eye sockets. I'm following the muscle structure of the orbicularis oculi to inform my decision-making while using the Multi-Cut tool.

As you cut into the mesh, make sure you continue the cuts through the rest of the model so you end up with a mesh made entirely from quads. Then, when we subdivide the mesh, we won't create any unwanted artifacts. The odd triangle isn't too much of an issue, but n-gons tend to create problems if a character is to be deformed.

To make it easier to form the region around the eyes, add a sphere to act as an eyeball and push and pull the forms around it. At this stage, don't worry too much about the topology as we'll be rebuilding this later. Focus mainly on getting the edges evenly spread throughout the model, with the masses in place, so we can build on the forms when sculpting.

11: Adding a mouth

To introduce the mouth, I again take advantage of the Multi-Cut tool and begin to make a few cut lines that mimic the orbicularis oris muscle. Once I'm happy with the placement of the vertices in the front perspective camera (**fullBody_camera_0**), I switch to the side camera (**fullBody_camera_90**) to push the lips back into the desired position. A few additional edge loops allow me to suggest the nasolabial fold.

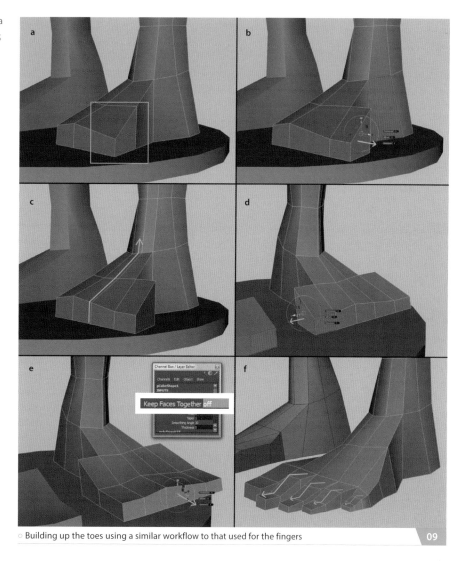
○ Building up the toes using a similar workflow to that used for the fingers   09

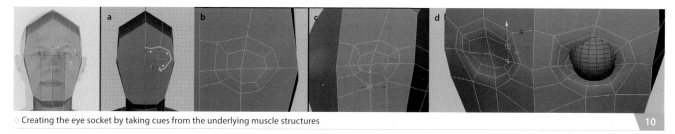
○ Creating the eye socket by taking cues from the underlying muscle structures   10

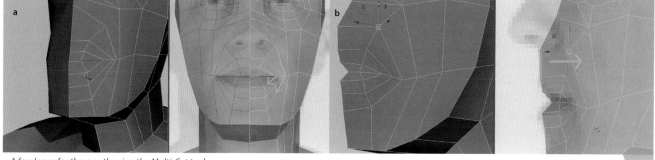
○ A few loops for the mouth using the Multi-Cut tool   11

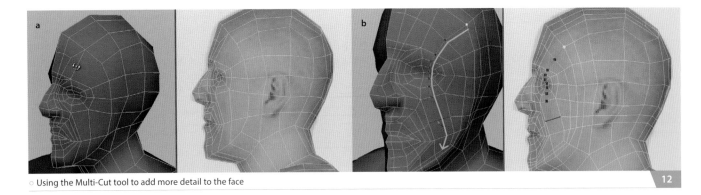

○ Using the Multi-Cut tool to add more detail to the face

12: Refining the face

From this stage onwards, it's simply a case of continuing to cut into the face using the Multi-Cut tool. My key aim here is to continue adding extra edge loops so that each face is similar in its size to its neighbor (or as close as possible).

Later, when it comes to subdividing the mesh, these even faces will create a more uniform result, rather than having some areas that are tightly packed and other areas that are more spread out.

To help speed up the process of pushing and pulling the vertices, I've activated Soft Selection (use the B key to turn on and off). You can control the size of the falloff by holding down the B key and LMB-dragging in the viewport, or jumping into Tool settings.

13: Extruding out the ear

To create the ear, I select three faces and extrude them. I could leave the ear as it is, but decide to continue with a few more extrudes to create the helix and antihelix of the ear. An extra edge loop helps to refine the shape of the ear to better match the reference.

After the ear is added, I spend a bit of time checking the mesh from top to bottom, adding extra edge loops here and there. Some of the edge flow is redirected using the Multi-Cut tool until I'm satisfied with the result.

14: Creating a unified mesh

With the base mesh ready to go, we need to create the final unified mesh to take into Mudbox for sculpting. Start by selecting the instanced geometry (the character's right-hand side) and deleting it. Then select the side we have left and go to Modify > Freeze Transforms to clean up the transform attributes. All the Translate and Rotate

channels should now have values of 0 and the Scale channels should all be at 1.

In edge mode, double-click the inside edge of the model to select every edge that sits

on the X-axis. Then set the input line menu of operations to Absolute Transform and pop a value of 0 into the X box (**Fig.14a**). All the vertices along the midline should now be perfectly flush against the X-axis.

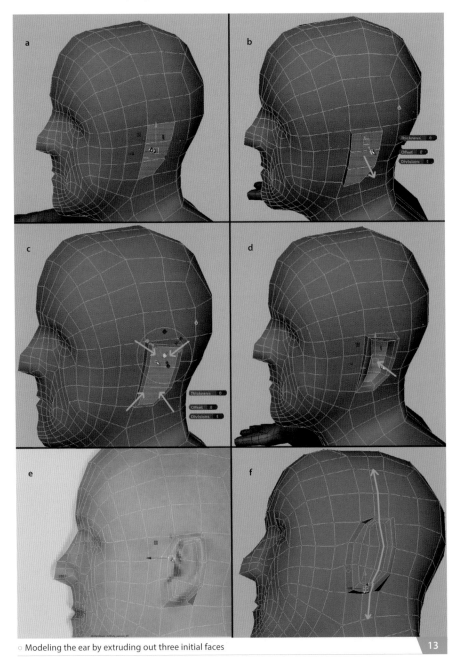

○ Modeling the ear by extruding out three initial faces

PRO TIP

Keeping your scene files clean and light

As you build your assets, all your actions are recorded in the INPUTS stack. Usually you can edit the last few commands, but if you step back, say, 10 or 20 commands, Maya will usually get a little upset and give you something you more than likely didn't expect.

Having heaps of history living on your mesh can also present performance issues as you work. To keep things nice and snappy, I like to delete the history of the model as I work. To do this, simply select the mesh and go to Edit > Delete by Type > History.

○ Deleting the history from your models to keep the scene running smoothly

"By setting such a low threshold, only the vertices that sit on top of one another will be merged together. You should now have a single, unified, watertight mesh"

Jump back into object mode, select the model, and hit Ctrl+D to duplicate it. With the duplicated mesh selected, place a value of -1 into the Scale X channel to flip the mesh over to the character's right-hand side.

To combine the two models together, select both meshes and go to Mesh > Combine. If you select any of the vertices that run down the midline and move them to one side, you will find an open seam present.

To create a watertight mesh, select all the vertices that run down the midline (I simply marquee-select all the vertices in the area) and go to Edit Mesh > Merge Components (Options). When the dialog box pops up, set the Threshold to 0.0001 and hit Merge (**Fig.14b**).

By setting such a low threshold, only the vertices that sit on top of one another will be merged together. You should now have a single, unified, watertight mesh. Before moving on, quickly rename the mesh to **paul_geo**.

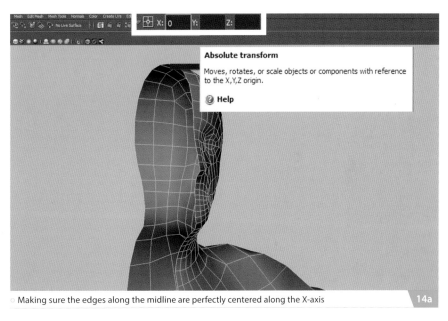

○ Making sure the edges along the midline are perfectly centered along the X-axis　14a

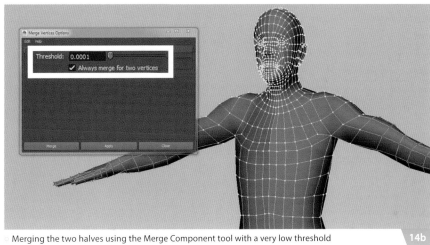

○ Merging the two halves using the Merge Component tool with a very low threshold　14b

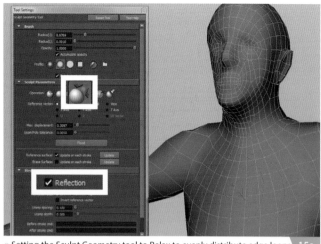

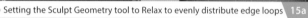

○ Setting the Sculpt Geometry tool to Relax to evenly distribute edge loops **15a**

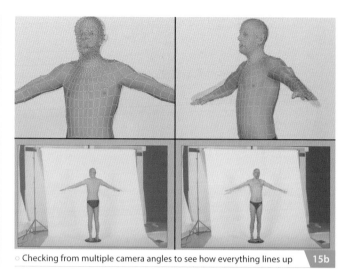

○ Checking from multiple camera angles to see how everything lines up **15b**

"Asymmetry will give me more work to do later, but it really helps to make the character more believable"

15: Using the Sculpt Geometry tool

Before we call the model finished, let's give it a bit of a clean-up with Maya's Sculpt Geometry tool. Select the model and go to Mesh Tools > Sculpt Geometry Tool (Options). Under Sculpt Parameters, set the Operation to Relax and then, under Stroke, enable Reflection (**Fig.15a**).

To interactively increase and decrease the size of the brush, hold down the B key and LMB-drag over the mesh. You can also increase and decrease the strength of the stroke by holding down the M key and LMB-dragging on the model. Using the Sculpt Geometry tool, paint over the mesh to make the edge loops more evenly spaced. The vertices along the midline usually need a bit of attention to remove the "pointy-ness".

Once you've cleaned up the mesh, you should be good to send it to Mudbox. Note I've added some asymmetry (mainly in the face) (**Fig.15b**). This will give me a bit more work to do later on but, as I said before, it really helps to make the character more believable. If you want to save time or use another method to add asymmetry (with blend shapes, perhaps), please do so.

16: Preparing cameras and exporting assets

Currently, if we send the scene file to Mudbox, it will take a few steps to line up all the reference images with the model. To make everything sync up in one hit, we need to

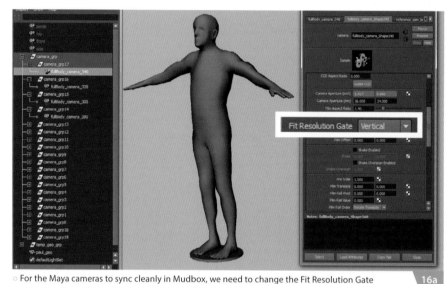

○ For the Maya cameras to sync cleanly in Mudbox, we need to change the Fit Resolution Gate **16a**

make a change to the Maya cameras. Start by selecting **fullBody_camera_0** and opening up the Attribute Editor (Ctrl+A). Now scroll down to Film Back and set the Fit Resolution Gate to Vertical (**Fig.16a**). Do the same for all the cameras and we should be good to go.

We're going to export the geometry and cameras out as an FBX file, so let's make sure that we have that plug-in enabled. Go to Window > Settings/Preferences > Plug-in Manager, and when the dialog box opens up, look for **fbxmaya.mll** (.mll for Windows, .lib

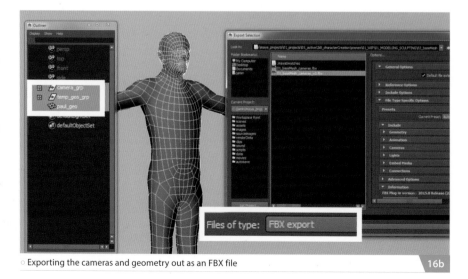

○ Exporting the cameras and geometry out as an FBX file **16b**

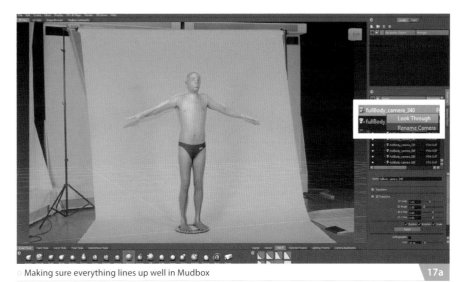

○ Making sure everything lines up well in Mudbox   17a

○ The final base mesh, ready for sculpting   17b

for Mac OS X, and .so for Linux) and check the Loaded and the Auto Load boxes.

Now, from the Outliner, select **camera_grp**, **temp_geo_grp**, and **paul_geo**, and go to File > Export Selection. Save it as **01_baseMesh_cameras_v1** and make sure you set the Files of type to FBX export (**Fig.16b**).

17: Testing the scene file in Mudbox

Open up Mudbox now and go to File > Open. Select the FBX we just created and make sure that everything lines up correctly.

Upon loading the file, you may be presented with a dialog window regarding **turntable_geo**. This is due to the fact that the turntable has a lot of edges that meet at a single vertex. Ignore this for now by hitting Keep This Mesh.

If you are presented with a second dialog box that detects errors with the base mesh (**paul_geo**), go back and fix the mesh before reloading the scene file. If you click the Keep This Mesh button in Mudbox, it will actually highlight the problem areas you need to fix.

Once Mudbox is happy with your meshes (minus the turntable), go to the Object List, hold down the RMB over any of the cameras, and go to Look Through (**Fig.17a**). Hopefully everything lines up correctly and you can start sculpting (**Fig.17b**).

🔍 PRO TIP
Using the Mesh > Cleanup tool

One way to check for any errors in your mesh is to simply send it to Mudbox and let it do its error-checking magic. You can also do something similar in Maya, using the Cleanup tool. To use this tool, select the mesh you'd like to check and go to Mesh > Cleanup.

You have a number of options, but here are my preferred settings: set the Operation to Select matching polygons and then set the Fix by Tessellation to 4-sided faces. Hit Apply and all the 4-sided faces should be selected (see image on the right here). Now go to Edit > Invert Selection (Ctrl+Shift+I) and all the triangles and n-gons should be selected. You should now be able to hit F on the keyboard to frame the trouble spots so you can go in and fix them manually.

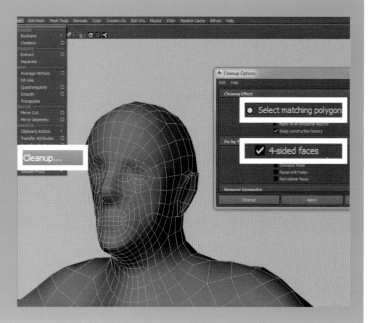

○ Using the Cleanup tool in Maya to check for any triangles and n-gons

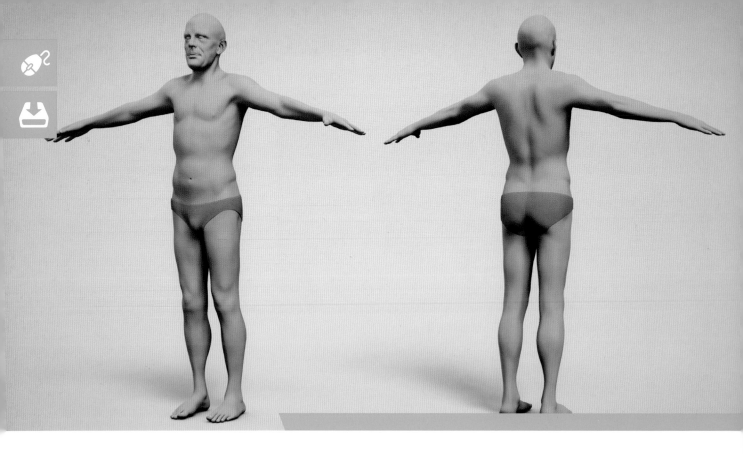

Retopology in Maya and UVs

Retopologizing the character model

Now we'll be taking the model that we worked on in Mudbox and retopologizing it in Maya to create an animatable mesh. My main objective will be to create a mesh which is suitable for deformation, so all the edge loops will be carefully considered in pursuit of this. To make the process more efficient, we'll mainly be using the Modeling Toolkit (MT). We'll start by building one side, then mirror it over to make a symmetrical mesh, and finally add asymmetry to match the reference.

01: Modeling heads-up

Before we start to retopologize, I just want to share some of the dos and don'ts I tend to follow when creating a mesh intended for deformation. Firstly, I like to stick to quads (four-sided faces), because quads subdivide predictably and cause fewer artifacts on a mesh that needs to deform (Fig.01a).

If you do have the odd triangle here and there, it shouldn't be too much of an issue, but I would stay away from n-gons (faces

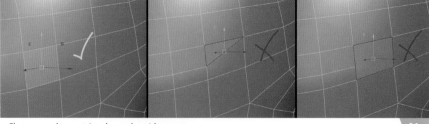
○ Choose quads over triangles and avoid n-gons　01a

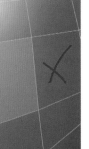
○ Try to make the faces squarer in shape　01b

with more than four edges). I try to keep each face at a size relative to its neighbor, and I also like to keep the faces as square as possible, rather than rectangular (Fig.01b).

This is because I find square faces easier to handle during the enveloping process, and they cause less of a headache regarding texture distortion.

The direction and layout of the edges will dictate how the character deforms, so make sure that the major edges all have a purpose. If you are not intending for your model to deform, then of course you can cut some corners. Though if you are, the more effort you put in to make your topology mimic skin, muscle, and wrinkle flow, the better the deformation will be.

02: Intro to the Modeling Toolkit

Let's now look at how we'll be using the MT. If you don't have the MT open, go into the Plug-in Manager (Windows > Preferences) and turn it on (Fig.02a). The main tool of interest for us from the MT is the Quad Draw. This will allow you to draw faces on a mesh that has been turned into a Live Surface.

Select the sculpt that we exported from

Sculpting the forms

Adding realistic surface anatomy with Mudbox

Please turn to the back of the book to find this chapter, in which we'll be using Mudbox to sculpt the muscle groups, body fat, and skin wrinkles that'll give the model an impression of life and weight.

If you'd like to move the current vertices, edges, or faces around, do so simply by grabbing and dragging them with the LMB. To create an edge loop, hover over a face, hold down the Ctrl key, and LMB-click. If you'd like to delete a face or a row of edges, hold down the Shift and Ctrl keys together. The edge of the face beneath the cursor will go yellow, and you can click the LMB to blow it away.

My favorite feature of the MT is the way you can relax the vertices in the same way you would do with the Sculpt Geometry Tool – only with the Quad Draw, it's built in. To do so, simply hold down the Shift key and use the LMB to paint over the surface. When doing so you'll find the vertices still stay fixed to the live surface. However, you can also enable Soft Selection (B) to have a falloff applied to the tool (Fig.02c).

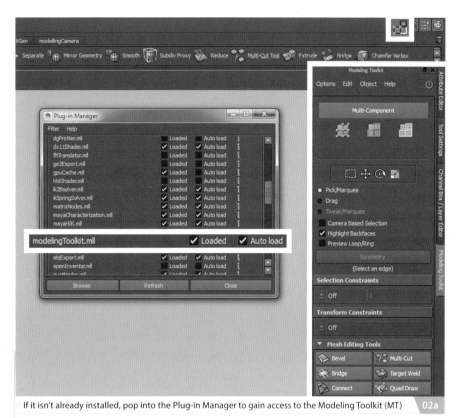

If it isn't already installed, pop into the Plug-in Manager to gain access to the Modeling Toolkit (MT) **02a**

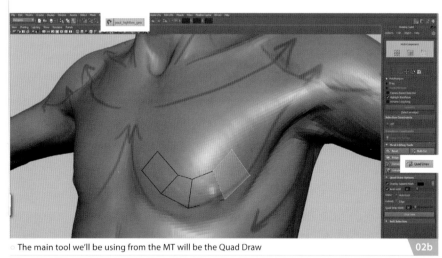

The main tool we'll be using from the MT will be the Quad Draw **02b**

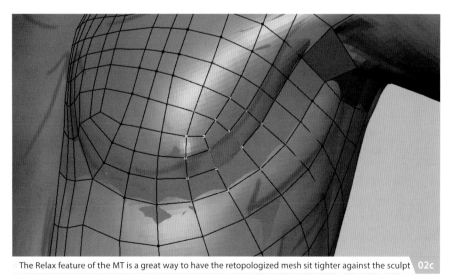

The Relax feature of the MT is a great way to have the retopologized mesh sit tighter against the sculpt **02c**

03: Retopologizing the torso

Let's begin the retopology with the torso. Following the guidelines, begin by creating a row of faces that follows the contours of the chest, and then work it over the shoulder region and towards the back.

Anatomically, we are not quite playing by the rules here, but I have found that by creating an edge flow like this, you can achieve some pretty nice deformation without too much fuss. Don't create too many faces at this stage because you can always insert extra edge loops later on in the process.

Focus on the flow, always bear the anatomy in mind, and think about where natural crease lines occur on the human body. Remember, you'll only need to work on one side as we'll mirror it over later on.

04: Transfer Attributes

To have our retopologized mesh sit tightly against the sculpted mesh, I tend to use the Transfer Attribute tool a lot. First, you'll have to click on the magnet icon to stop the sculpt mesh from being a live surface. Then select the sculpted mesh and Shift-select the current retopologized mesh. Now go to Mesh > Transfer Attributes (Options). When the dialog window pops up, go Edit > Reset Settings and hit OK to run the tool. The retopologized mesh should then snap snugly against the sculpt.

A word of warning: as soon as you've used this tool, make sure to select both meshes and go to Edit > Delete By Type > History. Failing to do so often results in a crash soon after. I'll be using this tool constantly throughout the process of retopologizing the mesh. Sometimes I'll even subdivide the retopologized mesh (Mesh > Subdivide) and perform Transfer Attributes to get an idea of what the final outcome will be. If you do this make sure to undo and return to the original mesh.

05: Retopologizing the arm

Once you've blocked out the torso, hide that piece of geometry by hitting Ctrl+H or popping it into a Display Layer. We could have continued to model the arm from the torso geometry but I like to work on the different regions of the body separately, allowing me a bit more freedom when creating the edge flow. Later on we'll be bringing the two parts together.

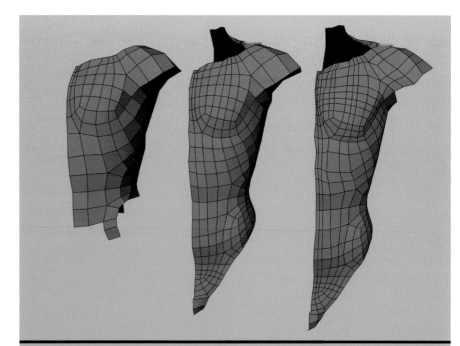
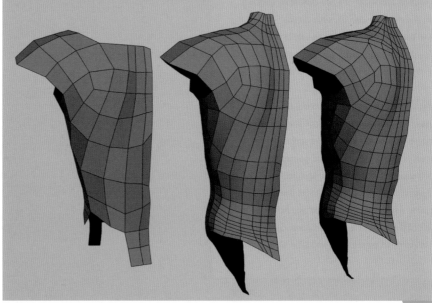

○ Blocking out the torso and defining the muscle masses   03

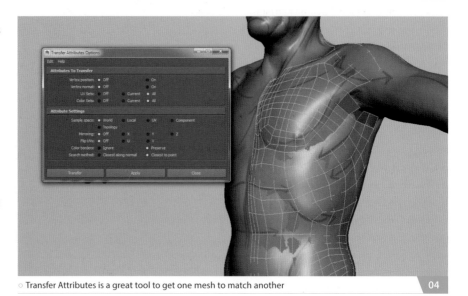

○ Transfer Attributes is a great tool to get one mesh to match another   04

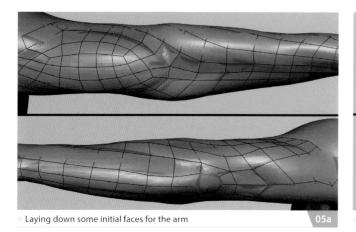

Laying down some initial faces for the arm **05a**

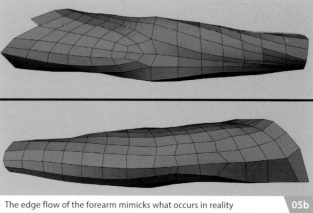

The edge flow of the forearm mimicks what occurs in reality **05b**

Using the same methodology, begin to create a fresh set of faces that loosely follows the guidelines of the arm. I say "loosely" here as I made a conscious decision to create faces around the bicep but not the tricep; the reason being that once this mesh is retopologized, I'd have enough resolution in the mesh to give me good volume to deform the tricep (Fig.05a).

As the hand is facing palm-side down, I make sure to create a flow of faces that runs from the elbow region to the thumb side of the hand, mimicking the natural flow of the skin when the palm is facing down (Fig.05b).

If you actually grab a pen and draw a line on your own arm, running from your elbow to the thumb, and rotate your forearm to go from supine to prone, you'll get a clearer idea of the how the skin flows here.

06: Attaching the arm to the torso

Once you are happy with the arm, unhide the torso, select both the arm and torso, and go to Mesh > Combine. With the combined mesh selected, go to Edit > Delete By Type History. We can now merge the vertices of the arm to the torso to close the gap. To do this, first line up the vertices of the open arm with those of the open torso where the two should meet (Fig.06a).

I then use the Merge Vertex tool and drag and drop the vertices of the arm on top of the corresponding vertices of the torso (Fig.06b). At this stage, you may find that you'll need to insert extra edge loops to match up the number of vertices from both sides and close the gap. After you've added the edge loops, make sure you go in and clean up the mesh. For this I use the Sculpt Geometry tool with the Operation set to Relax.

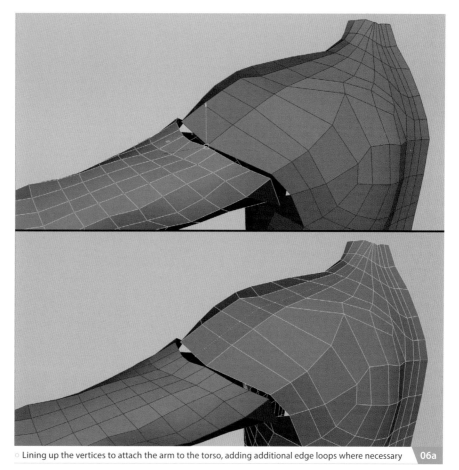

Lining up the vertices to attach the arm to the torso, adding additional edge loops where necessary **06a**

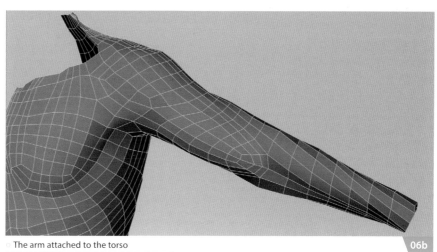

The arm attached to the torso **06b**

07: Retopologizing the hand

I work on the hand away from the body again, to avoid feeling governed by my previous work. I begin by creating the thenar and hypothenar masses before moving on to the fingers. The index finger is created first, independently of the body of the hand. This is so I can produce one finger (in this case, the index) and then duplicate it to make the others (Fig.07a). Some point-pushing is in order, of course, to match the length of each finger. For the thumb I also duplicate the finger geometry, but make sure to delete a couple of edges as the thumb only has two phalanges.

Once I'm happy with the fingers and thumb, I bring them together and create the "webbing" that's present between each digit. Following on from this, I combine the fingers with the body of the thumb, make some tweaks, and leave the hand there for now (Fig.07b).

08: Retopologizing the leg

Moving on to the lower limb, I begin by creating a row of faces that follow the contours of the gluteus maximus. I then create another row of faces flowing from the ASIS down to the pubic symphysis, and then in between the legs to meet the gluteal mass. Continuing from the ASIS, more faces are added to create the pelvic crest (Fig.08a).

Using the reference lines, I continue down the thigh, following the sartorius, and afterwards fill in the space for the quadriceps and patella. The same approach is taken for the posterior aspect of the thigh and leg (Fig.08b).

09: Retopologizing the foot

With the leg created, it's now hidden to spend time on the foot. Following the same workflow as employed on the hand, I work on

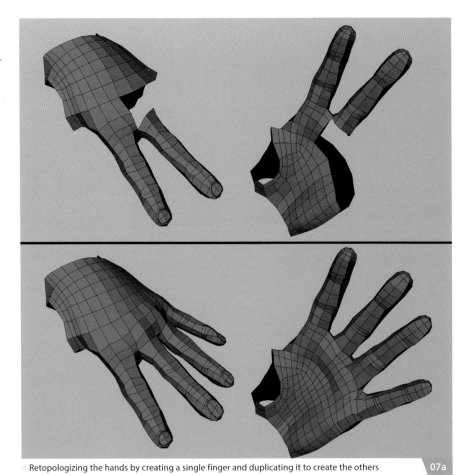

Retopologizing the hands by creating a single finger and duplicating it to create the others   07a

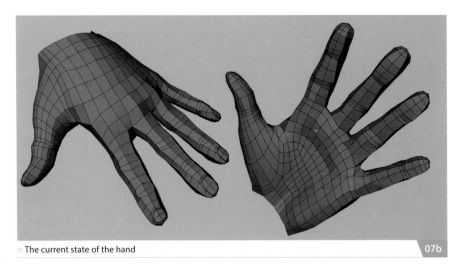

The current state of the hand   07b

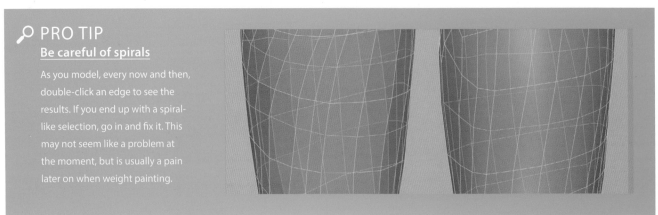

🔎 PRO TIP
Be careful of spirals

As you model, every now and then, double-click an edge to see the results. If you end up with a spiral-like selection, go in and fix it. This may not seem like a problem at the moment, but is usually a pain later on when weight painting.

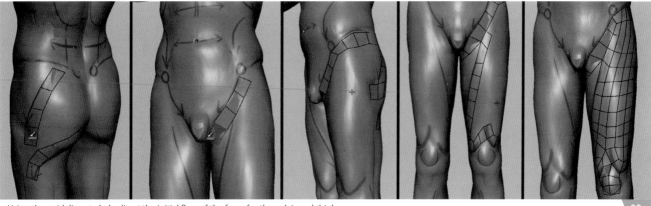

○ Using the guidelines to help direct the initial flow of the faces for the pelvis and thigh

08a

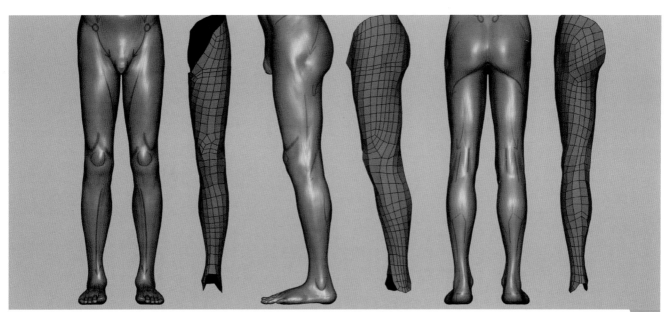

○ The front, side and back view of the retopologized leg

08b

"One main toe is created, and all the others are reshaped duplicates of this"

the body of the foot separately from the toes. Again, one main toe is created, and all the others are reshaped duplicates of this (Fig.09a). Once all the parts are in place, it's a process of combining these parts and then cleaning up a bit. As with between each finger, don't forget to add the "webbing" between the toes (Fig.09b).

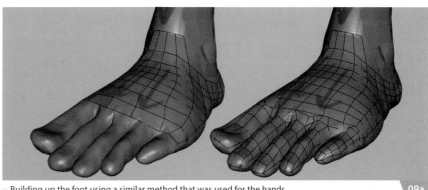

○ Building up the foot using a similar method that was used for the hands

09a

10: Retopologizing the face
Moving on to the face now (over the page), I begin by creating loops around the mouth and lips that mimic the orbicularis oris muscle. More faces are then added to create the nasolabial fold and chin (Fig.10a). I start out this process with quite large-sized faces, but as more resolution is needed to shape the region, extra edge loops are of course added. The eye is next, with a row of faces being

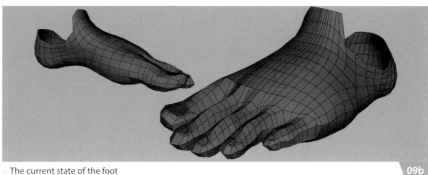

○ The current state of the foot

09b

created for the outer edge of the eyelids. A conscious choice I make here is to follow the flow of the skin as opposed to the muscle (the orbicularis oculi). This is because I seem to get better results for creating wrinkles and folds when deforming the face by using this technique. Once I'm happy with this region, I combine this mesh with the mouth portion and create faces to flow between the two forms (Fig.10b).

The nose is introduced soon after, as is the brow. The cheek is also filled in, and again the Transfer Attribute is used to tighten things up (Fig.10c).

11: Continuing with the face

Continuing with the face, the forehead and part of the neck are created. Next, I make some polygons that follow the sternocleidomastoid and the temporalis muscles. Other than the ear, the bulk of the face should be in place now, and it's just a case of filling in the gaps in between its major forms.

"Additional edge loops may be necessary to close the open seams"

12: Retopologizing the ear

For the ear, I create a row of faces for the helix, and then begin to add additional faces to create the antihelix, tragus, and so on. As we have the sculpt as reference, fleshing out the ear shouldn't take too long. Once you are happy with it, combine it with the main mesh of the head and weld the two parts together. Again, additional loops may be necessary to close the open seams between the two forms.

13: Eye and nose cavity

Moving on from this, a temporary eye bag and a nostril are added. The eye bag is only temporary, but by creating it now, you should be better able to go in and refine the eyelids around the eyeball geometry.

14: Create a mouth bag

You'll also need to create a mouth bag for the model, so that when the character opens his mouth it's not simply a gaping hole. This piece of geometry begins as part of the geometry of the face, which is then separated; I do this so it doesn't freak out when using the Transfer Attributes tool, which would have forced it to stick to the closest surface.

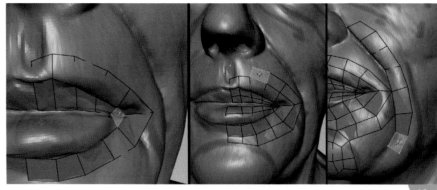

○ Mimicking the orbicularis oris muscle to retopologize the mouth, and creating additional faces for the nasolabial fold   10a

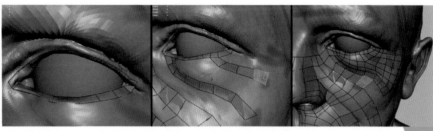

○ Creating the eye region by thinking about the natural skin and wrinkle flow rather than muscle flow   10b

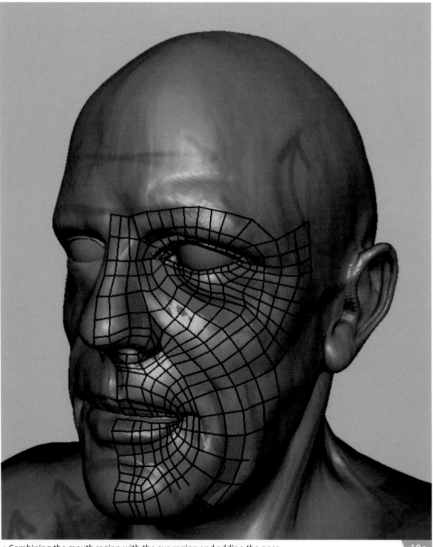

○ Combining the mouth region with the eye region and adding the nose   10c

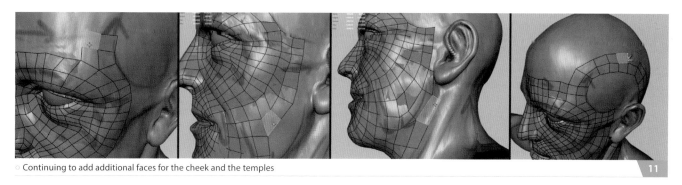

○ Continuing to add additional faces for the cheek and the temples

11

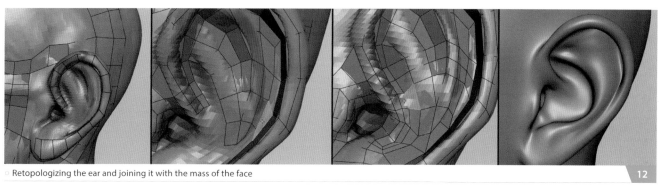

○ Retopologizing the ear and joining it with the mass of the face

12

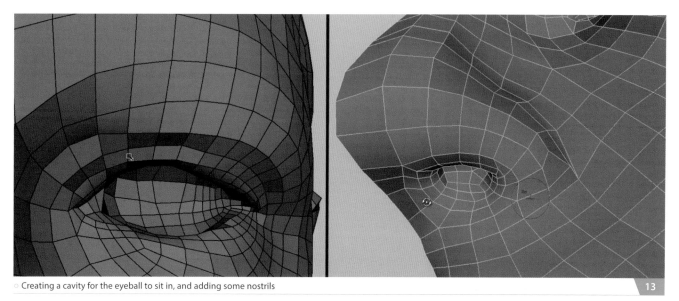

○ Creating a cavity for the eyeball to sit in, and adding some nostrils

13

15: Attaching the parts together

At this stage, the bulk of the character should be there (over the page). Now you can start combining the parts to create a single piece. Do this in the same way we attached the arm to the torso. Start by joining the leg to the torso and then go in, weld the vertices, and add any extra loops necessary to close the gaps. Do the same for the hand and foot, but leave the mouth bag out for now.

"At this stage, the bulk of the character should be there. Now you can start combining the parts to create a single piece"

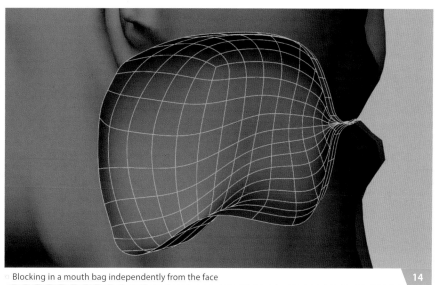

○ Blocking in a mouth bag independently from the face

14

16: Mirror over and combine

With the combined mesh selected, go to Edit > Delete By Type > History. Select all the vertices that should run down the center and make sure they are flush against the X-axis. You can do this (as we did when creating the base mesh) by using Absolute Transform with a value of 0 in the X box.

Next, duplicate the mesh and plug a value of -1 into the Scale X to flip it over, then go to Modify > Freeze Transforms to invert the normals and clean out the -1 in the Scale X channel. Then select both halves of the character and go to Mesh > Combine. Now select all the vertices that run down the middle of the mesh and go to Edit Mesh > Merge Components. A harsh line is probably still running down the middle of the mesh, but you can get rid of this by going to Normals > Soften Edge.

17: Add the asymmetry

The middle of the mesh is most probably a little sharp where the two halves come together. To soften this, use the Sculpt Geometry tool and set the mode to Relax. Turn on Symmetry and start to paint over the model to get rid of any "pointedness".

Following on from this, begin to add asymmetry back into the face. I do this by switching to vertex mode and using the Move tool with Soft-Selection turned on. You can also use the Transfer Attribute tool, but make sure the eyes and ears line up before doing so. Also make sure the mouth bag and eyeball cavities are not connected, or else they'll explode.

18: Updates to the eye region

At this stage, I'm pretty happy with the bulk of the mesh, but feel as if the eyes could do with a bit more attention. For this region, I chop them off and rework them to get a more pleasing result. The inner eye cavity is also re-created to better encompass the eyeball. This is then combined back into the head along with the mouth bag. From here onwards, I no longer use the Transfer Attributes tool as I find it destroys these parts.

19: Refine the mesh

At this point, the final mesh is almost complete, but I highly recommend that you go through and check that you're happy with the topology. If there's something that's bugging you,

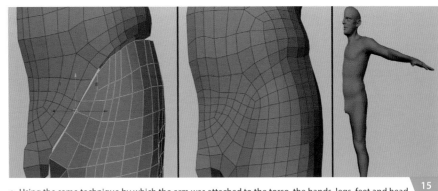

○ Using the same technique by which the arm was attached to the torso, the hands, legs, feet and head are all joined to form a unified mesh   **15**

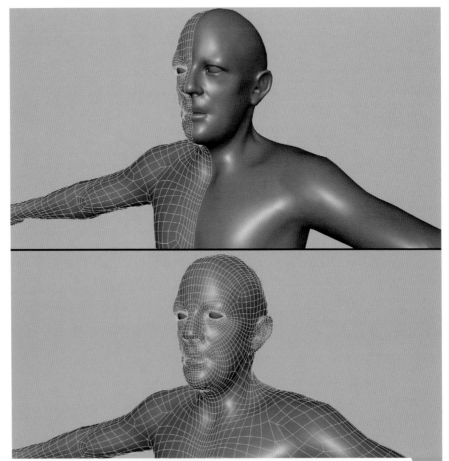

○ Once you are happy with one side, duplicate it, mirror it over, and combine the two halves together   **16**

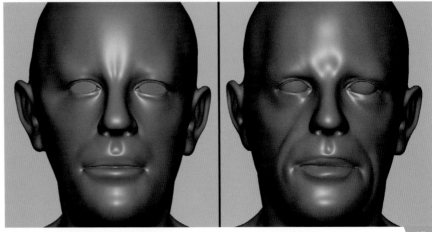

○ Add the asymmetry back into the face. I turned on Soft Selection to speed this process up   **17**

fix it now. With referencing, we can always make small changes later on, but don't leave something that you aren't happy with hanging around. I also suggest you let someone else cast their eyes over the model. Someone in rigging or texturing will be able to give a different perspective on what's working well and what could be refined (Fig.19a, 19b).

20: Check for errors

Once you're happy with the topology, let's test it for any errors that would, without a doubt, come back to haunt you. Maya has some pretty good tools to check the integrity of a model, but I like to simply save it out as an .obj file and open it up in Mudbox. As we found with the turntable geometry, Mudbox will very quickly let you know if it's not happy with the mesh, and will also highlight the regions that have offended it.

21: Multiple mesh resolutions

You should now have a model that has passed the Mudbox test and is almost ready for UVing. The resolution of this model (at around

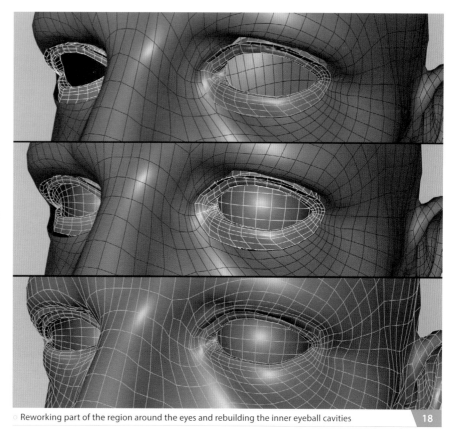

○ Reworking part of the region around the eyes and rebuilding the inner eyeball cavities   18

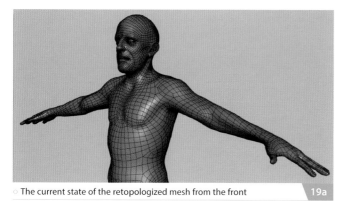

○ The current state of the retopologized mesh from the front   19a

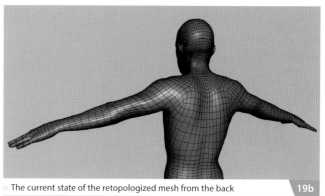

○ The current state of the retopologized mesh from the back   19b

🔎 PRO TIP
Test the deformation with joints

As I like to build up the retopologized mesh as different parts, it's very easy to throw a few joints in and then test how the model will deform. I don't do any weight-painting here, but if you are working as part of a team, you could always pass the different parts of the model to the rigging team for testing. That way, you can make any changes and fixes as early as possible.

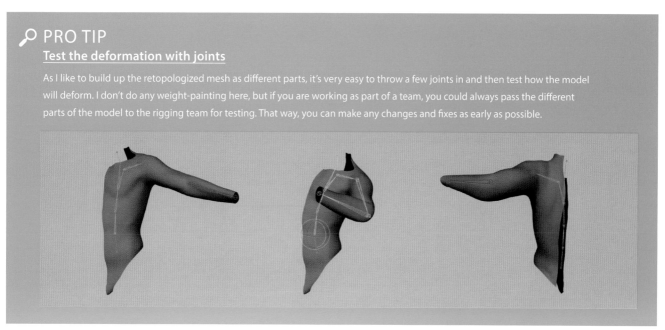

14000) is more than adequate and should give you some pretty nice deformation.

However, lately I've been experimenting with meshes with a higher resolution count and have found that I get more room to maneuver when attempting to create wrinkles, folds, and so on. For that very reason, I duplicated this mesh and went to Mesh> Subdivide (**Fig.21a**). Rename the original mesh **paul_midRes_geo** and the new subdivided mesh can be called **paul_highRes_geo**.

We now want to get the high-res mesh to sit tighter against the sculpt without the use of the Transfer Attributes tool, as this can be destructive around the eyes and corners of the mouth. To do this, we'll be using the Relax feature from the Quad Draw tool.

"We want to get the high-res mesh to sit tighter against the sculpt without the use of the Transfer Attributes tool"

First, select the sculpt and make it a live surface, then select **paul_highRes_geo** and activate Quad Draw (**Fig.21b**). Now hold down the Shift key, and paint over the model to have it sit tighter with the sculpt. I've also enabled Soft Selection here and there to speed up the process.

Remember to stay away from the corners of the mouth and the eyes, though.

22: Transfer high-res details

Once you're happy with **paul_highRes_geo**, export it out as an .OBJ file and import it into the Mudbox scene with the final sculpt. We now want to transfer the sculpt details over to our retopologized mesh.

To do this, go to Mesh > Transfer Details, set the Target Model to **paul_highRes_geo**, and the Source Model to **paul_sculpt** – Level 4. Then open up the Advanced options and enable "Transfer Base as Sculpt Layer" and "Test Both Sides". Hit Transfer Details when ready.

With the details transferred over, you'll probably find a few troubled areas that have been highlighted in yellow (**Fig.22a**). You'll also notice a sculpt layer has been

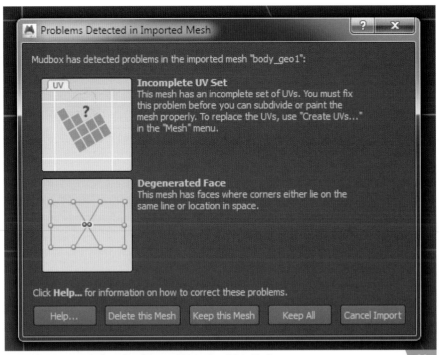

○ A quick way to test the integrity of the model is to drop it into Mudbox — 20

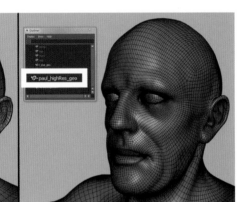

○ Duplicating the final model and then subdividing it once to create a high-resolution mesh — 21a

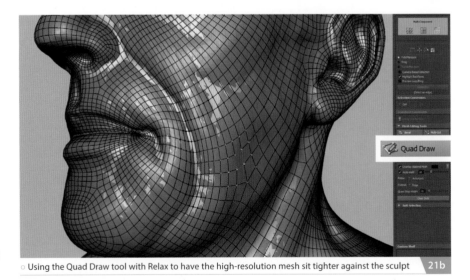

○ Using the Quad Draw tool with Relax to have the high-resolution mesh sit tighter against the sculpt — 21b

created with the high-res details applied. Now you can take the Erase brush and paint out the problem areas, and manually make any necessary fixes using the sculpt

tool of your choice (**Fig.22b**). We have yet to add the high-frequency details, such as fine wrinkles and pores; we'll be adding these during the texturing stage.

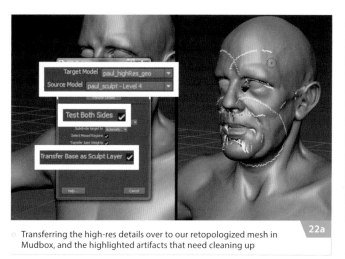

Transferring the high-res details over to our retopologized mesh in Mudbox, and the highlighted artifacts that need cleaning up

22a

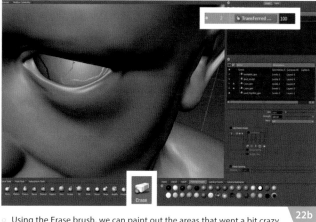

Using the Erase brush, we can paint out the areas that went a bit crazy when transferring the details over

22b

23: Create some eyes

Now that the main model is sorted, we need to jump back into Maya to create some eyes. Here's a quick overview of how I do this.

First, I create a sphere, rotate it 90° on its X-axis, and then reduce the Subdivisions Axis down to 8, and the Subdivisions Height Down to 14. I then alter the topology to get rid of the triangles (**Fig.23a**), and pull the front out slightly with Soft Selection enabled to create the bulge of the cornea. The model is then subdivided twice and scaled around a sphere to bring its roundness back. This model is then duplicated and scaled in slightly to form the combined sclera and pupil (**Fig.23b**).

With Soft Selection enabled once more, I select a vertex on the front and in the middle, and push in slightly to better simulate a real eye. The faces acting as the pupil are deleted, and a flat-shaped polygon is added in its space to act as the pupil. We could have left the sclera and pupil as one object, but I like to separate them for shader purposes.

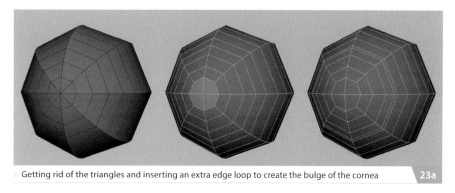

Getting rid of the triangles and inserting an extra edge loop to create the bulge of the cornea

23a

The different parts that make up the final eyeball

23b

24: Add teeth, gums and a tongue

For the teeth, I attach a reference image of Paul baring his gnashers onto a camera (**Fig.24a**), and use basic box modeling techniques to create the teeth and gums. The upper teeth are combined into a single mesh, as are the lower teeth. The upper and lower gums are left as individual meshes (**Fig.24b**). Once the teeth and gums are in place, I make sure the mouth bag surrounds them without penetrating.

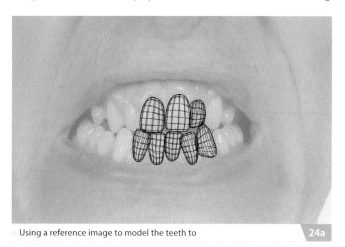

Using a reference image to model the teeth to

24a

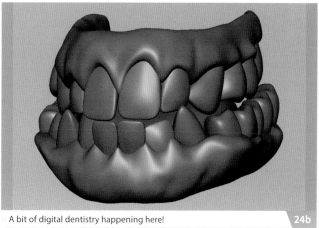

A bit of digital dentistry happening here!

24b

25: Separate the fingernails

At this stage, you should be good for UVing, then creating textures and shaders. One last thing I do, however, is create separate fingernails. Although the current model works fine, I like to sometimes have the nails as separate objects, again for shader purposes. Like the teeth, I also combine each set of fingernails together, as I'll be skinning these to the finger joints later on, rather than parenting them to the joints. Once the teeth are in place, a set of briefs are added to cover his modesty. To create the briefs, I simply set **paul_highRes_geo** as a live surface and use the Quad Draw tool to block them out.

"You can find details of the naming conventions that I am using in the 'documents' directory of the project folder"

26: Finishing up and publishing

You should now have a scene file that consists of a mid-resolution mesh, a high-resolution mesh, eyes, teeth, gums and a tongue, and finger- and toenails. Before moving on though, we do need to make sure that we rename all

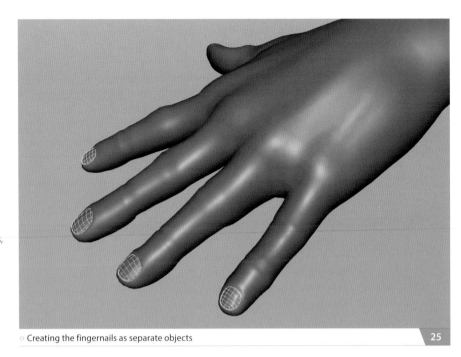

○ Creating the fingernails as separate objects   25

of the objects and use groups to add clarity to the scene, to make life as easy as possible.

For example, I group all of the high-resolution meshes under **paul_hr_geo_grp**, and all the mid-resolution meshes under **paul_mr_geo_grp**. I can then take both groups and place them under a group, which I've labeled

paul_geo_grp (Fig.26a). You can find details of the naming conventions that I am using in the **documents** directory of the project folder. I also created a few shaders to help visually separate the different objects in the scene.

Before publishing the model, we need to lower him so that he sits on the world plane. We'll also

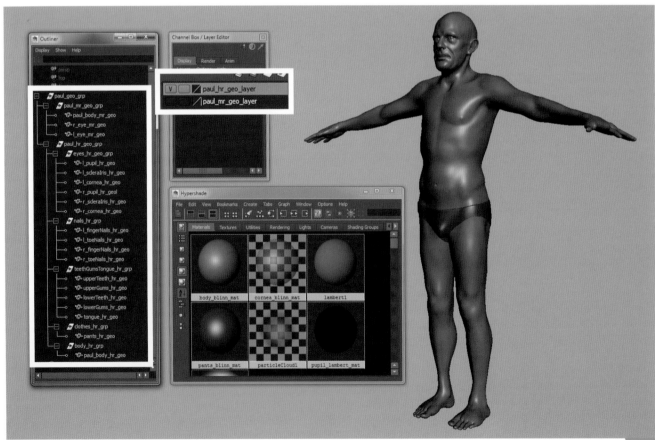

○ Renaming all the assets in the scene, and grouping them to add clarity   26a

have to update the Mudbox mesh so it doesn't cause problems later on. Start by selecting the top group node within the hierarchy (**paul_geo_grp**) and translate it down slightly so that the models sit on the world plane.

Now, with **paul_geo_grp**, go to Modify > Freeze Transformations to zero out the Translate values in the Channel Box. We then need to move the pivot of **paul_geo_grp** to the world plane as well.

To do this, go to Modify > Reset Transformations. Check all the models, and do the same to other meshes and groups, if necessary (**Fig.26b**). For the eyes and nails, I simply do a Modify > Center Pivot.

"The model can be picked up by the rigging team, or by the shading and texturing team"

Now, select **paul_body_hr_geo** (this was originally called **paul_highRes_geo**) and go to File > Export, and save it as an .OBJ file. Open the latest Mudbox scene (where we transferred the high-res details over to the retopologized mesh), drop down to the lowest subdivision and import the .OBJ file as a new Sculpt Layer. You should see the model shift down slightly. Now flatten the sculpt layers and save this scene file.

The last thing to do is to jump back into Maya, save the latest scene file as a local copy, and then publish the scene file. To do this, simply re-save it in the following directory: scenes\02_PUBLISHED\01_MODELLING_SCULPTING as paul_mod_PUBLISHED.ma.

At this stage, the model can be picked up by the rigging team or by the texturing and shading team. Bearing that in mind, you could now jump straight into section 03 (UVs, texturing, and shading) or tackle section 04 (rigging) first before coming back to texturing and shading (**Fig.26c**).

Either way, once the following two sections are complete, we'll bring everything together again.

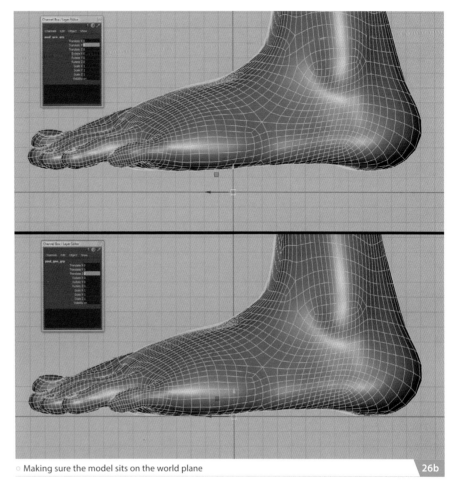

○ Making sure the model sits on the world plane
26b

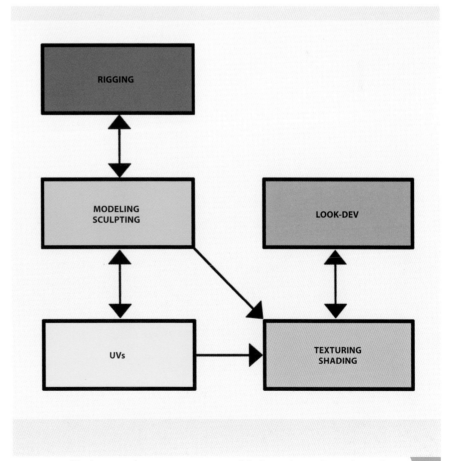

○ Now you could either create the rig, or start texturing and shading and create the rig afterwards
26c

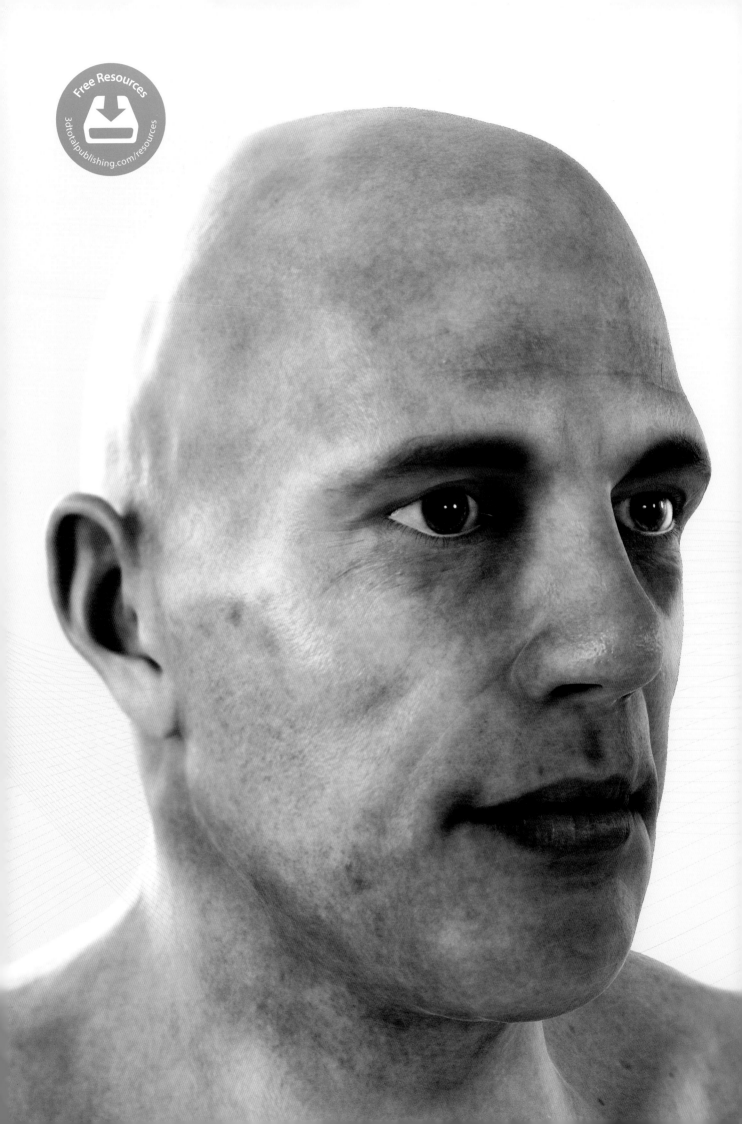

Texturing and shading in Maya and Mudbox

Understanding the eyes and skin, and creating UVs and maps

The character's taking shape, but he doesn't have any skin or shaders yet. In this section, we'll look briefly at the science behind the skin and eyes, and then use that knowledge to create realistic skin textures for your model. After that, we'll create shaders for further realism and set up a "look development" environment for experimenting with different lighting setups and scenarios. By the end of these chapters, your character will have achieved a new level of realism with convincing skin and eyes.

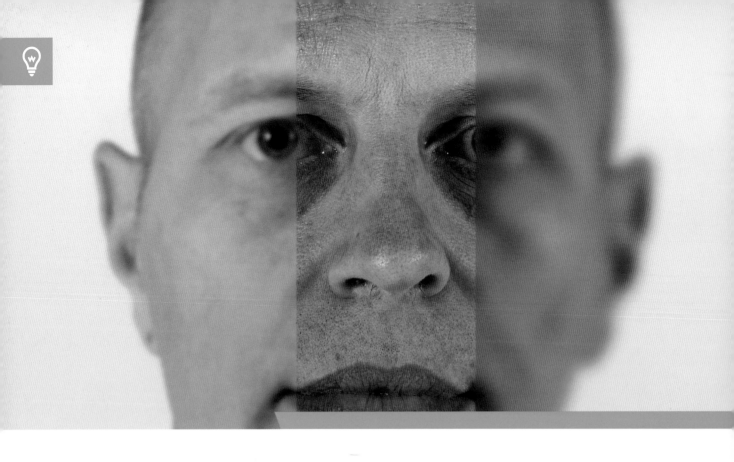

Skin and eyes

Breaking down the anatomy of the skin and eyes

This section will be devoted to texturing and shading the skin and eyes. Before we turn to the software, we are going to look at the biological structure of the skin and eyes, and see how these anatomies can inform the digital processes to come.

Our first CG step will be creating UVs for the character. We'll then grade the reference images to be used in the texturing process. Using this data, we'll create color maps, add displacement detail, and output all the additional maps needed for the shaders. Finally, we'll enter a look development environment to create the asset's final look.

Skin

The skin is the body's thinnest and largest organ, measuring around two square meters on an average-sized adult. It provides a protective barrier between the body and what is very frequently a hostile environment.

The skin is composed of two main layers: the epidermis above and the dermis below. Beneath

"Doing justice in CG to this complex organ, which appears so varied from person to person, and from one body part to the next, is a labor of love"

these is the subcutaneous layer, which is rich in fatty tissue and carries the major blood vessels and nerves to the skin above (**Fig.01**).

Doing justice in CG to this complex organ, which appears so varied from person to person, and from one body part to the next, is a labor of love. Take a look at your face in the mirror: see how the color varies from feature to feature, how some parts are oilier and have deeper pores than others, and how lines form around the eyes and corners of the mouth.

My approach to producing digital skin is more artistic than technical. I have a look in mind which can be backed up by reference, and strive for that look by tinkering with texture and displacement maps, while being very conscious

of and informed by the biological makeup of the skin outlined in the following paragraphs.

The epidermis in most areas of the body is less than 0.17mm thick. This figure rises in areas such as the soles of the feet, which are exposed to a lot of pressure and friction. The epidermis is composed of between three and five layers, depending on the area of the body. The cells at the surface of the skin are dead and continuously being shed, then replaced by cells which have migrated from lower layers in the epidermis. This continues even while we sleep.

Let's relate this biological information to the epidermal map that we'll create during the texturing process. As the visible portion of the epidermis is actually composed of dead cells, when viewed in isolation, it is very desaturated in color. This desaturation will need to be mimicked in the creation of the map.

Before the dermis is the dermal-epidermal junction, a membrane which effectively glues the dermis and the epidermis together.

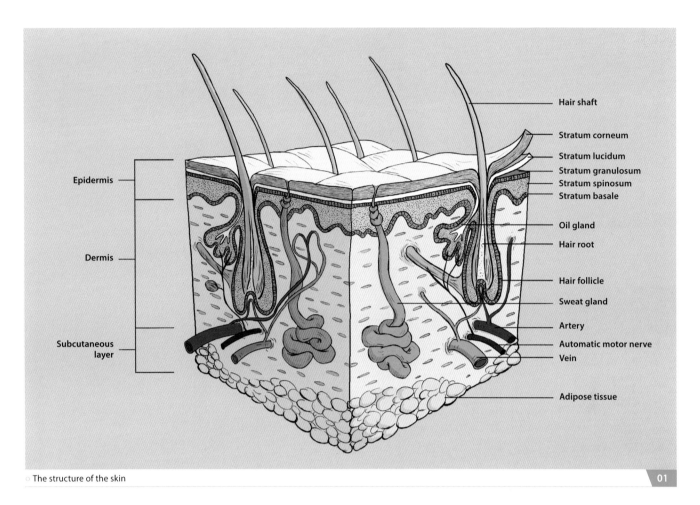

The structure of the skin

01

The dermis is sometimes known as the "true skin", and is much thicker than the epidermis, varying from 0.5mm (eyelids and penis) to 4mm (soles and palms) thick. It contains nerves and nerve endings, muscle fibers, hair follicles, sweat and sebaceous glands, and blood vessels. The dermis performs a number of functions such as heat regulation, protection from injury, and processing sensory information such as pain or heat.

"The subdermal texture map should be reddish in color, as the red wavelength penetrates the furthest and scatters beneath the epidermis"

Relating this to CG again, the subdermal texture map (which represents both the dermis and subcutaneous layer) should be reddish in

color, as the red wavelength penetrates the furthest and scatters beneath the epidermis (Fig.02, 03, and 04). The texture map should also be blurry as the red light bounces around this region. This is where we should include color variation as well, such as for the veins, to add a layer of complexity to the shader.

Of additional importance when considering shaders is the oily film which is visible

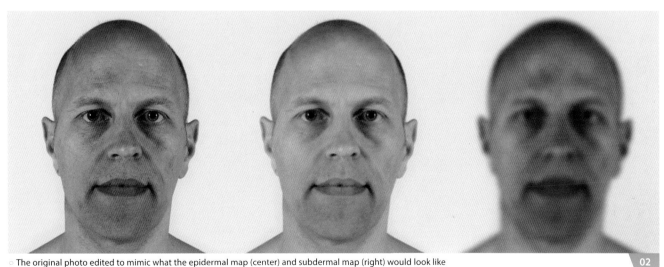

The original photo edited to mimic what the epidermal map (center) and subdermal map (right) would look like

02

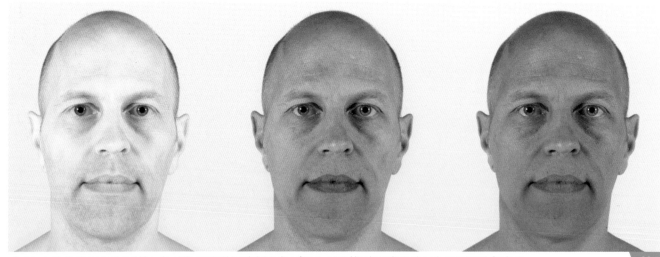

○ Left to right: the red, green, and blue channels. Notice the red channel's softness, caused by the red wavelength penetrating furthest | 03

on the surface of the skin, to a greater or lesser degree from person to person, and depending on the area of the body.

This film is composed of secretions from the sweat and sebaceous glands mixed with cells being shed from the epidermis. Because the surface film reflects light, and because blue light barely penetrates, I'll be adding a blue tint to the reflection and specular maps (Fig.05).

Eyes

The adult eyeball measures around 2.5cm in diameter. Only one sixth of the eyeball is exposed; based on the digital texturing and shading work we will do, it is this

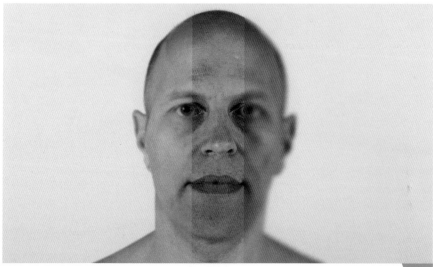

○ The original photo (center), epidermal map (left), and subdermal map (right) shown together | 04

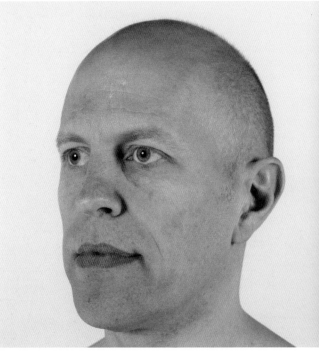
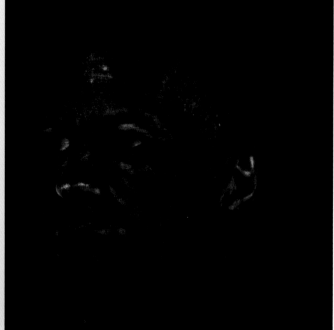

○ If we extract the specular component, we will notice a blue tint | 05

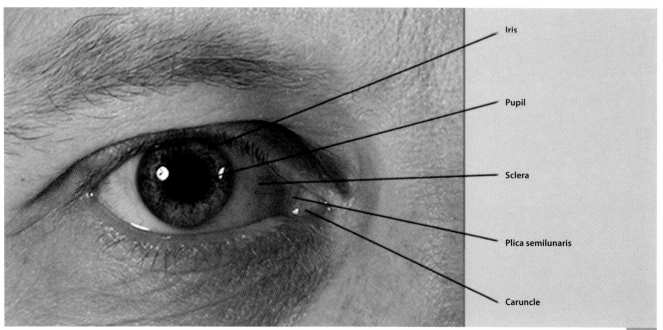

Iris

Pupil

Sclera

Plica semilunaris

Caruncle

○ The main elements of the eye that we will want to incorporate in our CG model and textures   06

sixth that we'll focus on, as the remainder of the eyeball is recessed and protected in its orbit. We will take a look, therefore, at the sclera, iris, pupil, and cornea.

The sclera is a tough, white fibrous tissue that almost encircles the eyeball, giving it shape and protecting its inner parts. The visible, anterior part of the sclera is the "white of the eye". The iris, the colored portion of the eye, is made up of

circular and radial muscles which are arranged in a donut shape, the hole in the middle being the pupil, through which light enters the eye.

A principal function of the iris is to regulate how much light enters the posterior cavity of the eyeball through the pupil. When light stimulates the eye, the circular muscles of the iris contract, shrinking the pupil as a result. In contrast, when the eye needs to see in poor

light, the radial muscles of the iris contract, therefore increasing the size of the pupil.

Covering the iris and pupil is the cornea, which is a transparent coat protected externally by an epithelial layer.

Having looked at the structure of skin and the eyes like this will help us to understand how we can recreate them in CG.

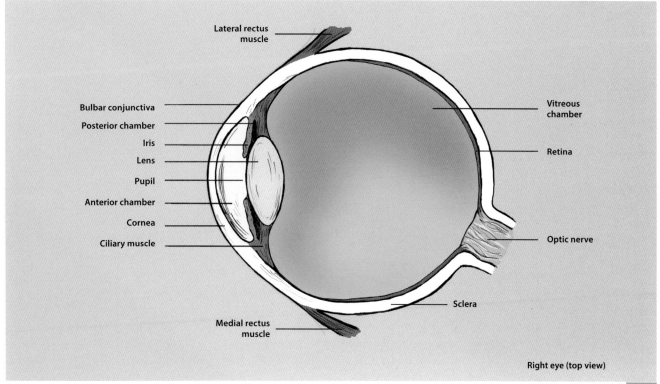

Lateral rectus muscle

Bulbar conjunctiva
Posterior chamber
Iris
Lens
Pupil
Anterior chamber
Cornea
Ciliary muscle

Vitreous chamber

Retina

Optic nerve

Sclera

Medial rectus muscle

Right eye (top view)

○ The structure of the human eye   07

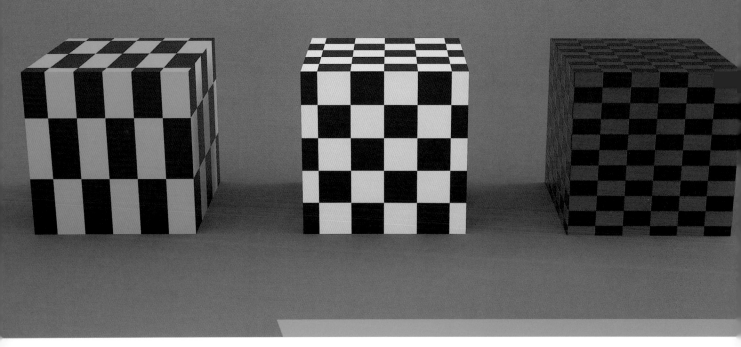

Checking for UV distortion

How to identify and repair distorted UVs

So this is where computer graphics meets taxidermy: here we'll be digitally unwrapping our 3D assets as if we were peeling the skin off a creature and laying it flat on the ground. "Ouch", you say, closely followed by: "Why?"

It's simply so we can assign 2D images to 3D models. You could skip this by using Ptex (ptex.us) – a texturing system that doesn't rely on UVs – but like everything, Ptex has its pros and cons (which you can discover for yourself). UV unwrapping is an important process to cover, and in some cases, such as for (mobile) games, Ptex is simply not viable.

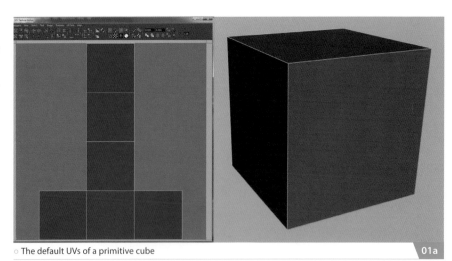

○ The default UVs of a primitive cube

01a

UVs can be used for many things, such as transferring properties. Let's say you have five characters who have the same UVs and who also need skinning. By having all the same UVs, you can skin one character and transfer those weights to the other four. Ptex is getting a strong foothold, but UVs are still widely used in the film and games industries because they have a wider application than just texturing your assets.

Some years ago, you would find that it was best practice to unwrap assets into as few pieces as possible in order to avoid revealing texture seams. These days, with the advent of 3D paint programs, it is easy to paint over the seams. So now, when you are UV unwrapping an object, whether it is a character, a vehicle, or even a light bulb, the thing you should watch out for instead is minimizing UV distortion.

UV distortion is caused when the representation of an asset in 2D space doesn't sync up closely enough with the representation of the asset in 3D space. The best way to combat this is by ensuring that the size relationship of one polygonal face to its neighbor is consistent in both 2D and 3D space. To get started, let's quickly take a look at how we can examine levels of UV distortion.

01: Viewing UV shells

In a clean Maya scene, start by creating a polygon primitive cube and a cylinder. Translate them to slt side by side, then go to Window > UV Texture Editor to examine their UVs. Now you'll see how they are represented in 2D space (**Fig.01a** and **01b**). These flattened shapes are UV shells, or UV islands. The window you're currently in will also be the main window we'll use to edit the UVs.

"Ideally, we want our models to be in the white color zone, but if there are only subtle hints of red or blue we should be fine"

02: Examining UV distortion

At the moment, we could be fooled into thinking that both objects have good UVs. Let's take a closer look with the UV distortion tools.

With just the cube selected, in the UV Texture Editor enable the UV distortion map by clicking on the icon as illustrated in **Fig.02a**.

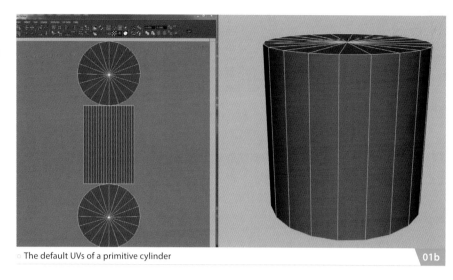

○ The default UVs of a primitive cylinder **01b**

The cube is colored white, indicating there's no distortion to the UVs (**Fig.02b**).

Now select the cylinder and view the results. You'll find the UVs are pale red or pale blue in places. Blue indicates that the UVs are stretched, while red indicates that they are compressed. Ideally, we want our models to be in the white color zone, but if there are only subtle hints of red and blue we should be fine. If they were deep red or deep blue then that would be a cause for concern.

If we compare the object in 3D space to 2D space (return to **Fig.01b**) you can see what's causing the problem: the long rectangular faces that surround the cylinder in 3D space are clearly wider than those in the 2D space.

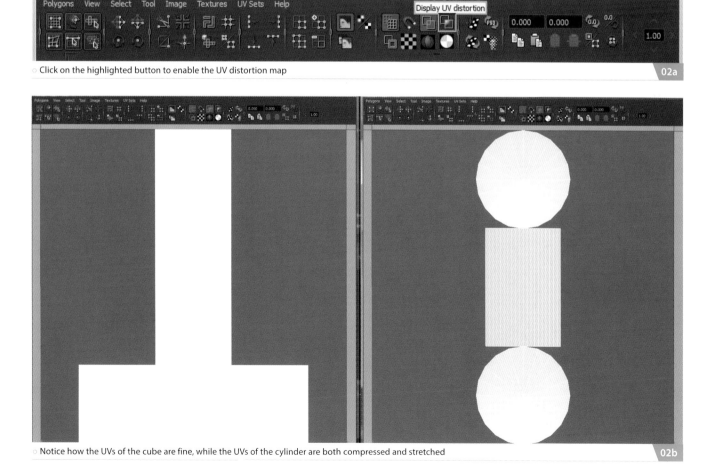

○ Click on the highlighted button to enable the UV distortion map **02a**

○ Notice how the UVs of the cube are fine, while the UVs of the cylinder are both compressed and stretched **02b**

03: Removing UV distortion

To correct this, with the cylinder still selected, hold down the RMB and go to UV > UV Shell. Now select the UV shell where the distortion is occurring. Jump into the UV Texture Editor, and with the standard Scale tool activated, scale the selected UV shell to make it wider. As you do so, notice how the distortion map is becoming whiter. Instead of affecting the entire shell, we could also affect individual UVs or multiple UVs by going to UV > UV.

04: Using a checker image

Maya 2015 also comes with a "Display checkered tiles" option, as illustrated in Fig.04a, giving you another method for checking UV distortion (Fig.04b).

Although this is useful, I tend to use the old-school method of slapping a checkered pattern onto the color input of the shader. To do this, simply select the object, and in the Attribute Editor, scroll to the right-most tab to get to the shader attributes.

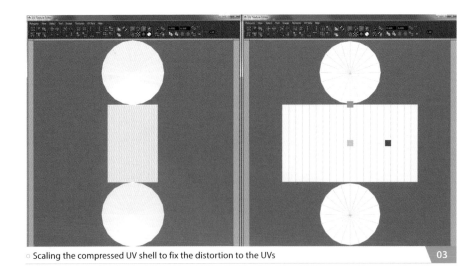

○ Scaling the compressed UV shell to fix the distortion to the UVs

03

Click the inputs icon (the small checkered square to the left of the Color parameter), and select Checker in the Create Render Node window that pops up (Fig.04c).

If you hit 6 on the keyboard, you'll activate texture mode and see a checkered pattern on the object. To make this a more useful

way of viewing distortion, go to the place2dTexture1 node and increase the repeat U and V to about 20 (Fig.04d).

If the window for the place2dTexture1 node is no longer open in the Attribute Editor, you can access it by going to the Utilities tab in Hypershade (Window > Rendering

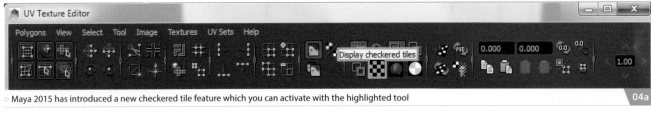

○ Maya 2015 has introduced a new checkered tile feature which you can activate with the highlighted tool

04a

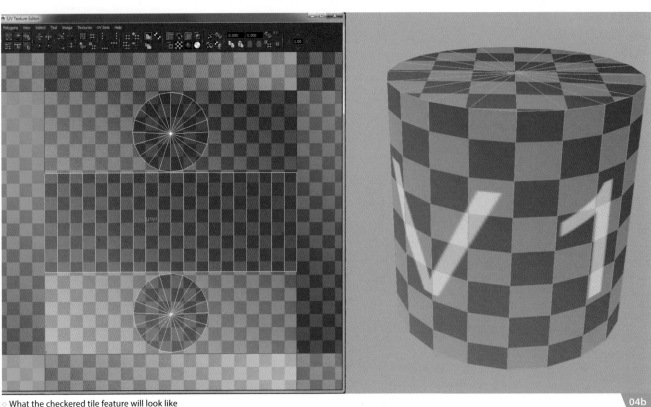

○ What the checkered tile feature will look like

04b

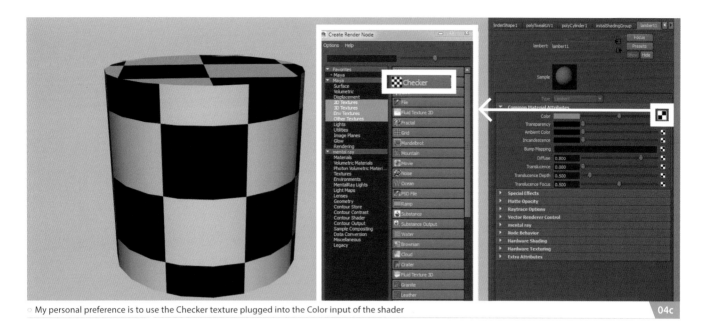

○ My personal preference is to use the Checker texture plugged into the Color input of the shader
04c

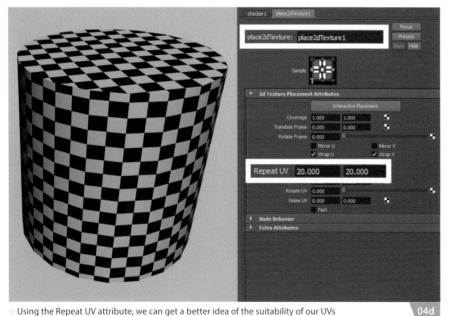

○ Using the Repeat UV attribute, we can get a better idea of the suitability of our UVs
04d

Editors), or by clicking on the inputs icon by the Color attribute for the shader.

"If you see a square-like checkered pattern on the model, you should be good to go"

The results should update in the 3D viewport, and if you see a square-like checkered pattern on the model, you should be good to go. If you see a more rectangular-shaped checkered pattern, then some clean-up will be necessary to correct the proportions (Fig.04e).

We'll look at the clean-up tools when we start UV unwrapping the main character, which we'll jump into next.

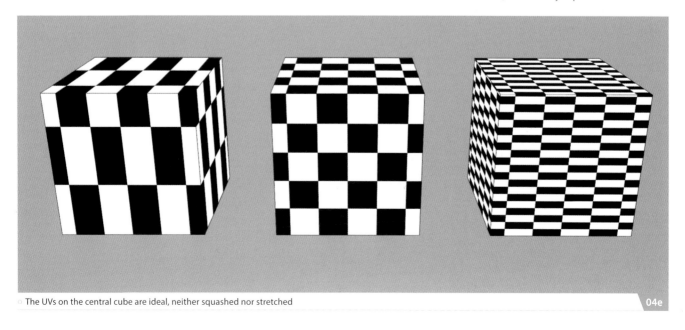

○ The UVs on the central cube are ideal, neither squashed nor stretched
04e

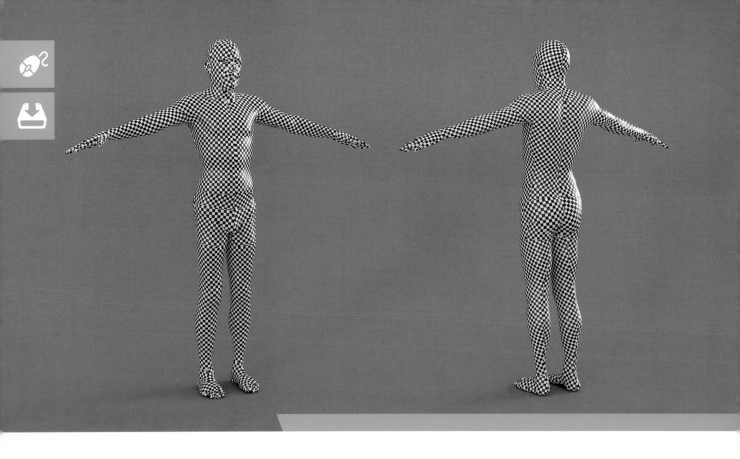

Unwrapping our character

Preparing the model for the texturing process

At this stage, we'll take our main asset and lay out the UVs to ready the model for texturing. I'll be adding more seams than would probably appear normal, but this is all to aid the process of creating undistorted UVs. Once we have the initial UVs laid out, we'll look at some of the tools we can use to clean up areas that haven't unfolded cleanly enough.

01: Bringing in the model

I'm not going to Reference the model in at this stage, but instead I'll be opening the Published model file (named "paul_ mod_PUBLISHED") as I would an ordinary file. Once you have the scene file loaded, make sure you save a local copy in a WIP > 02_TEXTURING_SHADING directory. I've actually created a folder called 01_UVs within that space and saved it in there.

Once we have finished UVing the model, we will simply overwrite the original paul_mod_PUBLISHED file so that anyone else who calls in that file will be able to see the UVs in place there.

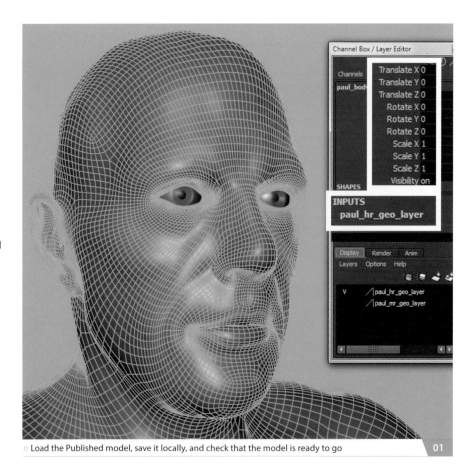

○ Load the Published model, save it locally, and check that the model is ready to go   01

100

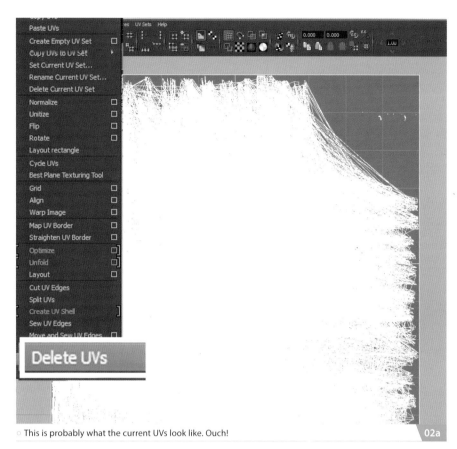

This is probably what the current UVs look like. Ouch!

02a

Lastly, we need to check that the model is clean and has no history, the Translate and Rotate values are at zero, and the Scale attributes have a uniform value of 1.

02: Deleting the existing UVs

With the model selected, open up the UV Texture Editor and examine the current UVs. It's not the prettiest picture, is it? Delete these UVs by going to Edit UVs > Delete UVs on the modeling menu (Fig.02a).

Now let's quickly edit the display settings for the UV Texture Editor. In the UV Texture Editor, go to View > Grid (Options). In here, set the "Length and width" to 6, "Grid lines every" to 1, Subdivisions to 2, and enable Tiles.

With the model still selected, go to Create UVs > Planar Mapping (Options). Set the "Projection from" to the Z Axis and hit Apply (Fig.02b). We're doing this simply to give us some UVs to begin with. The next stage in the process is to cut the UVs up so that the unfolding algorithm can do its magic.

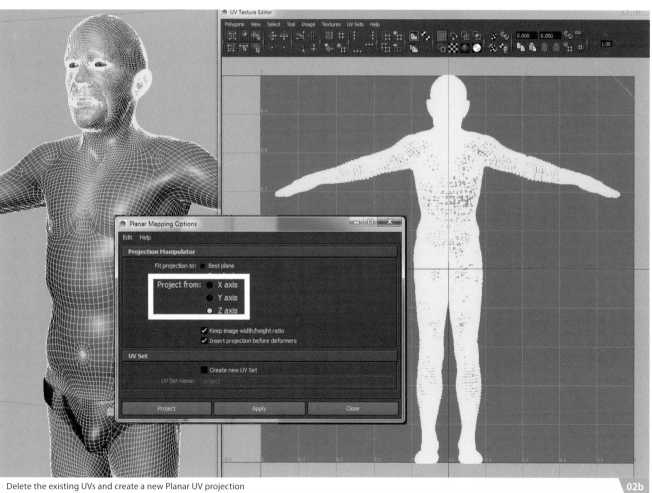

Delete the existing UVs and create a new Planar UV projection

02b

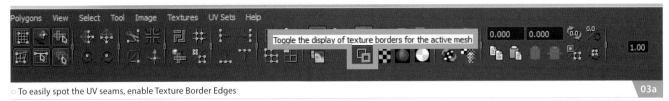

○ To easily spot the UV seams, enable Texture Border Edges
03a

03: Viewing the texture seams

To enable us to see the seams as we cut the model, with the model selected, go to Display > Polygons > Texture Border Edges.

We won't see anything now as we have yet to make any cuts, but you'll see the results when we do. You can also toggle this mode on and off in the UV Texture Editor if you want to, by clicking on the icon as illustrated in **Fig.03a**. If you'd like to increase the width of the seams to make them more easily viewable, go to Display > Polygons > Edge Width (**Fig.03b**).

At this stage, hide the briefs, eyes, nails, and so on, so we can focus on unwrapping the main model.

04: Cutting up the UVs

Start things off by selecting an edge loop that goes around the base of the neck (**Fig.04a**), and then go to Edit UVs > Cut UV edges. If you've enabled Texture Border Edges, you should see a thicker line around that edge loop.

In the 3D viewport, hold the RMB over the model and go to UV > UV Shell. Select the head above the cut line and jump into the UV Texture Editor. You should now be able to separate the selected UV shell from the rest of the body using the Move tool (**Fig.04b**).

05: Cutting up the torso

Moving on to the torso, select an edge loop that will allow you to separate the pelvic mass from the trunk, and go to Edit UVs > Cut UV Edges.

Every now and then, you'll probably find that selecting an edge loop will give you more edges then you bargained for, and the loop may go off at a tangent. In situations like this, I simply go in and manually select the edges I'd like to cut, or select one edge and then double-click the edge where I'd like the selection to terminate.

Continuing with the torso, I end up adding a cut line that runs down the center of the back, from the cut line of the head to the

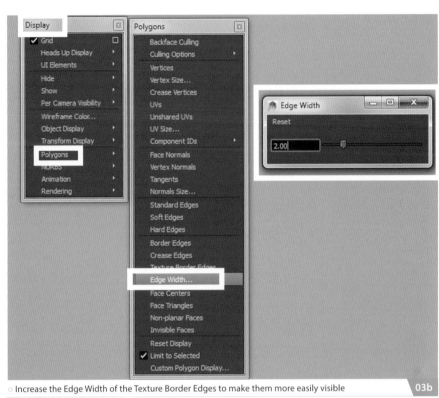

○ Increase the Edge Width of the Texture Border Edges to make them more easily visible
03b

cut line of the hip. I then make a similar cut line running down the front of the torso. An edge loop just past the shoulder mass on both arms is selected and then cut.

A cut line is then added from that cut line and run over the shoulder to meet the cut line of the head. Again, this is done on both sides. Two additional cut lines are then added down the side of the torso to separate the front portion from the back.

Now we come to finishing off the torso. Start by adding a cut line around the upper portion of each leg. Cut down the middle of the pelvic mass from front to back,

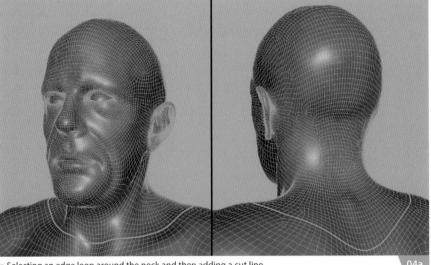

○ Selecting an edge loop around the neck and then adding a cut line
04a

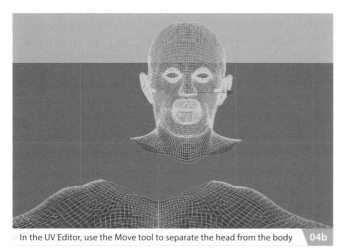
○ In the UV Editor, use the Move tool to separate the head from the body   04b

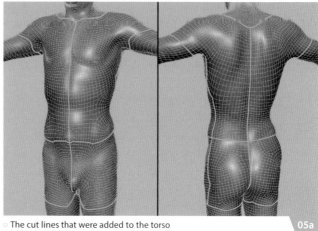
○ The cut lines that were added to the torso   05a

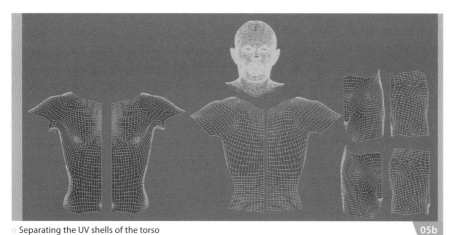
○ Separating the UV shells of the torso   05b

continuing with the same cut line that runs down the middle of the torso (Fig.05a). Do the same along the sides of the pelvis and then make a final snip beneath his manly bits. After this, select each UV shell and separate them in the UV Texture Editor (Fig.05b).

06: Cutting up the legs

Moving on to the legs, start by selecting an edge loop that runs around the ankle and make a cut line there. Then select a line of edges that runs up the back of the leg, from the latest cut line at the ankle to the cut line situated on the upper portion of the leg, and make a cut.

Next, select an edge loop that will separate the sole of the foot along with the bottom of each toe. Lastly, add a couple of extra cut lines around the ankle region so they can be unfolded easily later on. Make sure you do the same for the other leg.

07: Cutting up the arms

Handle the arms similarly to the legs. Select an edge loop and make a cut at the wrist. Then a line of edges on the back of the arm, from the wrist to the cut line on the upper arm, needs to be selected and cut. For the

○ The cut lines of the legs and the feet   06

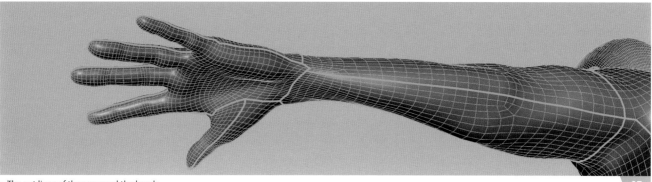
○ The cut lines of the arms and the hands   07

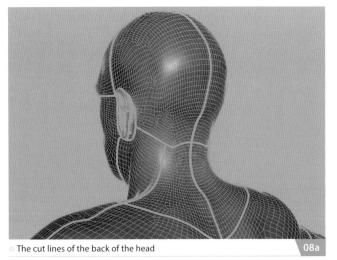

○ The cut lines of the back of the head   08a

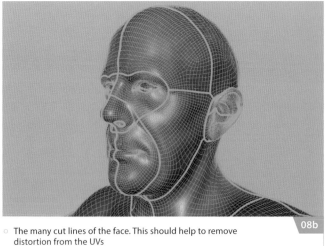

○ The many cut lines of the face. This should help to remove distortion from the UVs   08b

hand, select an edge loop that separates the palm from the back of the hand and then deal with the thumb on its own.

If at any stage you're not happy with the cuts you've made, simply select those edges and go to Edit UVs > Sew UV edges and try again.

08: Cutting up the head

For the head, I start by adding a cut line to separate the eye cavity and mouth bag from the rest of the head. A cut line is then added through the mouth bag and eye cavity to ease the unfolding process later. The nostrils are also separated, only I don't split those through the middle.

Additional cut lines are then introduced around the neck and down the back of the head (Fig.08a). These cut lines are pretty much continuations of the cut lines from the torso and shoulders. An edge loop that goes around the ear is selected and cut and then a line of edges that passes from one ear to the other and underneath the chin is selected and cut.

The bulk of the face is next (Fig.08b). Again, you'll see more cut lines than you're probably used to, but it's all in the name of reducing UV distortion. First I select an edge loop running over the nose and under the chin and add a cut line.

I then split down the front of the face using the center line, and also add another cut line under the nose so that part can be handled separately. The nose is a common place where UV distortion is apparent, so doing this should help reduce it.

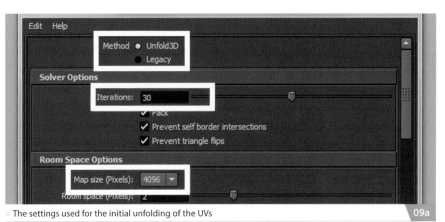

○ The settings used for the initial unfolding of the UVs   09a

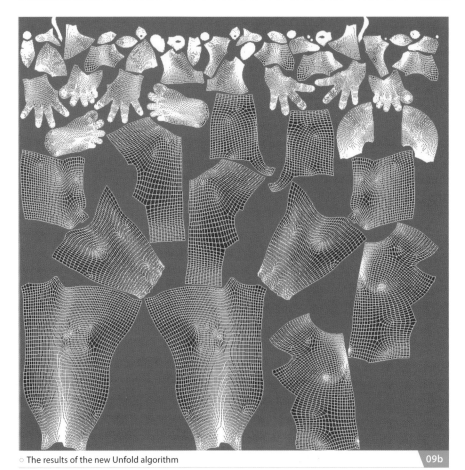

○ The results of the new Unfold algorithm   09b

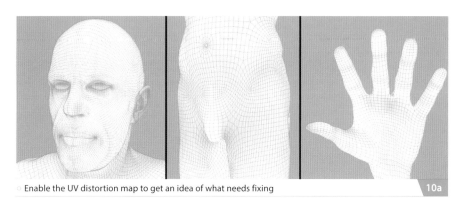

Enable the UV distortion map to get an idea of what needs fixing

10a

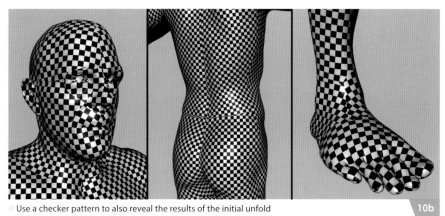

Use a checker pattern to also reveal the results of the initial unfold

10b

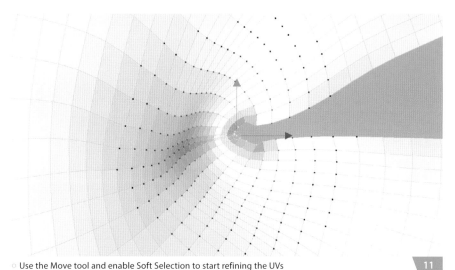

Use the Move tool and enable Soft Selection to start refining the UVs

11

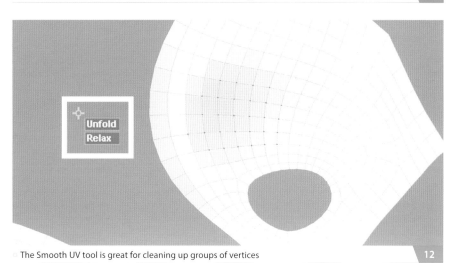

The Smooth UV tool is great for cleaning up groups of vertices

12

The same edge loop that is cut under the nose continues to be cut around the eyes and brows. A selection of edges running from the ear to the edge loop around the eyes is also cut. Lastly, the ears have more attention paid to them: separate the ear canal first and then add additional cuts around the ear to finish things off (for now).

09: Unfolding the UVs
So now we have the moment of truth. Start by deleting the history off the model to keep the scene file a little lighter. With the mesh selected, jump into the UV Texture Editor and select all the UVs, then go to Unfold (Options) in the same window. Set the Method to Unfold 3D, the Iterations to 30 (for better results), and the Map Size to 4096 (as we'll be creating 4K maps) (**Fig.09a**). Hit Apply and Close, give it a couple of minutes, and hopefully you'll have some pretty decent flattened UVs (**Fig.09b**).

10: Assessing the UV distortion
Now enable the UV distortion map and have a look at the results (**Fig.10a**). Hopefully the map will primarily be white in color, with hints of light red and blue in places. If you have areas of deep reds and deep blues, go back and re-adjust the cut lines before unfolding once more. I end up adding a new cut line through the ear and unfolding again, as I have a bit too much redness in that area.

Next, apply a checkered pattern to the color input of the shader and increase the Repeat U and V on the place2dTexture1 node to see how the unfolding has turned out (**Fig.10b**). It's also worth applying a colored checker image to the color input of the shader to get a different response. You can find plenty of colored checkered images online by doing a quick search.

11: Cleaning up the UVs (part A)
With the initial unfold complete, it's time to go in and clean up those troublesome areas where some redness and blueness is apparent. To do this, we have a few tools at our disposal. First, we can jump into UV mode and simply translate and scale a single UV or selection of UVs. I sometimes do this with Soft Selection enabled to quickly affect a region.

12: Cleaning up the UVs (part B)
We then have the Smooth UV tool. To activate this tool, go to Tool > Smooth UV Tool or hold

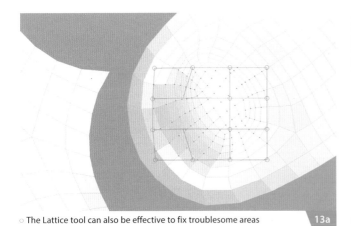

○ The Lattice tool can also be effective to fix troublesome areas **13a**

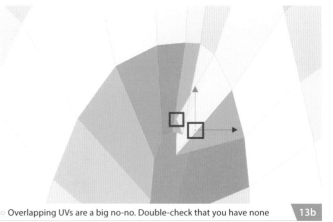

○ Overlapping UVs are a big no-no. Double-check that you have none **13b**

down Ctrl+RMB and select it from the marking
menu. A little tool should be unveiled, revealing
two words: Unfold and Relax. With this tool, you
can select some UVs and continue to unfold
them by LMB-dragging on the Unfold word.
The Relax feature used to be quite useful, but I
tend to just use the Unfold portion of this tool
now. This and the method in step 11 are the two
that I rely on most heavily to clean up the UVs.

"You don't need a 100% pure white map, but do get rid of any heavy reds and blues"

13: Cleaning up the UVs (part C)

We also have the Lattice tool. With a group of
UVs selected, go to Tool > UV Lattice Tool, or
use the same marking menu as was used to
get to the Smooth UVs tool. Once activated, a
small grid will appear allowing you to affect the
UVs in the same manner you would using the
Transform > Warp tool in Photoshop (**Fig.13a**).
If you jump into the Options for the Lattice tool,
you can also increase or decrease the columns
and rows of the lattice, which can be very useful.

With these tools at your disposal – experiment
with some of the other tools available as
well – spend some time cleaning up the UVs
as much as possible. You don't need a 100%
pure white map, but do get rid of any heavy
reds and blues. Between the fingers and toes
is usually a hot spot for this. A major thing to
look out for is overlapping UVs, which can cause
plenty of headaches later when texturing or
creating normal/displacement maps (**Fig.13b**).

14: Testing the UVs in Mudbox

Once you're happy with your UVs, select them
all, and go to Polygons > Layout in the UV

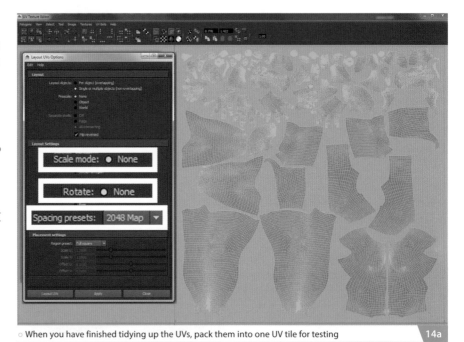

○ When you have finished tidying up the UVs, pack them into one UV tile for testing **14a**

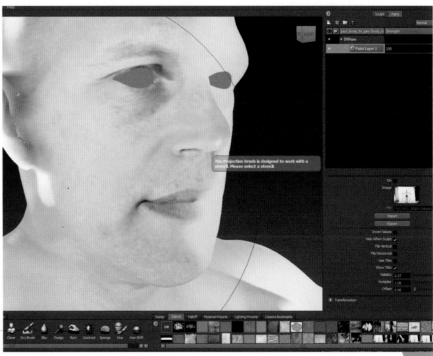

○ Use the Projection brush and check that there are no problems around the seams of your UVs **14b**

"I end up popping the UVs for the head on the first tile, and then laying out the remaining tiles with the body parts going from head to toe"

Texture Editor (Options). Under the Layout Settings, set the scale mode to None, Rotate to None, and the Packing preset to 2048 (Fig.14a). Hit Apply and all the UV shells should be within the 0 to 1 UV tile. With all the UVs still selected, scale them in uniformly so that they are away from the edges of the UV tile. Now export the model as an .obj file.

Jump into Mudbox and open your latest scene file. Drop the model down to the lowest subdivision and go to File > Import UVs. In the dialog window, locate and select the model you just exported from Maya with the latest UVs. If you now jump into the UV window in Mudbox, you should see that the UVs have been updated.

Create a new paint layer and paint over the model to test out if the UVs will be suitable. I usually use the Projection tool and paint through an image to get a quick idea of what the final result will be (Fig.14b). If texture seams are apparent or you notice any distortion, tidy up the UVs. It may not be the best fun you've ever had, but it really is worthwhile.

15: Laying out the final UVs

Now jump back into Maya so we can arrange our UVs. Instead of using just the 0 to 1 UV tile, I'll be using a total of 6 UV tiles. You can use more or less if you desire – it really depends on how you'll be framing your character.

A nice rule is to double the resolution of your UVs to the screen size they will be presented on. For example, if you're doing a close-up of the face on a 2K screen, you'll ideally want the resolution of the face to be at 4K.

In the UV Texture Editor, grab all the UVs and scale them up uniformly so that the unwrapped leg takes up one UV tile from top to bottom (but not too close to the edges). Now switch to UV shell mode and simply lay out the remaining UVs from left to right. I end up popping the UVs for the head on the first tile, and then laying out the remaining tiles with the body parts going from head to toe.

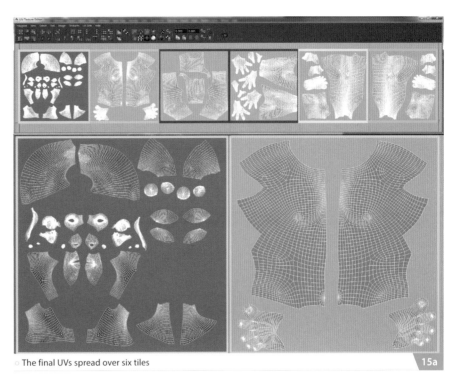

○ The final UVs spread over six tiles 15a

Once you're happy with how they've been laid out, proceed to unwrap the eyes, nails, teeth, gums, tongue, and underwear. With all the geometry unwrapped, ensure all history has been deleted from the models and overwrite the paul_mod_PUBLISHED.ma file with this file. As a result of this, anyone calling that file in through Referencing will have the model with updated UVs. The next stage will be grading our reference images.

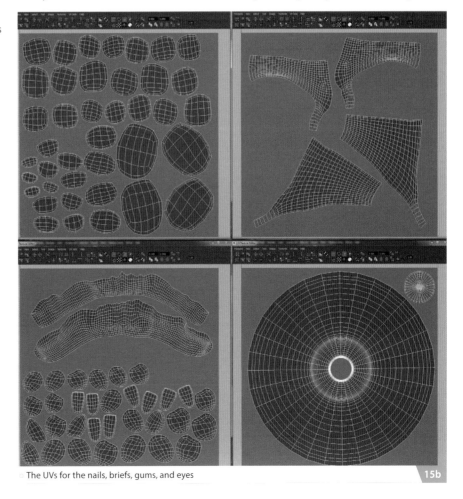

○ The UVs for the nails, briefs, gums, and eyes 15b

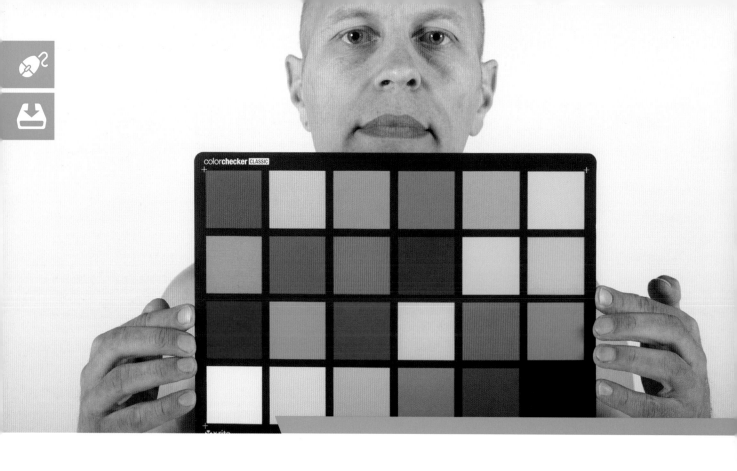

Preparing the reference images

Getting the reference images ready for texturing

In this chapter we will take the reference images and grade them to be used for texturing. Firstly, we will use them to create the color map, from which all additional maps will be created. Following that, we will look at how we can manipulate them to be used to add displacement detail to the sculpt. We'll also look at how we can remove the specular component from the images, and take advantage of Actions in Photoshop to avoid repetition.

01: Grading the images

To begin with, we need to take the original set of images that were taken during the photo-shoot (**Fig.01a**) and grade them. You'll find all the reference images used for this chapter in the following Maya directory from **www.3dtotalpublishing.com/resources**: /sourceImages/01_WIP/02_texturingReference. In this directory there are two folders: 01_RAW and 02_TIF. The 01_RAW directory contains

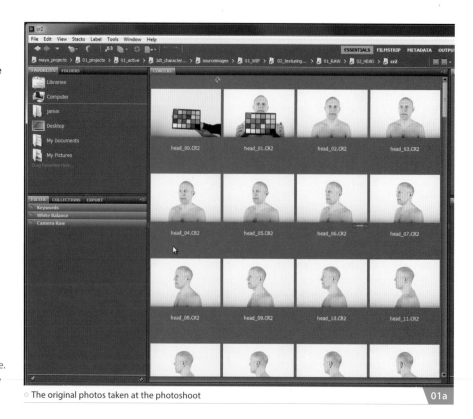

○ The original photos taken at the photoshoot

01a

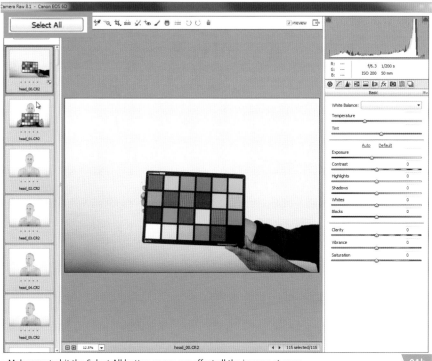

○ Make sure to hit the Select All button so we can affect all the images at once   **01b**

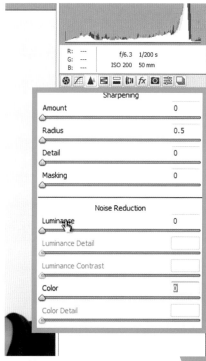

○ Disable Sharpening and Noise Reduction   **01c**

all the images taken on the shoot, and the 02_TIF directory holds some empty folders (01_FULL_BODY, 02_HEAD, and 03_HAND), to which I will save the graded reference images.

If you open up the 01_RAW directory, you'll find three folders: 01_FULL_BODY, 02_HEAD, and 03_HANDS, and in each of those will be two folders. The cr2 folder contains all the RAW photo files, and the jpg folder contains the photos in JPEG format.

> ## "Using the Macbeth chart, we will grade the images so that they match the lighting conditions of the texture shoot"

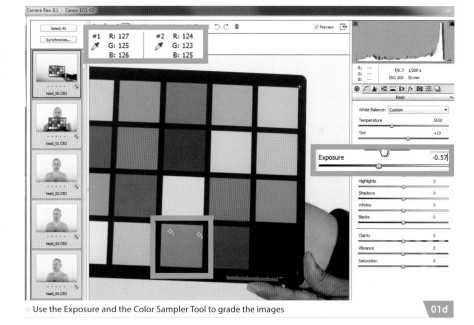

○ Use the Exposure and the Color Sampler Tool to grade the images   **01d**

For this example, I will just run through grading the head images, but the process I employ is the same for the body and the hands. Jump into Photoshop, load Bridge, and navigate to: 01_RAW > 02_HEAD > cr2. LMB-click on the first image (the Macbeth chart), and then Shift+LMB on the final image to select all the images in the directory (Fig.01b). Now press the RMB and go to Open in Camera Raw.

With all the images loaded into Camera Raw (I'm using version 8.1, by the way), and with the first image selected, hit the Select All

button in the top-left corner. Any changes that we make to the first image will now be applied to all the images. Next, using the Macbeth chart, we will grade the images so that they match the lighting conditions of the texture shoot more accurately. To do this, we will be using the white-colored square and the 18% gray square (bottom row, third from the right), which is a mid-gray.

Before we grade the images, jump to the Detail tab, and in the Sharpening section,

set the Amount to 0, the Radius to 0.5, and the Detail to 0. Under Noise Reduction, set the Color to 0 (Fig.01c). Now jump to the Lens Corrections tab and check the Enable Lens Profile Corrections box.

Switch back to the Basic tab now and we'll start grading the images (Fig.01d). In the top toolbar, start by selecting the White Balance Tool (I), and then click on the white box on the Macbeth chart. The effects are slight for these images, but it has removed a slight tint. Now

109

select the Color Sampler Tool (S), and LMB-click on two different spots on the 18% gray square. By using the Exposure attribute now, we want to get the RGB values of the color samples as close as we can to 128, 128, 128 (mid-gray). I end up dropping the Exposure down to -0.57.

With the images graded, we now want to save them out. Click on the Workflow Options at the bottom of the Camera Raw window, and check the following settings are being used: Space: sRGB IEC6 1966-2.1, Depth: 16 Bits/Channel (Fig.01e). Also, make sure Resize to Fit is disabled. Now click on the Save Images button, and then click on Select Folder. In here navigate to: /sourceImages/02_WIP/02_TIF/02_HEAD, and create a new directory called 01_GRADED.

Under File Naming, give the image sequence the following name: **paul_head_graded_**, and set the extension to 3 Digit Serial Number. Set the Begin Numbering to 001 and the File Extension to .tif. The Format should be set to TIF, the Metadata to All, and the Compression to None. Hit Save when ready and you should find the images in the directory that we specified.

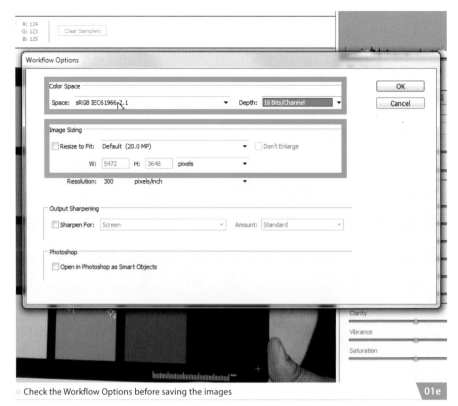

○ Check the Workflow Options before saving the images   `01e`

"We need to remove the specular component of the images, as we don't want them to be part of our diffuse (color) map"

With the head photos graded, run through and do the same for the full body images and the hand images.

02: Removing the specular component

We need to remove the specular component from the images, as we don't want them to be part of our diffuse (color) map. This is something that you can do at the shoot by using a Cross-Polarizing Filter (CPF). Although I did have one to hand during the shoot, it wasn't the greatest ever made, so I've decided to tackle the specular component at this stage.

One way we could remove the specular component is to use Photoshop's Shadows/Highlights tool, found under Image > Adjustments (Fig.02a). With a bit of tinkering of the settings and then some further adjustments using layer tricks and masking, all those shiny bits can be eradicated. Rather

than going through this process, however, I'm using a nifty little plug-in called ShineOff (**http://imagetrendsinc.com**). It won't hurt your wallet too much, and for what it saves you time-wise, I really can't complain (Fig.02b).

Once you have the plug-in installed, open up the first graded head image and duplicate the current layer by going Layer > Duplicate Layer, or in the Layers window, drag and drop the current layer onto the "Create a new layer" icon. Go to Filter > Image Trends

Inc > ShineOff to bring up the ShineOff parameters, of which there is only one: Shine Removal. Whack this value up to 150% (feel free to experiment) and hit OK.

If you now enable and disable that layer, you can see how much effect it has on the original image. The majority of the spec will be gone but the shadows will remain. We could paint the shadows out, but as we have a heap of reference images from different angles, we should be able to paint through other images

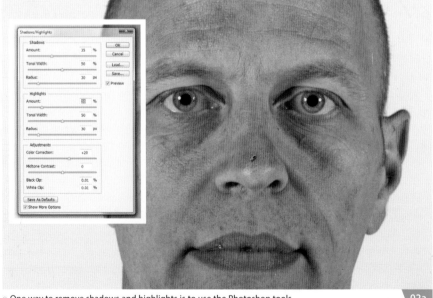

○ One way to remove shadows and highlights is to use the Photoshop tools   `02a`

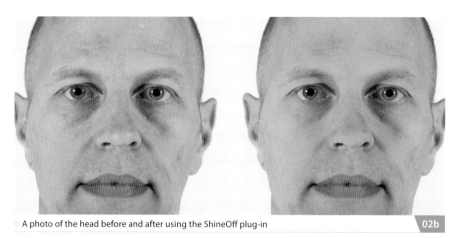

A photo of the head before and after using the ShineOff plug-in

02b

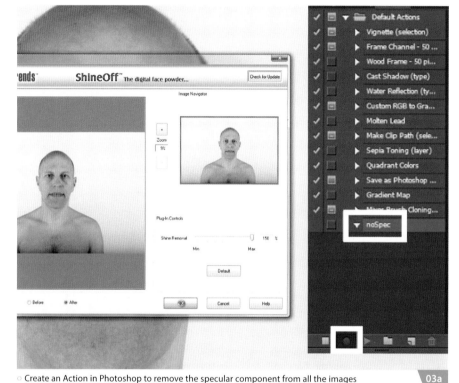

Create an Action in Photoshop to remove the specular component from all the images

03a

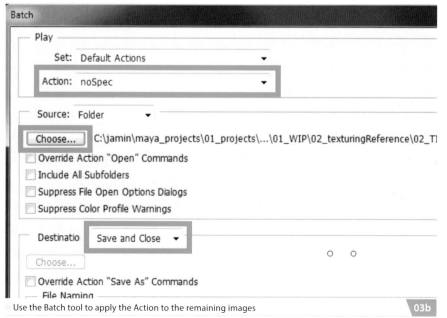

Use the Batch tool to apply the Action to the remaining images

03b

to remove them. Alternatively, we can use some layer tricks in Mudbox to paint out the shadows, which we'll look at later. Right now, we want to apply this same filter to all the graded images. To do this, we'll use Photoshop Actions.

03: Using Actions in Photoshop

Using Actions will allow us to automate a process and apply that same process to a set of images, therefore avoiding a lot of repetition. Start by duplicating the entire set of graded images and dropping them into a new folder called 02_NO_SPEC. Then use a rename tool (there are plenty of free ones online) and rename them **paul_head_ noSpec_###.tif**. Now load the first head image from the graded set, and save a copy of that image into a new TEST directory and rename it **paul_noSpec_test.tif**. This way, we won't alter our existing graded images.

Now open up the Actions window by hitting Alt+F9 or by navigating to Windows. When the Actions window pops up, click on the "Create new action" icon and name the action **noSpec**. From this point onwards, every move that we make is being recorded, which is indicated by the red circle on the Action window, so try to do only the steps that are necessary (Fig.03a).

Go to Filter > Image Trends Inc > ShineOff. Set the Shine Removal to 150% and hit OK. Then go to File > Save (which will overwrite our test file). Lastly, stop the recording by hitting the Stop button on the Actions window. If you take a look at the noSpec action in the Actions window, you will see that it has recorded the steps.

We now want to apply this Action to all of our images. To do this, go File > Automate > Batch. Make sure the Action is set to noSpec, leave the Source as Folder, and then click on the Choose button. When the Browse for Folder window pops up, navigate to and select 02_NO_SPEC. Leave the Destination as Save and Close, and then hit OK (Fig.03b). Now sit back, grab a tea or coffee and a packet of biscuits, and come back when it – and the biscuits – are complete.

Once the head images are done, repeat the step for the full body images and the hands. You don't have to do all the images of the full body, but make sure you have at least one revolution of the character. You'll find that the images of the model at full frame are not super-sharp, so

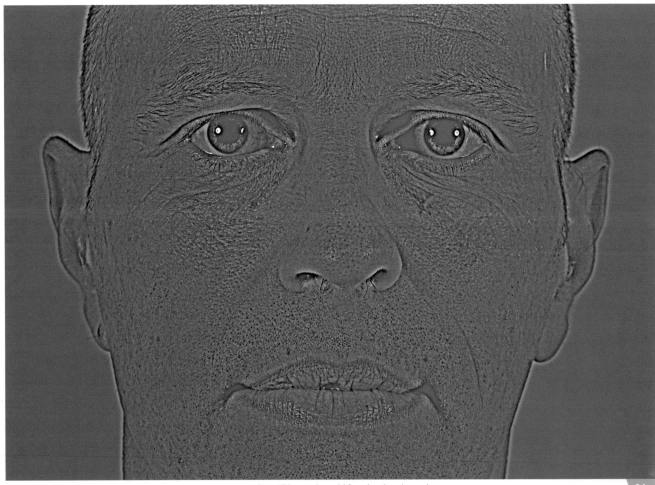

○ Take the head photos and manipulate them to create an image that will be used to add fine detail to the sculpt   04a

"I want to create a set of images that can be used to add displacement detail to the character"

on a separate shoot we captured some close-up images of different body parts. These have been supplied in the 03_EXTRA directory, so feel free to use them but do make sure to grade them.

04: Creating images for displacement

Now I want to create a set of images that can be used to add displacement detail to the character. These images will be used in conjunction with some Surface Mimic scans later on in Mudbox.

Again, I've duplicated all the graded images and placed them into a new folder called 03_DISP. The images have also been renamed **paul_head_disp_###.tif**.

I've only copied over the images of the model looking straight ahead, not down

or up. You can apply the following steps to those images too, but it could be overkill.

Open up the first head image and save it into the TEST directory as **paul_disp_test.tif**. Now, unlike removing the specular

component, creating the images to be used for displacement *does* take a little experimenting. I suggest you take the image that we create here into Mudbox and test it out on the model. I would still create an Action as you do it, in case you like the results.

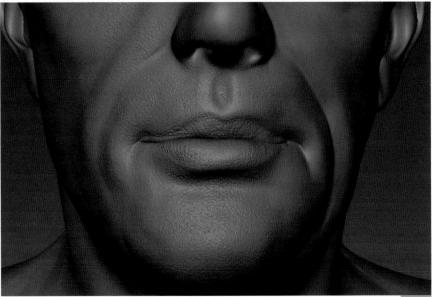

○ Test out the displacement image before committing to it   04b

Okay, so here is the process. Start by going Filter > Sharpen to give it a bit of a kick. Then go to Image > Adjustments > Hue/Saturation, and set the Saturation to -100. Then have a play with the Levels (Image > Adjustments) to further bring out some of the details.

Lastly go to Filter > Other > High Pass. A value between 5 and 10 works well, but experiment (Fig.04a). I end up using a value of 4.6. If need be, use Levels again to bring out the details. Save the file, stop the Action, and test it out.

To test out the displacement image, jump into Mudbox and open up the scene file with your latest sculpt. Subdivide the mesh to level 4 or 5 and create a new sculpt layer. In the Stencils tab, hit the Load Stencil button and load the displacement image we just created (Fig.04b).

You can also load this image into the Stencils attribute that lives under the camera itself. If you do this through the cameras we set up in Maya, you can get a one-to-one sync with the sculpt, the diffuse map, and the displacement images.

"Jump into Mudbox and open up the scene file with your latest sculpt"

With the stencil loaded, set the sculpt brush to either Sculpt or Bulge (I prefer Bulge), and start projecting the stencil onto the sculpt with a low strength.

Once you're happy with the results, jump back into Photoshop and apply the Action to all the images.

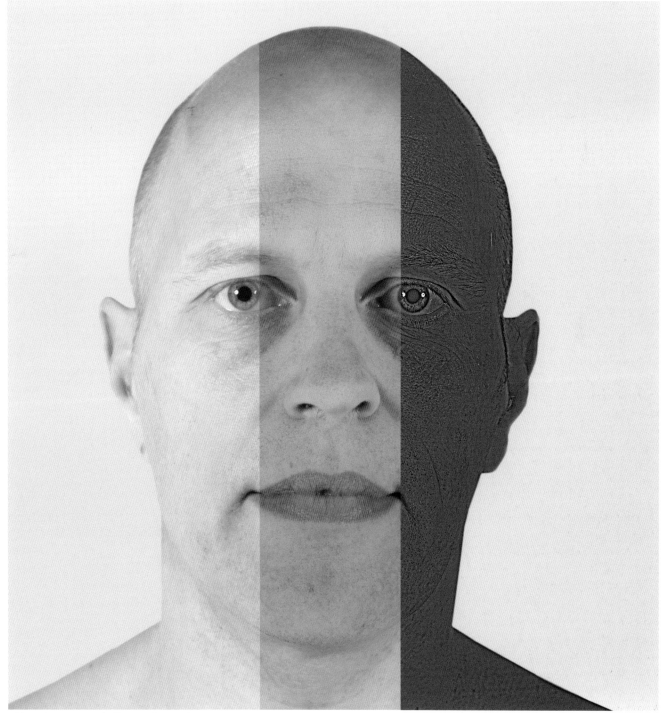

The various maps needed for texturing our character

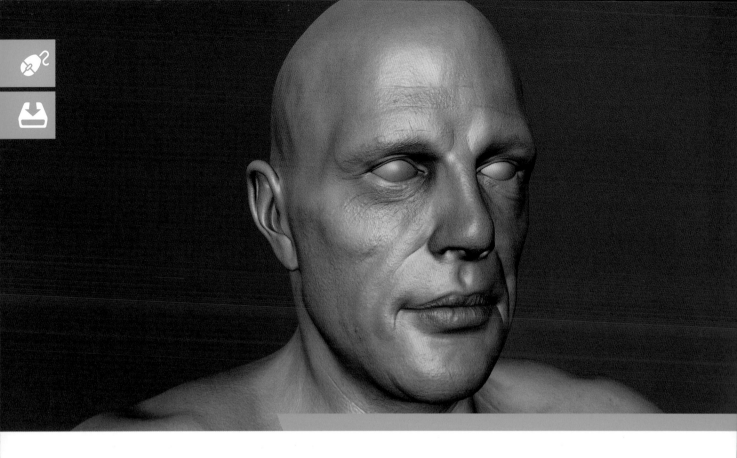

Painting the color map

Bringing the character to life with a diffuse map

In this chapter we'll be painting the diffuse map for the character. This map, also called a color map, will be used as the basis to generate the subdermal, epidermal, and reflection maps.

Using the reference images that we've graded and removed the specular component from, we're going to take the cameras that were set up during the sculpting process and project these images through them onto the model.

Once the images have been projected onto the model, we'll clean them up and remove any remaining shadows and highlights.

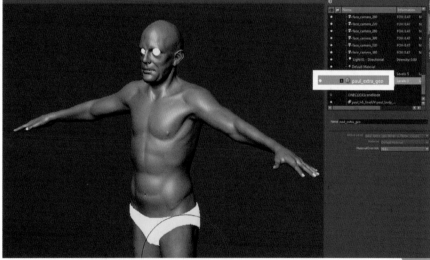

○ The additional bits of geometry have been merged together   01a

01: Setting up the scene

Before we start creating the diffuse map, I'll explain how the current scene has been set up. First I subdivide the nails and eyes in Maya (Mesh > Smooth). I then take all the extra bits of geometry (the nails, teeth, gums, eyes, and briefs) and merge them together (Mesh > Combine). I name this merged geometry

paul_extra_geo, export it out of Maya, and drop it into a Mudbox scene containing just the male sculpt geometry and all the cameras that we previously sent over (**Fig.01a**).

The fewer objects we have in Mudbox, the better it will perform. When we do need to texture these extra objects, we'll have to

import each model individually. So we don't paint on the combined geometry, enable the padlock in the Object List to lock it.

Next I give **paul_extra_geo** a different shader. You'll need to do this or you won't be able to paint the main mesh without affecting the combined mesh (**Fig.01b**). You can do this by RMB-clicking over the combined mesh and going to Select Model. Press the RMB once more, and go to Assign New Material > Mudbox Material. Feel free to give the new shader a different color as well.

With our geometry organized, we now want to take care of the cameras. If you still have the cameras in the Mudbox scene that we used during the modeling/sculpting phase, we should be good to go. If you don't have the cameras ready, jump back into the scene we set up in section 02, re-export the cameras, and bring them back into the Mudbox scene.

As our texture images are the same set used for the modeling (just graded, with the spec removed but at the original size), we can essentially project through the cameras and everything should line up accordingly. Some tinkering with camera positions may be needed, but for the most part they should be correct.

Tip: you can also switch between the cameras by pressing the RMB in the viewport (away from the model) and going to Switch View (**Fig.01c**).

02: Head projections

With our scene set up, let's begin creating the diffuse map. I'll primarily focus on the head here, but I'll also give you an overview of painting the body later on. You should be able to simply repeat the same process and then do a little tinkering at the end.

Switch to the Paint tab on the Layers window, and with the Paint Brush or Projection tool active, click on the model. This will prompt you to create a new Paint Layer (you can also click on the white paper icon on the Paint tab to do this). Here are the settings I'm using: Size: 4096, Save As: TIFF [16 bit Integer, RGBA], Channel: Diffuse. I know that using 16-bit may be going a little overboard, and the overheads in terms of file size will be very high in comparison

to using 8-bit files, but I find it gives me a wider range to work with when editing the images in post-production. I can always save the 16-bit files into 8-bit files if need be.

To make things a little snappier as you work in Mudbox, you can hide parts of the model based on the UV tiles. To do this, press Shift+A over the model, anywhere but the head. The region that the cursor's hovering over should go yellow. Hit H to hide that section. For now, as we're mainly working on the head, I would hide all the other parts of the mesh (**Fig.02a**).

Go to the Object List window to access the cameras. (If you want to have both the Object List and Layers window open, just go to Windows and select any you'd like to open.) In the Object List, RMB-click over face_camera_0 and go to Look Through. Remember to use only the 2D pan and zoom when looking through the projection cameras. Now click on

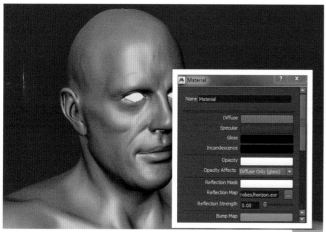
○ A new shader is applied to **paul_extra_geo**   01b

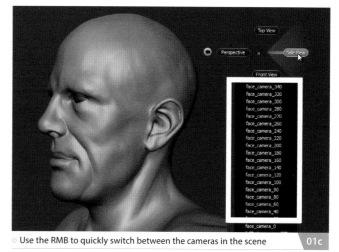
○ Use the RMB to quickly switch between the cameras in the scene   01c

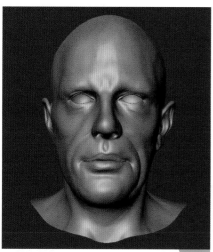
○ Hide all the geometry other than the area you need to work with   02a

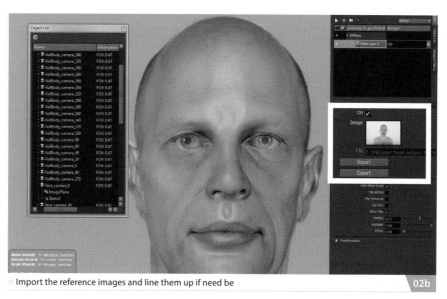
○ Import the reference images and line them up if need be   02b

the little plus icon next to face_camera_0, and click on Stencil. When the properties window pops up for the Stencil, click on the Import button, then navigate to and select the first image of the head from the 02_NO_SPEC directory (Fig.02b). Hopefully the image lines up correctly, but if not, translate it into position by holding down the S key and using the mouse buttons to align the image.

"Don't worry about painting over the existing texture as we'll clean this up later on"

Now that the reference image is in place, select the Projection brush, and make sure the Strength is set to 100 and the Color is set to white. When ready, start painting the model (Fig.02c). By the way, the model at this stage is only subdivided to Level 3 (around 400,000-odd polygons). Once you have projected through the first image, create a new paint layer by clicking on the white paper icon in the Layers window.

Now switch the camera to face_Camera_20 (the cameras are set up in 20° increments, but feel free to pop a camera at every 10°), add an image to the Stencil parameter of that camera, and again paint through the image onto the model (Fig.02d). Don't worry about painting over the existing texture as we'll clean this up later on. Make sure to spend a little time lining up the image before painting through. Try to use the corners of the mouth or the position of the eyes as guides.

Once you've painted through the second image, create a third layer, go to the next head camera, add a stencil again and project through once more. Continue to do this until you've painted through all the cameras, each on their own paint layer. By the way, don't concern yourself with getting the ears looking great – we'll come back and give them some attention later.

03: Cleaning up the head projections

You should now have projected the relevant reference image through the relevant camera all the way around the model, and each projection should have its own layer. At this stage, I don't recommend closing Mudbox as you may struggle to reload the scene file,

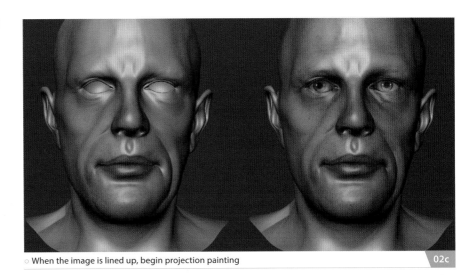

○ When the image is lined up, begin projection painting　02c

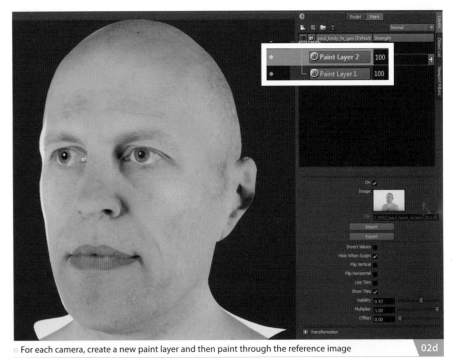

○ For each camera, create a new paint layer and then paint through the reference image　02d

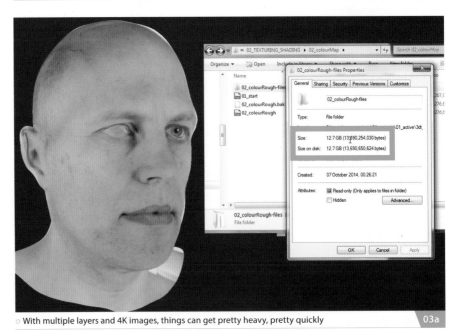

○ With multiple layers and 4K images, things can get pretty heavy, pretty quickly　03a

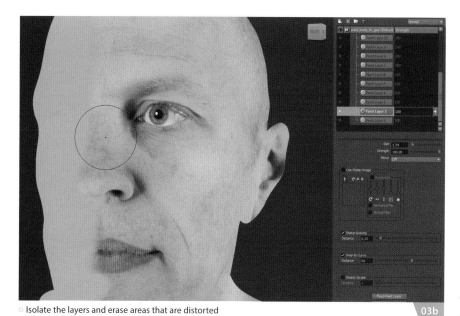

○ Isolate the layers and erase areas that are distorted

03b

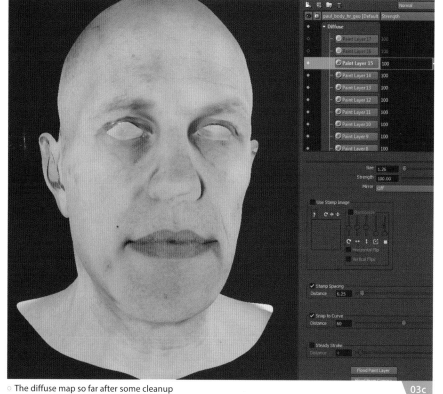

○ The diffuse map so far after some cleanup

03c

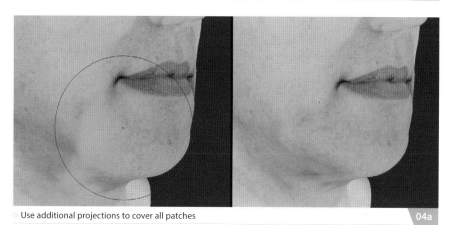

○ Use additional projections to cover all patches

04a

since Mudbox will save a 4K 16-bit image for each tile of the model for every layer. For me, this can generate an image directory of 12GB or so. Trying to load that scene file at a later stage will result in memory issues. So right now, we are going to do some tidying up and flatten the display layers, creating a more manageable and saveable file (Fig.03a).

To tidy up the projections, we'll take the best parts of each (the bits without stretching and distortion) and erase all the others. Start by hiding all but the first two layers. With the second layer active, take the Erase brush (set the Strength to 100), erase all the areas where the projection is distorted, and blend the two maps together (Fig.03b). As you do this, hide each of the two active layers here and there to view the effect of the layer in isolation. Once you've blended the first two layers together, hide the first layer and work with layers two and three. This time, layer three should be active and you should be erasing parts from that projection.

As you continue this all the way around the head, try your best to paint out areas that have shadows, but don't worry about fully removing them at this stage. Later we'll look at a couple of different techniques to do that job. If any details are getting lost or "soft", we'll re-project those parts back onto the model later on. To get a clearer idea of just the diffuse map without any lighting information, I also recommend disabling the lights by hitting Shift+L every now and then.

Once you're happy with your blended layers (Fig.03c), in the Layers window, RMB-click over any of the layers, and go to Merge Visible. Saving this file now creates an image directory of only 700MB or so, making it a doddle to load back into Mudbox.

04: Continuing with the cleanup (A)
We now want to re-project from multiple angles to bring back any details that may have been lost, and also to remove as much shadow information as possible. Start by creating a new paint layer, and again, activate the Projection brush. Find areas that need improving and look through a camera to work on that area. Project using a stencil again, this time projecting only onto the region of interest, and use the erase brush to blend the projection with the surrounding area (Fig.04a).

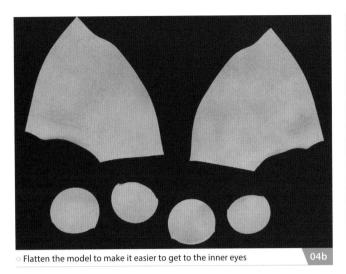

○ Flatten the model to make it easier to get to the inner eyes   04b

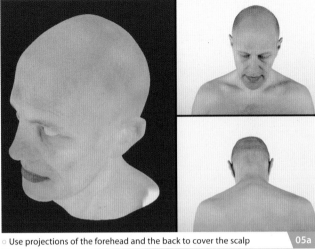

○ Use projections of the forehead and the back to cover the scalp   05a

It may be worth reducing the strength of the erase brush slightly, but I wouldn't go too low as this can result in "softening" the details. Enable and disable the new layer to see if it helps the overall map. Once you're happy with the area you've cleaned up, merge the layers together, then create a new layer and fix the next area that needs some attention.

Continue until you've brought many of the lost details back and removed at least 70-80% of the shadows. You'll find that areas such as the inner eyes and inner lips need fixing. Cleaning up these regions in the 3D viewport can be tricky, so try flattening the model based on its UVs. To do this, go to UV & Maps > Flatten to UV Space. For the inner eyes, I end up taking an image of the back of the neck and projecting it onto the flattened UVs (Fig.04b). When you're ready to unflatten the model, go to UV & Maps > Unflatten from UV Space.

05: Continuing with the cleanup (B)

Now you're ready to tackle the scalp and ears, and remove the remaining shadows and highlights. The scalp is easy: I simply use two images (the first image is of the head down, revealing a lot of the forehead, and the second is an image of the back) and project through these images to cover the entire scalp (Fig.05a). I initially work on a new layer for the scalp and then erase the borders to blend the patch in with the existing diffuse map.

The ears follow much the same technique as the scalp. I use multiple images of the ear to give me the majority of the detail and color information. I then use numerous other images of skin patches to clean up the areas of heavy

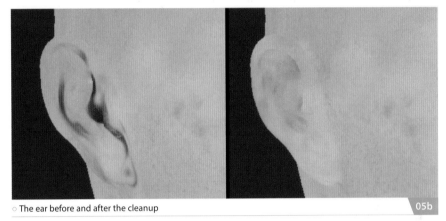

○ The ear before and after the cleanup   05b

shadow. Lastly I use the Burn brush to add more redness to the earlobes (Fig.05b).

I now need to remove the remaining shadows and highlights. For the shadows, I create a new paint layer and set the blend mode to Lighten. I pick the Airbrush and select the bw_cellNoise

stencil to add variation to the brush, but you can experiment with other Mudbox stencils (Fig.05c). I then sample a lighter color that's close to the shadow patch and paint over the area that needs fixing. I set the paint layer's strength to 60% to blend it with the overall map. For the highlights, I do the same, only

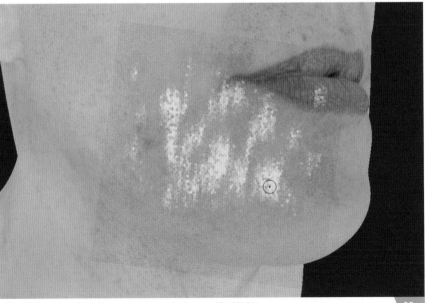

○ Use Mudbox stencils and layers to remove shadows and highlights   05c

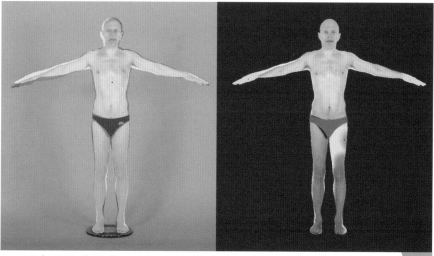

Line up the images for the body and begin painting through onto the model 06a

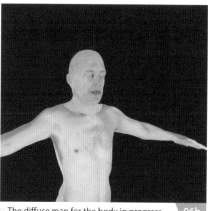

The diffuse map for the body in progress 06b

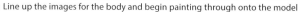

The current diffuse map of the character 06c

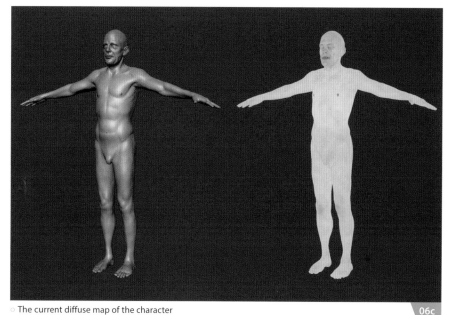

We can give life to characters in Mudbox

with the paint layer's blend mode set to Darken. Once you're happy with the diffuse map, merge all the layers together and save the scene file.

06: Painting the body

For the body, I follow the same procedure as for the head (**Fig.06a**). Using the existing cameras from the modeling/sculpting phase, I create a number of layers and project the reference image from each camera (**Fig.06b**). The layers are cleaned up and merged. At this stage, I decide not to paint hair. However, in Maya 2015, XGen has been implemented and I highly recommend you have a play if you don't want a bald character. To paint out the hair, I use images of the back (where there's no hair) and project them onto the arms and chest.

Once the body is blocked out and the layers merged, I create a new layer to blend the diffuse layer of the head with that of the torso – without accidentally destroying existing layers. I also create a base layer, drop it at the bottom of the stack, and fill it with a flat skin color. This is so I know every part of the model is covered (**Fig.06c**). Lastly I use the Burn brush with a combination of stencils to add further variation to the diffuse map: bw_grimeScratched, bw_neckSkin, and bw_cellNoise stencil. The elbows, knees, and knuckles need particular attention.

All the layers are merged together and I'm ready to move on to creating additional maps. Although we're leaving the diffuse map here for now, once we start developing our shader, there will be a lot of back and forth between Maya, Mudbox, and Photoshop to really fine-tune the diffuse map, as with all the additional color maps.

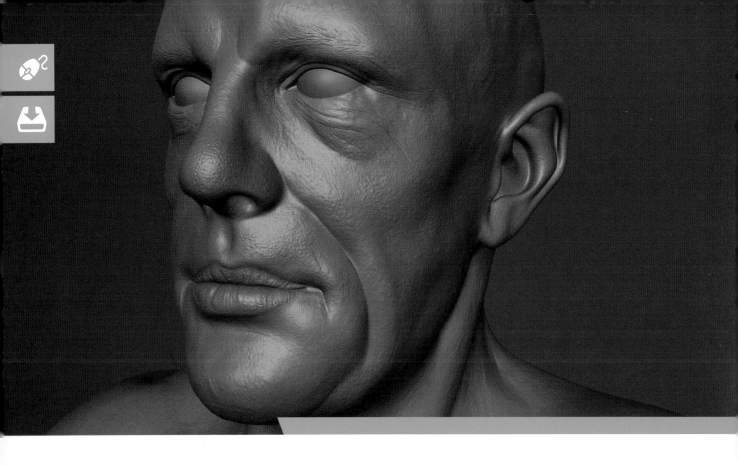

Creating the additional maps

Adding realism with displacement maps and more

Now we're going to add the displacement detail to the sculpt. A person's character can be captured through adding unique facial lines. We'll take our existing diffuse map and use it to create the subdermal, epidermal, and reflection maps. We'll also look at baking out an AO and cavity map that we can use to enhance our reflection map. All of these maps will be exported, along with a displacement and a normal map, ready for the look development stage.

01: Adding the displacement detail

We'll start by adding the displacement detail. We could have done this earlier in the character creation process, but I like to add finer details once the diffuse map is in place. This way I can use the color information as a guide for placing the wrinkles, scars, and so on.

As mentioned earlier, I'll use a combination of the displacement images that we created and images from Surface Mimic (**http://surfacemimic.com**) (**Fig.01a**). Surface Mimic's high-res scans are great for projecting details

onto a model. It'll pull me slightly away from the skin details of our model Paul, but my intention is to create a believable character, not a one-to-one representation of him.

Start by subdividing the mesh. This should take you to Level 4 and give you an object made

from around 17-million polys, the highest I'll be taking the model for this project. In the Sculpt layer window, create a new layer and look through **face_camera_0**. Load the first displacement head image into the camera's Stencil, and line it up with the model if need be. Select the Bulge brush (feel free to experiment

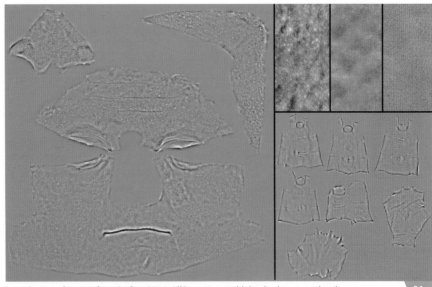

○ A selection of images from Surface Mimic I'll be using to add the displacement detail   01a

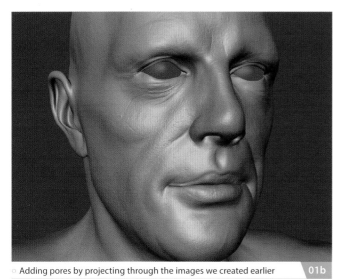

Adding pores by projecting through the images we created earlier `01b`

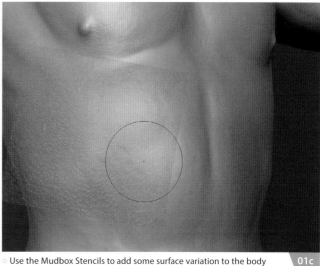

Use the Mudbox Stencils to add some surface variation to the body `01c`

with other brushes) and set the Strength to a very low value. Start projecting through the image to add the fine detail, and then switch cameras and do the same. As the resolution of the model is quite high, I advise against creating a layer for each camera – just work with one or two additional sculpt layers (**Fig.01b**).

I mainly project the Surface Mimic images through the Perspective camera, rotating and scaling the images to place them correctly. I use **Face_MaleThirties_Sam_Full** for the head, and **Body_SkinPatch** for the body. I also use some default Mudbox stencils to add further surface detail to the sculpt. After the fine detail is laid down, I cut into the model with the Knife tool to accentuate wrinkles and add additional variation to the surface of the skin (**Fig.01c**).

Once you've added the displacement detail, merge all the layers down to just one layer. I like to keep one layer active, so I can use the Strength attribute to increase or decrease the amount of displacement over the entire model. I usually crank this up above 100%, as some details can get lost when using a skin shader.

02: Exporting the diffuse map

Now let's look at exporting out the maps, starting with the diffuse map. I'll be exporting out .TIF files, and by default Mudbox will compress the files when you save them. This isn't good, as Maya will not play well with compressed .TIFs. We could re-save the files in Photoshop, but this is still not ideal. Instead, we can change a preference in Mudbox to stop it compressing the files. Go to Windows

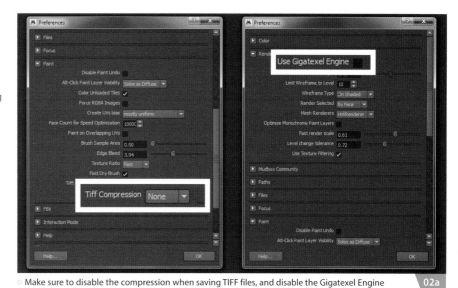

Make sure to disable the compression when saving TIFF files, and disable the Gigatexel Engine `02a`

> Preferences, navigate to the Paint tab, and set TIFF Compression to None. In the Render tab, I've also disabled the Gigatexel Engine, as I sometimes find that if I've framed a certain part of the mesh and use the Adjust Color tool, it only affects the region of the map that's loaded, rather than the entire map (**Fig.02a**).

RMB-click over the Diffuse channel and go to Export Selected. In the Save As window pop-up, create a new folder in the sourceImages > 01_WIP directory and call it **diffuse**. In the new folder, name your file **diffuse**, set the Save as Type to TIFF [16-bit Integer, RGBA] (feel free to use 8-bit) and hit Save (**Fig.02b**).

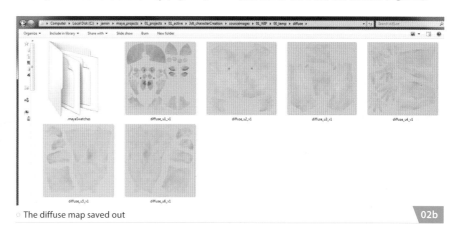

The diffuse map saved out `02b`

03: The subdermal and epidermal maps

Now duplicate the diffuse map and rename the new layer **subdermal**. RMB-click over the subdermal map and go to Adjust Color. When the Adjust Color window pops up, select More Contrast from the Presets menu (**Fig.03a**). Crank up the Saturation slightly and use Curves to add more variation to the map. This takes a little experimenting, and later on we'll push this further using a combination of Photoshop and Mudbox in the look development process. For now, export this layer (again as a 16-bit TIFF), name the file **subdermal**, and save it in a new directory, also called **subdermal**.

Duplicate the diffuse layer once more and call the layer **epidermal**. RMB-click over the epidermal layer and go to Adjust Color. This time, take the Saturation down and adjust the Hue to make it slightly yellowish-pink (**Fig.03b**). Again, don't concern yourself too much as we'll be editing later on. Save the layer as epidermal and pop it into a new directory, also called **epidermal**.

04: Generating AO and cavity maps

I'll now generate an AO (Ambient Occlusion) pass and a cavity map. Both of these will be used in conjunction with a desaturated diffuse map to create the reflection map. Let's begin by generating the AO map. To do this, go to UV & Maps > Extract Texture Maps > New Operation. When the Extract Texture Maps window pops up, select Ambient Occlusion Map. In the Target Models box, hit the Add All button. Select all the geometry, except **paul_body_hr_geo** (Level 0), and hit the Remove button. Do the same for the source mode also. The **paul_body_hr_geo** should be set to Level 4 here.

Under Output Map, set Quality to Fast and Method to Subdivision. Then under Image Properties, set Image Size to 4096x4096 (4K). Now save the images out into a new directory called **ao** (**Fig.04a**). Again, I have saved the images out as 16-bit TIFF files. Before hitting the Extract button though, ensure that Preview as Diffuse is enabled. This will add the map to a new layer in the Paint Layers window. When ready, hit the Extract button, and go and enjoy a cup of tea, as this could very well take a while.

With the AO pass created, you may find some areas are a little too dark, for

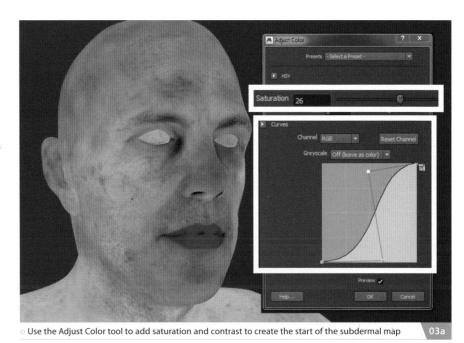
○ Use the Adjust Color tool to add saturation and contrast to create the start of the subdermal map 03a

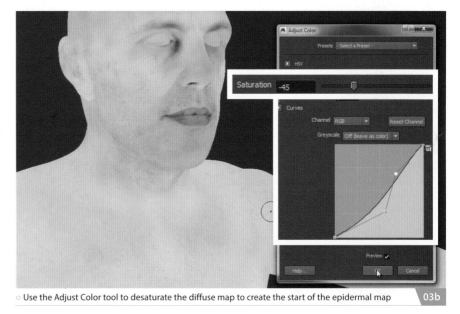
○ Use the Adjust Color tool to desaturate the diffuse map to create the start of the epidermal map 03b

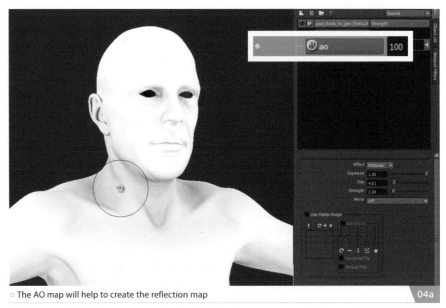
○ The AO map will help to create the reflection map 04a

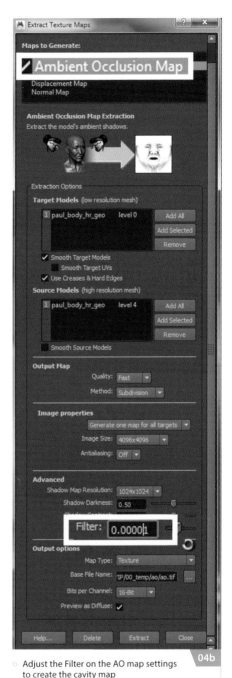

Adjust the Filter on the AO map settings to create the cavity map

04b

> "This time set the Filter to 0.0001, to create a map that gets into all the tight nooks and crannies"

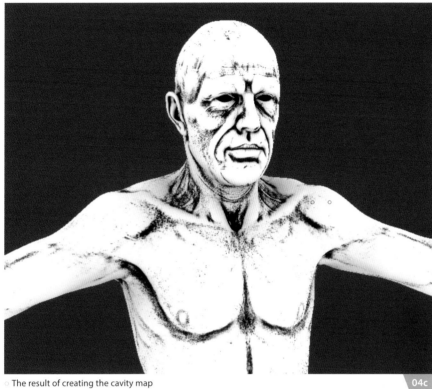

The result of creating the cavity map

04c

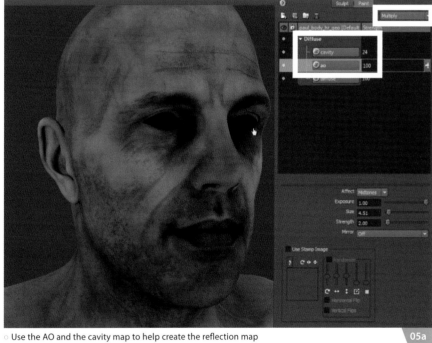

Use the AO and the cavity map to help create the reflection map

05a

example in between the legs. To brighten these areas, use the Dodge brush.

We need to create the cavity map. Go to UV & Maps > Extract Texture Maps, only this time select the same operation that created the AO pass. This will bring back the settings we previously used. Set the Filter to 0.0001 to create a map that gets into all the tight nooks and crannies (Fig.04b). Make sure to save the

files in a directory called **cavity**, and hit Extract. Preview as Diffuse should be enabled. Once the map is generated (Fig.04c), use the Dodge brush to brighten up between the legs.

05: Creating the reflection and the spec maps

Now we can start to build the reflection map. You should have both the AO map and cavity map in the Paint layers stack. If

you haven't already, make sure the diffuse map is also in the stack and placed at the bottom of the pile, and use the Adjust Color tool to desaturate it. I've also adjusted the Curve and used the Value parameter to get a bit more variation in the map (Fig.05a).

Now set the blend mode for both the AO and cavity maps to Multiply, and lower the Strength of the cavity map. I end up taking it down to

123

around 25%. Merge the layers together and use the Dodge brush to brighten up areas such as the forehead, nose, beneath the eyes, the cheeks, and the lips. When you're happy with the map, save it out into a directory called **reflection**, and give the map the same name. The reflection map will be used to create

"Use the Dodge brush to brighten up areas such as the forehead, nose, beneath the eyes, the cheeks, and the lips"

the broad, oily film that covers the skin. I want to create a second map, which I'll call the **spec** map, to add a second layer of oil to the skin, only with a tighter reflective quality (**Fig.05b**). At this stage, you should still have the reflection map on a layer. Now create a new layer, select the Paint

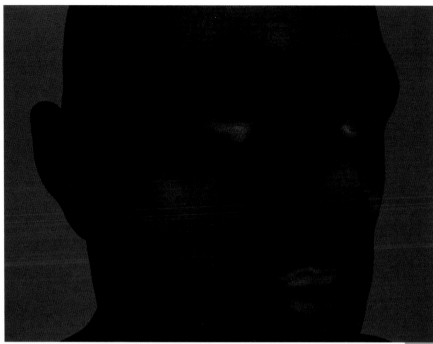
○ With the reflection map in place, we can create a spec map　05b

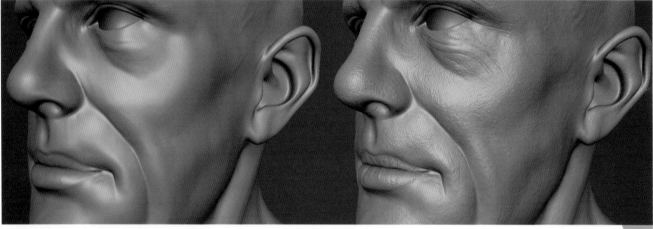
○ The model with and without the displacement detail　06a

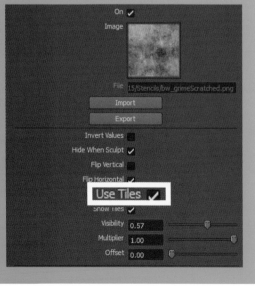

🔍 PRO TIP
Tile the Stencils

One of the things I like to do is to enable the Use Tiles feature of stencils. This way, I can easily paint over a wider region without having to constantly move the stencil or the camera. Time-saving tricks like this will make life much easier when dealing with larger surface areas.

○ Enable the Use Tiles feature to make it easier to project the same stencil over a larger surface area

Brush tool and set the color to black. In the Paint Brush properties window, scroll down and hit the Flood Paint Layer button. Then select the Erase tool and, with a low Strength, begin to paint away at the areas that are usually a little oilier, such as the nose, brows, lips, cheeks, ears, and under the eyes.

When ready, merge the layers together and export the layer into a new directory, called **spec**.

06: Exporting the displacement map

Now to export the displacement map (**Fig.06a**). You should still have all the displacement detail on a sculpt layer. I initially set the strength of this layer to 120% but later upped it to 150%.

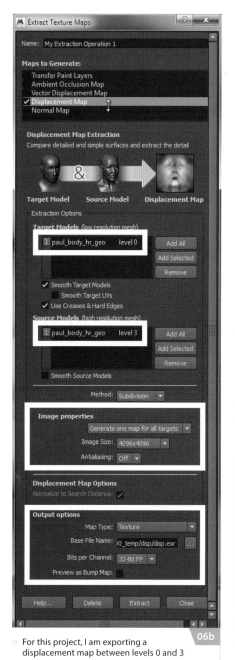

For this project, I am exporting a displacement map between levels 0 and 3

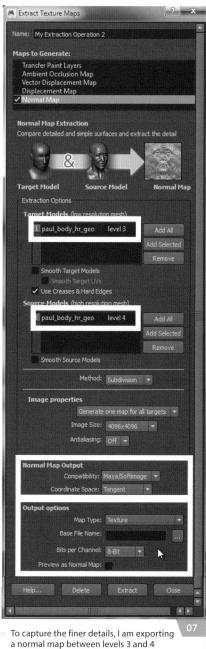

To capture the finer details, I am exporting a normal map between levels 3 and 4

The reason I go beyond 100% is because some of the details can get lost when using a skin shader. Go to UV & Maps > Extract Texture Maps > New Operation, and select displacement map in the dialog box. Make sure **paul_body_hr_geo** is in the Target Models box and is set to Level 0. Then make sure the same model is in the Source models box and it is set to Level 3. This is one level lower than the highest resolution; I've dropped it down one level because I'll be using the normal map to create the high-frequency detail (**Fig.06b**).

> "The maps we have created are not done and dusted, and will require many a further tweak"

Ideally, we would use the highest-resolution model to add the displacement detail in Maya, but it has a major effect on render times. If you have the time, though, I would go for that. Now set the Method to Subdivision and the Image Size to 4096x4096 (4K). Then click on the Base File Name … button and set the Save as Type to OpenEXR [32-bit Floating Point, RGBA]. Call the file **disp** and save it into a new directory, also called **disp**. By using a 32-bit file format, we can plug this directly into our skin shader and have it work correctly. Make sure Preview as Bump Map is disabled, and hit Extract.

07: Exporting the normal map
Now we're ready to create the final map that we need: the normal map. Once again, go to UV & Maps > Extract Texture Maps > New Operation, and this time set it to normal map. Make sure that **paul_body_hr_geo** is set as the Target Model and the Source Model. However, this time, set the resolution of the Target Model to Level 3 and the resolution of the Source Model to Level 4.

By doing this, we will only take out the high-frequency detail. Make sure Compatibility is set to Maya/Softimage and Coordinate Space is Tangent. Now save this file as a 4K 16-bit TIFF file and pop it into a new directory called **normal**. We now have all the maps we'll be using to create the shader. However, as mentioned on many occasions, the maps we have created are not done and dusted, and will require many a further tweak.

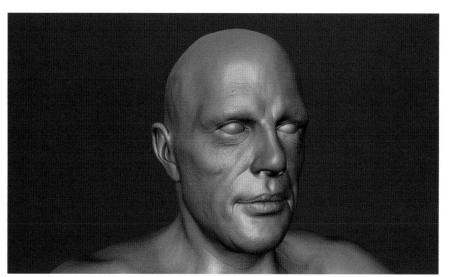

Displacement detail adds realism to our character's skin

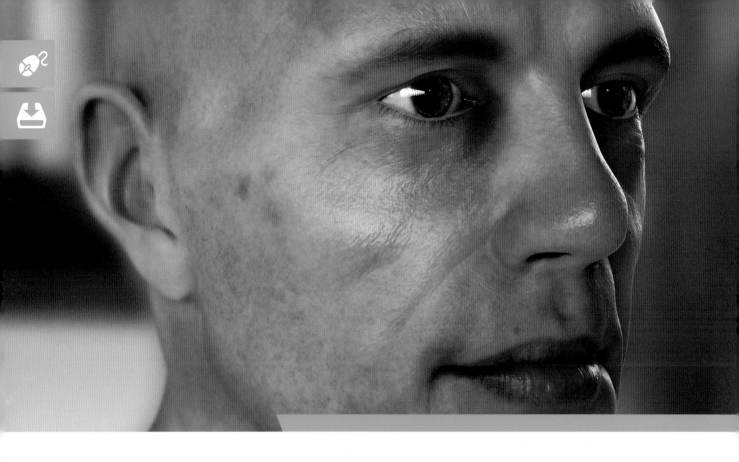

Look development

Creating a look development environment and testing shaders

Now we can create the shaders in Maya, but first we'll study the look development environment that's already been set up and make some tweaks. We won't go into detail on setting up the look development scene as I want to start building the shaders as soon as possible. If you want to create your own look development scene, look at the lighting section to see how I set up this base scene.

Once the look development scene has been assessed, we'll add an HDRI to our lighting environment, and an area light for some contrast. We'll make basic shaders for our chrome and gray balls, test our displacement and normal maps, then develop our skin shader, from the subdermal layer to the surface of the skin.

I'll give an overview of how I create the eye shader, but it's in your hands to experiment with it. Bear in mind that the idea of look development is *not* to get the final look; it's to experiment, try things, and have a play. There isn't space to share all the variations

and tests I go through, but I recommend you don't simply follow the final values and parameters I use. Come to your own conclusions on how characters should look!

01: The look development scene
Load the **lookDevEnv_final.ma** scene from the following Maya directory: scenes/01_WIP/02_ TEXTURING_SHADING/02_lookDev. This scene contains a mentalraylbl node (the red wireframe sphere) that'll allow us to map an HDR image (**Fig.01a**). I've enabled the Emit Light attribute for the mentalraylbl node so we can take full advantage of the HDR images providing the majority of our lighting for the scene. We then have a curved plane that we can use for a

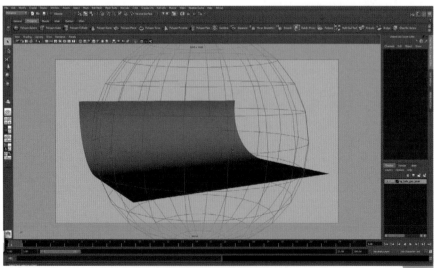

○ The scene file that we will use as the base for the look development 01a background. This geometry is useful for adding contact shadows to the feet, but increases render times, so I'll occasionally hide it.

I've created a new camera and called it **lookDev_cam**. It has a Focal Length of 50mm, which is what we've been using throughout, but feel free to change that. I've parented two spheres to the camera (**greyBall_geo** and **chromeBall_geo**) and positioned them in the top-right corner of the frame. Later on, we'll attach mid-gray and reflective shaders to the spheres, allowing us to view the environment that the character was rendered under.

I open up the Render Settings, add a File name prefix and set the Image format to OpenEXR (.EXR). I've also set the Frame/ Animation ext to **frame_#.ext** and the Frame Padding to 2. With this frame extension, we can now output a sequence of images and have them open correctly in NUKE or After Effects, depending on your preference. The Image Size is quite high, but rather than reduce it, I tend to use the Test Resolution settings, found in the Render View, under Options.

Under the Features tab, I've enabled Global Illumination (GI), Final Gathering (FG) and Ambient Occlusion (AO). This increases the rendering process, but the lighting will be more realistic. In the Indirect Lighting tab, you'll see the settings I'm using for the GI and FG. The FG settings are quite low as the updated mentalraylbl Light Emission settings do a great job and create less noise in the renders than they used to. In the Quality tab, under Framebuffer, I've also set the Data Type to RGBA (Float) 4x32 Bit so that our renders come out correctly.

The scene has been prepared for a linear workflow (covered in more depth in section 06) but make sure to open the Render View and go to Display > Color Management (**Fig.01b**). In the Attribute Editor, make sure Input Color Profile is set to Linear sRGB and Display Color Profile is set to sRGB. This ensures that we're working and viewing images in the correct color space. I haven't enabled the Maya Color Management feature (in Render Settings) because Maya only color-corrects input images and not color swatches (which also need correcting unless you're using pure

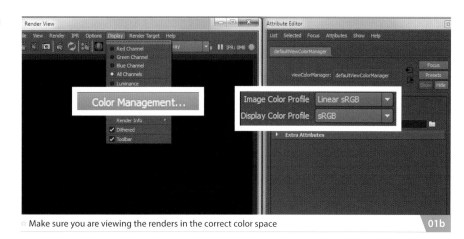

○ Make sure you are viewing the renders in the correct color space   01b

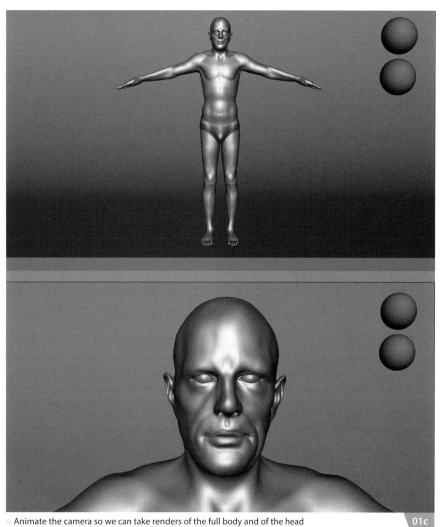

○ Animate the camera so we can take renders of the full body and of the head   01c

black or white). So I tend to handle all color correcting myself as it simplifies the process.

Go to File > Create Reference and bring in the latest published model. Check that this model has UVs and no history on it in the Channel Box. Next, at frame 1, look through the **lookDev_cam** and position it so that the anterior aspect of the model is in full view.

From the Outliner, select the **lookDev_cam**, and hit S on the keyboard to set a key. Now go to frame 10, zoom in to the head with the same camera, and set another key (**Fig.01c**).

At the moment, if you scrub through the Timeline, the camera will gently transition between the positions of the two keyframes. I do not want this; I want it to either be in one position or the other. With the camera still selected, go to Window > Animation Editors > Graph Editor. Select all the animation curves in here, and go to Tangents > Stepped. Now if you scrub through the timeline, the position of the camera will be fixed until it hits the next keyframe.

02: Adding an HDRI

Now let's add an HDR image for the lighting. On the day of the shoot, I didn't capture a HDRI (which would have been ideal) so I'll use a selection of images from the good old World Wide Web. I'm pulling HDRIs from three main sources: PanoCapture (**http://panocapture. com**), HDRI-Hub (**http://hdri-hub.com**) and sIBL Archive (**http://hdrlabs.com/sibl/archive**).

The main HDRI I'll be using is the **ScanRoom_06.hdr** from PanoCapture's Scan Room 8 HDRI Map Pack - a great set of HDRIs taken from a studio lighting session, the type of conditions I like to test shaders under. I'll also be using a selection of HDRIs from the other two sites to test the shaders under different conditions . Take a look at what they have on offer and pick the HDRIs you find the most interesting. I save the HDRIs I'll be using in a directory called **HDRI**, in the following Maya directory: sourceImages/02_PUBLISHED.

Back in Maya, select the **mentalrayIbl** node, and in the Attribute Editor make sure you are in the **mentalrayIblShape1** node. Click on the little folder icon next to Image Name and select the HDRI that you'll be using. Again, I'm using **ScanRoom_06.hdr**. You'll now see the image mapped onto the sphere, and rotating the sphere will affect the lighting. We'll be doing this later on to test the shaders.

03: Gray and chrome ball shaders

Now let's do a quick render to see the results. Look through the **lookDev_cam** and jump to frame 10 (close-up of the head). Select all the geometry in the scene, open up Hypershade (Window), and RMB-click over lambert1. In the marking menu, drag and drop the cursor over "Assign initialShadingGroup To Selection". Now that everything has the default shader, open up the Render View so we can do an initial render (**Fig.03a**). Set the Test Resolution to a size of your choice, then go to Render > Render > lookDevShape. This ensures that we're rendering through the correct camera.

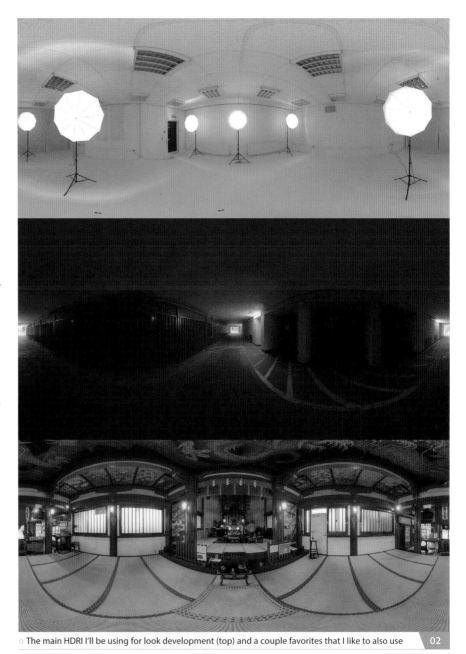

○ The main HDRI I'll be using for look development (top) and a couple favorites that I like to also use   02

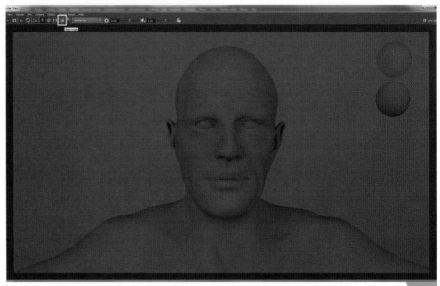

○ An initial render with the default shaders and lighting produced by the HDRI   03a

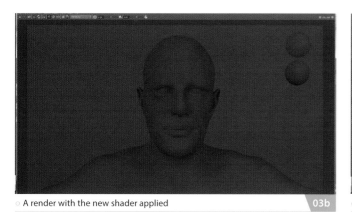

○ A render with the new shader applied   03b

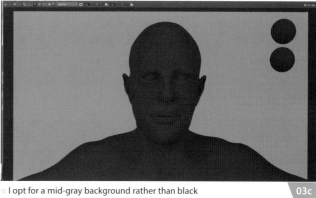

○ I opt for a mid-gray background rather than black   03c

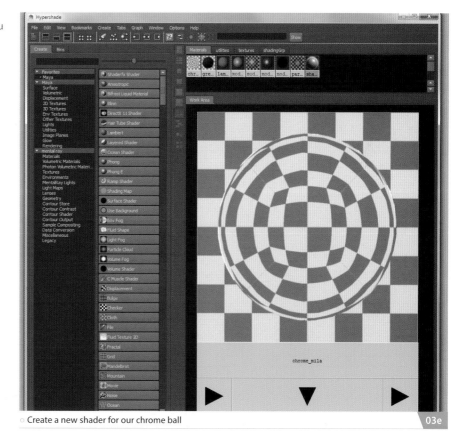

○ The Color Gain attribute will allow you to edit the intensity of the HDRI   03d

You should have a result like Fig.03a, which you can save by clicking the icon highlighted in the image. Let's now create our mid-gray shader. Open up the Hypershade, and in the left-hand column, highlight Materials from under mental ray and then select **mila_material**. With the material selected, jump into the Attribute Editor and rename it **grey_mila**.

This **grey_mila** looks like a mid-gray shader, but the color swatch has a gamma of 2.2. We need to invert this gamma so that it renders correctly, so click on the input (checkered) icon to the left of Color to bring up the Create Render Node window. Under Maya, highlight Utilities, then click on the gamma node and rename it **grey_gamma**. Set the Gamma to 0.455, 0.455, 0.455. This is the inverse of 2.2 (to be covered in the lighting section). Click on the Value color swatch, set the mode to RGB, 0 to 255, and set the R, G, and B to 128. Now select all the geometry in the scene, apply the new shader, and do a new render (Fig.03b).

The result of applying the new shader feels a little dark. To brighten things up, I won't play with the shader's value, but instead the intensity of the **mentalraylbl** node, which we'll do in a bit. I also want to hide the background

○ Create a new shader for our chrome ball   03e

plane for the close-up shots to save render time. To do this, animate the visibility of the background plane so that it's only visible on the full-frame shot. If you do a render now, the

background plane will be gone, and you'll see the HDR image in the render. To hide this from the render, select the **mentalraylbl** node, and open up the Render Stats tab in the Attribute

Editor. Uncheck Primary Visibility and then do another render. Leave the visibility on if you like – this is a personal choice as I like to use a chrome ball to view the HDRI that is being used.

If you render without the HDR image, the background is black, which is fine, but my personal preference is for gray (Fig.03c). To change it to gray, select the **lookdev_cam** in the Outliner and open up the Attribute Editor. Scroll down and open up the Environment tab, where you'll find the Background Color, which will also need color-correcting, unless we're using pure black or white. Unfortunately there's no input icon for us to plug a gamma node into. However, we can MMB-drag and drop a gamma node onto the Background Color attribute from the Hypershade to make the connection. For now, I've used the existing gamma node (**grey_gamma**) rather than creating a new one. Once the gamma node is plugged in, do another render.

To brighten things, select the **mentalraylbl** node and open the Advanced tab in the Attribute Editor. Click on the swatch for Color Gain and increase the value to 2/3 (Fig.03d). (Alternatively, you could leave this setting and increase the strength of the area light during the next step to brighten things.) Render again.

You can also rotate the **mentalraylbl** node to change the lighting. Later on, we'll add an area light to bring a bit more contrast to the lighting, and tinker further with the Color Gain of the **mentalraylbl** node until we're truly satisfied.

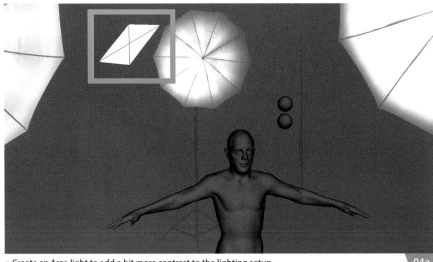

○ Create an Area light to add a bit more contrast to the lighting setup | 04a

Next, let's create the shader for the chrome ball (Fig.03e). Select **chromeBall_geo** in the viewport, hold down the RMB, and go to Assign New Material. Select **mila_material** from the stack and rename the new material **chrome_mila**. In the Attribute Editor, with the shader selected, click on the +Layer button. In the dialog window, select Weighted Layer, and then select Glossy Reflection from the "Choose elemental component" window. Leave the weight value at 1 and set the Roughness to 0. This will create a perfect mirror ball. I also rotate the **mentalraylbl** node slightly, as I'm getting quite a strong blue tint over the model.

04: Area lights and chopping up the model

The lighting we're getting from the HDRI is fine, but feels too flat. To spice things up

a little and add more contrast, I've added an area light (Create > Lights) (Fig.04a and 04b). I've positioned the light above and to the left of the model (but out of the render view) and scaled it down so the shadows are slightly sharper. To make it easier to position the light, you can look through it by selecting the light, going to the Viewport menu, and then Panels > Look Through Selected.

For the light to have a more realistic falloff, I've set the Decay Rate to Quadratic. After doing this, we'll need to crank up the light's Intensity (I've set mine to 6000). Still in the Attribute Editor, scroll down to the mental ray > Area Light tab and enable Use Light Shape. I set High Samples to 32 and High Sample Limit to 8. This reduces the noise in our renders. I also enable the Visible checkbox so that the light pops up

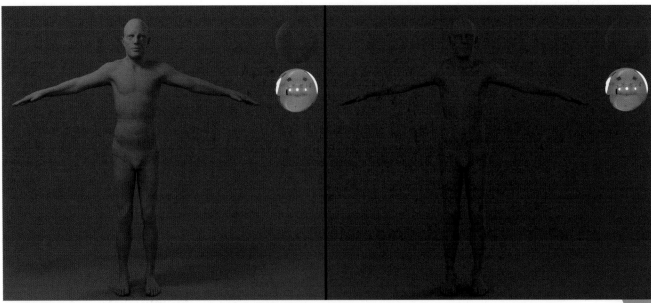

○ The difference, without and with the Area light for the full body composition | 04b

in reflections. There are many other things we can do to the area light to make it believable, such as attaching a Physical Light node or Blackbody node, but this should do just fine. Experiment with the placement and scale of the area light until you're happy, and then parent the area light under the **mentalraylbl** node.

Now select the main model and duplicate it twice, leaving the first duplicate as it is. Delete all the second duplicate's faces, other than those of the head (use the UV shells as a guide, and only keep the faces on UV tile 1).

Animate the visibility of the two duplicates so that when the camera is pulled back (frame 1), we see the complete model, and when the camera is zoomed in (frame 10), only the head is visible (**Fig.04c**). This will speed up the initial render times so we can focus on getting the head right before giving attention to the rest of the body.

05: Testing the displacement and normal maps

Now I want to bring in the displacement map and normal map. I do this at an early stage because these details can get lost when using a skin shader. I can see if they're coming through correctly, and crank up the settings later if needed. I'll test this out on the head model, as it's where the majority of the detail has been added.

Select the head model, and in the Attribute Editor, look for the shape node. On that tab, open up the Displacement Map section and disable Feature Displacement. This subdivides

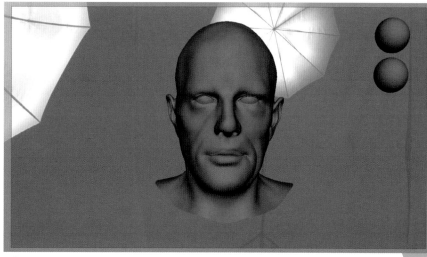
◦ If you zoom in (frame 10) only the head will be visible, which will help speed up render times   04c

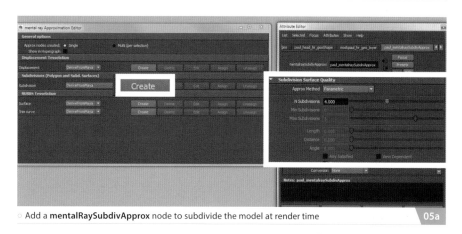
◦ Add a **mentalRaySubdivApprox** node to subdivide the model at render time   05a

the mesh at render time, but we'll use a mental ray node instead (**Fig.05a**). To add this node, with the model still selected, go to Window > Rendering Editors > mental ray > Approximation Editor. In the dialog box, click the Create button next to Subdivide to make a **mentalRaySubdivApprox** node. The values I use are: Approx Method: Parametric, N Subdivision:

4, and I enable Fine. Feel free to tweak these values, but they're the ones I am happy with. Create a new **mila_material** shader and rename it **paul_skin_mila**. In the Hypergraph, jump to the Utilities tab and drag and drop the **grey_gamma** node onto the Color attribute of **paul_skin_mila**. With the shader selected, hit the Inputs and Outputs icon to reveal the

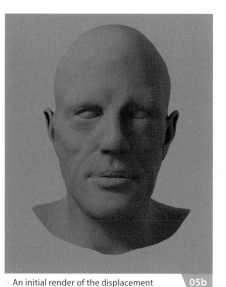
◦ An initial render of the displacement   05b

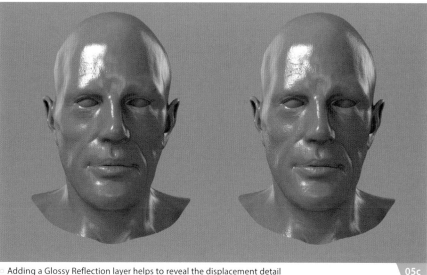
◦ Adding a Glossy Reflection layer helps to reveal the displacement detail   05c

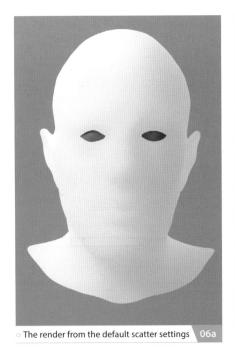

○ The render from the default scatter settings 06a

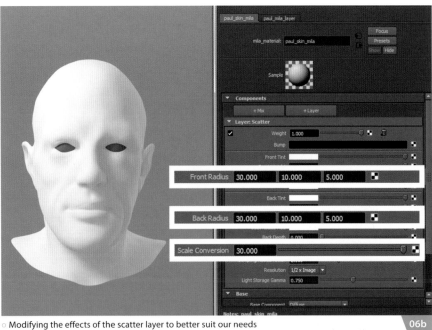

○ Modifying the effects of the scatter layer to better suit our needs 06b

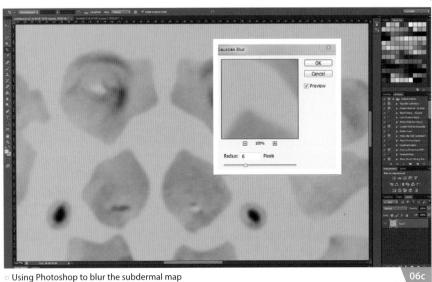

○ Using Photoshop to blur the subdermal map 06c

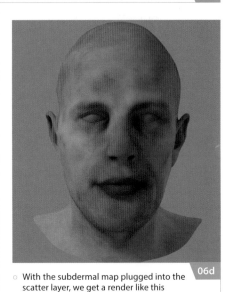

○ With the subdermal map plugged into the scatter layer, we get a render like this 06d

Shading Group (SG). Select the SG node and name it **paul_skin_mila_SG**. The SG node is what we'll connect the displacement to. Select the SG node and click on the input icon next to the Displacement mat. When the Create Render Node window pops up, search for and then click on the Displacement node. Rename the new node **paul_disp**, and click on the input icon besides Displacement. Select File from the pop-up window, rename the File node **paul_disp_file**, and rename the **place2dTexture paul_disp_place2dtexture**.

Select the **paul_disp_file**, disable the Filter Type (I do this for all input images), and click on the folder icon next to Image Name. Search for and select the first displacement image that we exported from the previous chapter. If we want

to add all six UV tiles, we can set the UV tiling mode to 1 based (Mudbox). This is the same for all the textures, so remember to enable this later. Scroll down to Color Balance and enable Alpha is Luminance. Apply **paul_skin_mila** material to the head model and render.

This displacement detail should be coming through, but it's hard to see (**Fig.05b**). To make it easier to see the effects, add a reflection layer to the shader. With **paul_skin_mila** selected, in the Attribute Editor, click on the +Layer button. Select Weighted Layer and Glossy Reflections, set the Weight to 0.1, and kick off a new render (**Fig.05c**).

Now let's test the normal map. Under the Glossy Reflections tab, click on the input icon next to

the Bump attribute. When the Create Render Node window pops up, select Bump 2d from the Utilities set, and rename this new node **paul_normal_bump2d**. Set the Use As to Tangent Space Normals, and click on the input icon next to Bump Value. Plug a File node into here, then rename that file node **normal_file**, click on the folder icon, and select the first normal image that we exported previously. Do another test render to see the results. If you want to increase or decrease the effects, use the Bump Depth attribute that lives on the **bump2d** node. If this all works for you, delete the Glossy Reflection layer and let's start adding the scatter layers.

06: Subdermal scatter layer
Select **paul_skin_mila** and create a new layer. Set this as a Weighted Layer, and select

Scatter from the Choose elemental component window. This should now be living at the top of the stack for our shader, and as the Weight is set to 1, we'll have a pure scatter effect. Jump into the Hypershade now and graph the network for the **paul_skin_mila** material. You should see a **mila_scatter1** node has been created; rename it **subdermal_mila_scatter**. You can also rename the **mila_layer1** node **paul_ mila_layer**. Before you do a render, I suggest disconnecting the displacement node and the **mentalRaySubdivApprox** node, or else you may be waiting for a very long time. Once you hit render, you should see something like **Fig.06a**.

The results are a little extreme to say the least, and as this is just the scatter component, it took a while to come through. When we start to add the additional layers, the render times will decrease, but for now we need to improve this scatter layer. First we can increase the Scale Conversion. Larger numbers will result in less scattering, and smaller numbers in more scattering. I end up setting this attribute to around 30 (**Fig.06b**).

We can then edit the Front and Back Radius. The three boxes (from left to right) beside each set of the Radius attributes correlate to the red, green, and blue wavelengths. We know that the red wavelength penetrates deepest, so let's increase its value to 30 for both the Front and Back Radius. Do another render and experiment to see what results you can achieve.

We now want to plug our subdermal map into the scatter layer, but first we need to blur the map using Photoshop. (Before making any changes, always make a backup of the originals!)

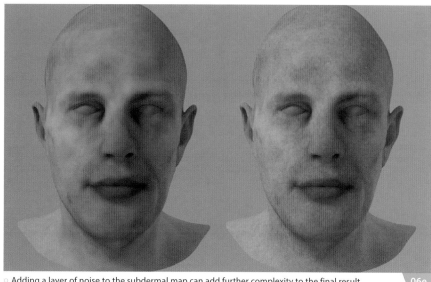

○ Adding a layer of noise to the subdermal map can add further complexity to the final result   06e

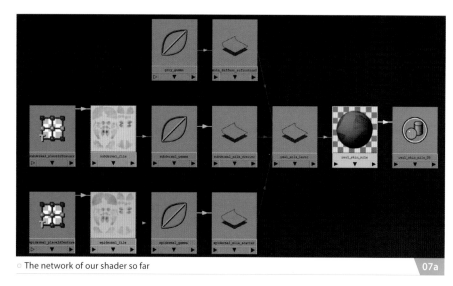

○ The network of our shader so far   07a

Load the subdermal map for the head into Photoshop, and apply a Gaussian Blur with a Radius of 6 or so (**Fig.06c**). Jot down all the changes that you make to the images as you go, as you'll need to do the same for the remaining five subdermal maps. Save the image and jump back into Maya. In Maya, open up the Hypershade, select **paul_skin_mila** and graph it so we can see the inputs and the outputs. We now need to plug our subdermal map into a

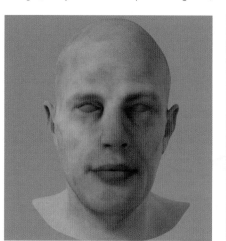

○ With the epidermal map plugged into the shader, we get something like this   07b

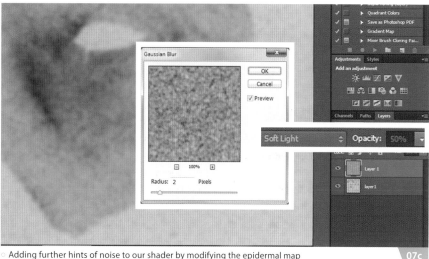

○ Adding further hints of noise to our shader by modifying the epidermal map   07c

133

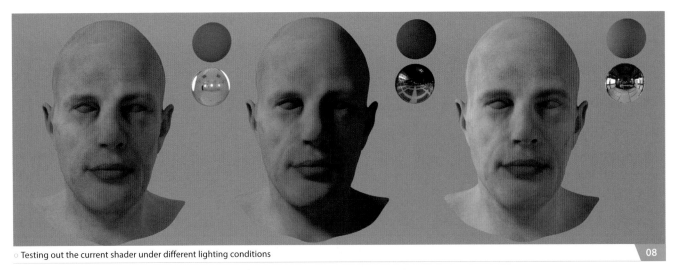

○ Testing out the current shader under different lighting conditions

08

gamma node before plugging it into the scatter layer. To do this, start by selecting the existing **grey_gamma** node and hit Ctrl+D to duplicate it. As this node was duplicated, it already has a Gamma of 0.455. Rename this node **subdermal_gamma** and then click on the input icon next to Value, and select File. Rename the file node **subdermal_file**, click on the folder icon and select the subdermal image that we just edited in Photoshop. Select **paul_skin_mila** so that it pops up in the Attribute Editor and MMB-drag and drop the **subdermal_gamma** node onto the Front Tint and the Back Tint attributes. Once again, do another render (**Fig.06d**).

I'll now demonstrate some of the processes I go through to add further noise and variation to the subdermal map. In Photoshop, load the latest subdermal map of the head. Create a new layer, sample a color from the map, and fill the layer with it using the Paint Bucket tool. Go to Filter > Noise > Add Noise, set the Amount to a value of your choice (mine's 82.43) and hit OK. Set this layer's blend mode to Soft Light, reduce the layer's Opacity to 50%, and add Gaussian Blur (I set the Radius to 3.5). Save the image without flattening and render in Maya. You may need to go to the **subdermal_file** node and Reload to make sure it calls the updated image.

If happy with the results of the render, copy the new layer of noise that we added to the subdermal map of the head and apply it to the remaining subdermal maps (**Fig.06e**). Once done, flatten the images down.

07: Epidermal scatter layer
We now want to add the epidermal scatter layer. I should mention that with the new MILA

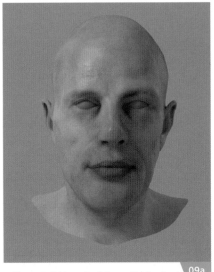

○ The material is pretty flat – a reflection layer will help reveal more of the model's shape

09a

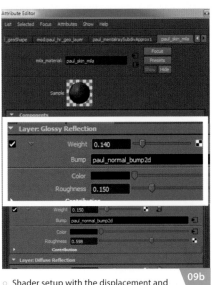

○ Shader setup with the displacement and normal map plugged back into the MILA mat

09b

material, we could get away with using just the subdermal scatter layer and then adding a diffuse layer on top. I, however, still like to add an epidermal layer as I find this adds an extra level of complexity to our shader – plus, these small habits of mine are hard to let go.

With **paul_skin_mila** selected, add a new layer, make it a Weighted Layer and set it to Scatter. Take the weight down to about 0.3 (you'll have to experiment with this) and give it the same values as the subdermal layer. Remember to pop into the Hypershade and rename the nodes appropriately.

Duplicate the **subdermal_gamma** node and rename it **epidermal_gamma**. Plug a File node into the input of the Value attribute and rename this new node to **epidermal_file** (**Fig.07a**). Click on the folder icon and find the first epidermal map. Now MMB-drag and drop the

epidermal_gamma node onto the Front Tint and Back Tint of our epidermal scatter layer.

Before we do a render, jump into Photoshop and load the first epidermal map. Apply a Gaussian bur to this map with a Radius of around 2.5. Save this file, reload the image back in Maya and then do a render (**Fig.07b**). Like we did with the subdermal map, jump into Photoshop and add a new layer of noise. Set the Amount of noise to a different value (I go with 171.82) so it's offset from the subdermal layer. Set the blend mode of the layer to Soft Light and lower the Opacity to 50%. Apply a Gaussian Blur to this layer with a Radius of around 2 (**Fig.07c**). Save this image now, reload the texture and do a new render.

08: Adding the diffuse layer
Now we want to add the diffuse layer. Select **paul_skin_mila** and add a new Weighted Layer.

This time, however, add a Diffuse Reflection from the Choose elemental component window. Set the Weight of this new layer to 0.4 to begin with, increase the Roughness to around 0.4, and appropriately rename the associated nodes in the Hypershade. Duplicate the **epidermal_gamma** node and rename it **diffuse_gamma**. Plug a File node into it and connect the first diffuse map to that node. Again, rename all the nodes as you go. When that's done, select **paul_skin_mila** and MMB-drag and drop the **diffuse_gamma** node into the Color attribute of the Diffuse Reflection layer, and do a new render.

To add a more color variation to the layer, load the first diffuse map into Photoshop and create a new noise layer. I set the amount to 153 (you can choose otherwise) and the blend mode to Soft Light. Reduce the layer's Opacity to around 20% and apply a Gaussian Blur with a very low Radius (around 1). Save this image, reload it back in Maya, and do a new render. It's worth doing a couple of extra renders with the HDRI changed, so that we can see the effects of our shader under different lighting conditions.

09: Adding the reflection layers

For the reflection map, simply select **paul_skin_mila** and add a new layer. Make it a Weighted Layer and pick Glossy Reflection. If we were to make a render now, we'd most likely get something similar to a dodgy-looking version of the T-1000 from *Terminator*, so reduce the Weight to 0.15 or so (**Fig.09a**). Increase Roughness to 0.6 to make the reflections more diffuse and less mirror-like.

Let's connect our reflection map to the layer now. In the Hypershade, duplicate one of the existing gamma nodes, rename the node **reflection_gamma**, and click on the input icon next to the Value. As always, select a File node and rename everything appropriately. Connect the first reflection map into the File node and then MMB-drag-and-drop **reflection_gamma** onto the Color attribute of the Glossy Reflection layer. Now connect the displacement node back into the SG node of the shader, and create a new **mentalraySubdiv** node (or apply the existing one if it's still kicking around). From the Hypershade, you can now MMB-drag-and-drop the **paul_normal_bump2d** node onto the Bump attribute of both the Glossy Reflection layer and Diffuse Reflection layer (**Fig.09b**).

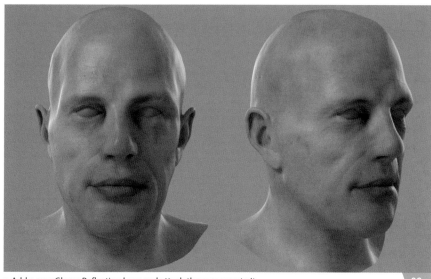

○ Add a new Glossy Reflection layer and attach the spec map to it   09c

○ You can use NUKE to push the images and quickly assess what works and what doesn't   10

I now want to add a blue tint to the Reflection map. Open up the first reflection image in Photoshop, create a new layer, and fill it with a blue color. Set the blend mode to Multiply and lower the Opacity to 30% or so. Save this image, jump back into Maya, and reload the texture.

Now let's add the spec map. Create a new Glossy Reflection Weighted Layer for the **paul_skin_mila** material. Duplicate an existing gamma node, rename it, and attach a File node to it. Plug the first spec map into the gamma node and MMB-drag-and-drop the gamma node onto the Color attribute of our new Glossy Reflection layer. For this new layer, set the Weight to 1.4 and Roughness to 0.15 to create sharper reflections in the hot spots. The final layer is a Fresnel layer. The "Fresnel effect" describes the amount of reflected and refracted light that we see on an object

depending on the angle from which it's viewed (**Fig.09c**). It's an effect you'll see on everyday objects, including skin. For example, take your phone and look at the screen at eye level. You should be able to see everything fine. Tilt the phone away from you so the screen starts to face upwards, and notice the reflection at the grazing angles – this is the effect of Fresnel.

To add this effect to our shader, select **paul_mila_skin** and add a new layer. Make it a Fresnel Layer and click on Glossy Reflections. Now set the Weight down to 0.7, the Fresnel IOR to 1.3 and the Roughness to 0.7. Do a new render to view the results and play with the values to see what you can come up with.

10: Tweak the results in NUKE

Now the first pass of the shader is created, I'll render out a sequence of images of the head turning over 10 frames, and then of the **mentalraylbl** node (with the area light parented to it) rotating around the model over 10 frames. These images are then dropped into NUKE (**www.thefoundry.co.uk/products/ nuke**), where I have a tinker with them to see how the shader holds up. Usually I add a Sharpen node, a Grade node, and sometimes a Saturation node. Using these nodes, I can make changes quickly and think about how I'd like to push the shader and textures.

I won't go into detail on using NUKE as it really isn't my forte, but here's an overview to get you editing. First, load an image or image sequence. To do this, press the R key to create a Read node, which will prompt you to select an image. With the image loaded, you can hit the 1 key to load it into the viewer. If you have multiple images in the Node graph, you can use the keyboard keys 2, 3, 4, and so on, to load them into the viewer and toggle between them.

To create further nodes, press the Tab key and begin typing the name of the node. First press Tab and type Sharpen. When the node pops up, drag it so that it attaches itself beneath

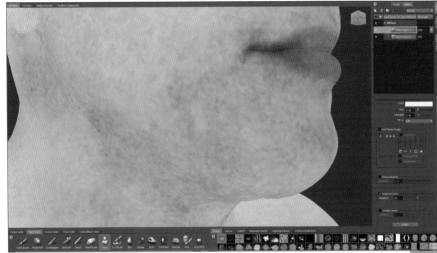

○ Now that the shader is blocked out, start pushing the texture maps and adding extra subtle details   11a

the Read node. Create a Saturation node and attach it beneath the Sharpen node. Finally create a Grade node and attach it beneath the Saturation node. For each node, you can edit the parameters in the Properties window. Have a tinker to see what you come up with.

11: Updating the maps

Now that the initial maps are plugged in, you'll probably find that they could be better. I like to

jump between Photoshop, Mudbox, and Maya to tweak the texture maps and shader (**Fig.11a**). For example, I might use Mudbox's paint layers to paint bluish-green veins onto a subdermal map, then flatten and import it back into Maya for rendering; or I might add extra layers of noise in Photoshop.

You may need to return to Mudbox to paint over any seams between the UV shells;

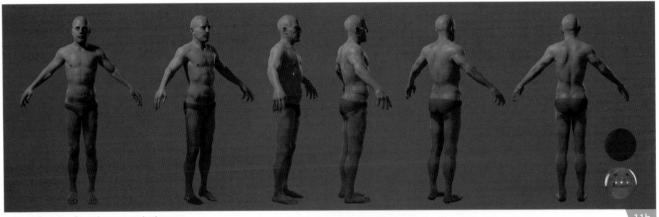

○ A set of renders from the current shader setup   11b

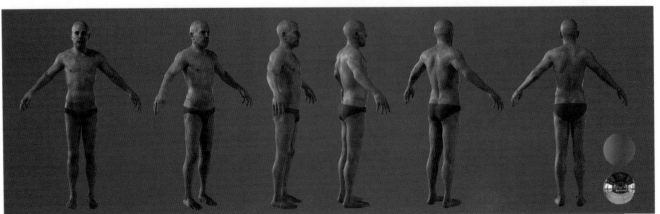

○ More test renders with a different HDRI   11c

"It takes time and there are no magic numbers, so experiment and enjoy"

the Clone tool is perfect for cleaning up issues like this. The subdermal map will get attention, as well as all the others, except the normal and displacement maps.

As you edit the maps, remember to play with the values of each layer of the shader. Once you're happy with the direction of the head, do the same for the body and remember to enable all the UV tiles in Maya so all the maps get picked up. It takes time and there are no magic numbers, so experiment and enjoy.

Note: as I was simultaneously rigging and working on look development, I ended up re-posing the model so that it felt more relaxed in the renders. I also darkened the gray background for the renders, purely for aesthetic reasons.

12: Overview of the eyes

I like to keep things simple for the eyes. First, I gather some reference, rather than using images from the shoot. A quick Google search for macro eye photography offers a wide selection to choose from.

Once I have a range of images, I import **l_scleraIris_hr_geo**, **r_scleraIris_geo**, and **paul_body_hr_geo** into Mudbox (**Fig.12a**). I create a new diffuse paint layer (2046x2046) for **l_scleraIris_hr_geo**, and project my texture images onto the model. If any reflections are present in your texture images, make sure to paint them out. I've created a diffuse map for each eye rather than duplicating, so that each eye is unique. When you're happy with the maps, save them out and open them in Photoshop.

We'll now create a bump map from the diffuse map. If you intend to do a close-up of the eyes, it may be beneficial to create a normal map. Take the diffuse map, desaturate it, then invert it. Save this as the bump map and jump into Maya (**Fig.12b**).

Creating a shader for the pupil is simple: just create a new MILA material and set the diffuse color to pure black (**Fig.12c**). You can

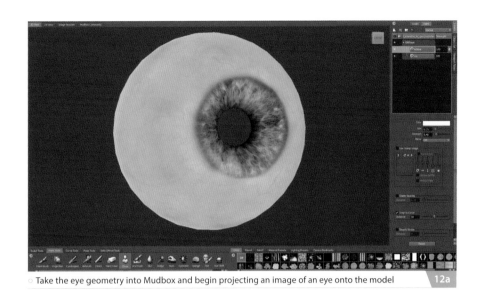
○ Take the eye geometry into Mudbox and begin projecting an image of an eye onto the model　12a

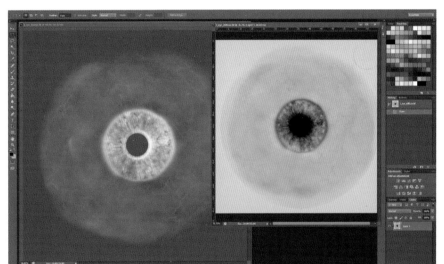
○ Create the bump map for the eye by adjusting the diffuse map in Photoshop　12b

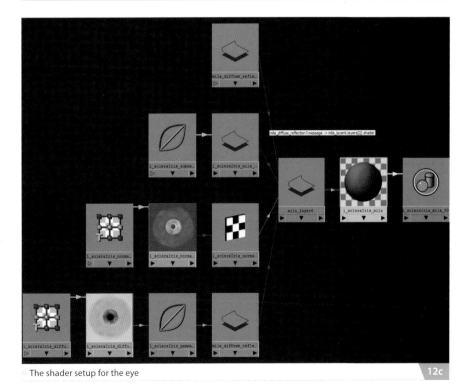
○ The shader setup for the eye　12c

137

apply this to both pupils. For the cornea, create a new MILA material and set the Base Layer to Transmissive. Set the Color to white, Reflective Weight to 1, Roughness to 1.25, and IOR to 1.55. Create a Fresnel Layer and set it to Glossy Reflections. Set the Weight to 1, Fresnel IOR to 1.3, and Roughness to 0.6. This can be applied to both corneas.

Create a new MILA material and assign it to the **l_scleralris_geo**. Add a Weighted Layer and make it a Scatter layer. Set the Weight to 1, Front and Back Radius to 5, 2.5, and 1.25. Set the Scale Conversion to 30. Plug a gamma node into the Front and Back Tint and give it a pinkish color. Create a new Weighted Layer and set it to Diffuse Reflection. Set the Weight of this layer to 0.85 and plug the **scleralris** texture into the Color attribute via a gamma correct node. You can also plug the bump map into the

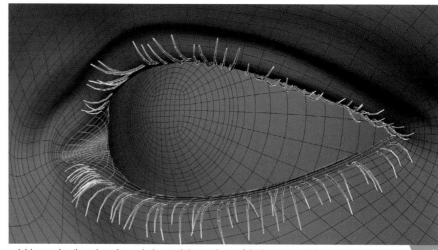

○ Add extra details such as the eyelashes and the wet layer of the bottom eyelid   12d

Bump attribute through a **bump2d** node (make sure to set the node from Use As to Bump). With the shaders ready, do a few test renders from multiple angles and under different

lighting conditions. To take things further, you could model some eyelashes (or use a hair system) and add extra geometry to create the wet layer that sits on the bottom eyelid

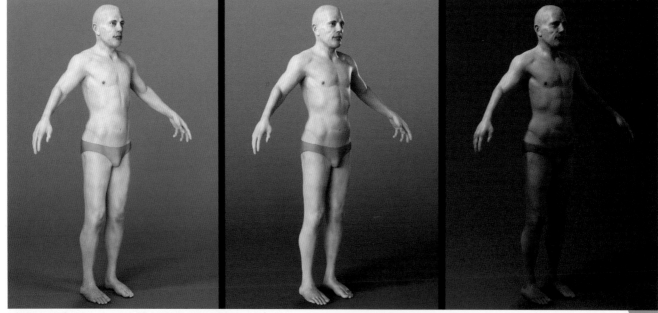

○ Renders of the full body under different lighting conditions   12e

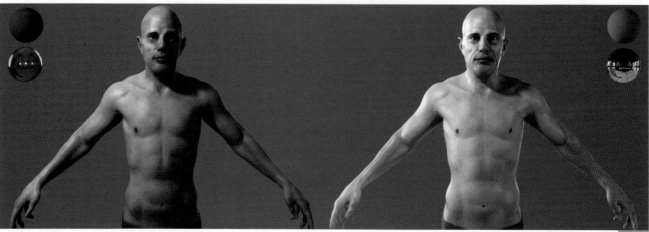

○ Renders of the torso under different lighting conditions   12f

(Fig.12d). However, remember that you'll need to re-publish the main model file with these extra bits and rig them they are picked up down the pipeline. Once the eyes are complete, go for the nails, gums, teeth, and briefs if you wish to.

13: Publishing the shaders

Now we need to prepare our scene for Publishing. Jump into the Hypershade and go to Edit > Delete Unused Shaders to remove any shaders not connected to objects.

I've been calling in texture images from the 01_WIP directory in the **sourceImages** folder, and could leave that as it is, but as this file will be published, I'd rather the File nodes point to maps in a 02_PUBLISHED directory. So I've copied only the relevant texture maps to a new directory called TEXTURES in the 02_PUBLISHED folder, and re-directed all the File nodes in Maya.

Now select all the geometry in the Outliner and delete it. For anything that's being Referenced in, RMB-click on it and go to Reference > Remove. Then delete any additional cameras, lights, and layers from the scene. The shaders are all that should be left in the scene.

Save a local copy of this scene file, and another copy in this Maya directory: scenes/02_PUBLISHED/02_TEXTURING_SHADING. Call the scene file **paul_shaders_PUBLISHED.ma**. And that's it – our character now looks the part!

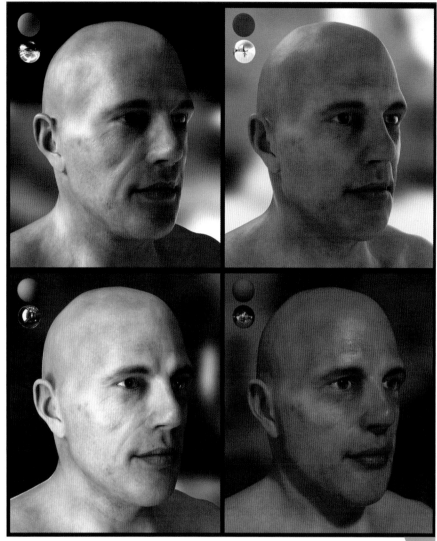

12g

○ Testing the head against the background images to see if the character will successfully sit within the plate

○ Remove any unnecessary objects and publish the scene file

13

139

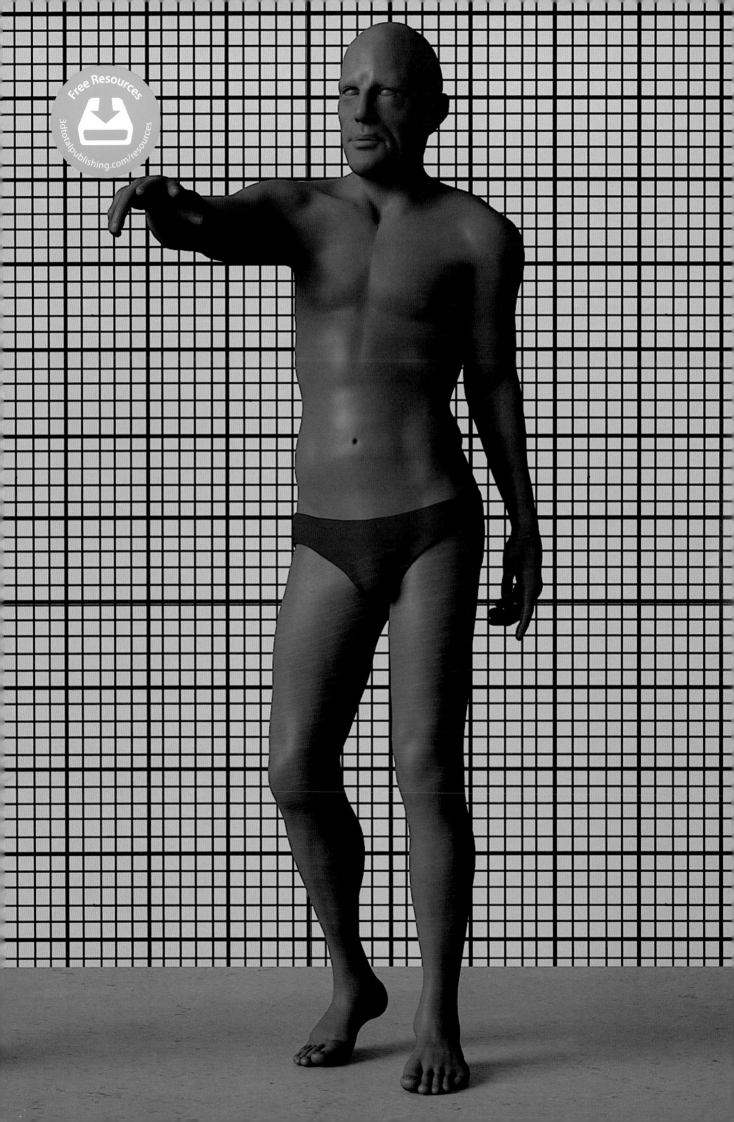

Rigging and deformation in Maya

Rigging and skinning your character ready for animation

How better to bring your character fully to life than with some animation? This section will break down the process of rigging your model for animation: adding joints so that he'll twist and bend in the right places and testing how the model deforms, from the head down to the toes. All of this will be informed by knowledge of human joints and muscle mechanics to ensure that your character can move with all the weight and tension of a real person.

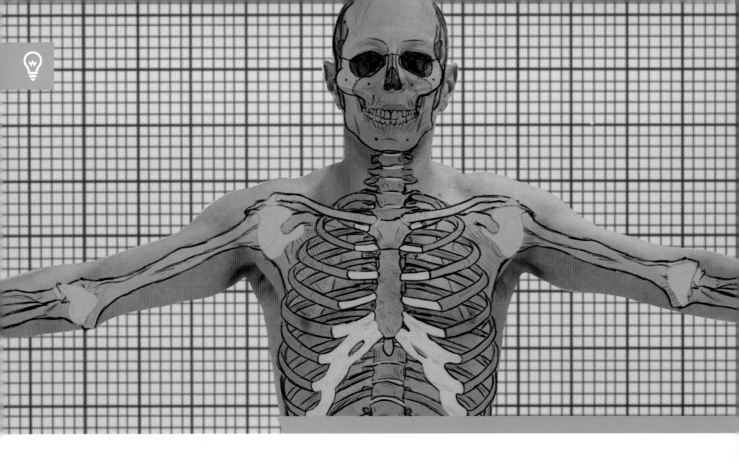

Joint mechanics

Understanding different joint types

This fourth section will be devoted to the process of rigging, a vital stage that bridges the modeling and animating processes. The rigger builds the internal structure – the skeleton – of the model, and with it the controls that will be used by the animator to bring that model to life.

A good rig is one that fulfills the needs of the animator, capable of performing the actions required of it. However, it must also be "animator-friendly": efficient, robust, and well-organized.

Like other stages of the CG pipeline, rigging has real-world roots. The rig of a character, like we said above, may be seen as its skeleton. So when it comes to rigging a character, real or fantastical, an understanding of anatomy and joint mechanics is imperative.

Equally, when rigging a vehicle, a basic conception of the mechanics of that vehicle should guide the process.

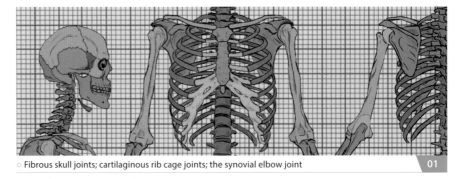

○ Fibrous skull joints; cartilaginous rib cage joints; the synovial elbow joint   01

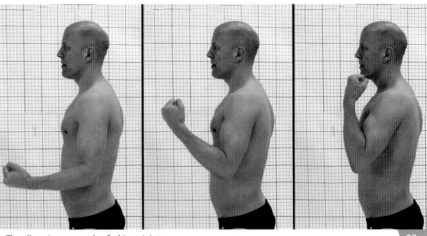

○ The elbow is an example of a hinge joint   02a

We aren't going to create a rig mimicking the human body exactly. Sometimes we'll deliberately pull away from anatomy to keep things simple or efficient. First we'll see what it is in reality that we're seeking to recreate.

This chapter begins with a brief study of rigging's foundations in anatomy. Having already looked at bones and muscles in section 02, we'll focus here on joint mechanics and develop an understanding of how muscles work.

An overview of the joint types

Without joints, the human body would be an immovable hulk. Joints hold bones firmly together, while also permitting movement between them, however large or small. An understanding of joint mechanics assists greatly in creating believable articulation in a character.

The following information provides an overview of joint mechanics to inform decision-making during the rigging process and at other points during the pipeline.

Classified according to their structure, there are three main types of joint:

• **Fibrous joints** are held together so tightly by fibrous tissue that they are largely immovable. For example, the sutures of the skull, which are fixed by around the age of around 20.

• **Cartilaginous joints** are connected by cartilage, which does allow limited movement. For example, the cartilaginous joints between the first 10 pairs of ribs and the sternum allow for the chest to swell slightly on inhalation.

• **Synovial joints** are characterized by synovial fluid filling the joint cavity. Not only are these joints the most numerous and complex in the human body, they are also by far the most mobile, and therefore they require our deepest attention.

There are three main types of synovial joint and they are divided according to the kind of movement that they allow, as follows here.

Synovial joints: uniaxial

Uniaxial joints permit action around one axis, in only one plane. Hinge and pivot joints

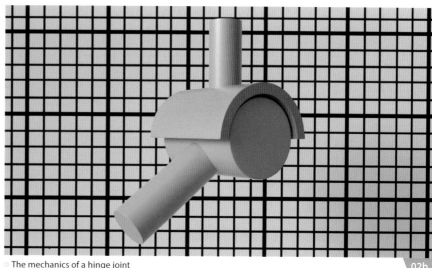

The mechanics of a hinge joint   02b

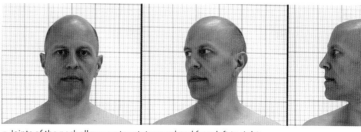

Joints of the neck allow you to rotate your head from left to right   02c

are two kinds of uniaxial joint, as illustrated in the images on these two pages.

Hinge joints are where the articulating ends of bones create a hinge-shaped unit. Their movement is purely back and forth: flexion and extension. The elbow provides a good example (**Fig.02a** and **02b**).

Pivot joints are also known as rotary joints, and consist of a round bone rotating around another bone. The name implies what movement they allow. The joint between the first and second cervical vertebrae, allowing the head to turn from side to side, is a clear example (**Fig.02c** and **02d**).

Synovial joints: biaxial

Biaxial joints permit movement around two perpendicular axes in two perpendicular planes. Saddle and condyloid joints (**Fig.03a**) are types of these.

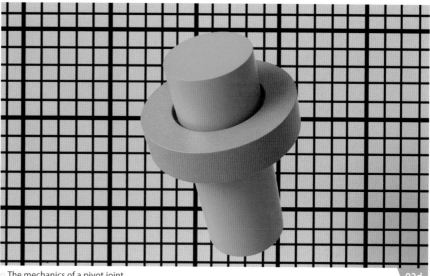

The mechanics of a pivot joint   02d

Saddle joints are so named because one concave and one convex joint surface form a saddle shape (**Fig.03b**). The sole example of this in the human skeletal system is the first metacarpophalangeal joint at the base of the thumb, which provides us with our all-important opposable thumbs.

Condyloid joints are where the articular surface of the bone which inserts into the joint, and the cavity that it fits into, are oval in shape (**Fig.03c**). Condyloid joints allow flexion, extension, abduction, adduction, and rotation. Examples of these are the metacarpophalangeal joints (knuckles) of fingers 2, 3, 4, and 5.

Synovial joints: multiaxial
Multiaxial joints permit movement around three or more axes and in three or more planes.

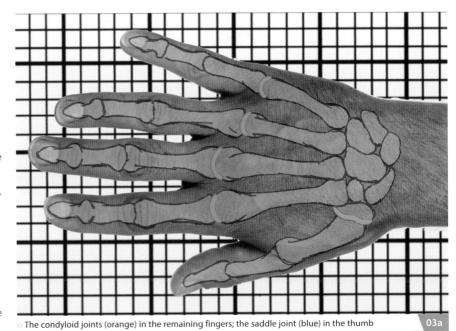

○ The condyloid joints (orange) in the remaining fingers; the saddle joint (blue) in the thumb   03a

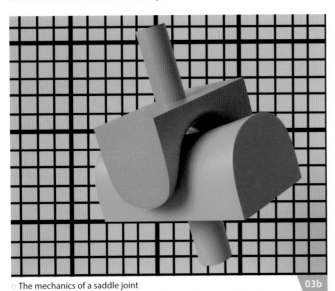

○ The mechanics of a saddle joint   03b

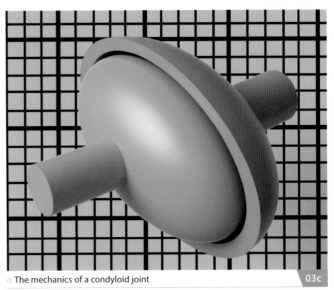

○ The mechanics of a condyloid joint   03c

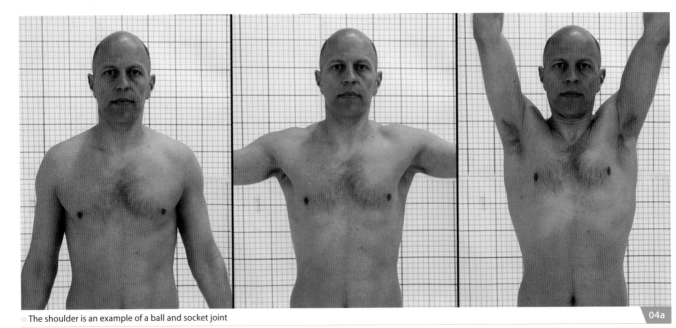

○ The shoulder is an example of a ball and socket joint   04a

144

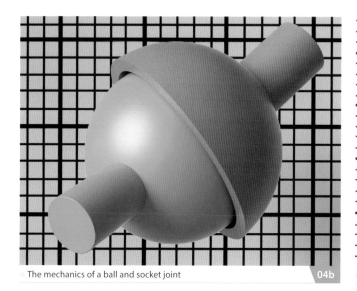

The mechanics of a ball and socket joint · 04b

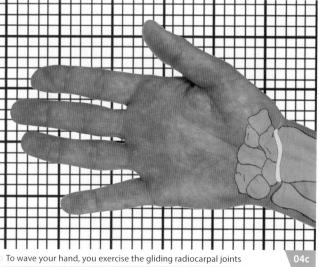

To wave your hand, you exercise the gliding radiocarpal joints · 04c

Ball and socket joints allow for the greatest range of movement of any joints in the body. A ball-shaped articulating surface of a bone fits into a concave cup on another. An example is the glenohumeral joint of the shoulder (**Fig.04a** and **04b**).

Gliding joints have relatively flat articulating surfaces which allow very limited sliding motion along different axes. Waving your hand to and fro, for example, employs the gliding radiocarpal joints (**Fig.04c** and **04d**).

Scapulohumeral rhythm

Before we move away from joint mechanics, I would like to take a brief look at the scapulohumeral rhythm. This term refers to the interplay of bones involved in raising your arm above your head.

As you raise your arm the first 30°, the glenohumeral (shoulder) joint rotates while the scapula remains still. As the arm continues to rise, the scapula begins to assist in the movement.

Once the arm is rotated to 90°, the scapula will have rotated 30°. This produces a 2:1 ratio between the humerus and the scapula when the arm is raised between 30–90°. Once the arm is at 90°, the shoulder joint is locked in its socket. To raise the arm any further, the clavicle pivots in conjunction with the scapula, thereby allowing the arm to reach 180°.

It goes without saying that an appreciation of mechanics such as these is essential for credible CG work to be produced.

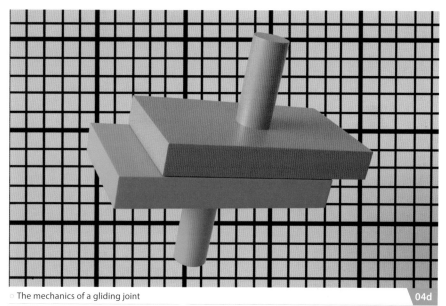

The mechanics of a gliding joint · 04d

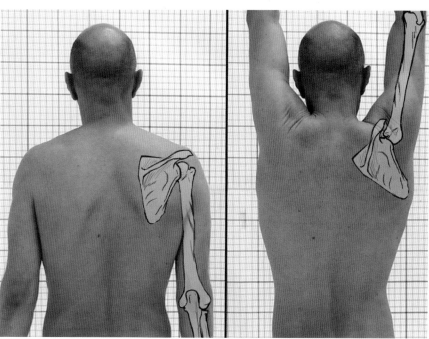

Think about the relationship between the scapula, humerus and clavicle as you raise the arm

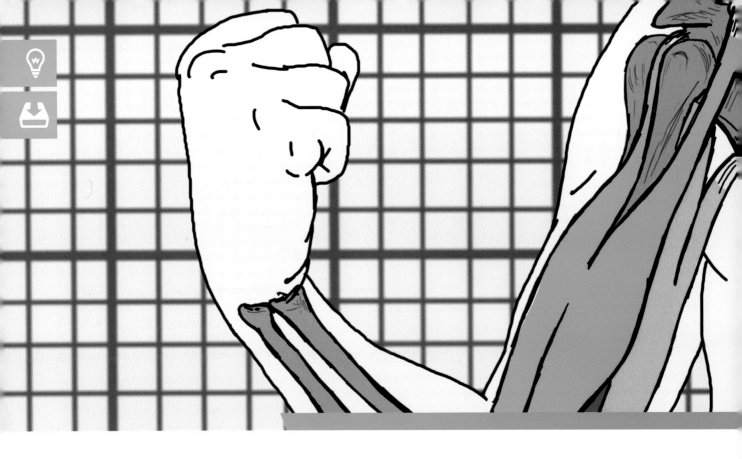

Muscles and motion

Understanding muscles and how they work

Now we've looked at the muscles and at joints, let's see how the two work together to produce movement. An appreciation of this stands a CG artist in very good stead and a simple example will illustrate why.

In order to raise the forearm towards the shoulder, the bicep is activated, contracting to produce a bulge in the upper arm. This kind of simple yet crucial cause-and-effect movement in the body is rarely consciously considered by an audience, but as they are literally a part of our body and taken totally for granted, believability is sacrificed when they are absent from CG work.

The following chapter gives a concise overview of what happens on a muscular level when your body moves.

Skeletal muscles, which drive joints, are capable of one function: contraction. When a nerve impulse arrives in skeletal muscle fibers, they contract, and then relax after the requisite time. As most muscles

span at least one joint, and attach to both articulating bones, the contraction pulls on the bones and creates movement.

Muscles work in groups, not singly. The principal muscle, which is known as the "prime

mover", pulls on both articulating bones of a joint, but other muscles work in conjunction with the prime mover to ensure that only one bone moves. Alongside the prime movers there are antagonist muscles, which relax while the prime mover is contracting. Going

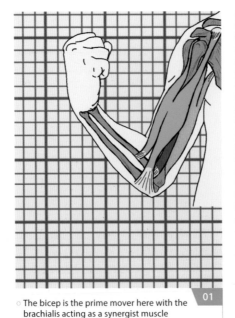

○ The bicep is the prime mover here with the brachialis acting as a synergist muscle

01

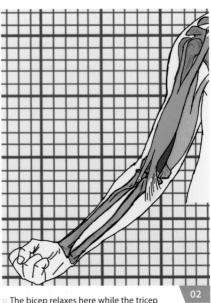

○ The bicep relaxes here while the tricep contracts to extend the arm

02

back to our example of raising the forearm, the bicep (prime mover) contracts while the tricep (antagonist) relaxes (Fig.01).

In addition to this, synergist (helper) muscles contract at the same time as the prime mover, for example to help stabilize a part in order to make the contraction of the prime mover more effective.

So if we return to our example: the bicep contracts, the tricep is relaxed, the brachialis and brachioradialis synergist muscles contract, and hey presto, the forearm is raised. To return the forearm to its original position, the bicep and tricep simply swap roles: the bicep relaxes while the tricep contracts (Fig.02).

The good news is that unless you happen to be creating a highly toned, hyperrealistic character, you won't need to get bogged down in the details of all the muscles involved in every articulation of every joint.

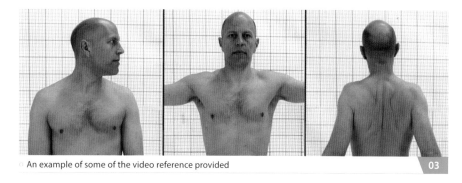

An example of some of the video reference provided 03

"Think about which muscles and joints create these articulations"

What you will need, however, is enough to keep the illusion alive and well in the eyes of your audience, who will be well-versed in the movement of the human body.

Accompanying this book is a wealth of footage taken of the model we're using as the basis for our work here (see riggingReference directory at www.3dtotalpublishing.com/resources). I asked the model to assume a wide variety of poses employing different muscles and joints. Please do take the time to look through them.

Think about which muscles and joints create these articulations; notice where muscles bulge, where skin folds. Every key pressed on the keyboard has a better chance of achieving good results if decisions are reinforced by an appreciation of how the human body moves (Fig.03 and 04).

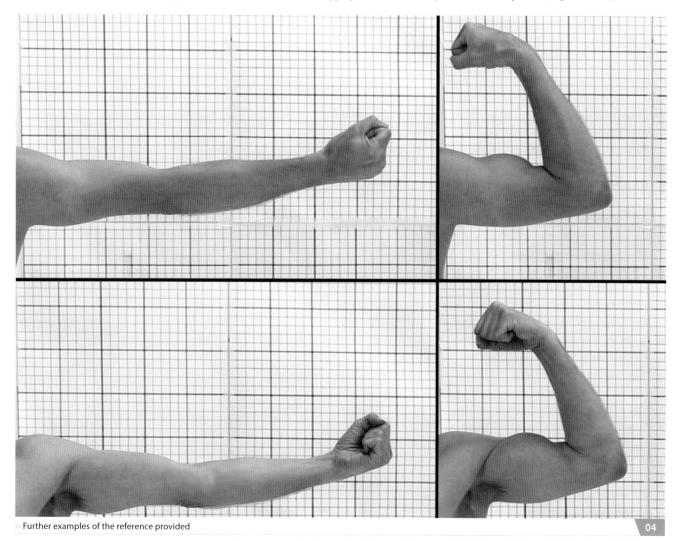

Further examples of the reference provided 04

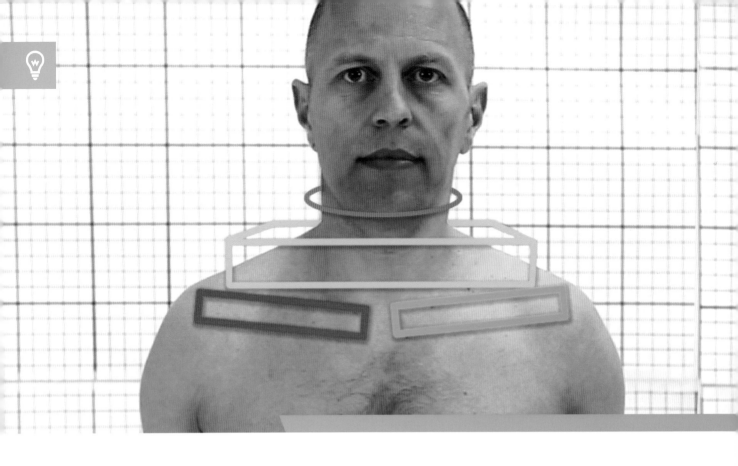

Planning a rig

Things to consider before starting your rig

Before jumping in and creating a rig, I grab a bit of paper and plan things out before hitting the keyboard. The first thing I do in this planning stage is break down the type of movement that the rig will need to perform.

Try to get hold of the storyboards, animatics, video references, and so on, and examine them. You'll be able to better create a rig that is fit for purpose (**Fig.01**). Being fit for purpose is key; why spend time creating parts of a rig that will never be used?

So you know what the rig will need to do. The next thing is to work out how to best create a rig that is animator-friendly: you will need to open up communication lines with the animators. Find out what kind of controls they like: forward kinematics (FK) or inverse kinematics (IK)? Both? Do they want automated clavicles? Would they like pole vector controls for elbows and knees?

It's your rig, but it's the animators who'll be using it, so bear their needs in mind throughout the creative process.

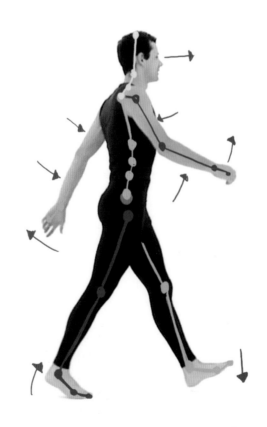
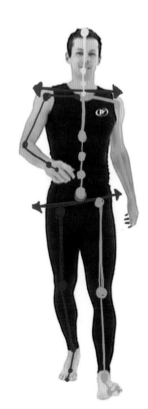

○ Breaking down the reference to analyze what your rig will require

As the rigger, I know that the objective is for the rig to handle a walk cycle. This may sound simple enough, but I want it to maintain volume in areas such as the shoulders, elbows, and knees. I need there to be a sense of anatomy beneath the surface. Basically, I don't want a walking jelly man.

For the torso, I could stick with a simple FK spine, but I'll want to have independent control over the pelvis and chest. The arms will primarily be swinging back and forth, so I could also stick with an FK setup. I know the legs and feet will need to make contact with the ground, so I'll need some kind of setup that stops them from penetrating the ground plane, which would suggest IK (Fig.02). For the head, I'll want it to follow the orientation and position of the neck, but I'll also sometimes want it to follow the orientation of the torso or hips.

So that's my wish list as a rigger. We now need to examine the needs of the animator, which happily here is also me!

Firstly, I'd like to work with as few controls as possible, as I value being able to work as freely as I can, but I also want enough controls to get the animation done efficiently. For example, there are 5 lumbar, 12 thoracic, and 7 cervical vertebrae in the spine, but if a rigger handed me

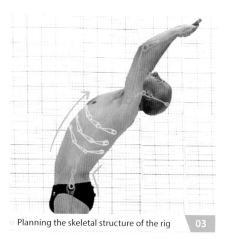

Planning an IK leg setup as the legs will need to interact with the environment 02

a rig with 24 controls for the spine alone, I'd be overwhelmed. Three or four FK controls would do nicely, perhaps with the added ability to translate and stretch the spine slightly (Fig.03).

I would like to be able to switch the arms and legs between FK and IK mode, giving me a bit more freedom to decide how I can approach a shot. For the fingers, I want the ability to control each digit independently, but I also want a few controls that will allow me to quickly pose the hand, so that I can, for instance, relax the fingers or create a fist without too much fuss. The same goes for the toes.

Lastly, for the foot, I'd like one control that allows me to roll the foot back onto its

Planning the skeletal structure of the rig 03

heel, rock onto the ball of the foot, and then forward onto the tips of the toes.

With all this information to hand, it's time to start designing the rig on paper. A few preliminary sketches should help define where the joints will go, the controls that we'll be creating, and the general look of the rig.

As you do this, think also about where the body is most flexible and where it's more rigid (Fig.04). Take the spine, for example: the lumbar region is extremely flexible, while the thoracic region is less so as it carries the rib cage.

Moving from paper to keyboard now, it may also be worth your while to take the model, chop it up into masses such as the torso mass or the upper limb mass, and then run a few tests to see what would and wouldn't work. The more you think, plan, and test, the less time you'll spend having to rework should the rig fall short (Fig.05).

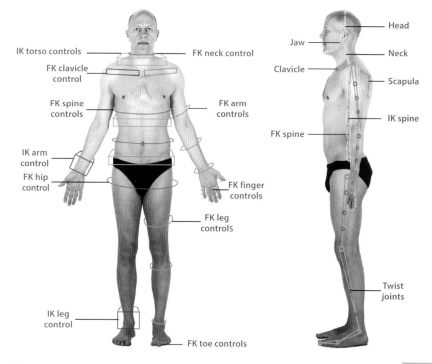

Thinking about the type of controls the rig will require before hitting the computer 04

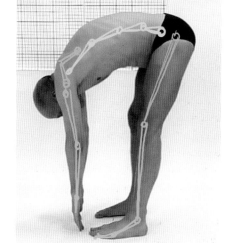

Planning the different controls required 05

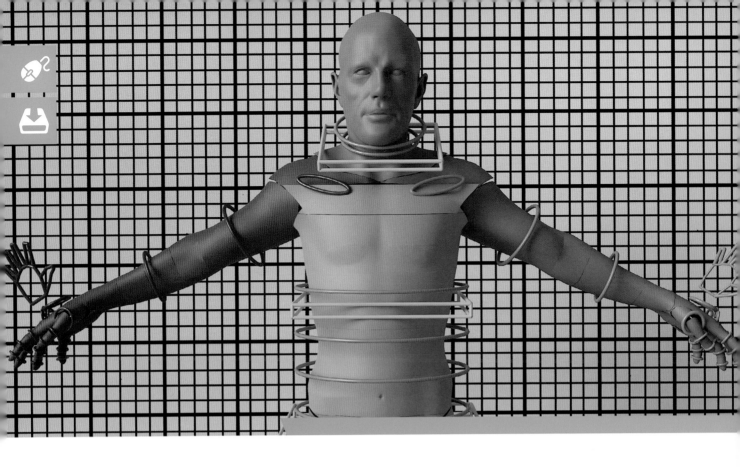

Rigging fundamentals

Learning the basics of rigging

We're now ready to rig! Let's get acquainted with the concepts, tools, and techniques that could well become your new best friends.

01: Parenting and hierarchies

If you examine any rig, what you'll find at its core is a series of relationships and connections, much like a family tree. One way to build these connections is through parenting.

Parenting is the process of allowing one object (parent/master) to lead another object (child/slave). The useful thing about parent-child relationships is that although the child object will follow the parent object however it is transformed, the child object will still have the ability to be manipulated independently, which can come in very handy.

By creating parent-child relationships you start to build hierarchies. A hierarchy of a few tiers is simple enough to comprehend, but when it comes to rigging, you'll soon be creating hierarchies that resemble the family trees from *The Lord of the Rings*. Therefore, it's important

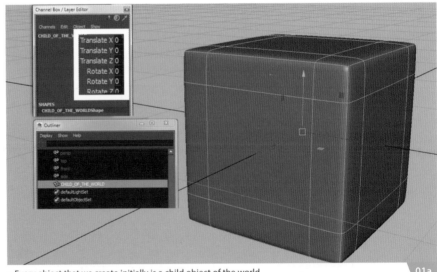

○ Every object that we create initially is a child object of the world   01a

to make sure that you're fully aware of all the connections you're making and, crucially, that you name everything as you go. Every object that you initially create in Maya (presuming you have Interactive Creation disabled) will be a child of the world and created in the world center (Fig.01a). If you translate that object

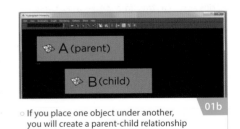

○ If you place one object under another, you will create a parent-child relationship   01b

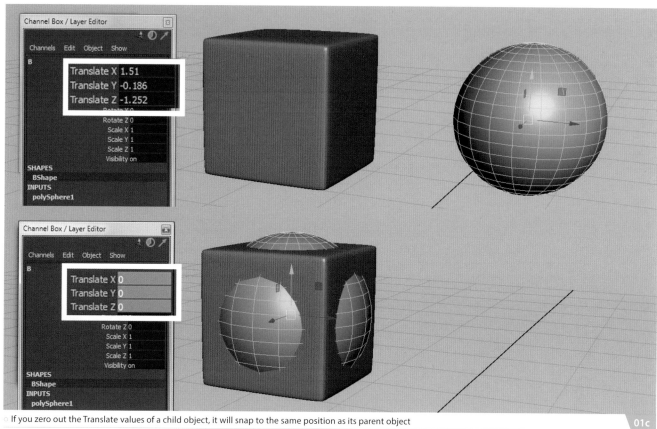

If you zero out the Translate values of a child object, it will snap to the same position as its parent object `01c`

around and then want to return it to the world center, you can do so by simply popping values of 0, 0, 0 into the Translate channels.

Now let's say you have two objects, which we'll refer to as A and B, and you position them randomly in the scene. By default, both objects will be children of the world, but let's say you parent object B under object A, as in Fig.01b. Now, if you zero out the Translate values for object B, you'll notice that it pops to the same position as object A, its parent (see Fig.01c). This is significant as it means we are able to give objects a new position anywhere in the world space and it becomes their new world center.

Having seen how we use objects, we'll now take a look at using group nodes to build parent-child hierarchies. A polygon cube, a NURBS sphere, a camera, and so on, all have shape nodes as well as transform nodes associated with them, allowing you to grab them in the viewport. If you jump into the Attribute Editor with any one of those objects selected, you'll notice a tab with <objectName>Shape.

Sometimes, however, you'll want to perform parenting tasks with objects that you do not

want selected in the viewport. This is where group nodes come in handy (Fig.01d). To create a group node, simply hit Ctrl+G. If you have an object selected while doing this, you'll get a node called group1; if you don't have an object selected, you'll get a null1 node. Both

do the same thing: they are simply transform nodes with no shapes associated with them.

Have a look in the Attribute Editor to see what comes with them. They are very useful as they allow you to organize and structure your rig,

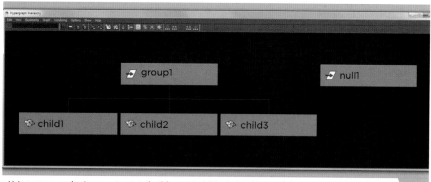

Using group nodes is a great way to build parent-child relationships and also nest objects together `01d`

Constraints don't affect object hierarchy but create an additional node that describes the relationships `02a` while also playing a crucial role when creating controls. But more on that later (page 157).

02: Constraints

Constraints are another way to build relationships in Maya. They differ to parenting as rather than affecting the hierarchical structure, they simply create a constraint node that lives under the constrained (slave) object (Fig.02a). Where parenting also affects all of the transform attributes, with constraints you can define which attributes they should affect (Fig.02b).

For example, an orient constraint will only affect the Rotate attributes. The constraint node that

gets created also comes with a weighting value that allows you to define how much influence the master object has over the slave object.

Unlike parenting, which still allows you to manipulate the child object, the constraints' weighting value needs to be disabled in order for you to do so. Furthermore – and this is another advantage of using constraints – it is possible to have multiple objects influencing a single object and use weighting value to decide which master object should have control over the slave object (Fig.02c). This paves the way for creating FK/IK blending and space-switching later on.

03: Joints

Now we come to joints, which I regard as the nuts and bolts of rigging, literally and metaphorically. Joints will be the main influence on how your model deforms, so it's important that we have a solid understanding of how joints work in Maya.

A joint looks like a sphere with a cross through it. When you create a chain of joints, you'll notice a triangular shape drawn between the joints – this is known as the joint segment, as shown in Fig.03a. What sets joints apart from every other object in Maya is that they have a unique characteristic. While every object, be it a cube,

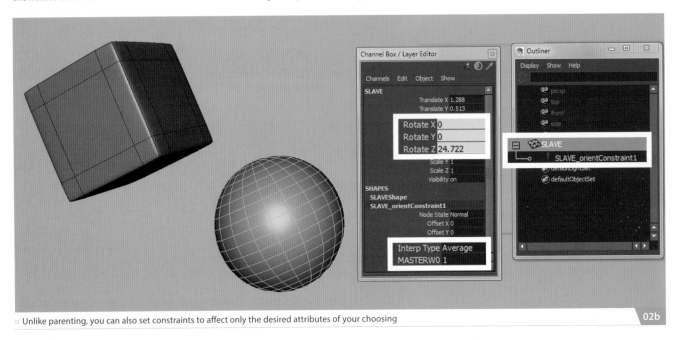

○ Unlike parenting, you can also set constraints to affect only the desired attributes of your choosing

02b

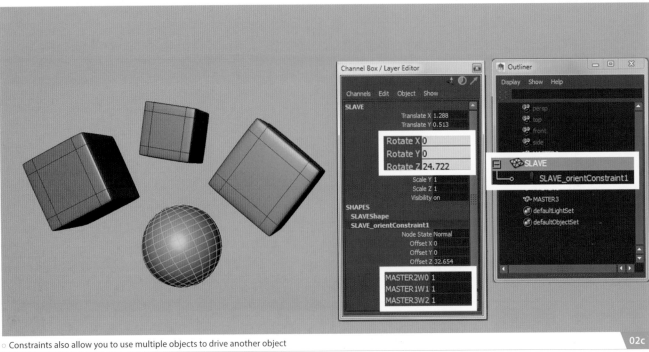

○ Constraints also allow you to use multiple objects to drive another object

02c

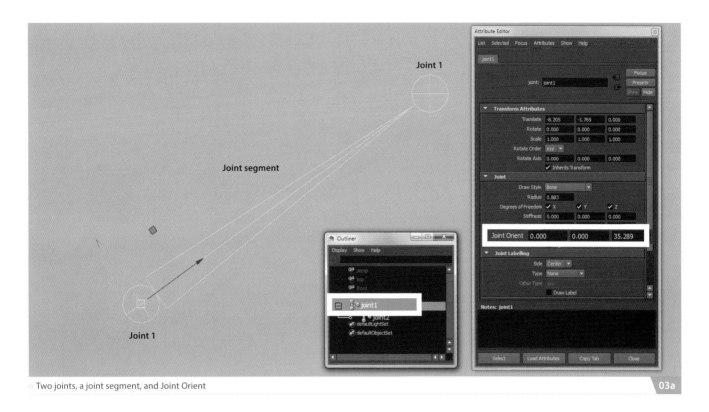

○ Two joints, a joint segment, and Joint Orient

03a

camera or light, has a transform node associated with it, allowing you to translate, rotate, and scale the object, joints also have an orientation. This orientation attribute, known as Joint Orient (Fig.03a), gives joints an axis on which they can be oriented. This may not seem mind-blowing, but when you start to create your rig, you'll see its benefits as you place the joints.

If you have more than one joint in a chain, this creates a parent-child hierarchy. You'll notice that the parent joint will always aim at its child joint (make sure the Move tool

is set to Local). If you find that this isn't the case, I strongly suggest rebuilding that part of the joint structure; the chances are that you'll find the behavior of your joint may be unpredictable or misaligned when you rotate it.

As joints will be the main driving force behind the rig, we'll want to make sure their creation has been handled correctly. Here are some guidelines that I follow in order to ensure this.

Firstly, all Rotate channels on all joints and controls throughout the rig should have a

default value of zero. This ensures that we can revert to the original pose cleanly and simply. Next comes positioning the joints. For the root joint of any chain, you can translate it on any axis. For all child joints, however, only translate them through one attribute – the one which relates to the length (Fig.03b). By default, this is set to the Translate X attribute, but we will be switching this to Translate Y later. This may seem like it will restrict how we place the joints, but I can assure you that it won't. What it will do is ensure that you have a clean skeleton for your rig.

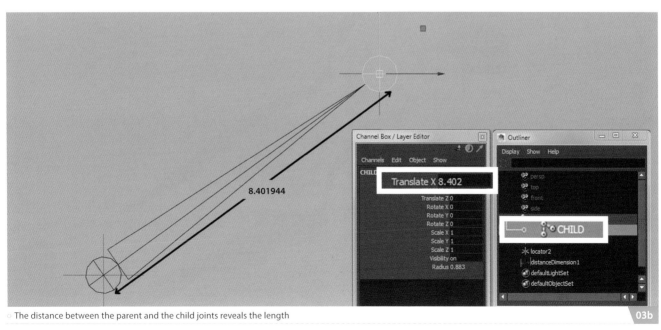

○ The distance between the parent and the child joints reveals the length

03b

Note that we need to maintain consistency throughout the rig. We can do this by making sure we follow a strict naming convention. (See the namingConventions_PUBLISHED document in the \3dt_characterCreation\documents\ PUBLISHED directory.) Every joint will have a suffix of **_jnt**; every IK (see below) handle will have a suffix of **_ik**, and so on. By following this kind of pattern, you make life easier for yourself should you need to debug anything. Plus, if there will be multiple people working on the rig, or if someone else has to finish what you started, they can get up and running a lot faster.

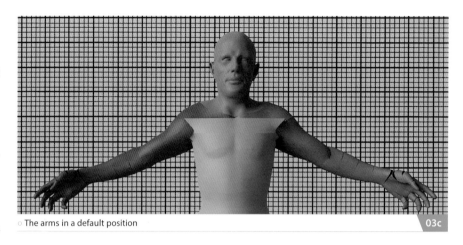
○ The arms in a default position | 03c

We must also think of the animator, ensuring that the behavior of the rig (Fig.03c) is uniform throughout. Flexion throughout the rig should be handled by the same rotate axis with positive values. Extension should be handled by the same axis but with negative values. So if the animator wished to flex the elbow joint on both arms, this can be achieved by rotating a single axis in one direction (Fig.03d and 3e). The animation data produced by this motion can then be easily read in the Graph Editor, a tool covered on pages 247–248 and 250.

04: FK and IK

We now need to spend some time looking at forward kinematics (FK) and inverse kinematics (IK), which are the two main types of movement that an animator will work with. It's important to know what they are, how they differ, and when to choose which.

In forward kinematics (Fig.04a), the movement originates from the root joint, traveling down the chain using rotations. For example when kicking a ball, the leg will rotate backwards from the hip joint and then rotate further backwards from the knee. Following this, the leg will rotate forwards from the hip and the motion will continue from the knee, then finally from the ankle to bring the foot into contact with the ball. Rotations work from root to tip. FK creates very smooth, very naturally occurring arcs of motion.

In inverse kinematics (Fig.04b), a chain of joints is controlled using translations rather than rotations. The translations originate at a point at the tip of the chain and are manipulated by what is known as the IK handle. As opposed to FK, where rotation moves from root to hip, in IK the rotations of the joints are calculated automatically from the IK handle up towards the root of the joint chain.

Because IK movement originates from the tip and works towards the root, it is the best choice when an animator needs an asset to make contact with (rather than penetrate) its environment. IK, for instance, is a good choice for the legs in walk cycles, as each foot needs

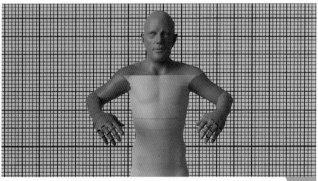
○ Flexion of the elbows for both arms is achieved using positive Z rotation | 03d

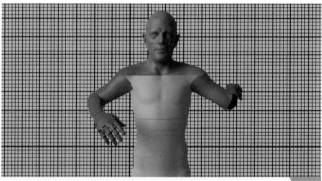
○ Ouch! What happens when consistency is not maintained in the rig | 03e

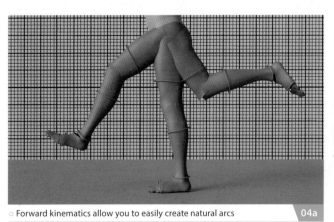
○ Forward kinematics allow you to easily create natural arcs | 04a

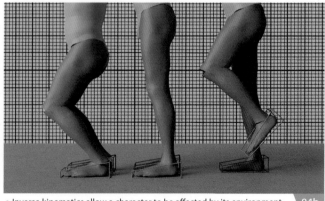
○ Inverse kinematics allow a character to be affected by its environment | 04b

to hit the ground with every step. However, in that same walk cycle, it may be advantageous to use FK in the arms to take advantage of its smooth rotations for the swing needed there.

Each method of movement has its pluses and minuses from the animator's point of view. Deciding which to use will often be based on the nature of the movement required by the animator. As we said before, open channels of communication need to exist between rigger and animator, and this is an example of when it is important.

05: Rotate Order and Gimbal Lock

Rotation order is often overlooked in CG, when it should be integral to riggers' and animators' work. The term refers to the order of operation in which the orientations are evaluated. By default, all objects have a rotate order of XYZ (found in the Attribute Editor – see Fig.05a).

When looking at this rotation order setting, it is read most easily from right to left. XYZ means that Z will carry both Y and X, and Y will carry X. X has no effect on the other two axes. By default, when you rotate an object in Maya you are

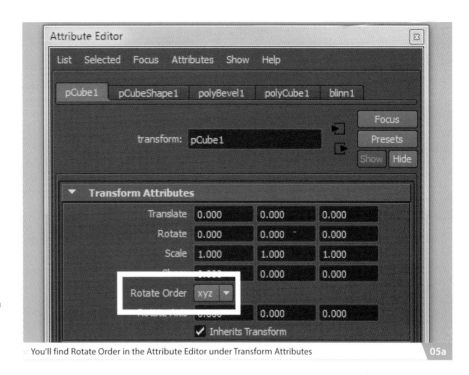

You'll find Rotate Order in the Attribute Editor under Transform Attributes

05a

viewing the rotations in local space, so it seems as if no single axis is carrying another (Fig.05b).

However, by switching your rotate settings to Gimbal mode, you'll be able to see a true representation of what the axes are doing. This leads us to the heartache that is Gimbal Lock.

Gimbal Lock is the term used to describe the situation when two of the rotation axes are sitting on top of each other (Fig.05c). The result of this is that both axes will produce a similar rotational result, and you'll have pretty much lost the ability to rotate the selected object on one axis. Of course, you'll only see this if

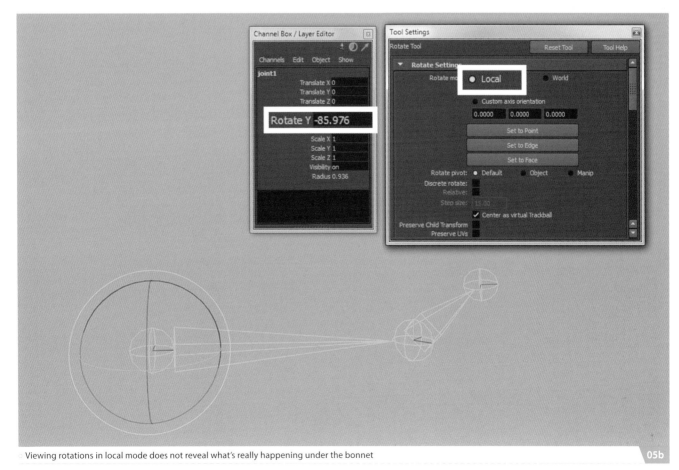

Viewing rotations in local mode does not reveal what's really happening under the bonnet

05b

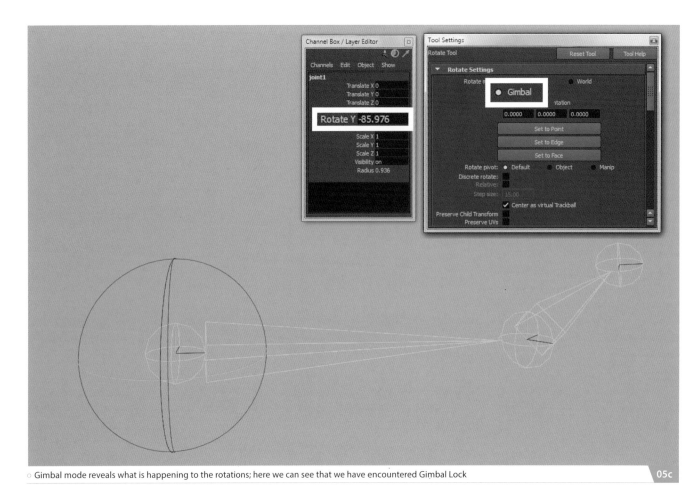

○ Gimbal mode reveals what is happening to the rotations; here we can see that we have encountered Gimbal Lock   05c

"As a rigger or animator, you need to think about the kind of movement that's needed for a particular task"

you are working in Gimbal mode; if you are working in local mode, it will seem as if you always have the three axes readily available. Gimbal Lock isn't something you'd choose to be in. So how do you best avoid it? The simple answer is that as a rigger or animator, you need to think about the kind of movement that's needed for a particular task and then consider what rotational order is best suited to it.

To get a feel for rotation order and Gimbal Lock, create a primitive object such as a cube. Set your rotate mode to Gimbal and rotate the cube one axis at a time. Look at the results with the default rotate order (XYZ), then change them around and view the results once more.

06: Animation controls

At this point we bring parenting, hierarchies, constraints, and rotation order together and look at creating animation controls.

On a very simple rig, just animating the joints may well do the trick. However, a purely joint-based setup has considerable limitations, so some controls need to be put in place to achieve greater flexibility and potential. Additionally, rigs are not always

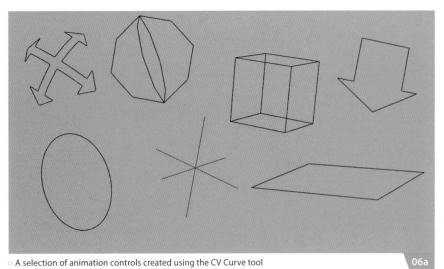

○ A selection of animation controls created using the CV Curve tool   06a

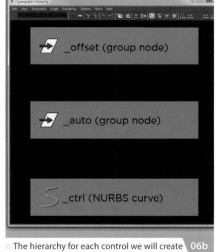

○ The hierarchy for each control we will create   06b

totally safe in animators' hands. During the process of animation, bits and bobs can be deleted – erroneously, I prefer to believe! In general, recreating a deleted control will result in less of a headache than having to rebuild a joint, so it's definitely worth reading on.

Using curves for animation controls is advantageous as they are non-renderable, so you don't need to worry about hiding them before you begin rendering. The curve could be in the form of a custom-designed one made using the CV Curve tool (Fig.06a) or it could simply be a NURBS Primitive such as a circle. Another plus point of using curves is that their shape can easily be edited, so your rig can be customized without too much hard work. For example, I like to use circles for FK controls and squares for IK controls. Naturally, you'll find your own way, but the important point is that using curves will simplify the process for you.

For every control, I create a small hierarchy (Fig.06b) using group (transform) nodes, which allows me to place and orient the control in the exact same location as the joint it will control. This is of great importance as it provides for secondary levels of control, while also allowing the animator to return the control back to the default position and orientation by zeroing out the Translate and the Rotate channels.

The hierarchy should be arranged as follows: the top node in the hierarchy is purely for placement and will have a suffix of _offset to show this. The second node in the hierarchy will have the suffix of _auto to show that this can provide a secondary level of control. The final object in the hierarchy will be the

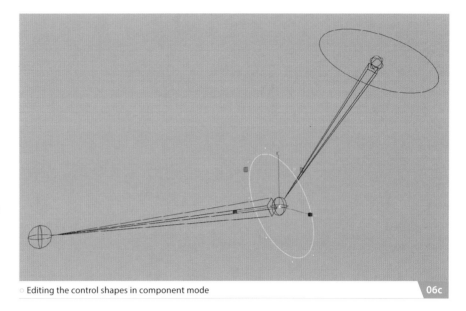

Editing the control shapes in component mode
06c

animation curve, and the animator will be able to select it in the Maya viewport.

Controls can be positioned in one of the two ways detailed below. Both methods will give you the same end result, so whichever you choose will simply be a matter of preference.

"Naturally, you'll find your own way, but the important point is that using curves will simplify the process for you"

The first method is as follows: select the _offset node, Shift-select the joint it will control, and hit P on the keyboard. This parents the _offset node under the joint. Now zero out the Translate and Rotate values for the _offset node so the whole control hierarchy snaps to the same position as the joint. You'll also notice that the orientations

line up. Now simply select _offset and hit Shift+P to unparent it from the joint. As a result, there should be some transform values back on the _offset node. These are the coordinates of where this node is in world space. Leave them as they are. Select _auto or _ctrl and you will see that they both have 0 values for all the rotation and the Translate channels, plus the orientations still line up to the joint. Perfect.

The second method is to select the joint that needs the control, then Shift-select the _offset node and go to Constraints > Parent (Options). Disable Maintain Offset and hit Apply. The entire control hierarchy should snap into place. Now delete the parentConstraint node that lives below the _offset node in the Outliner, and your control will be in place.

Later we'll use a small script to automate creating and positioning controls, as creating each one manually can be a laborious process.

With the controls in place, the next thing will be to have them drive the relevant joint. We will do this with constraints. For example, we would select the _ctrl object, Shift-select the relevant joint, and go to Constrain > Orient (Options). Make sure Maintain Offset is disabled and hit Apply. Finally, we will need to edit the shape of the control so it is easily selectable by the animator. To do this, we will switch to component mode and use the control vertices (CVs) to edit the control's shape (Fig.06c). By editing the components, we are ensuring that the transforms for the controls stay in the correct place.

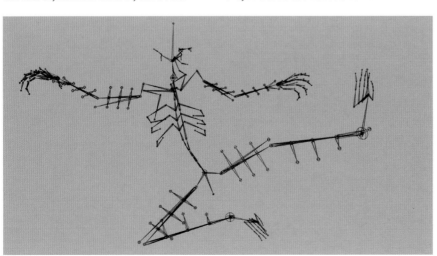

You must consider what kinds of movement your character will perform

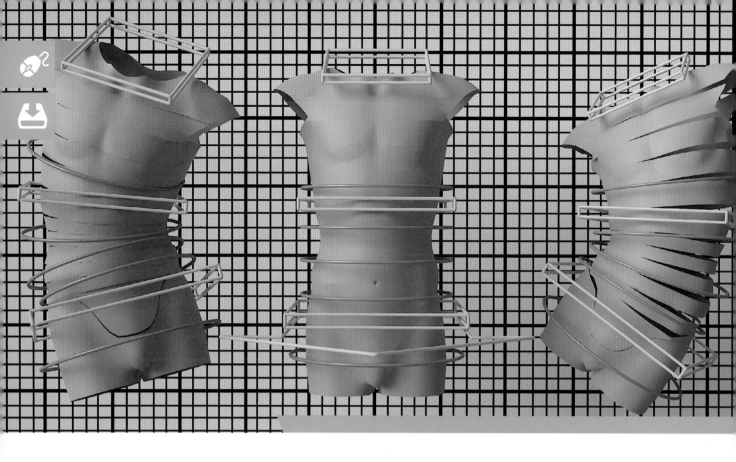

Rigging the torso

Starting our rig with the torso

Now that we have a brief overview of what a rig consists of, let's start creating one for our model. We'll build the rig up in parts: the torso, the neck and head, the arms, the hands, and so on. We'll link these parts together with a combination of parenting and constraints.

The benefit of this approach is that we can experiment with independent parts of the body without accidentally destroying other parts. It also makes it very easy to do things like space-switching (more on this in the next chapter and on page 212). If I find later on that part of the rig isn't behaving as it should, I can fix that region without too much of a knock-on effect on the rest of the rig.

We'll kick off our rigging conquest with the torso. I like to start with this as it creates the framework to which we can attach the neck, the head, the upper limb, and the lower limb. The torso that we'll be creating will be an FK/IK setup, will have independent hip and chest controls, and we'll also be adding

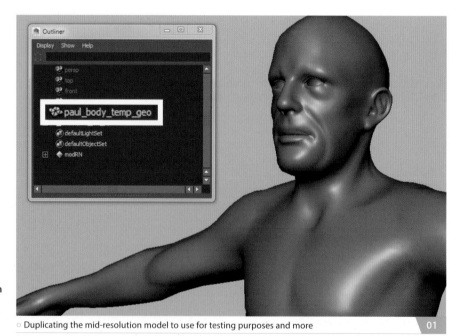

○ Duplicating the mid-resolution model to use for testing purposes and more   01

additional joints to simulate breathing and create the illusion that our character has a rib cage. Throughout the rigging process, we'll be using a few scripts which you will find in the scripts directory of the Maya project (3dt_characterCreation/scripts/).

01: Referencing the model

Let's start by bringing in the model as a reference. That way, should any changes be made to the model, we can automatically pick them up without having to go hunting for the latest file. To do this, go to File > Create

Reference (Options). Under the Namespace Options, set the mode to "Use selected namespace as parent and add new namespace string", and then pop the word "mod" into the box. Then click the Reference button and select the file **paul_mod_PUBLISHED. ma**, which you should find under /02_ PUBLISHED/01_MODELLING_SCULPTING.

With the model in the scene, take the **mod:paul_body_mr_geo** (the mid-resolution model) and hit Ctrl+D to duplicate it. Hit Shift+P to bring it out from its current hierarchy, and rename it **paul_body_temp_geo**. This model will be used for testing while we rig, and we'll continue to duplicate it and then chop it into parts. The chopped-up parts will then be parented to the skeleton of the rig so we can quickly evaluate how it articulates.

Pop the model **paul_body_temp_geo** into a new Display Layer and call that layer **temp_geo_layer**. Save this scene file, making sure you save it in the 01_WIP/03_RIGGING directory. I create a new folder in here called **01_torso** and pop the file in there as **01_start**. As we create each part of the rig, I'll be creating a new folder and dropping the latest scene files in there to be picked up.

"Give yourself time to experiment as you rig and try out different techniques and methods"

02: Straight spine versus S-shaped spine

Before we build the actual joint structure for the spine, I just want to explain why I'll be stepping away from what is anatomically correct here.

The human spine is situated closer to the back than the front of the torso, consists of 24 bones, and is S-shaped. We could mimic this, but as with everything in CG, we should aim to simplify it to make things easier for both the rigger and the animator. So straight away we'll want to reduce the number of joints we're adding.

Next, consider the position of the spine: placing a digital spine closer to the back of the torso doesn't always yield the best deformation, so I'll be placing our spine closer to the middle of the torso.

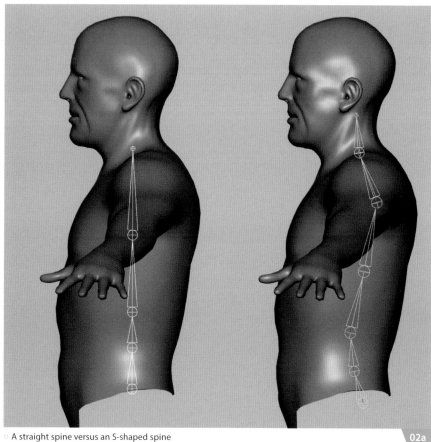

A straight spine versus an S-shaped spine

02a

Last, what about the S shape? When creating realistic characters, it's usually advisable to follow the natural shape of the spine, and I myself have done this on many occasions and achieved more than adequate results. For a while, though, I've pushed away from this and gone for a straighter spine because it simplifies the process when twisting a character (**Fig.02a**).

With an S-shaped spine, I always find that I have to use two rotational axes to achieve a clean twisting motion (anatomically referred to as left or right rotation) due to the orientation of the joints. With a straight spine, I can handle this with just one axis (**Fig.02b**). And did I lose anything, deformation-wise, by going from an S-shaped to a straight spine? No – or if I did, it was so minute that it wasn't noticeable to my simple eyes. It all comes down to trying things out and evaluating the results. Give yourself time to experiment as you rig and try out different techniques and methods.

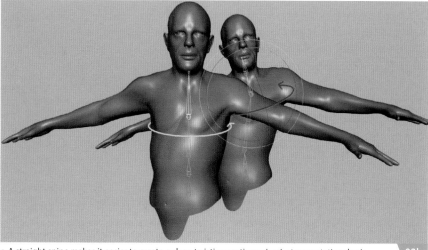

A straight spine makes it easier to create a clean twisting motion using just one rotational axis

02b

159

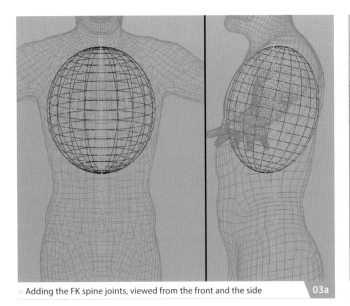

○ Adding the FK spine joints, viewed from the front and the side   03a

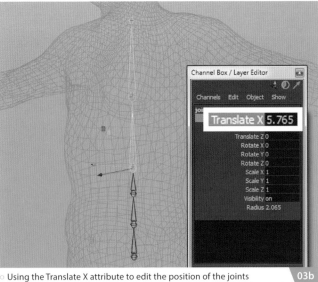

○ Using the Translate X attribute to edit the position of the joints   03b

03: Creating the FK joint chain

Now that you know why we'll be creating a straight spine, let's do just that for the FK side of things. To aid in your joint placement, feel free to create a sphere, re-shape it, and pop it into the area where the rib cage would sit. That way, you can use it to guide you on where you should place more joints (the lumbar region) and where you should place fewer joints (the thoracic region).

Switch to the Animation menu (F2) and in the side view, go to Skeleton > Joint Tool. Using the LMB, click once in the middle of the torso (in line with the ASIS points) to create the first joint. Then hold the Shift key (allowing you to create a straight joint chain) and LMB-click three more times to go from the root joint up to the bottom of the rib cage. Continuing to hold the Shift key, click again at the middle of the rib cage and then make a last click at the base of the neck (Fig.03a). When you have six joints created, hit Enter on the keyboard to terminate the tool.

If you need to edit the position of any of the joints, remember that you can translate the root joint on any axis (although for the spine, you should not do so in the X-axis as this would de-center it) and you should only use the length of the joint to position any child joints. So far, the length is still being determined by the Translate X attribute (Fig.03b).

04: Rename the FK joints

To rename the joints, we could do so one at a time, but this can be a laborious process. To speed things up, we'll use the **cometRename**

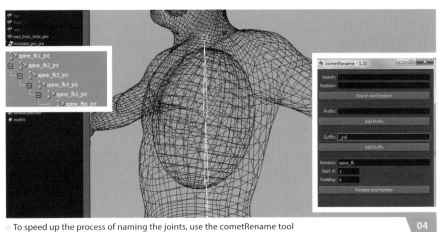

○ To speed up the process of naming the joints, use the cometRename tool   04

tool created by Michael Comet (**www. comet-cartoons.com**). If you have yet to load his tools in, I would recommend you do so now. His tools and scripts are fantastic and will save you hours, if not days.

With the tool now installed on your Menu Bar, go to Comet > Tools > cometRename. Select all the joints that need renaming from root to tip and, in the Rename box of the tool, type **spine_fk**. Leave Start #

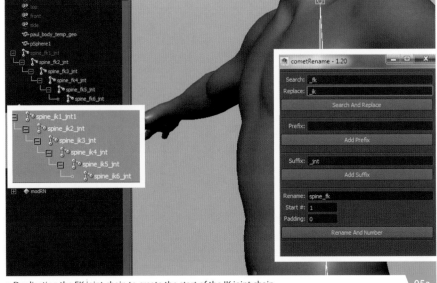

○ Duplicating the FK joint chain to create the start of the IK joint chain   05a

at 1 and hit Rename And Number. With the joints still selected, pop _jnt into the Suffix box and hit Add Suffix. Easy peasy.

05: Create the IK joint chain

To create the IK joint chain, select **spineFK1_jnt** and hit Ctrl+D. We won't be working with the FK joint chain now, so select it and then hide it by hitting Ctrl+H. Select all the joints of the duplicated joint chain. In the cometRename tool, type **_fk** in the Search field and **_ik** in the Replace field, then hit Search And Replace (**Fig.05a**). We are now going to add more joints to the current IK joint chain as this will yield better results when used in conjunction with the splineIK that we'll be adding.

To add more joints, we will be using the truly awesome **jointSplitter.mel** script by Brian Escribano (**www.meljunky.com**). With this tool, we can add a single joint or multiple joints that will be evenly distributed between two existing joints. For this tool to work, you have to ensure that the joints you wish to apply them to all have unique names within the scene.

Open up the script in a MEL tab in the Script Editor. To execute the script, highlight all the text (Ctrl+A) and hit Enter on the numpad. Once you have executed the script, a small user interface should pop up.

Now select **spine_ik1_jnt1** and hit Select Start Joint on the user interface. With Jnt Qty set to 1, hit Split Joints. An additional joint should now be created, sitting perfectly between the two joints. Do the same for select **spine_ik2_jnt** and for **spine3_ik_jnt**. For **spine_ik4_jnt** and **spine_ik5_jnt**, increase Jnt Qty to 2 and then hit Split Joints (**Fig.05b**). You now have your IK joint chain.

The next thing to do is correctly rename the joints. To do this, select the joints in order from root to tip. Using the cometRename tool, type **spine_ik** into the Rename field and hit Rename And Number. Then add the suffix of _jnt. You should now have an IK chain that consists of 13 joints (**Fig.05c**) and an FK chain that consists of 6 joints.

06: Adding the Spline IK

Now go to Skeleton > IK Spline Handle Tool (Options). Reset the settings for the tool

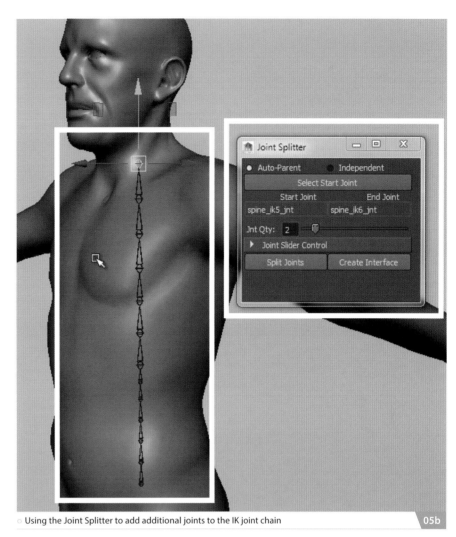

○ Using the Joint Splitter to add additional joints to the IK joint chain   05b

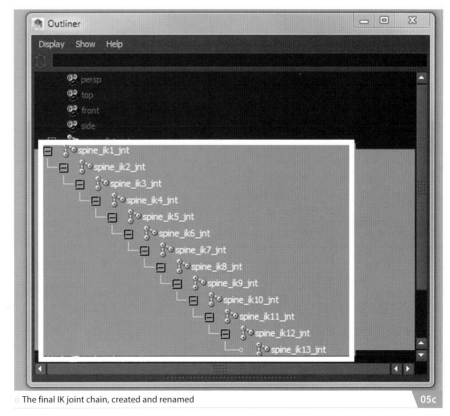

○ The final IK joint chain, created and renamed   05c

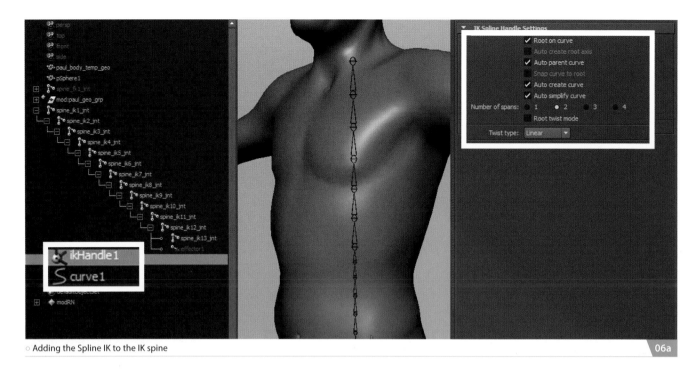

○ Adding the Spline IK to the IK spine 06a

and then increase the Number of spans to 2 (Fig.06a). If you pop your cursor into the 3D viewport, you'll notice there's a crosshair present, indicating that you're in the tool.

Click on the root joint (spine_ik1_jnt) and then on the joint at the tip (spine_ik13_jnt) of the chain. Go into the Outliner; you'll see that you now have an ikHandle1 and a curve. Rename them spine_ik and spine_crv, respectively. Unlike the IK we explored in the last chapter, with Spline IK, it's not the IK handle that's used to manipulate the joints, but the curve itself.

To experiment with this, switch to component mode (F8), select the CVs of the curve, and translate them around. Make sure you undo this so you go back to the default state. So, how do we deform the curve that in turn deforms the joints? There are a few ways to do this, such as using clusters, but for this rig, we're simply going to skin the curve to some joints.

In the side view, use the Joint tool to create a single joint. Click anywhere in the view but keep it far away from the current joint chain, so it doesn't automatically parent to it. In the Channel Box, increase the joint's radius so we can easily pick it out from the rest.

We now want to position this joint at the base of the spine, so hold down the V key (Snap to Points) and drag and drop it into place. Rename this joint spine_hip_ik_jnt, then duplicate

it and snap it to the same position as spine_ik7_jnt. Rename this joint spine_mid_ik_jnt. Duplicate this joint one more time and position it at the tip of the IK joint chain. Rename this joint spine_chest_ik_jnt. You should now have three independent joints in place.

Next, select the three new joints and spine_crv (it's easier to do this in the Outliner; Fig.06b) and go to Skin > Smooth Bind (Options). Set Bind to Selected joints. Leave everything else as it is and hit Bind Skin (Fig.06c). You can now use

the three new joints to drive the IK spine. Again, if you translate them around, make sure you use undo to get them back to the default pose.

07: Creating the low-resolution mesh

As you build the rig, you need to test it as thoroughly as possible. I like to chop the model into slices and parent those slices to the joints. This not only allows you to test the rig, but also creates a low-resolution mesh that the animator can use. As this geometry

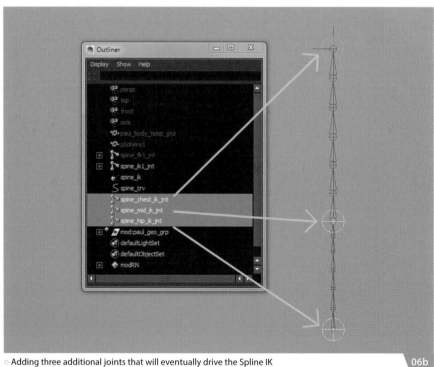

○ Adding three additional joints that will eventually drive the Spline IK 06b

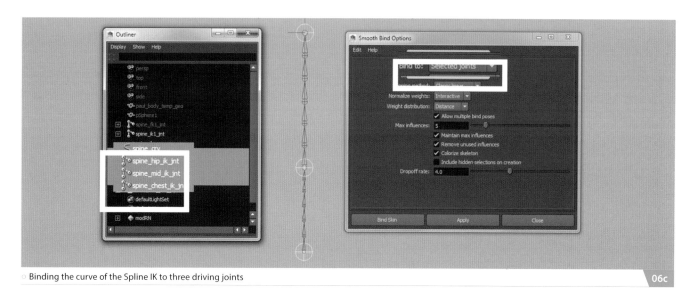

○ Binding the curve of the Spline IK to three driving joints
06c

will be simply parented to the joints, the playback of this rig should be pretty snappy in comparison to a rig that has to calculate the bind information. There are a few ways to chop up the model, so use whatever method suits you. I use a combination of the following techniques depending on the task at hand.

Select the faces you'd like to chop off and go to Mesh > Extract. Alternatively, you can select some faces and go to Edit Mesh > Duplicate (found under the face section), or simply duplicate the model and delete all the unwanted faces (Fig.07a). As you chop up the model, think about where the joints are and try to separate the different parts of the mesh to coincide with the placement of the joints.

For the torso, I duplicate **paul_mr_mod_geo**, then delete unwanted faces from around the arm and hip. Use Mesh Tools > Cut Faces Tool with the Shift key on the keyboard held down (to create straight cuts) and slice through the geometry horizontally at the same position for every joint (Fig.07b). Select the faces of each slice and go to Edit > Extract to separate the parts. Next, make sure you select all the sliced parts and go to Edit > Delete by Type > History.

You may notice in the Outliner that a few transform nodes are created from the extraction process. Sometimes they get deleted when you delete the history; other times, they'll still be there. Make sure you delete them.

You can then parent each relevant piece of geometry under the relevant joint. I really recommend that you go in and rename all

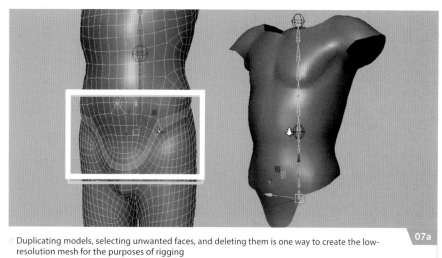

○ Duplicating models, selecting unwanted faces, and deleting them is one way to create the low-resolution mesh for the purposes of rigging
07a

the parts. Again, use the jointRename tool and use the same naming convention to match the joints for the geometry. Also add a suffix of **_lr_geo** to all the pieces. With the geometry parented to the joints, you should be able to translate **spine_hip_ik_jnt**, **spine_mid_ik_jnt**, or **spine_chest_ik_jnt**

around and get a good idea of how the character will deform. Remember to undo the joints back to their default positions.

08: Creating the IK spine controls
For each of the IK joints, we'll create a control. As the controls are intended primarily for

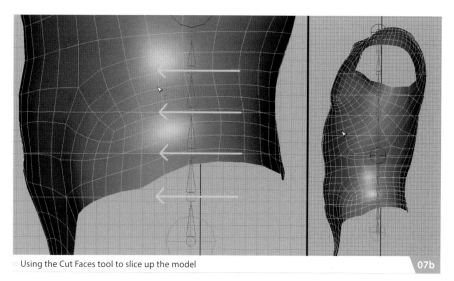

○ Using the Cut Faces tool to slice up the model
07b

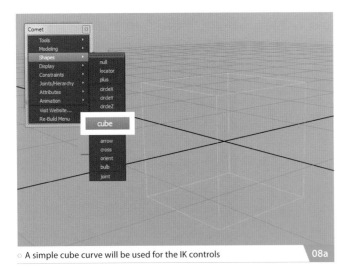

○ A simple cube curve will be used for the IK controls   **08a**

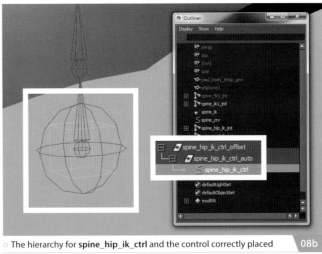

○ The hierarchy for **spine_hip_ik_ctrl** and the control correctly placed   **08b**

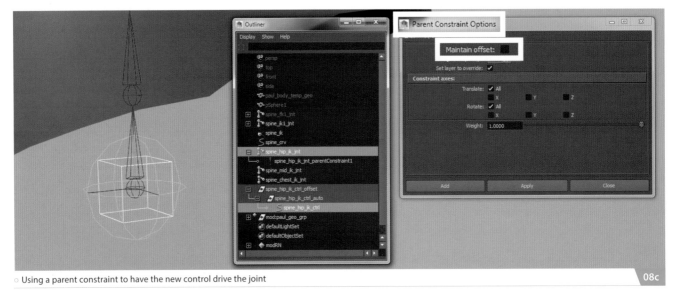

○ Using a parent constraint to have the new control drive the joint   **08c**

translation, I would like to have shapes that resemble a cube. We could create a polygon cube to use as a reference for this, by activating the CV Curve tool and, with the curve angle set to 1, snapping points to the polygon cube to create our cube-like curve. But to speed things up, I'll create a cube shape using cometTools. To do this, go to Comet > Shapes > cube.

Either way, you should end up with a curve shaped like a cube in the center of the world space (**Fig.08a**). If your cube is not centered, make sure you pop a value of 0 into all the Translate and Rotate channels and leave the scale with a uniform value of 1.

Rename this curve to **spine_hip_IK_ctrl** and then, with the curve selected, hit Ctrl+G twice to create two group nodes above it. Call the top-most node **spine_hip_ik_ctrl_offset** and the node below **spine_hip_ik_ctrl_ auto**. Select **spine_hip_ik_ctrl_offset** and

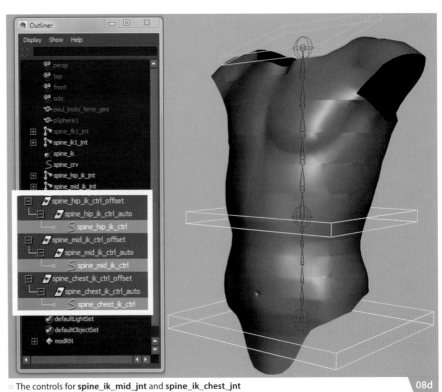

○ The controls for **spine_ik_mid_jnt** and **spine_ik_chest_jnt**   **08d**

then Shift-select **spine_hip_ik_jnt**. Hit P in order to parent **spine_hip_ik_ctrl_offset** under **spine_hip_ik_jnt**.

You should now see that there are some values in the Translate channels for **spine_hip_ik_ctrl_offset**, indicating how far away the **_offset** node is away from the joint. Zero out the Translate values on **spine_hip_ik_ctrl_offset** and your control should pop into the correct position (**Fig.08b**).

> "You should now be able to drive the hip with the control and get it back into the default position by zeroing out the Translate and Rotate values"

Now you need to select **spine_hip_ik_ctrl_offset** and hit Shift+P in order to unparent it from the joint. We now want the control to drive the joint. To do this, select **spine_hip_ik_ctrl** and **spine_hip_ik_jnt** (in that order) and go to Constraint > Parent (Options). In the options, make sure that Maintain Offset is disabled and then hit Apply.

You should now be able to drive the hip with the control (**Fig.08c**) and get it back into the default position by zeroing out the Translate and Rotate values.

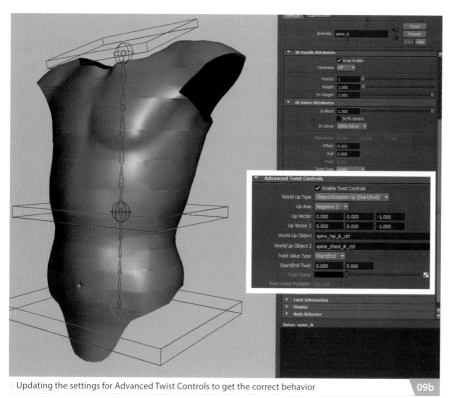

○ Enable Twist Controls for the Spline IK – things will look a little crazy to begin with   **09a**

To shape our control, we need to switch to component mode and translate the CVs. This will ensure that we don't add any transform values to our control. To do this, simply grab the control and hit F8.

Feel free to shape the control however you see fit. I've just made sure that it is easily selectable from most angles by scaling the CVs around

the mass of the pelvis. That's one control down. Now do the same for **spine_mid_ik_jnt** and **spine_chest_ik_jnt** (**Fig.08d**). Remember to name the controls using the same conventions that we have used for the hip control.

09: Adding the twist

To allow for some twisting motion, select **spine_ik** and jump into the Attribute Editor. Open up the IK Solver Attributes > Advanced Twist Controls tab and check the Enable Twist Controls box (**Fig.09a**). This will allow us to pick two controls to drive the twisting from the root and the tip of the IK joint chain. Things may look a little crazy initially.

To fix this, set World Up Type to Object Rotation Up (Start/End) and set Twist Value Type to Start/End. Next, in the World Up Object field, type **spine_hip_ik_ctrl** and in the World Up Object 2 field, type **spine_chest_ik_ctrl**. These are the two controls that will drive the twisting: one at the root of the IK chain and one at the tip. Set Up Axis to Negative Z and then Up Vector and Up Vector 2 to 0, 0, -1 (**Fig.09b**). You should now be able to twist using the two controls.

10: Adding some stretch

At the moment, if we translate **spine_hip_ik_ctrl**, the entire spine comes along with it when really we'd like it to stay between the hip and chest joints. You'll notice, however, that **spine_**

○ Updating the settings for Advanced Twist Controls to get the correct behavior   **09b**

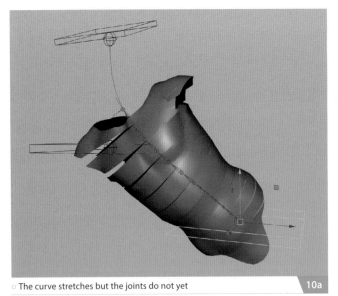

○ The curve stretches but the joints do not yet   10a

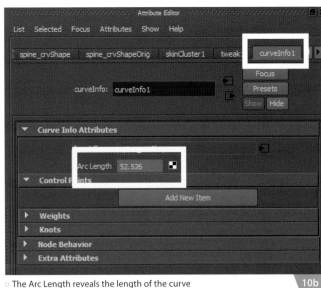

○ The Arc Length reveals the length of the curve   10b

crv does stay between the hip and the chest, growing in length to accommodate this. We'd like to have our joints do the same thing, and we'll use the curve to help us do so (**Fig.10a**).

First, we need to find out the length of **spine_crv**. To do this, select the curve and in the MEL box in the bottom-left corner, type: **arclen –ch 1**. This reveals a hidden node housing information on how long the curve is. If you select the curve now and jump into the Atttribute Editor, you should find a tab called **curveInfo1**. Alternatively, you can select the curve, open up Hypershade or the Node Editor, and click on the Inputs/Outputs button to bring it up. Quickly rename the **curveInfo1** node to **spine_curveInfo**.

On examination, the Arc Length for my spine is 52.526 (**Fig.10b**). Your length may

be slightly different, so do note it down and use that value for the upcoming steps. Next we'll use the Arc Length value to drive the stretching of the joints.

We'll use utility nodes to neutralize the Arc Length value so we can pass it through to the joints. In the Node Editor (Window > Node Editor), press TAB, type **multiplyDivide**, and hit Enter to create the node. Double-click the node to drop it into the Attribute Editor, rename it **spineLength_md**, and then set the Operation to Divide.

Expand both the **spine_curveInfo** and the **spineLength_md** nodes in the Node Editor by clicking on the expand icons on the right of each node. This allows you to see the attributes associated with both nodes. LMB-click on the output of Arc Length (on the **spine_curveInfo**

node) and feed it into the Input > Input 1X of **spineLength_md**. If you examine **spineLength_md** in the Attribute Editor, you'll see that the Arc Length value is being fed into the Input 1X attribute. Copy the same value of Input 1X and paste it into Input 2X.

By taking Input 1X (52.526) and dividing by Input 2X (52.526), we'll output a value of 1. As the length of **spine_crv** varies, the **spineLength_md** node will figure out the difference, and we can feed this value into the joints to have them lengthen correctly (**Fig.10c**).

In the Node Editor, create a new multiplyDivide node and call it **spine_ik2_md**. Now select **spine_ik2_jnt** and copy the value from the Translate X channel (its length) and paste it into the Input 2X of **spine_ik2_md**. Plug the Output X attribute from the

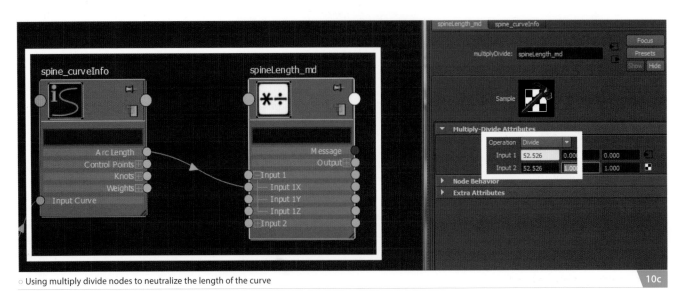

○ Using multiply divide nodes to neutralize the length of the curve   10c

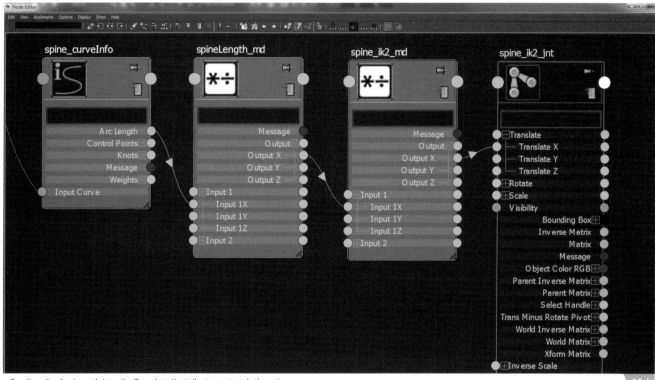

Feeding the Arc Length into the Translate X attribute to stretch the spine

10d

spineLength_md node into the Input X attribute on **spine_ik2_md** (**Fig.10d**).

We now want to pass the output of **spine_ik2_md** onto **spine_ik2_jnt**. To bring **spine_ik2_jnt** into the Node Editor, select it from the Outliner and MMB-drag-and-drop it into the Node Editor. Then feed the Output X of **spine_ik2_md** into the Translate X of **spine_ik2_jnt**.

As the majority of the joints have different lengths, we'll have to create a multiplyDivide node for each joint and make sure the length of each joint is being passed into those multiply divide nodes. Do this now.

If you lose any of your nodes as you do this, open up Hypershade and have a look under the Utilities tab. Once you've done

this, you should be able to translate any of the IK controls and the spine should no longer pull away from **spine_crv** (**Fig.10e**).

11: Creating the FK controls
Now let's move on to the FK controls, which will eventually drive the IK controls. Start by unhiding the FK joint chain by selecting the root joint in the Outliner and pressing Shift+H.

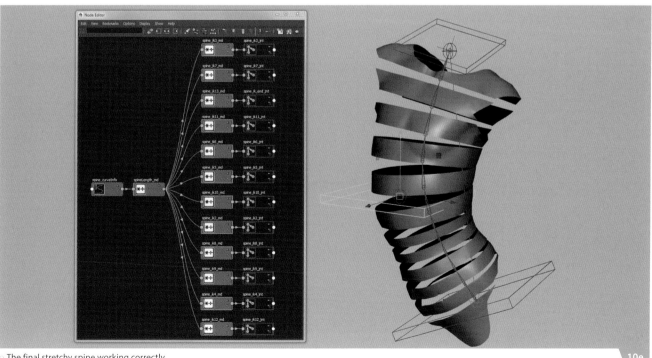

The final stretchy spine working correctly

10e

The first thing we want to do is orient the FK joint chain so flexion is created by positive X rotation. This will be the case for most of the joint chains from now on. The reason we avoided this for the IK spine joint chain was so we could easily set up the advanced twisting.

Grab **spine_fk1_jnt** and go to Skeleton > Orient Joint (Options). Set the Primary Axis to Y, the Secondary Axis to Z, and the Secondary Axis World Orientation to Y (+) (**Fig.11a**). Test out the joints to make sure that you're getting the correct behavior.

By setting the orientations like this, you will have probably noticed that Y is now aiming down the chain, and the Translate Y attribute now relates to the length of the joints. Instead you could have this as X pointing down the chain with positive Z rotation creating flexion. To be honest, it doesn't matter. The only thing that matters is that you keep it consistent throughout the rig.

Now we need to create the FK spine controls. We could do this manually, like we did for the IK controls, but to speed up the process, let's use a quick script I knocked together. In the Script Editor, open up a clean Python tab and bring in the **createControls.py** script from the scripts directory of this project (**Fig.11b**).

This script will look for any joint with the suffix of **_jnt** and create a control with the same name, only replacing the **_jnt** with **_ctrl**. It will then create two group nodes above the control and rename them appropriately.

Then it will correctly place the control by using a parent constraint. Last, the parent constraint will be deleted and the joint will be constrained to the control using the constraint defined in the final line of code.

I know it sounds like a lot of work, but for 10 lines of code (I'm not including the comments), it should really help to speed things up. Before using the script, edit the final line to read as follows, as we only want to orient-constrain the FK joints to their respective controls:

```
21 cmds.orientConstraint(ctrl, s, mo=0)
```

Now, select **spine_fk1_jnt**, **spine_fk2_jnt**, **spine_fk3_jnt**, and **spine_fk4_jnt**, highlight

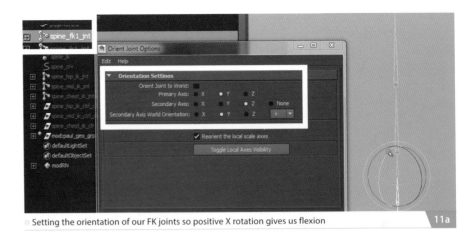

○ Setting the orientation of our FK joints so positive X rotation gives us flexion   11a

○ To create the FK spine controls, use the createControls.py script   11b

all the text in the Script Editor, and hit Enter on the numpad. If you look in the Outliner now, hopefully you'll have a control for each of the four joints and each control will consist of a hierarchy. You should now be able to

edit the shape/size of the controls, but please remember to do so in component mode.

Next we need the control hierarchy to mimic the joint hierarchy. To do this, parent

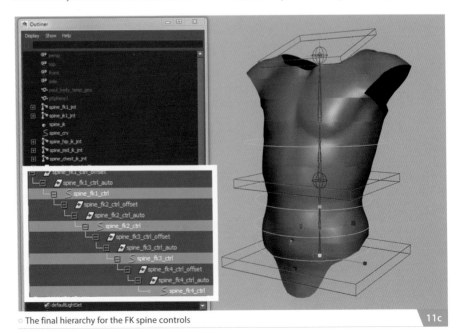

○ The final hierarchy for the FK spine controls   11c

spine_fk4_ctrl_offset under spine_fk3_ctrl.
Then parent spine_fk3_ctrl_offset under
spine_fk2_ctrl, and last, parent spine_f2_
ctrl_offset under spine_fk1_ctrl (Fig.11c).
Test out the rotations and hopefully
everything will be working in order.

12: The FK IK setup

Now we want to drive the IK spine with the
FK spine. To do this, start by parenting spine_
mid_ik_ctrl_offset under spine_fk3_ctrl. Then
take spine_chest_ik_ctrl_offset and parent
it under spine_fk4_ctrl. Now test out all the
controls by translating and rotating them.
Make sure that when you zero out the values
for the Translate and the Rotate channels, the
controls revert back to their default positions.

13: A quick cleanup

We've got joints, controls, group nodes,
curves, and so on, in our scene at the moment.
Although we've been labeling everything,
let's do a bit of housework so the Outliner is
less cluttered. It may sound boring, but the
more often you do this, the easier it will be to
create and maintain the rig in the long run.

So let's start by selecting spine_ik1_jnt, spine_
fk1_jnt, spine_hip_ik_jnt, spine_mid_ik_jnt,
and spine_chest_ik_jnt, and hitting Ctrl+G.
Rename this group torso_jnt_grp. Next,
select spine_hip_ik_ctrl_offset and spine
_fk1_ctrl_offset, and hit Ctrl+G. This time,
rename the group torso_ctrl_grp. Now select
spine_crv and spine_ik, group them together,
and call this group torso_doNotTouch_grp.

14: Adding the rib cage

To help give a sense of a skeletal structure
beneath the model, let's add some joints
that will be used to simulate the effects of
a rib cage. So that we can easily draw the
joints, unhide the high-resolution model
and set it as a Live surface. We can now
use this model to snap the joints to.

On the character's left side, start from the back
of the torso and create a four-joint chain that
works its way towards the front. Create two
additional joint chains, each consisting of four
joints, one beneath the other, to represent
the rib cage (as illustrated in Fig.14a).

For now, just work on the character's left-hand
side, as we'll mirror these joints later. With the

joints in place, disable the high-resolution mesh
as a Live surface and select the root joint of each
new joint chain, translating them in slightly so

they sit within the character. Next we'll take care
of the orientation of the joints so that positive
X rotation allows for the rib cage to expand.

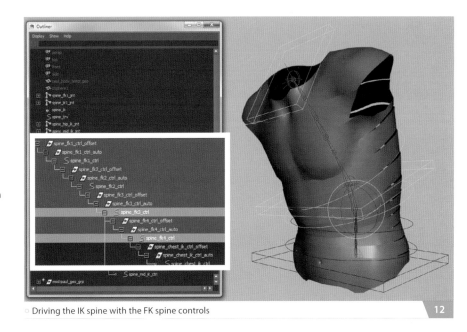

○ Driving the IK spine with the FK spine controls   12

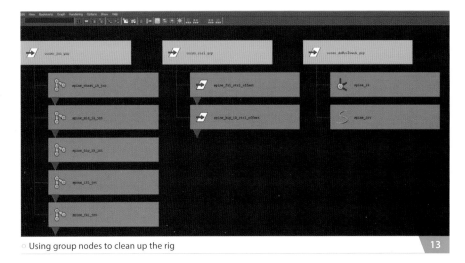

○ Using group nodes to clean up the rig   13

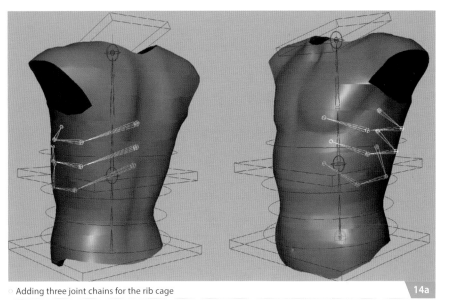

○ Adding three joint chains for the rib cage   14a

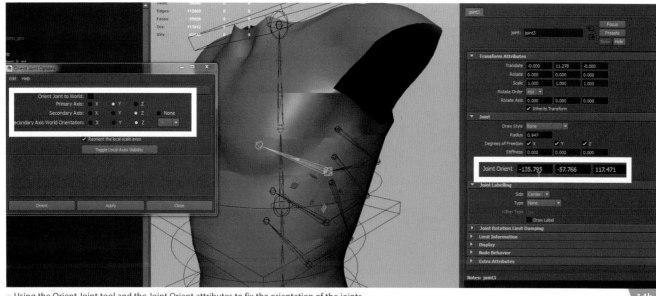

○ Using the Orient Joint tool and the Joint Orient attributes to fix the orientation of the joints

14b

Select the root joint of the first chain and go to Skeleton > Orient Joint (Options). Set the Primary Axis to Y, Secondary Axis to Z, Secondary Axis World Orientation to Z (-), and hit Apply. Check the joint, then move on to the next joint in the chain. Use Joint Orient in the Attribute Editor to orient this joint until it gives you the desired behavior (**Fig.14b**). To interactively edit the values in the Attribute Editor, hover the cursor over the box you'd like to edit, hold down the Ctrl key, and use either the LMB, MMB, or RMB to edit the values.

You could also use the cometJointOrient tool (Comet > Joints/Hierarchy), which yields faster results, or simply rotate the joints and use Freeze Transforms so that the Rotate channels end up with a default value of 0. Do this for all the joints and test out the rotations.

With all the joints oriented correctly, let's rename them using cometRename. Select all the joints from the first chain from root to tip and type **l_ribA** in the Rename field. Hit Rename And Number and then, with the same joints selected, add the Suffix of **_jnt**. Follow the same naming convention for the remaining joint chains, replacing the A with B and then C.

We now want to mirror the joints over to the other side. Select **l_ribA1_jnt** and go to Skeleton > Mirror Joint. Set the Mirror across to YZ and the Mirror Function to Behavior. Then, in the "Search for" field, type **l_** and in the "Replace with" field, type **r_**. Hit Apply and then repeat the step for the remaining joint chains.

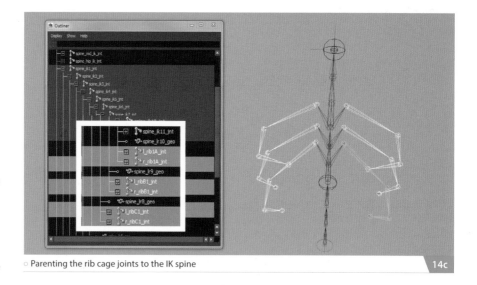

○ Parenting the rib cage joints to the IK spine

14c

Now it's time for some parenting. Select both **l_ribA1_jnt** and **r_ribA1_jnt** and parent them under **spine_ik10_jnt**. Then select **l_ribB1_jnt** and **r_ribB1_jnt** and parent them under **spine_ik9_jnt**. Last, select **l_ribC1_jnt** and **r_ribC1_jnt** and parent them under **spine_ik8_jnt** (**Fig.14c**).

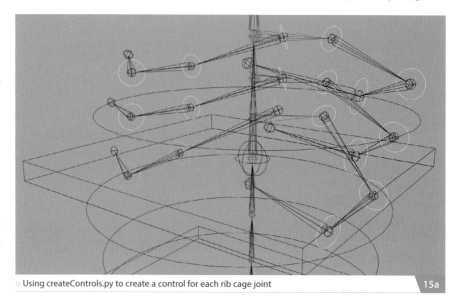

○ Using createControls.py to create a control for each rib cage joint

15a

15: Adding the rib controls

I'd like to add a control for each joint of the rib cage (minus the end joints). This might seem like we'll have more controls than necessary, but it'll give the animator an additional set of controls to deform with. We'll hide some controls later to simplify the rig, but we'll also allow the animator to reveal them as he or she desires to obtain the additional control.

Let's use the createControls.py script again to create the controls. Load that script into the Script Editor and edit the following lines to read like so:

16   ctrl = cmds.circle(nr=(0, 1, 0), r=1.5, n=ctrlName) [0]

21   cmds.orientConstraint(ctrl, s, mo=0)

This will change the radius of the circle and orient-constrain each joint to its control. Now select **l_ribA1_jnt**, **l_ribA2_jnt**, and **l_ribA3_jnt** and run the script (**Fig.15a**).

Jump into the Outliner and create the parent-child relationship between our new controls so they deliver the correct behavior. To do this, parent **l_ribA3_ctrl_offset** under **l_ribA2_ctrl**. Then parent **l_ribA2_ctrl_offset** under **l_ribA1_ctrl**. Do this for all six control hierarchies. Then select the **_offset** nodes for all six rib control hierarchies, group them together (Ctrl+G), and call that group **rib_ctrl_grp**.

To have the rib controls follow the spine joints, but keep the controls and joints as two separate hierarchies, we'll use constraints. In this order, select **spine_ik10_jnt** and **l_ribA1_ctrl_offset** and go to Constrain > Parent (Options). Enable Maintain Offset (so the control doesn't flip out) and hit Apply. Once you've completed and checked the first joint chain, repeat the process for the remaining rib cage joints (**Fig.15b**).

16: Adding the COG control

The center of gravity (COG) control is usually the main control that drives a character. In most cases, this would be positioned at the hip. In reality, however, a person's center of gravity changes depending on their pose or action. For example, when standing with both legs parted and the hips spaced in between, the center of gravity would be around the hip. But now imagine doing a forward roll.

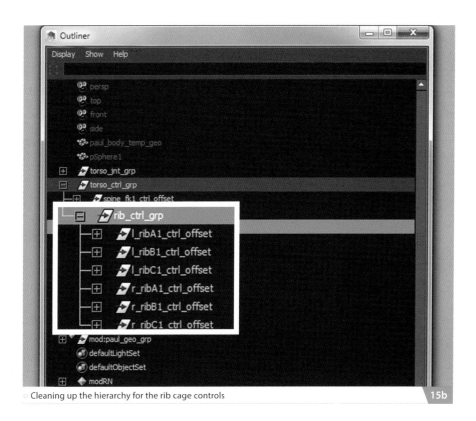
○ Cleaning up the hierarchy for the rib cage controls
15b

Your body would be in the shape of a ball and therefore the center of gravity for this motion would be in the center of that form.

To allow for this change, you'd need to add the ability to move the pivot of the COG control. As this is not necessary for the animation we'll be producing, we won't add this function. (If you did want to add the effects of editing the position of the COG, try experimenting with some curves, locators, and constraints.)

Now, to create this COG control, go to Comet > Shapes > arrow. Make sure it's in the world center and rename it **COG_ctrl**. Now create the control hierarchy by grouping it to itself twice. Rename the top group **COG_ctrl_offset**

and the next node down **COG_ctrl_auto**. Parent **COG_ctrl_offset** under s**pine_hip_ik_ctrl**, zero out the Rotate and Translate values, and then unparent it.

Next, jump into component mode (F8) and edit the shape of **hip_ ctrl** so that it's more easily selectable.

17: Adding the hip control

At the moment, we can use **spine_hip_ik_ctrl** to move the hip around. That's all good but it also affects some of the spine. Although this behavior is intended, I'd also like to rotate the hips without having any effect on the spine, as it makes it easier to handle tasks such as having the character sit down.

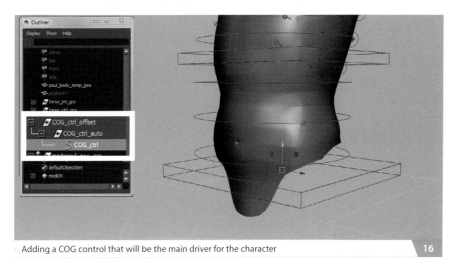
○ Adding a COG control that will be the main driver for the character
16

To create the joint chain that will handle this, jump into the side view and load the Joint tool. Holding down the V key (snap to points), LMB-click close to **spine_hip_ik_jnt** (but not on it). It should draw the joint on top of **spine_hip_ik_jnt**.

Hold down the Shift key and draw a second joint at the base of the pelvic mass. Rename the two joints, from root to tip: **hip_fk_jnt** and **hipEnd_fk_jnt**. (**Fig.17a**). Next, let's orient the joint. Select **hip_fk_jnt** and go to Orient Joint (Options). In here, set the Primary Axis to Y, the Secondary Axis to Z, and the Secondary Axis World Orientation to Z (+).

"Using a parent constraint will allow us to connect it to the rest of the rig with little bother, while keeping the lower portion of the rig separate from the torso"

Now select **hip_fk_jnt** and use the createControls.py script to create a control for it. Make sure you edit the final line of the script to read like so:

```
21  cmds.parentConstraint(ctrl, s, mo=0)
```

Although we're only going to drive **hip_fk_jnt** by rotations, using a parent constraint will allow us to connect it to the rest of the rig with little bother, while keeping the lower portion of the rig (we'll add the legs later) separate from the torso.

So to get everyone playing happily, take **hip_fk_ctrl_offset** and parent it under **spine_hip_ik_ctrl**. Make sure you add some geometry to the hips, as we did for the torso, and that you re-shape the new hip control in component mode so the animator can grab it easily (**Fig.17b**).

18: Finalizing the torso rig

Now let's bring everything together and also clean up the Outliner (**Fig.18a**). Start by selecting both **spine_fk1_ctrl_offset** and **spine_hip_ik_ctrl_offset** and parenting both of them under **COG_ctrl**.

Select **spine_fk1_ctrl**, Shift-select **spine_fk_jnt**, and go to Constrain > Point. You should now be able to translate the COG control around and have everything follow along.

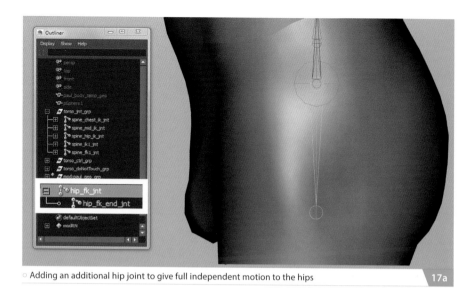

○ Adding an additional hip joint to give full independent motion to the hips   17a

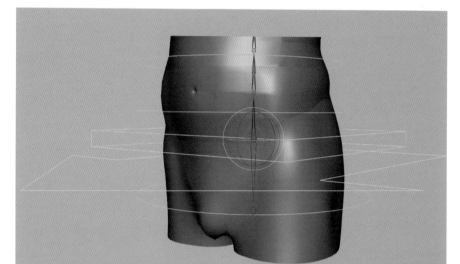

○ A new control added to drive the new hip joint   17b

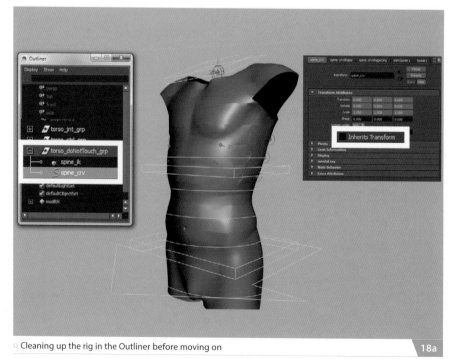

○ Cleaning up the rig in the Outliner before moving on   18a

"We want to lock and hide both attributes that we don't want to hand over to the animator"

To stop the torso rig breaking later (when we add **global_SRT_ctrl**), select **spine_crv** and disable Inherits Transform in the Attribute Editor. You'll find this on the left-most tab that houses the transforms. If you don't disable this, you can end up adding a double transformation to your rig, which isn't what you want. Next, take **COG_ctrl** and drop it under **torso_rig_ctrl** to keep things organized.

We want to lock and hide both attributes that we don't want to hand over to the animator, and also parts of the rig that we don't want anyone to accidentally grab in the viewport. Select all the FK controls (including the rib controls), highlight the Translate and Rotate attributes in the Channel Box, hold down the RMB, and go to Lock and Hide Selected (**Fig.18b**). Then select all the IK controls and lock and hide the Scale attributes. Select **spine_ik**, **spine_crv**, disable the Visibility attribute, and then lock it off.

We should now have completed the torso portion of our rig. Next, we move on to the neck and the head.

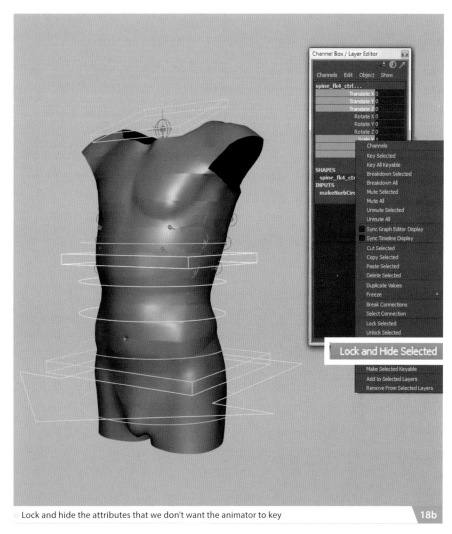

○ Lock and hide the attributes that we don't want the animator to key   **18b**

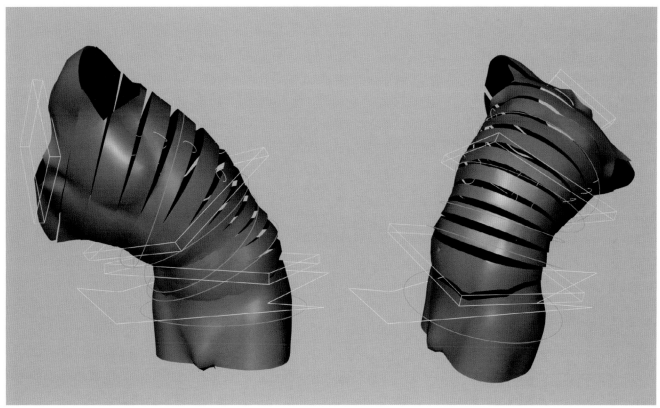

○ Make sure to test the rig out before moving on

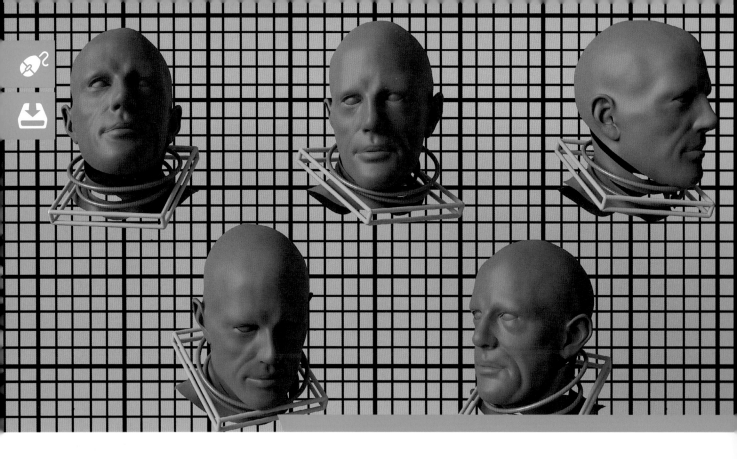

Rigging the neck and head

Setting up the rig for the neck, head, ears, and eyes

With the torso rig complete, we have a base to start adding the neck, head, arms, and legs. You could go in any one of these directions but we'll tackle the neck and head next. We're going to create FK joints and controls for the neck, head, eyelids, and ears.

For the eyeballs we'll be using aim constraints so we can lock the eyes on a particular point. There is no reason why you can't go for an IK neck setup as was done for the spine, if that works better for

you. I simply prefer an FK setup, and, in any case, through space-switching we'll be adding IK-like capabilities to the head.

01: Creating the head joints

Let's start with the main joints for the neck and head. In the side view, activate the Joint tool, hold down the V key, and point-snap the root joint to start at the tip of the spine joint chain. Make sure you click slightly away from it, so it creates a new chain rather than parenting itself to the spine. Click again between the

neck root joint and the ear, then make another click just below and in front of the ear. Still in the tool, hold down the Shift key and make one more click at the top of the head.

Let's take care of the orientation of the joints. Select the root joint of the new chain, go to Skeleton > Orient Joint (Options), and set Primary Axis to Y, Secondary Axis to Z, and Secondary Axis World Orientation to Z (+). Rename the joints from root to tip: **neck1_jnt, neck2_jnt; head_jnt; head_end_jnt (Fig.01a)**.

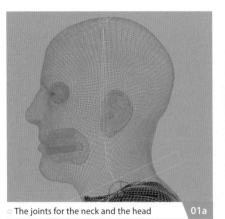
○ The joints for the neck and the head 01a

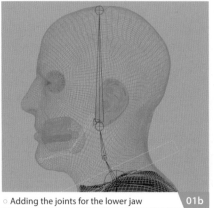
○ Adding the joints for the lower jaw 01b

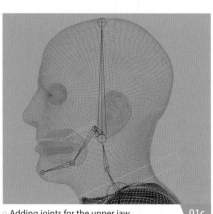
○ Adding joints for the upper jaw 01c

> "I actually had the joints rotate in the opposite direction to the lower jaw so that should the animator rotate them together, they could make the mouth open wider"

Now we turn to the jaw joints. Create a new joint chain starting from just in front of the ear and ending at the chin. To visually mimic the shape of the actual jaw bone, I actually add an extra joint. With the jaw bone in place, as we've done previously, orient the joints to give you the correct behavior, and don't forget to freeze the transformations to zero out the Rotate values. Rename the joints from root to tip as follows: **lowerJaw1_jnt**, **lowerJaw2_jnt**, and **lowerJaw_end_jnt** (**Fig.01b**).

Next, let's create an upper set of jaw joints. Although this is not anatomically accurate, I do this so I have something to attach the upper teeth and gums to. Create a new three-joint chain, as illustrated in **Fig.01c**, and rename the joints from root to tip as follows: **upperJaw1_jnt**, **upperJaw2_jnt**, and **upperJaw_end_jnt**.

Again, take care regarding the orientation of the new joint chain using the Joint Orient tool. I actually had the joints rotate in the opposite direction to the lower jaw so that should the animator rotate them together, they could make the mouth open wider. Now take both **lowerJaw1_jnt** and **upperJaw1_jnt** and parent them both **under head_jnt**.

02: Creating the eye joints

First we need to find the center of the eyeball, in order to start our joint chain from that position. To do this, select the left eyeball geometry and, in the Attribute Editor, jump to the left-most tab (the Transform tab). Under Pivots, enable Display Rotate Pivot to reveal a small locator. Activate the Joint tool and in the side view, hold down the V key and point snap the first joint to this locator. With the Shift key held down, create a final joint at the bulge of the cornea (**Fig.02a**).

If you're following along with the videos, at this stage I rotate the joint to sit in line with the orientation of the eyeball. *Do not* do this as it makes more work when creating controls for the eyes. I had to go back and rectify this, and I'd like to save you that inconvenience. Instead, rotate the eyeball geometry to match the orientation of the joints, and leave the joint as it is.

Rename the joints from root to tip: **l_eye_jnt** and **l_eye_end_jnt**. Now duplicate **l_eye_jnt** and put a minus in front of the value in the Translate X attribute to pop it over to the

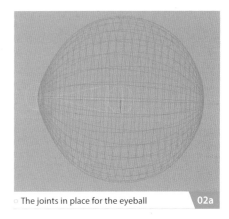

○ The joints in place for the eyeball   02a

right-hand side. Double check the position sits correctly within the eye. If your model is asymmetrical like mine, you'll need to slightly offset the position. Rename this joint chain **r_eye_jnt** and **r_eye_end_jnt**. The reason I did not mirror this joint over is so that both eyes will go in the same direction when rotated together rather than creating a cross-eyed look.

Now duplicate either one of the eye joints and pop a 0 into the Translate X attribute to center it. Rename this joint **eyes_root_jnt** and parent both **l_eye_jnt** and **r_eye_jnt** under this new joint. Lastly, take **eyes_root_jnt** and parent it under **head_jnt**. With the joints in place, duplicate the eye geometry, rename them **l_eye_lr_geo** and **r_eye_lr_geo**, and parent them under their respective eye joints (**Fig.02b**).

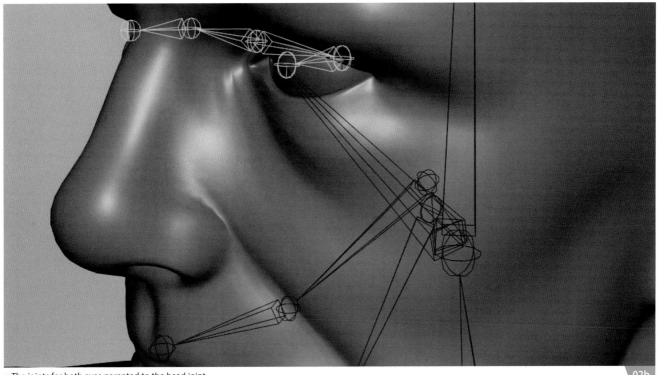

○ The joints for both eyes parented to the head joint   02b

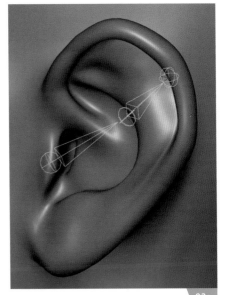

○ The joints for the ear running from the tragus to the helix   **03a**

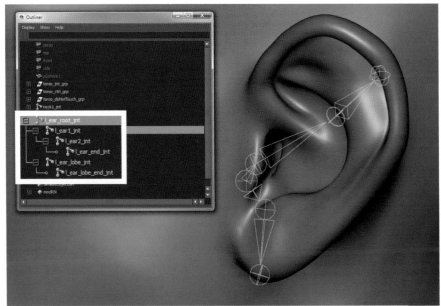

○ Additional joints for the ear lobe and the final hierarchy for the ear joints   **03b**

"Sometimes I don't rig the ears, but every now and then I do, as small movements can add a bit more life to a character"

03: Adding the ear joints

Next we come to the ears. Sometimes I don't rig the ears, but every now and then I do, as small movements added during animation can add a bit more life to a character. In the side view, create a three-joint chain from the tragus to the helix (**Fig.03a**).

Translate the joint chain to sit within the ear geometry in Perspective view, then use the Joint Orient tool to set the correct behavior. Next, rotate the joints to sit better in the geometry and go to Modify > Freeze Transformations to clean up the Rotate channels.

Back in the side view, create a two-joint chain from the tragus to the lobule and tidy up the position and orientation again. Duplicate the root joint for the initial joint chain we created and delete all the child joints from this new chain so you have a single floating joint. Position this joint to sit between the existing two joint chains and then go to Skeleton > Orient Joint (Options). Enable Orient Joint to World and hit Apply. Then parent the existing two joint chains under this single joint.

Now we will move on to the renaming of the joints. Select the parent joint and rename

it **l_ear_root_jnt**. The joint chains will then tail off in the hierarchy. Next rename the two-joint chain from root to tip as follows: **l_ear_lobe_jnt** and **l_ear_lobe_end_jnt**. Then rename the three-joint chain as follows, again do this from root to tip: **l_ear1_jnt**, **l_ear2_jnt**, and **l_ear_end_jnt** (**Fig.03b**).

Select **l_ear_root_jnt** and go to Skeleton > Mirror Joint. My model is asymmetrical, so I have to manually translate the ear into the correct position. With both ears lined up, parent both **l_ear_root_jnt** and **r_ear_root_jnt** under **head_jnt**.

04: Adding the eyelid joints

For the eyelid joints, select and duplicate **l_eye_jnt** and then rotate it to line up with the lower eyelid. Now go to Modify > Freeze Transformations to clean up the rotation values. Rename this joint, from root to tip: **l_lowerLid_jnt** and **l_lowerLid_end_jnt**. Now duplicate **l_lowerLid_jnt** and rotate that joint chain to fit in line with the upper eyelid (**Fig.04a**). Freeze the transformations again and rename the joints appropriately.

Like we did with the jaw joints, we want to be able to rotate both the upper and lower

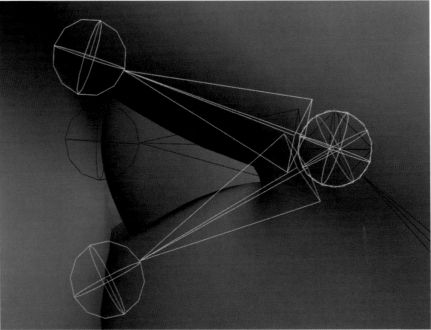

○ Adding a two-joint chain for both the upper and the lower eyelids   **04a**

eyelid joints together and have them open the eyes wider or close them tighter. To allow for this, select **l_upperLid_jnt**, rotate it on its axis by 180°, and then freeze its transformations to pass the rotations to the Joint Orient.

For the right eyelids, due to the asymmetry of the face, I make the decision to duplicate **l_eye_jnt** and repeat the process rather than mirroring the left eyelid joints. As we duplicate the eyelid joints from the eye joints, they should all be parented to **eyes_root_jnt**. If not, make sure they are.

At this stage, as we did for the torso, chop up the model, rename the pieces, and parent the geometry pieces to the relevant joint (**Fig.04b**).

05: Adding the FK controls

From the neck up, we are going to be creating all FK controls. Later on, however, we'll add some space-switching functionality to allow for the behavior of the head to be changed. Select the neck joints (**neck1_jnt** and **neck2_jnt**) and use the createControls.py script to create the controls. Make sure you change the final line to read as below, because we only need to orient-constrain most of the joints to the controls:

```
21  cmds.orientConstraint(ctrl, s, mo=0)
```

Select the newly created controls, hit F8, and in component mode, edit the shape of the controls so that they better fit around the model.

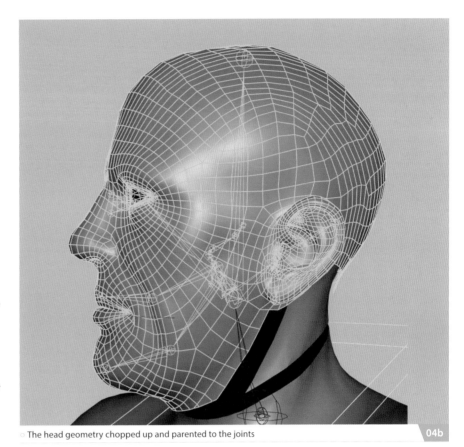

The head geometry chopped up and parented to the joints   **04b**

For the control hierarchy to work correctly, take **neck2_ctrl_offset** and parent it under **neck1_ctrl**. Select **head_jnt** and **lowerJaw1_jnt** and run the script again. Edit the shape of the controls and parent **lowerJaw1_ctrl_offset** under **head_ctrl**. Then take **head_ctrl_offset** and parent it under **neck2_ctrl**. As we won't be adding an additional jaw joint, rename

lowerJaw1_ctrl to **lowerJaw_ctrl** to avoid confusion for the animator. Make sure you do the same for the **_auto** and **_offset** nodes. Now repeat the same process for the ear controls but leave the eyes alone for now.

The last thing we need to do is point-constrain **neck1_jnt** to **neck1_ctrl** so that we can

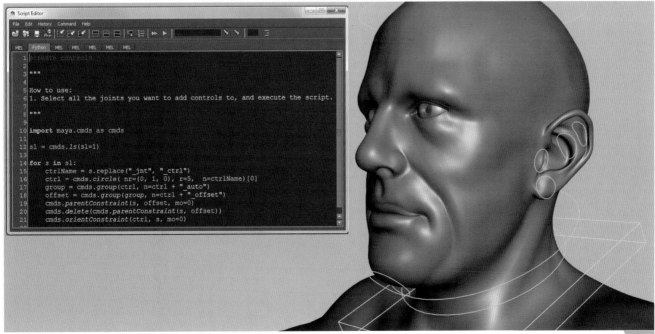

Using the createControls.py script to create controls for the neck, head, and ears   **05**

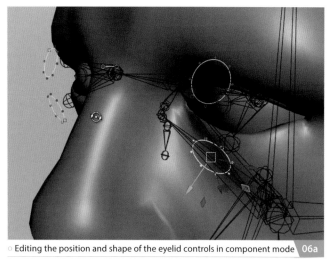

○ Editing the position and shape of the eyelid controls in component mode · 06a

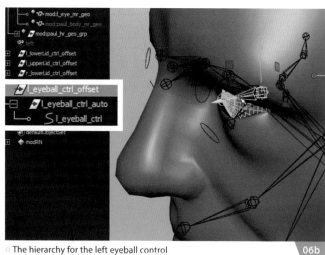

○ The hierarchy for the left eyeball control · 06b

connect the neck to the torso. To do this, select **neck1_ctrl**, Shift-select **neck1_jnt**, and go to Constrain > Point (with the default settings). We could have handled this with just one parent constraint, rather than an orient and point constraint, but I'll leave that decision to you.

06: Create the eye controls

Start by creating the controls for the eyelids. Select **l_lowerLid_jnt**, **l_upperLid_jnt**, **r_lowerLid_jnt**, and **r_upperLid_jnt** and execute the createControls.py script (set to orient constraint) to create the controls. Now switch to component mode (F8) and position the controls to be more easily selectable (**Fig.06a**). Select all four **_offset** group nodes for the eyelid controls now and parent them under **head_ctrl**.

Now for the eyeball controls. Start by going to Comet > Shape > Plus to create a curve that looks like a locator. Make sure it's positioned at the world center. Rename it **l_eyeBall_ctrl** and then hit Ctrl+G twice to create the control hierarchy. Name the top-most group **l_eyeBall_ctrl_offset**, and the next down **l_eyeBall_ctrl_auto** (**Fig.06b**). To position the control, parent it under **l_eye_jnt**, zero out the Translate and Rotate attributes to snap it into place, and then unparent it. Next, create the control for the right eye.

Once you have both sets of eye controls, select the **_offset** node for both and in object mode (it's very important to set it to Object), translate them both out in front of the character, as

illustrated in **Fig.06c**. In this order, select **l_eyeBall_ctrl**, Shift-select **l_eye_jnt**, and go to Constrain > Aim (Options). Reset the settings and then set Aim Vector to 0, 0, -1 (our joint is pointing at the control down this axis). Then set Up Vector to 0, 1, 0 and hit Apply.

Do the same for the right eye. You'll now be able to translate the new eye controls to drive the rotation of the eyeballs. Next, we want to create a new control that will carry both individual eye controls together (**Fig.06d**). Start by going to Comet > Shapes > square. Rename this to **eyes_ctrl** and group it to itself twice. Rename the top-most group **eyes_ctrl_offset** and the next group down **l_eyes_ctrl_auto**.

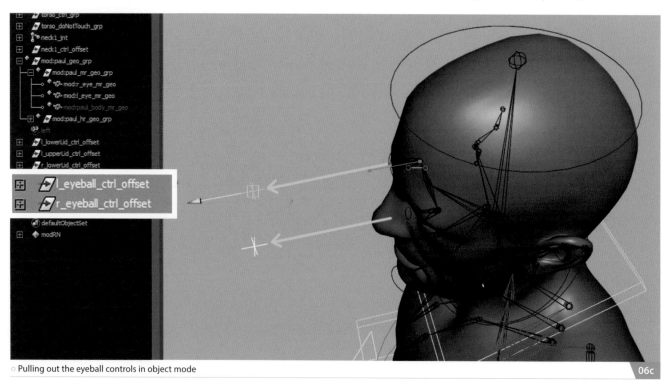

○ Pulling out the eyeball controls in object mode · 06c

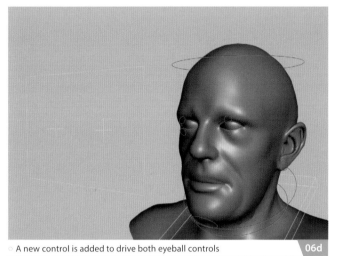

A new control is added to drive both eyeball controls　06d

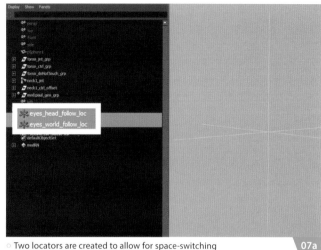

Two locators are created to allow for space-switching　07a

We now want to position this control perfectly between the two eyeball controls. Select both **l_eyeBall_ctrl** and **r_eyeBall_ctrl**, Shift-select **l_eyes_ctrl_offset**, and go to Constrain > Point (with Maintain Offset disabled). The control should snap into place.

Now select **pointConstraint1** that lives under **l_eyes_ctrl_offset** and delete it. Jump into component mode next, and scale and rotate the shape of the control. To rotate the control with increments, hold down the J key on the keyboard. Select both **l_eyeBall_ctrl_offset** and **r_eyeBall_ctrl_offset**, and parent them under **l_eyes_ctrl**.

07: Space-switching the eyes

For now, the eyes don't follow the head control, so let's add an optional feature allowing them to do so. Create two locators and rename them **eyes_head_follow_loc** and **eyes_world_follow_loc** (Fig.07a). Parent both new locators underneath **eyes_ctrl**, zero out the translation values, and then unparent them.

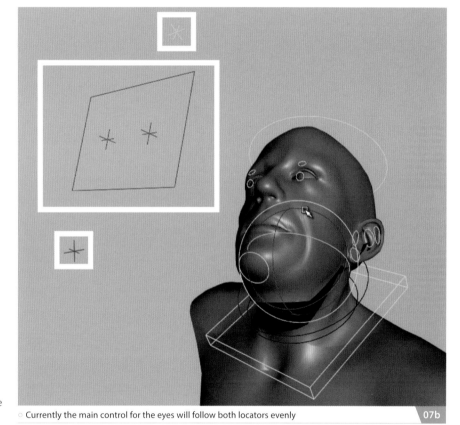

Currently the main control for the eyes will follow both locators evenly　07b

Select both locators, add **eyes_ctrl_auto** to the selection, and go to Constrain > Parent. Take **eyes_head_follow_loc** and parent it under **head_ctrl**. Then select **eyes_world_follow_loc**, hit Ctrl+G to group it to itself, and rename that group **world_follow_loc_grp**. Moving **head_ctrl** will now carry **eyes_ctrl** but only with 50% influence. The other 50% is driven by **eyes_world_follow_loc** (Fig.07b). We'll use a custom attribute and SDK to dictate which mode should have full control over the eyes.

Select **eyes_ctrl** and go to Modify > Add Attribute. Here we will create our custom

attribute. Give it a Long name of **eyesFollow**. Set the Data Type to Enum. Then under Enum Names, highlight Green and give it a New name of head. Then highlight Blue and give it a New name of world (Fig.07c). In the Channel Box you should now see our custom attribute.

Now go to Animate > Set Driven Key > Set. This is the window we will use to drive the attributes of one object with the attributes of another. Select **eyes_ctrl** and hit the Load Driver button on the SDK UI. This will drop the object into the top-left box and the attributes for that object into the top-right box.

Select **eyes_ctrl_auto_parentConstraint1** (under **eyes_ctrl_auto**) and hit Load Driver. This is the constraint that houses the weighting values that we can use to control whether the eyes should follow the head or not. The constraint should pop into the bottom-left box and its attributes in the bottom-right.

At this stage in the process, you need to select **eyes_ctrl** and set the Eyes Follow attribute to Head. Then select **eyes_ctrl_auto_parentConstraint1** and set Eyes World Follow Loc W0 to 0 and leave Eyes Head Follow Loc W1 at 1.

Back in the SDK window, highlight **eyes_ctrl** in the top-left box and Eyes Follow in the top-right box. Then highlight **eyes_ctrl_auto_ parentConstraint1** in the bottom-left box and both Eyes World Follow Loc W0 to 0 and Eyes Head Follow Loc W1 in the bottom-right box. Now hit Key on the SDK window. If you select **eyes_ctrl_auto_parentConstraint1**, you'll see that the weight attributes are now highlighted in red, indicating that they've been keyed. We have now defined that when the Eyes Follow attribute is set to Head, **eyes_ctrl** will follow the head. Let's reverse this next.

Set the Eyes Follow attribute to World now. Then select **eyes_ctrl_auto_parentConstraint1** and this time set Eyes World Follow Loc W0 to 1 and Eyes Head Follow Loc W1 to 0. Back in the SDK window, hit Key once more. We have now defined that when the Eyes Follow attribute is set to World, **eyes_ctrl** will not follow the head (**Fig.07d**). Test it out before moving on and make sure you are familiar with this SDK window as we will be using it for many, many tasks later on.

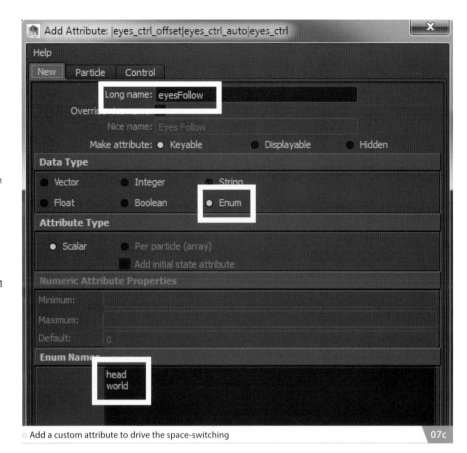

○ Add a custom attribute to drive the space-switching | 07c

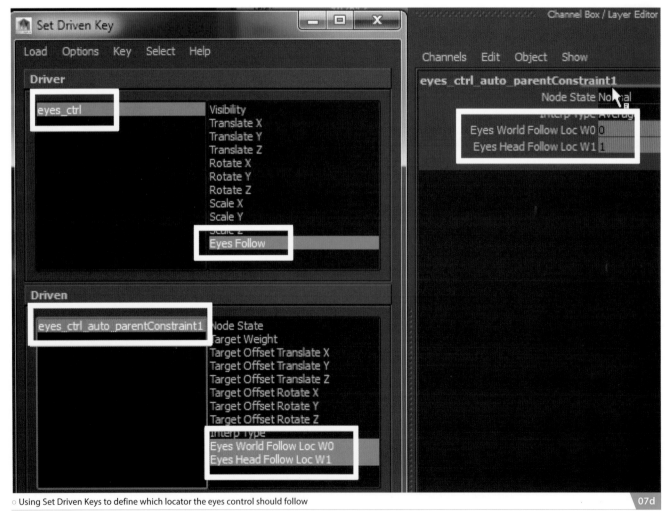

○ Using Set Driven Keys to define which locator the eyes control should follow | 07d

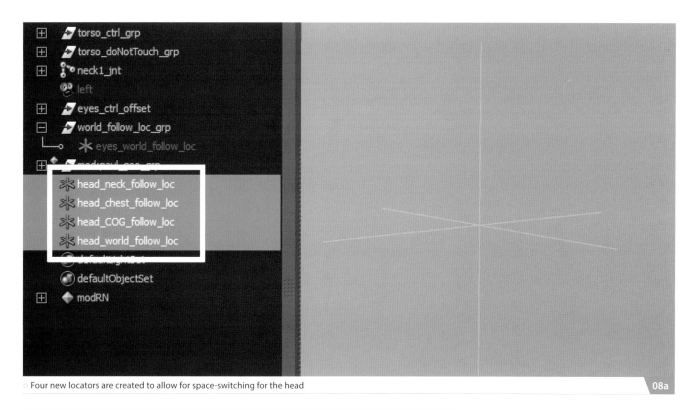

○ Four new locators are created to allow for space-switching for the head

08a

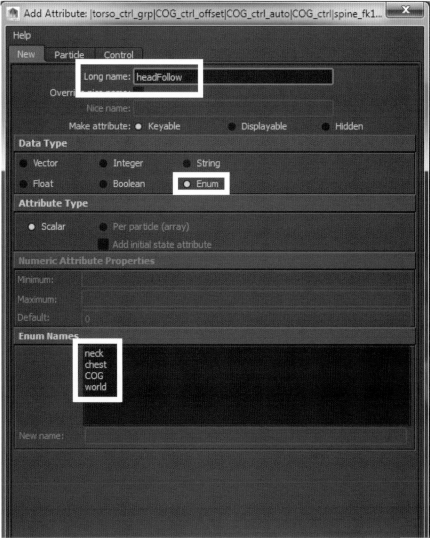

○ The custom attribute to allow the head control to follow either the neck, chest, COG, or world

08b

08: Space-switching the head

Now we'll do a similar thing with the head. This time, we'll allow the head to follow either the neck, chest, COG, or world. First we need to hook the head to the chest, so parent **neck1_ctrl_offset** under **chest_ctrl**. Create four locators called **head_neck_follow_loc**, **head_chest_follow_loc**, **head_COG_follow_loc**, and **head_world_follow_loc** (Fig.08a).

Take all four locators, parent them under **head_ctrl**, zero out the Translate and Rotate values (so they pop into the correct place) and unparent them. Select **head_ctrl** and go to Edit > Add Attribute. In the window that pops up, set the Long name to **headFollow**, the Data Type to Enum, and add the following entries: neck, chest, COG, and world (Fig.08b). Now select in this order: **head_neck_follow_loc**, **head_chest_follow_loc**, **head_COG_follow_loc**, **head_world_follow_loc**, and **head_ctrl_auto**, and go to Constrain > Orient.

The next thing to do is to open up the SDK window. In here, set **head_ctrl** as the Driver object and the **head_ctrl_auto_orientConstraint1** node as the Driven object.

Set the Head Follow attribute to Neck, and on the orient constraint node, set all the weights to 0 apart from Head Neck Follow Loc W0, which should remain at 1 (Fig.08c).

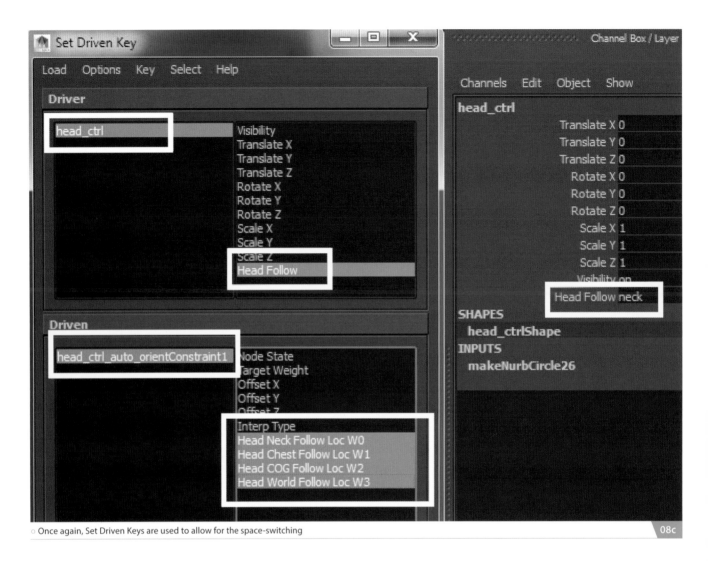

○ Once again, Set Driven Keys are used to allow for the space-switching
08c

Once you have done so, hit Key on the SDK window. Then set the Head Follow attribute to chest, zero out all the weights on the orient constraint node except for Head Chest Follow Loc W1, which needs to be 1, and then hit Key again. Do this for the COG and world attributes.

We now need to pop the locators under the relevant control so everything goes swimmingly. Start by parenting **head_neck_ follow_loc** under **neck_ctrl**. Then parent **head_chest_follow_loc** under **chest_ik_ ctrl_loc**. Parent **head_COG_follow_loc** under

COG_ctrl, and lastly parent **head_world_ follow_loc** under **world_follow_loc_grp**.

Test out the rig at this stage, making sure the head doesn't wander off as you articulate the torso (**Fig.08d**). Once you've tested the head,

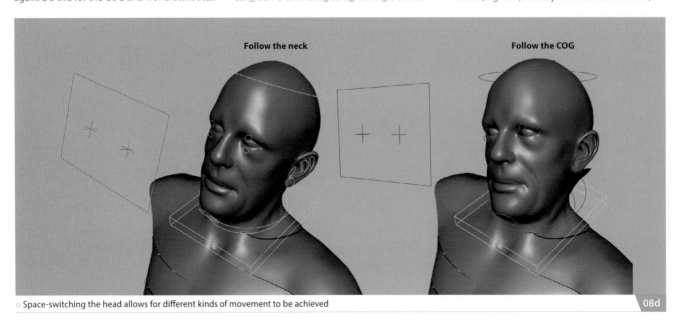

○ Space-switching the head allows for different kinds of movement to be achieved
08d

select all four locators, zero out the visibility in the Channel Box, and finally lock the attribute.

"At this stage, our rig should be a bit more organized but do make sure you test it out"

09: Cleaning up the neck and head

A bit of housework is in order now. Select **neck1_jnt**, hit Ctrl+G, and call this group **head_jnt_grp**. Select **eyes_ctrl_offset**, hit Ctrl+G, and call this group **eyes_ctrl_grp**. Now

rename **torso_doNotTouch_grp** to **torso_rig_doNotTouch_grp**. Select both **torso_jnt_grp** and **head_jnt_grp**, hit Ctrl+G, and call this group **rig_jnt_grp**. Select **torso_ctrl_grp**, **eyes_ctrl_grp**, and **world_follow_loc_grp**, and hit Ctrl+G. Call this group **rig_ctrl_grp**. Then take **torso_rig_doNotTouch_grp**, hit Ctrl+G, and call this group **rig_doNotTouch_grp**.

If you collapse everything down now, you should have three top-level group nodes for the rig: **rig_jnt_grp**, **rig_ctrl_grp**, and **rig_doNotTouch_grp**. At this stage,

our rig should be a bit more organized but do make sure you test it out.

Now lock and hide some of the attributes on the controls. Select the eye controls and lock and hide the Scale attributes. Select both neck controls, the head control, ear controls and eyelid controls, and lock and hide the Translate and the Scale attributes. For the jaw control, just lock and hide the Scale attributes.

The last thing to do is to color-code the controls, which I'll leave in your artistic hands.

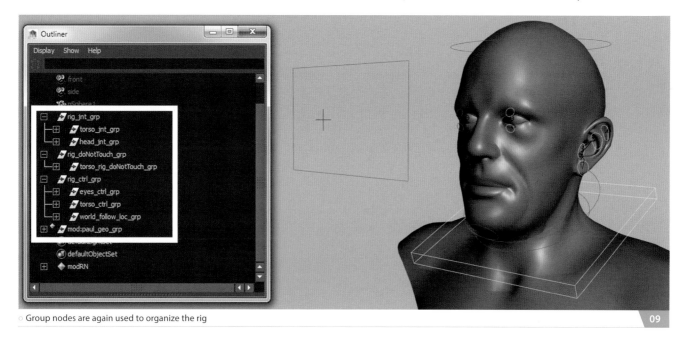

○ Group nodes are again used to organize the rig

09

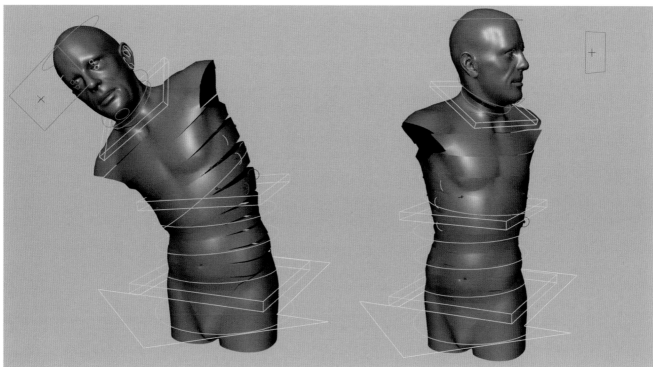

○ At this stage, check that the head follows the torso

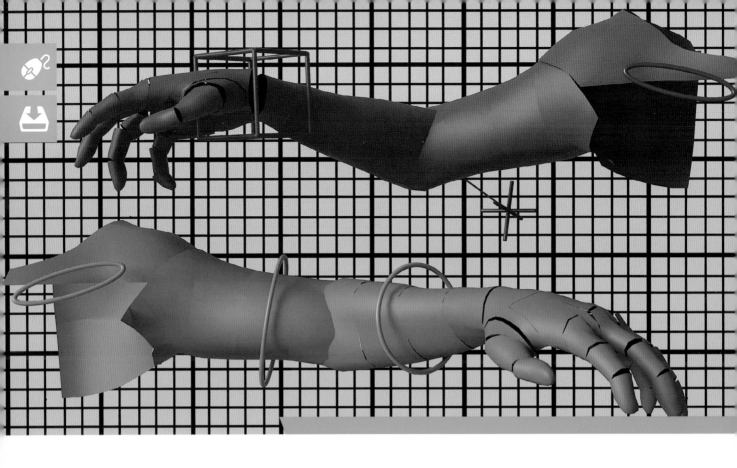

Rigging the arms

Rigging the arms and adding FK/IK blending

For the arms, we'll mimic the skeleton with digital equivalents of the clavicle, scapula, humerus, and radius/ulna. We'll cover FK/IK blending, giving the animator a choice of modes to work with, and introduce joints that will aid in deforming the forearm.

01: Creating the arm joints

Let's start off with the clavicle. In the front view, create a two-joint chain using the Joint tool. The first joint should originate close to the center line, below the neck (imagine how it attaches to the sternum), and the second joint should terminate at the acromion process. Switch to Perspective view and translate the root joint of our new chain out so that it sits close to the chest. Let's orient the joint so that Y points down the chain and we get the same orientation behavior as we have with our torso and head.

With the root joint selected, go to Skeleton > Joint Tool. Set Primary Axis to Y, Secondary Axis to Z, Secondary Axis World Orientation to X (+), and hit Apply (**Fig.01a**). Once you've done this, test out the joint rotations and double-check the placement of the joint in Perspective view. Don't forget to freeze the transformations so that the rotations get passed on to the Joint Orient. Rename the joints from root to tip, **l_clavicle_jnt** and **l_clavicle_end_jnt**.

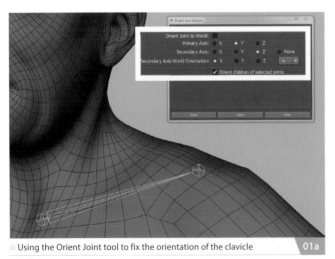

○ Using the Orient Joint tool to fix the orientation of the clavicle 01a

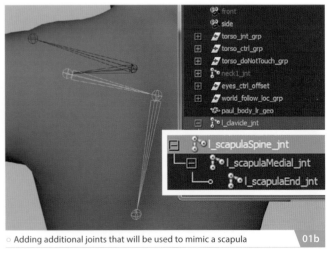

○ Adding additional joints that will be used to mimic a scapula 01b

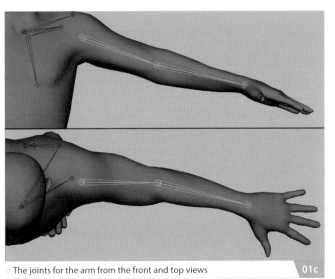

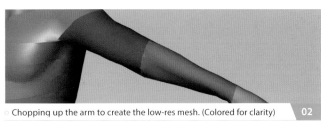

○ Chopping up the arm to create the low-res mesh. (Colored for clarity) `02`

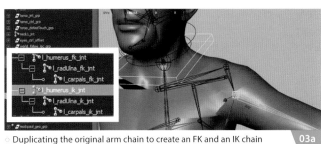

○ The joints for the arm from the front and top views `01c`

○ Duplicating the original arm chain to create an FK and an IK chain `03a`

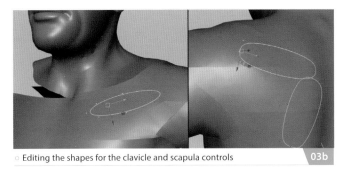

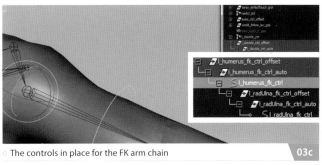

○ Editing the shapes for the clavicle and scapula controls `03b`

○ The controls in place for the FK arm chain `03c`

Now the scapula. In the back view, create a three-joint chain mimicking the spine of the scapula and medial border of the scapula as illustrated in **Fig.01b**.

Translate the joint chain into the correct position (easier to do in world mode) and go through the process of orienting joints and freezing transformations as we did for the clavicle. Rename the joints, from root to tip: **l_scapulaSpine_jnt**, **l_scapulaMedial_jnt**, and **l_scapula_end**. Then parent **l_scapulaSpine_jnt** under **l_clavicle_jnt**.

Now for the humerus, radius, and ulna. In the front view, use the Joint tool to create a three-joint chain: the first joint where the ball of the humerus would meet the scapula, the second joint around the elbow, and the end joint at the wrist. With the root joint of this chain selected, use the Orient Joint tool with the following settings: Primary Axis: Y, Secondary Axis: Y, Secondary Axis World Orientation: Z (+).

Check that these new joints rotate with the same behavior as the clavicle. Now, in the top and Perspective views, translate and rotate the

joints to fit better within the arm (**Fig.01c**). I add a slight bend to the joints so it's easier for the IK to figure out which way the chain should bend. Make sure you freeze the transformations.

I'd like to edit the orientation of the end joint of this chain so it's easier to attach the hand rig later on. Select the end joint and in the Orient Joint tool, enable Orient Joint to World and hit Apply. Now rename the joints from root to tip: **l_humerus_jnt**, **l_radUlna_jnt**, and **l_armEnd_jnt**. Parent **l_humerus_jnt** under **l_scapula_end_jnt**. (Note that in the video I call the end joint **l_carpals_jnt** but change it to **l_armEnd_jnt** later.)

02: The low-resolution arm mesh

Next we'll chop up the model (duplicate the original mid-resolution model first) and parent the parts to the arm joints. Rename the geometry using our established naming convention and delete the history from the chopped-up pieces.

03: Creating the FK arm controls

At the moment, we have one arm chain. This will be bound to the model (with additional

twist joints) and be driven either by an FK or IK joint chain. Let's create those extra joint chains now. Select **l_humerus_jnt** and duplicate the joint chain with Ctrl+D (**Fig.03a**). Open up the hierarchy for our new joint chain in the Outliner and you'll find the geometry has also been duplicated. Select those parts and delete them.

Rename all the joints to end with **_fk_jnt** rather than **_jnt** and also delete the 1 from the end of **l_humerus_fk_jnt1**. Select and duplicate **l_humerus_fk_jnt** and this time rename the joints to end with **_ik_jnt** rather than **_fk_jnt**. Again, delete the 1 from the end.

We'll now create the controls for the clavicle, scapula, and FK arm joint chain. Before we do, select both **l_humerus_jnt** and **l_humerus_ik_jnt** and hit Ctrl+H to hide them. Now select **l_clavicle_jnt**, **l_scapulaSpine_jnt**, and **l_scapulaMedial_jnt**, and load the createControls.py script. Make sure the final line is set to create orient constraints, then execute the script.

With the controls created, jump into component mode (F8) and reshape the controls so they're easier to identify and select (**Fig.03b**).

The next thing to do is to create the control hierarchy. Select **l_scapulaMedial_ctrk_offset** and parent it under **l_scapulaSpine_ctrl**. Parent **l_scapulaSpine_ctrl_offset** under **l_clavicle_ctrl**. Select **l_scapulaSpine_ctrl**, Shift-select **l_scapulaSpine_jnt** (or Ctrl-select in the Outliner), and go to Constrain > Point. We can now translate the scapula, allowing the animator more freedom over the rig. To do the same for the clavicle, select **l_clavicle_ctrl**, Shift-select **l_clavicle_jnt**, and go to Constrain > Point.

Let's turn to the joints for the FK arm now. Select both **l_humerus_fk_jnt** and **l_radUlna_fk_jnt** and execute the createControls.py script. Reshape the controls in component mode. The last thing to do is to create the control

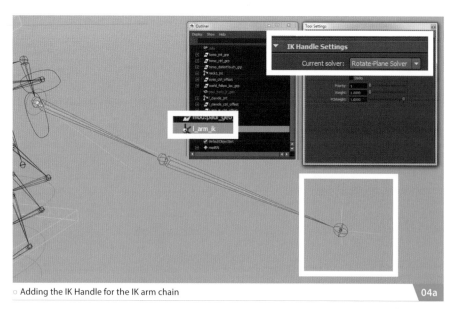

○ Adding the IK Handle for the IK arm chain   04a

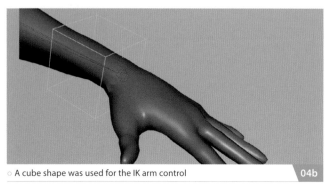

○ A cube shape was used for the IK arm control   04b

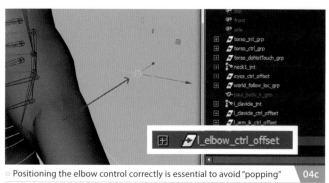

○ Positioning the elbow control correctly is essential to avoid "popping"   04c

hierarchy to get the correct behavior. Do this by parenting **l_radUlna_fk_ctrl_offset** under **l_humerus_fk_ctrl**, and parenting **l_humerus_fk_ctrl_offset** under **l_clavicle_ctrl**. Test out the controls of the entire arm to make sure they are working as expected (**Fig.03c**).

04: Create the IK controls

Now for the IK controls. Select **l_humerus_fk_ctrl** and hit Ctrl+H to hide the current controls. Hide **l_humerus_jnt** and **l_humerus_fk_jnt** and unhide (Shift+H) **l_humerus_ik_jnt**. I find this easier to do in the Outliner than in the viewport.

Now we need to add the IK handle. Go to Skeleton > IK Handle Tool (Options) and set Current solver to Rotate-Plane Solver (**Fig.04a**). This allows us to use an additional control to aim the joint in the middle between the root and the tip of the chain (in this case, the elbow joint).

In this order, click on **l_humerus_ik_jnt** (root of arm) and **l_armEnd_ik_jnt** (end of arm). You should now have an IK handle that you can grab to manipulate the arm. This IK handle is in world space, so make sure you undo it

back to its creation position after playing with it. Rename the IK handle **l_arm_ik**.

To create the control for **l_arm_ik**, go to Comet > Shapes > cube (**Fig.04b**). Rename the cube **l_arm_ik_ctrl** and hit Ctrl+G twice. Rename the top group node **l_arm_ik_ctrl_offset** and the next group node **l_arm_ik_auto**. The IK handle is in world space with no rotations applied to it, so can simply point-snap into place. Select **l_arm_ik_ctrl_offset**, hold down

the V key, and drag it onto the IK handle. In component mode, reshape the cube to better fit around the wrist, and parent **l_arm_ik** and under **l_arm_ik_ctrl**. You can now drive the IK arm with the new control and return it to its default position by zeroing out the translation values.

For the elbow, I'd like a control resembling a locator. We could create a new control, but let's duplicate and rename an existing one.

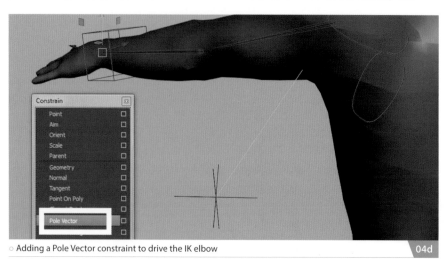

○ Adding a Pole Vector constraint to drive the IK elbow   04d

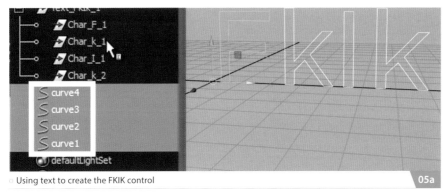

○ Using text to create the FKIK control **05a**

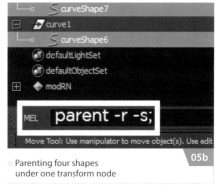

○ Parenting four shapes under one transform node **05b**

Select **l_eyeball_ctrl_offset** and hit Ctrl+D, then Shift+P to bring it out from its current hierarchy. Zero out the translation values to center it to the world center. Go to Modify > Search and Replace, type **l_eyeball** in the "Search for" field and type **l_elbow** in the "Replace with" field. Hit Replace to rename the control, then delete the 1 hanging on the end of **l_elbow_ctrl_offset**.

Positioning the elbow control will be tricky as the arm has a slight bend to it. The control must be placed correctly or you can get a slight popping in the joints, which is never a good thing (**Fig.04c**). To place it, select in this order: **l_humerus_ik_jnt**, **l_radUlna_ik_jnt**, and **l_armEnd_ik_jnt**. In the Outliner, Ctrl-select **l_elbow_ctrl_offset** and go to Constrain > Point (Options). Ensure Maintain Offset is disabled and hit Apply. The control should now be sitting in the middle of the arm chain. Select **l_radUlna_ik_jnt**, Ctrl-select **l_elbow_ctrl_offset** and go to Constrain > Aim (Options). Reset the settings and hit Apply. The control is now positioned correctly and we can delete the two constraint nodes under **l_elbow_ctrl_offset**.

Set the Move tool to object mode, select **l_elbow_ctrl_offset**, and move it out along its X-axis to a suitable position. Select **l_elbow_ctrl**, Shift-select **l_arm_ik**, and go to Constrain > Pole Vector (**Fig.04d**; by using a pole vector constraint, we can manipulate the pole vector of the IK solver without causing any flipping of the joint chain – this will also allow us to control the pole vector to position, which in this case is the elbow). Hopefully there's no movement in the joints, and you should be good to go.

05: Creating the FK/IK switch

We want to create a control allowing the animator to switch between the FK and IK controls. Go to Create > Text and in the Text field type **Fklk** and pick any font (**Fig.05a**).

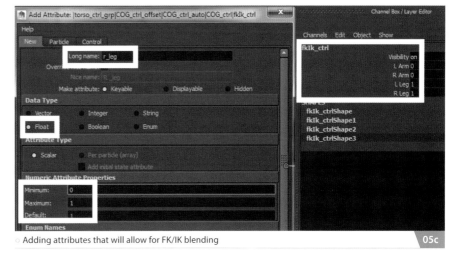

○ Adding attributes that will allow for FK/IK blending **05c**

Don't worry about the size as we'll be scaling the control to make it more easily selectable. Hit Apply and you should now have four curves at the world center.

At the moment, we can select each letter independently. I want to be able to select any letter and have it pick the set as a whole. To do this, jump into the Outliner and open up the **Text_Fklk_1** group. Select all four curves within that group, hit Shift+P to bring them out, and then delete **Text_Fklk_1**.

Still in the Outliner, hold down the RMB and enable Show Shapes. Select **curveShape6**, **curveShape7**, and **curveShape8** (all shape nodes), then Ctrl-select **curve4** (the transform node) last. In the MEL command line, type: **parent –r –s;** (**Fig.05b**). Execute that command and all the shape nodes should jump under the single transform node. Delete the old transform nodes. Selecting any one of the letters now results in selecting the whole word. In component mode, reposition and scale the letters so they're easier to select.

With the letters reorganized, disable Show Shapes in the Outliner. Rename the curve

fklk_ctrl, center it, and then go to Modify > Freeze Transformations and Modify > Center Pivot. Then position the control somewhere behind the character (I pop it behind the hips). Now parent **fklk_ctrl** under **COG_ctrl** so it follows along with the rest of the rig. If you like, you can freeze the transformations for **fklk_ctrl** again, but it's not really necessary.

With the fklk_ctrl selected, now highlight all the Translate, Rotate, and Scale channels, hold down the RMB and Lock and Hide Selected. We'll now add some custom attributes so we can switch between FK and IK mode (**Fig.05c**). With the control still selected go to Modify > Add Attribute and create the following attributes with these settings:

Long name	Data Type	Min, Max, Default
l_arm	Float	0, 1, 0
r_arm	Float	0, 1, 0
l_leg	Float	0, 1, 1
r_leg	Float	0, 1, 1

For our control, 0 will indicate that we're in FK mode and 1 will indicate that we are in IK mode. So by default, the arms will be in FK mode (easier to swing the arms with) and the legs will be in IK mode (easier for interaction with the ground).

06: FK/IK blending

In order to drive the original arm chain with the FK or the IK joint chain, we'll be driving the weight values for orient constraints (**Fig.06a**). Open up the hierarchy in the Outliner so you can see all three arm chains. Select the following in this order: **l_humerus_fk_jnt**, **l_humerus_ik_jnt**, and **l_humerus_jnt**. Go to Constraint > Orient (Options). Reset the settings and hit Apply.

Select in this order: **l_radUlna_fk_jnt**, **l_radUlna_ik_jnt**, and **l_radUlna_jnt**, and again create an orient constraint. If you now translate the IK controls or rotate the FK controls, you should notice that the original joint chain follows both with equal weighting. Let's now use our custom attributes to define which arm chain (FK or IK) the arm should follow.

Make sure the controls are all back to their default positions and go to Animate > Set Driven Key > Set. Select the fkIk_ctrl and hit the Load Driver button in the SDK window (**Fig.06b**). Select the two orient constraint nodes (**l_humerus_jnt_orientConstraint1** and **l_radUlna_jnt_orientConstraint1**) that we created (under **l_humerus_jnt** and **l_radUlna_jnt**) and hit Load Driven in the SDK window.

In the bottom-left window, select **l_humerus_jnt_orientConstraint1** and, in the Channel Box, set L Humerus Fk Jnt W0 to 1 and L Humerus Ik Jnt W1 to 0. Then select **l_radUlna_jnt_orientConstraint1** and, in the Channel Box, set L RadUlna Fk Jnt W0 to 1 and L RadUlna Ik Jnt W1 to 0. We have now enabled the FK joint chain to drive the arm and disabled the IK joint chain from doing so. Select **fkIk_ctrl** and make sure L Arm is set to 0 (FK mode).

Back in the SDK window, in the top-left box, highlight **fkIk_ctrl** (the driver object) and in the top-right box, highlight L Arm (the driving attribute). In the bottom-left box, highlight **l_humerus_jnt_orientConstraint1** (the driven object) and in the bottom-right box, highlight both L Humerus Fk Jnt W0 and L Humerus Ik Jnt W1. Hit Key on the SDK window and then do the same to **l_radUlna_jnt_orientConstraint1** too (**Fig.06c**).

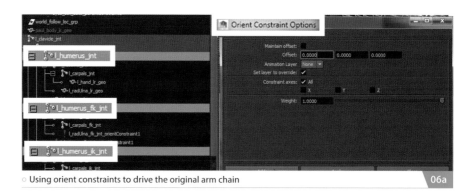

○ Using orient constraints to drive the original arm chain   06a

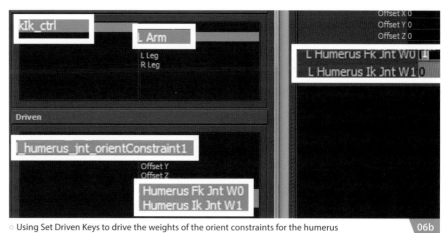

○ Using Set Driven Keys to drive the weights of the orient constraints for the humerus   06b

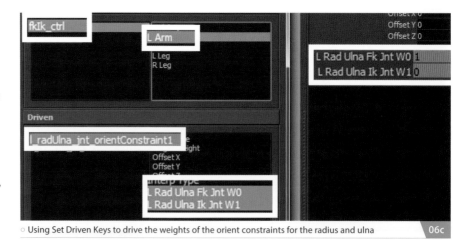

○ Using Set Driven Keys to drive the weights of the orient constraints for the radius and ulna   06c

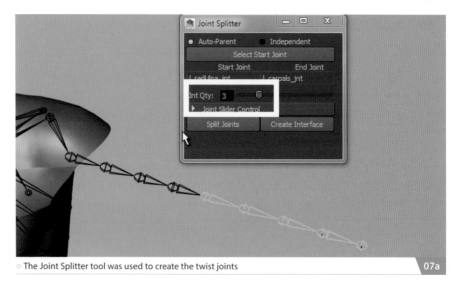

○ The Joint Splitter tool was used to create the twist joints   07a

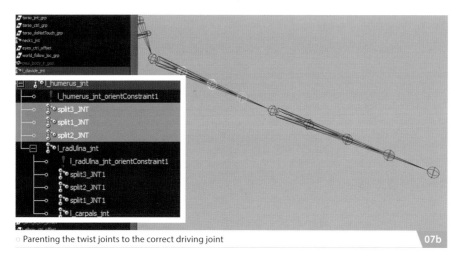

○ Parenting the twist joints to the correct driving joint　07b

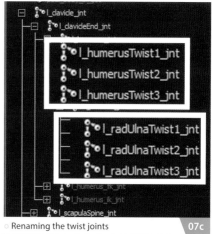

○ Renaming the twist joints　07c

Now we need to reverse the settings. Select **fklk_ctrl** and set the L Arm to 1. Then reverse the weight values for the **l_humerus_jnt_orientConstraint1** node and hit Key once more in the SDK window. Do the same for the **l_radUlna_jnt_orientConstraint1** node and then test out the arm. You should be able to drive the main arm with either the FK set of controls or the IK set.

07: Adding the twist joints

Start by unparenting the geometry that's currently attached to the arm joints. As we are adding additional twist joints, we will need to chop this geometry up further and add each new slice to the new twist joints.

Hide the geometry, the FK and the IK joint chains, and the FK and IK controls. Select **l_humerus_jnt** and bring up the Joint Splitter tool. Click Select Start Joint, set Jnt Qty to 3, and hit Split Joints. Following that, select **l_radUlna_jnt** and split the joint with the same settings.

We now have our twist joints but the constraint nodes that were associated with the original joints have also been duplicated. Under each new joint (not **l_humerus_jnt** and **l_radUlna_jnt**), go in and delete the duplicated constraint nodes.

Now a bit of reorganizing of our arm chain is in order. Start by selecting **l_radUlna_jnt** and hit Shift+P to unparent it. Then select **split1_JNT**, **split2_JNT**, and **split3_JNT**, and parent them all under **l_humerus_jnt**.

Now take **l_radUlna_jnt** and parent it back under **l_humerus_jnt**. Next, let's do the same for the forearm. Select **split1_JNT1**,

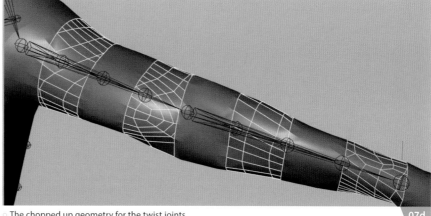

○ The chopped up geometry for the twist joints　07d

split2_JNT1, **split3_JNT1**, and **l_armEnd_jnt** and parent them all under **l_radUlna_jnt**. It's time now for some renaming. Using the cometRename tool, rename the twist joints of the humerus: **l_humerusTwist1_fk_jnt**, **l_humerusTwist2_fk_jnt**, and **l_humerusTwist3_fk_jnt**. Then rename the twist joints for the radius/ulna like so: **l_radUlnaTwist1_jnt**,

l_radUlnaTwist2_jnt, and **l_radUlnaTwist3_jnt**. We'll leave the twist joints here for now. Later on, once we've rigged the hand, we'll drive the radius/ulna twist joints using the palm control.

Finally, chop up the arm geometry so each slice can be parented under one of the new twist joints. Once done, test out the rig thoroughly.

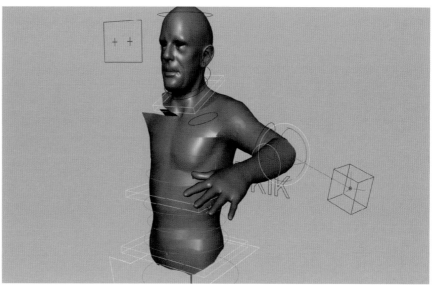

○ The final arm rig, currently in FK mode

189

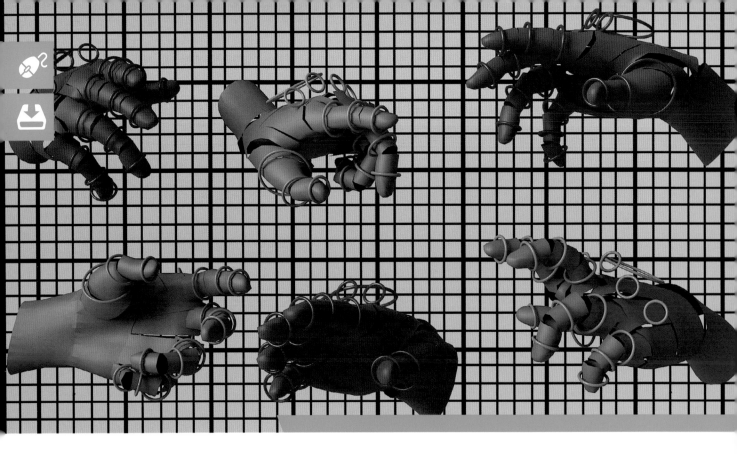

Rigging the hands

Tidying up the arm and moving on to the hands

In this chapter we are going to create the joints and controls for the hands. If body language can speak louder than words, it's imperative that an animator is given a hand rig that offers a great deal of flexibility as well as efficiency.

For this reason, we'll be adding a control which allows the animator to pose the whole hand, while also creating individual controls for each phalanx. With regard to the fingers, we are going to add the metacarpal bones to enable a credible fist to be formed. Before we start though, we'll first clean up the arm rig...

01: Cleaning up the arm rig

Before we dive in to the hand, I just want to do a little housework and add the ability to twist the IK arm from the **l_arm_ik** control. At the moment we can twist the arm using **l_elbow_ctrl**, but this twist will just give the animator another option.

Start by selecting **l_arm_ik_ctrl** and go to Modify > Add Attribute. Give it a Long name of

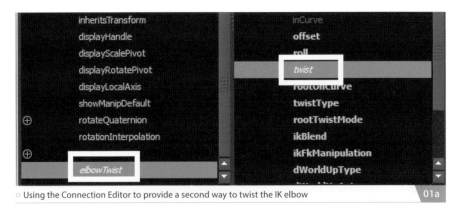

○ Using the Connection Editor to provide a second way to twist the IK elbow   01a

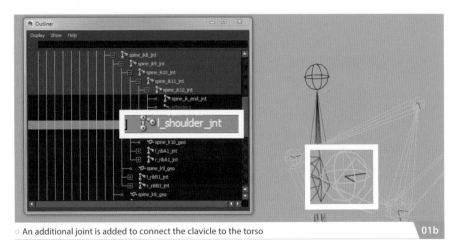

○ An additional joint is added to connect the clavicle to the torso   01b

elbowTwist, set the Data Type as Float, and then leave the Minimum and Maximum fields empty and Default at 0. Now go to Window > General Editors > Connection Editor (CE). The CE allows you to make one-to-one connections, which is precisely what we'd like to do in this instance. Select **l_arm_ik_ctrl** and on the CE window, hit Reload Left. This will be the driver object. Now select **l_arm_ik** and hit Reload Right on the CE window. This will be the driven object.

In the left-hand side of the CE window, you will see the Outputs for **l_arm_ik_ctrl**. Navigate to and select elbowTwist from the list (**Fig.01a**). On the right-hand side of the CE window, you'll see the inputs of **l_arm_ik**. This time, navigate to and select twist. You should now be able to twist the IK arm either using the elbowTwist attribute or through **l_elbow_ctrl**.

Let's turn to the house-keeping now. First, I'd like to attach the clavicle joint to the spine. To do this, we'll add an additional joint that acts as a bridge between the upper limb and the torso (**Fig.01b**). We can also use this joint

for skinning purposes later on. In the front view, use the Joint tool to create a single joint, then point-snap it to **spine12_ik_jnt** and translate it slightly to the (screen)-right of the spine. Rename this joint **l_shoulder_jnt** and increase the radius of the joint in the Channel Box to make it more easily selectable.

Then take **l_clavicle_jnt** and parent it under **l_shoulder_jnt**. Then parent **l_shoulder_jnt** under **spine12_ik_jnt**. Now take **l_clavicle_ctrl_ offset** and parent it under **spine_chest_ik_ctrl**.

Select **l_elbow_ctrl** and rename it **l_elbow_ ik_ctrl** to fit our naming convention. Do the same for the auto and offset node for that control. Then select **l_arm_ik_ctrl_offset** and **l_elbow_ik_ctrl_offset**, and hit Ctrl+G. Rename this new group **l_arm_ik_ctrl_grp**. You'll now have an empty group in the Outliner called **l_arm_jnt_grp**, so select and delete it.

Now select **neck1_jnt**, hit Ctrl+G, and rename that group **head_jnt_grp**. Take both **torso_jnt_grp** and **head_jnt_grp**, hit

Ctrl+G, and rename this group **rig_jnt_grp**. Take **eyes_ctrl_offset**, group it to itself, and rename that group **eyes_ctrl_grp**.

Now take **torso_ctrl_grp**, **eyes_ctrl_grp**, and **l_arm_ik_ctrl_grp**, and group them together. Call this new group **rig_ctrl_grp**. Lastly, take **torso_doNotTouch_grp** and **world_ follow_loc_grp**, and group them together. Rename this group **rig_doNotTouch_grp**.

After all the renaming and grouping madness, test that the rig still works correctly by rotating and translating the controls.

02: Create the finger joints

We'll start by creating the main joint that will drive the hand. For this joint, select **l_arm_end_ jnt** and hit Ctrl+D to duplicate it. Hit Shift+P to unparent the joint, then rename it **l_carpals_jnt**. Duplicate **l_carpals_jnt** and rename the new joint **l_carpals_end_jnt**. Then parent **l_carpals_end_jnt** under **l_carpals_jnt**. With **l_ carpals_end_jnt** still selected, use the Translate Y attribute to move it down the palm. To make

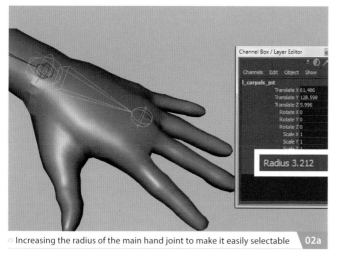

○ Increasing the radius of the main hand joint to make it easily selectable　02a

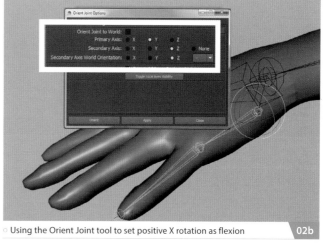

○ Using the Orient Joint tool to set positive X rotation as flexion　02b

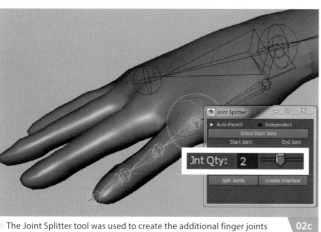

○ The Joint Splitter tool was used to create the additional finger joints　02c

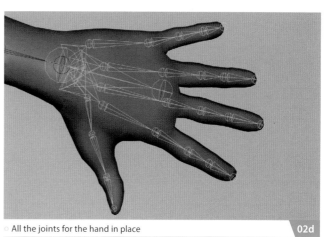

○ All the joints for the hand in place　02d

l_carpals_jnt more easily selectable, increase the Radius in the Channel Box (Fig.02a).

We'll go to the finger joints now and start with the little finger. Jump to the top view and use the Joint tool to create a three-joint chain. Pop the first joint at the base of where the metacarpal joint would lie, the second joint at root of the proximal phalanx (first knuckle), and then the third joint at the end of the finger. We'll be adding the additional joints in a while using the Joint Splitter tool. Switch to Perspective view now and translate the root joint up so that it sits within the body of the finger.

Using the Orient Joint tool, set the orientation so that positive X rotation equals flexion (Fig.02b). I used the following settings: Primary Axis: Y, Secondary Axis: Z, and Secondary Axis World Orientation: Z (-). Duplicate the root joint three times to create the additional finger joints, then position and rotate them to sit within the fingers.

Remember, you can translate the root joint on any axis, but for any child joints you should only use the Translate Y attribute (the length). You can rotate the joints, but do remember to freeze the transformations to send the rotation values to the Joint Orient.

As we'll be using the Joint Splitter tool to create the additional joints (Fig.02c), we need to make sure that the names of the joints do not clash, which they currently do. For now, go in and quickly add a "p" on the end of all the pinky finger joints, an "r" to the end of all the ring finger joints, an "m" for the middle finger joints, and an "i" on the end of all the index finger joints.

Now load the Joint Splitter tool, select the pinky joint that needs splitting, and set that as the Start Joint. Set Jnt Qty to 2 and hit Split Joints. Do the same for the rest of the fingers and then reposition the new joints and rotate them into place. Again, freeze the transformations when you are happy with the placement of the joints.

Back in the top view, create a four-joint chain for the thumb (we won't be using the Joint Splitter tool here). Select the root joint and open up the Orient Joint tool. Set Primary Axis to Y, Secondary Axis to Z, and Secondary Axis World Orientation to Z (-). Positive X rotation

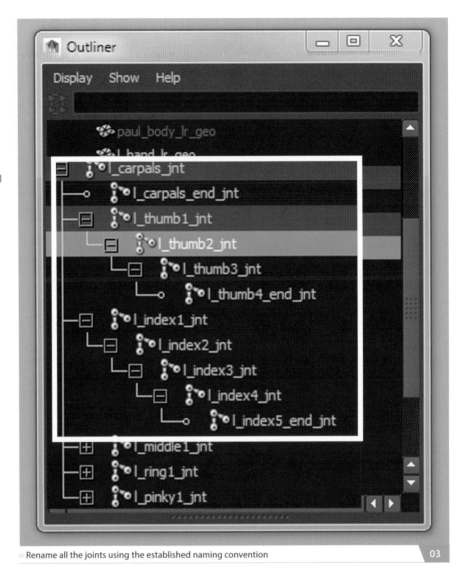

○ Rename all the joints using the established naming convention   03

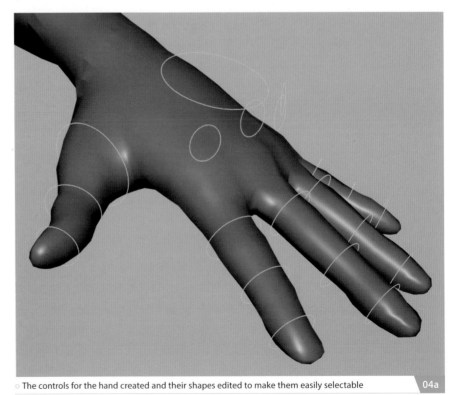

○ The controls for the hand created and their shapes edited to make them easily selectable   04a

should now curl the thumb in towards the pinky finger. Then select the root joint of the chain and translate and rotate it into the geometry of the thumb. Continue to rotate the rest of the finger joints so that when you rotate the joints they curl under the palm, rather than into it. At the risk of sounding like a broken record, remember to freeze the transformations for all the joints. Now take all the root joints for each finger and the thumb and parent them under **l_carpals_jnt**. Fig.02d shows all the joints for the hand in place.

03: Rename the joints

Time for some wholesome renaming. To speed things up, we'll again be using the cometRename tool. Load the tool and select all the joints of the pinky finger from root to tip. In cometRename's Rename field, type **l_pinky** and hit Rename And Number. Then type **_jnt** into the Suffix field and hit Add Suffix. Then select the end joint for the pinky (**l_pinky5_jnt**) and change **_fk** to **_end_fk**. Repeat the same process for the rest of the fingers, giving them the name of ring, middle, index, and thumb.

04: Create the controls

To create the controls for the fingers and palm, we'll be using the createControls.py script. Load the script into the Script Editor and update the following lines to read like so:

```
16  ctrl = cmds.circle( nr=(0, 1, 0),
    r=1.5, n=ctrlName)[0]

21  cmds.orientConstraint(ctrl, s, mo=0)
```

This will reduce the radius of the controls (feel free to experiment with the value) and orient constraint the joints to the controls. Now select all the finger joints (minus the end joints) and **l_carpals_jnt**, and execute the script. You should have all the controls created, each with its own auto and offset group node. Switch to component mode and edit the positions of the controls for ease of selection (Fig.04a).

Next we'll tackle the hierarchy for our hand controls so they mimic the FK setup of the joints, starting with the pinky (Fig.04b). Select **l_pinky4_ctrl_offset** and parent it under **l_pinky3_ctrl**. Parent **l_pinky3_ctrl_offset** and under **l_pinky2_ctrl**. Parent **l_pinky2_ctrl_offset** under **l_pinky1_ctrl**. Parent **l_pinky1_ctrl_offset** under **l_carpals_ctrl**.

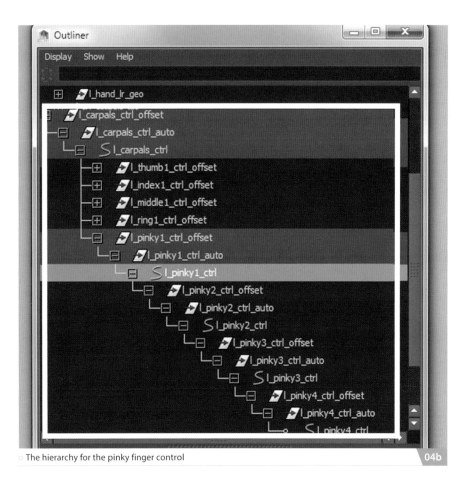

○ The hierarchy for the pinky finger control   04b

This is the same process to follow for all the fingers, so I'll let you take care of them now.

With the hierarchy in place, the controls now orient the joints correctly. Unfortunately, if we translate **l_carpals_ctrl**, the joints do not follow. To fix this, simply select **l_carpals_ctrl**, shift-select **l_carpals_jnt**, and go to Constrain > Point.

With the joints and the controls in place, we can chop up the geometry (Fig.04c – note that I've only colored the geometry for clarity here) and parent the slices to each joint. Rather than use the Cut Faces Tool here, I decided to grab a selection of faces and simply extract them, working my way from the tip of the finger towards the root.

05: Create the main fingers control

We are now going to create a control that will allow the animator to quickly pose the hand. In the top view, go to Create > CV Curve Tool (Options) and set the Curve degree to 1 Linear. Then, using that tool, draw a curve that goes around the body of the hand (excluding the fingers).

Next you need to snap the last CV to the first CV in order to close the curve. To do this, you can hold down the C key to activate Snap to curve. Then, using the CV Curve tool again, draw a curve for each finger as well as for the thumb. Once you have created all of the curves, you should have six curves in total and together they should mimic a very simplified hand (see Fig.05a).

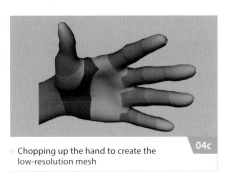

○ Chopping up the hand to create the low-resolution mesh   04c

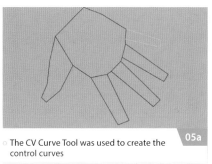

○ The CV Curve Tool was used to create the control curves   05a

Now rename the first curve (the body of the hand) **l_fingers_ctrl** and rename the remaining five curves as follows: **l_pinky_ctrl**, **l_ring_ctrl**, **l_middle_ctrl**, **l_index_ctrl**, and **l_thumb_ctrl** (Fig.05b). With all the curves renamed, select all the new finger curves and parent them under **l_fingers_ctrl**. With all the curves selected, go to Modify > Center Pivot.

Position **l_fingers_ctrl** close to the hand and scale it so that it's easily selectable. I've rotated the control by around 45° so it's easier to grab in the front or side view. For the control to follow our existing hand rig, parent **l_fingers_ctrl** under **l_carpals_ctrl**, then select all our new curves and go to Modify > Freeze Transformations.

Next we'll be adding some custom attributes to drive the hand, and have no need for the transform attributes that each curve currently has. Select all our new finger curves and highlight all the Translate, Rotate, and Scale attributes in the Channel Box. Hold down the RMB and Lock and Hide Selected.

06: Add the finger attributes

Now let's add custom attributes to our new controls. Select all the new control curves, go to Modify > Add Attribute and add the following:

Long name	Data type	Min, Max, Default
Curl	Float	-10, 10, 0
Scrunch	Float	-10, 10, 0
Spread	Float	-10, 10, 0

Select just **l_fingers_ctrl** and add this attribute:

Long name	Data type	Min, Max, Default
Relax	Float	-10, 10, 0

Select all the fingers' controls and add these attributes:

Long name	Data type	Min, Max, Default
metacarpal	Float	-10, 10, 0
Proximal	Float	-10, 10, 0
Medial	Float	-10, 10, 0
Distal	Float	-10, 10, 0

Select the thumb control and the add the following:

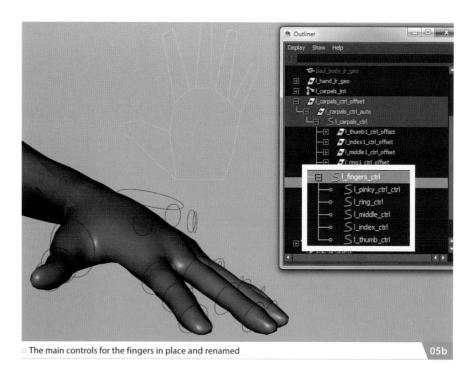

○ The main controls for the fingers in place and renamed   05b

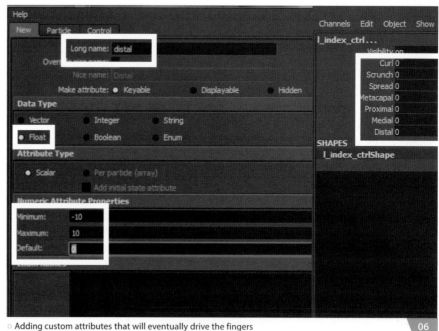

○ Adding custom attributes that will eventually drive the fingers   06

Long name	Data type	Min, Max, Default
metacarpal	Float	-10, 10, 0
Proximal	Float	-10, 10, 0
Distal	Float	-10, 10, 0

07: Finger curl with SDKs

We'll now drive the curling of the fingers using our custom control through Set Driven Keys (SDKs). As we do this, it's very important that we apply the SDKs to the **_auto** node of all our controls. This will allow us to be able to animate on top of the SDKs using the control curves around the fingers.

Open up the SDK window by going to Animate > Set Driven Key > Set. Select **l_fingers_ctrl** and click on the Load Driver button on the SDK window. Then select all the _auto nodes for the finger controls and click Load Driven (Fig.07a). Rather than finding and selecting the **_auto** nodes in the Outliner, select all the finger controls in the viewport and hit the up arrow on the keyboard. This should select all the **_auto** nodes by "pickwalking" up the hierarchy.

With all the objects in the SDK window, let's set up the finger curl (Fig.07b). First we need to key the default pose. In the SDK window,

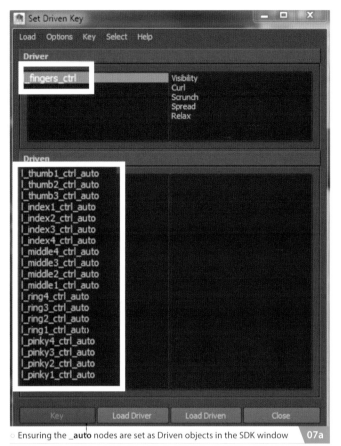

○ Ensuring the **_auto** nodes are set as Driven objects in the SDK window   **07a**

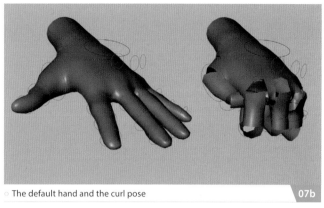

○ The default hand and the curl pose   **07b**

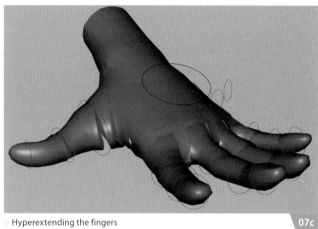

○ Hyperextending the fingers   **07c**

highlight **l_fingers_ctrl** from the top-left box, Curl from the top-right box, all the **_auto** nodes from the bottom-left box, and Rotate X from the bottom-right box. With everything at 0, hit Key on the SDK window. Then up the Curl attribute to 10 on **l_fingers_ctrl**. Using the **_auto** nodes, create a fist with the hand. Remember to only use the Rotate X attribute. I also add some rotation to the metacarpal controls, especially the pinky control, to create a nice arc from the knuckles. Once you're happy with the pose, hit Key on the SDK window.

If you go from 0–10 with the Curl attributes on **l_finger_ctrl**, you should be able to create a fist. Set the Curl attribute to -10 and then hyperextend the fingers as illustrated in **Fig.07c**. In this instance, I do not add any rotation to the metacarpal joints. Again, make sure you only use the Rotate X attribute. When ready, hit Key on the SDK window. Ensure that you test out the results before moving on.

08: The scrunch, spread, and relax poses

Let's create the scrunch pose next. If you are wondering what the scrunch pose should look like, imagine how you would pose your

hand to scrape your fingernails against a blackboard. Back in the SDK window, make sure that **l_fingers_ctrl** is still set as the Driver. Bring in all the **_auto** nodes for the finger controls but leave out the metacarpal controls. Make sure everything is at 0, highlight Scrunch in the top-right box, Rotate X in the bottom-right box, and hit Key to set the default pose. Then up the value of Scrunch to 10 and create a scrunch pose as illustrated in **Fig.08a**.

When you are happy with the pose, hit Key on the SDK window once more. Then take the Scrunch attribute down to -10 and create a pose like that in **Fig.08b**. Clearly, this is not a very natural pose, but for very fast movements it can help to add fluidity. One you are happy with the pose, hit Key once more on the SDK window.

Using the same technique, do the same for the Spread and Relax attributes. For the spread pose, the Driven attribute should be set to Rotate Z. I only use the auto nodes for the metacarpal controls and the proximal controls to create these poses. Increasing the Spread attribute to 10 would bring the fingers together, and decreasing the value to -10 would spread the fingers apart (**Fig.08c**).

For the relax pose, all the **_auto** nodes for the fingers were used (excluding the thumb). Rotate X was again used as the Driven attribute. In this case, upping the Relax attribute to 10 would relax the fingers, with the pinky being

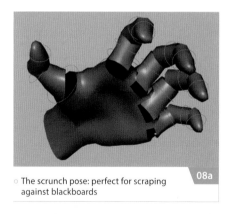

○ The scrunch pose: perfect for scraping against blackboards   **08a**

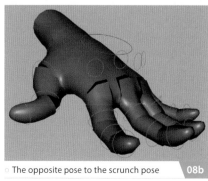

○ The opposite pose to the scrunch pose   **08b**

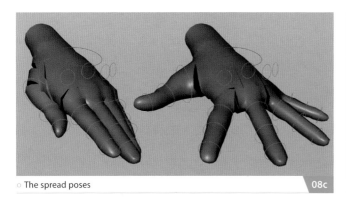

○ The spread poses
08c

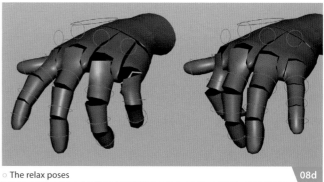

○ The relax poses
08d

the most relaxed and the index the least, and then -10 would make the index finger the most relaxed and the pinky the least (**Fig.08d**).

09: Copying the SDKs

So far, we can pose the hand as a whole. I'd now like to extrapolate the SDKs for the entire hand and pop them onto each individual finger. We could do this manually, like for the current SDKs, which would be a little slow and tiresome, or we could grab a script from the internet to speed up the process. Another way to handle this is to copy the animation curves from one attribute to another. This will be the route we take now.

First I'll give you a working example that you can use for the rest of the controls. In this example, we'll copy the SDKs from the Curl attribute of **l_fingers_ctrl** and paste them to the Curl attribute of **l_index_ctrl**. Open up the SDK window and set **l_index_ctrl** as the Driver object. Then select **l_index1_ctrl_auto**, **l_index2_ctrl_auto**, **l_index3_ctrl_auto**, and **l_index4_ctrl_auto**, and load them in as the Driven objects. Highlight Curl in the top-right box, all four **_auto** nodes in the bottom-left box, and Rotate X in the bottom-right window (**Fig.09a**). Then hit Key to set the initial pose.

Now with **l_index1_ctrl_auto, l_indexB2ctrl_ auto, l_index3_ctrl_auto, l_index4_ctrl_auto selected**, pop into the Graph Editor (Window > Animation Editors). Here you should see all the animation data for the SDKs you created in the previous steps. On the left-hand side are the attributes driving the motion. Take a look under **l_index1_ctrl_auto** and you'll see three different attributes are driving Rotate X: **l_fingers_ctrl.Curl, l_fingers_ctrl.Relax**, and the attribute we just added, **l_index_ctrl.Curl**.

What we want to do now is copy the animation data from **l_fingers_ctrl.Curl**

to **l_index_ctrl.Curl**. Before we do that, we need to edit a few settings. So in the Graph Editor window, go to Edit > Paste (Options). Set Time range to Clipboard, Paste method to Replace, Replace region to Entire curve, and then disable Connect (**Fig.09b**).

Now, highlight **l_fingers_ctrl.Curl** and select the animation curve. Hit Ctrl+C on the keyboard in order to copy it. Then highlight **l_index_ctrl.Curl** and hit Ctrl+V to paste the animation curve on to this attribute. If you use the Curl attribute now on **l_index_ctrl**, you should see that it is also creating the same motion as **l_fingers_ctrl.Curl**.

Next, all we need to do is copy and paste the animation for the rest of the controls. It

may seem like a long-winded process, but you should be able to get through it quickly once you've done it a few times (**Fig.09c**).

By copying the animation data, we ensure that regardless of whether the animator uses **l_fingers_ctrl** or each individual finger, he or she will always hit the same final pose when it's maxed out. This indicates that we've been successful in adding consistency to the rig.

Once complete, you should now have three levels of controls. You can use **l_fingers_ ctrl** to drive all the fingers at once; the individual finger controls allow you to make broad changes to each finger; the control curves around each phalange allow you to add minute changes to the fingers.

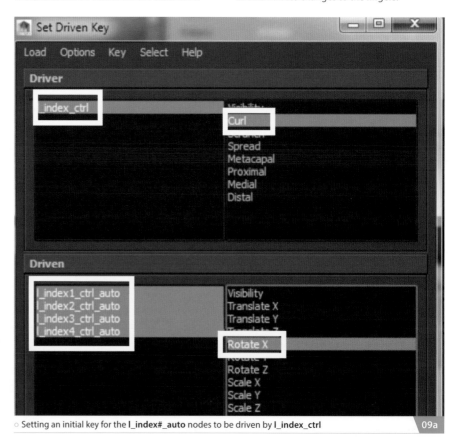

○ Setting an initial key for the **l_index#_auto** nodes to be driven by **l_index_ctrl**
09a

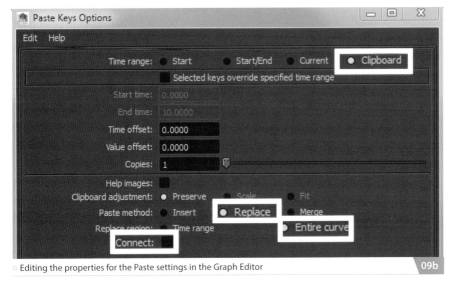

Editing the properties for the Paste settings in the Graph Editor `09b`

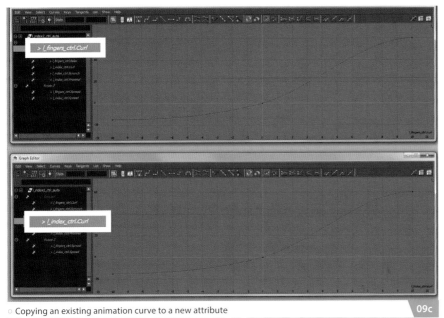

Copying an existing animation curve to a new attribute `09c`

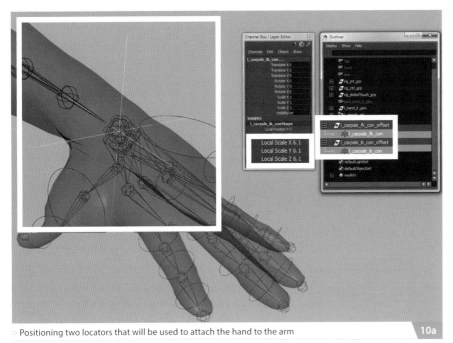

Positioning two locators that will be used to attach the hand to the arm `10a`

10: Connecting the hand to the arm

With the main strokes of our hand rig in place, it's time to attach it to the arm. Unfortunately, we can't simply parent **l_carpals_jnt** and constrain **l_carpals_ctrl** to **l_arm_end_jnt**. Doing this would yield good results when in FK mode, but in IK mode the orientation of the hand wouldn't stay in a locked-off position as you would want. This would result in the animator having to counter-animate, which is never a good thing. To get this working correctly, we'll need some locators and some constraints.

Create a locator and call it **l_carpals_fk_con**. With the locator selected, hit Ctrl+G and call that new group **l_carpals_fk_con_offset**. Take the **_offset** node now and duplicate it (Ctrl+D) and change the name to **l_carpals_ik_con_offset** (Fig.10a). Also change the name of the locator living under that group node to **l_carpals_ik_con**. Select both **_offset** nodes and parent them under **l_carpals_ctrl**. Zero out the translation and rotation values so they pop into place, and then unparent them. To make the locators more easily selectable, select them and increase the Local Scales X, Y, and Z in the Channel Box (you'll find this setting under SHAPES).

In this order, select **l_carpals_fk_con**, **l_carpals_ik_con**, and **l_carpals_ctrl_offset**, and go to Constrain > Parent. Then select **l_arm_end__fk_jnt** and **l_carpals_fk_con_offset**, in that order, and go to Constrain > Point and then Constrain > Orient (Fig.10b).

Let's go on to the IK side of things now. In this order, select **l_arm_end_ik_jnt** and **l_carpals_ik_con_offset**, and go to Constrain > Point. The hand should now follow both the FK and the IK arm. We now want to use a Set Driven Key to control which arm chain it should follow.

Open up the SDK window by going to Animate > Set Driven Key > Set, and with **fklk_ctrl** selected, hit Load Driver. Then select the **parentConstraint** node that lives under **l_carpals_ctrl_offset** and hit Load Driven. Set L Arm attribute to 0 (FK mode) on **fklk_ctrl** and, on the **parentConstraint** node, set L Carpals Fk Con W0 to 1 and L Carpals Ik Con W1 to 0. Hit Key on the SDK window. Now set **fklk_ctrl** to 1 (IK mode) and, on the **parentConstraint** node,

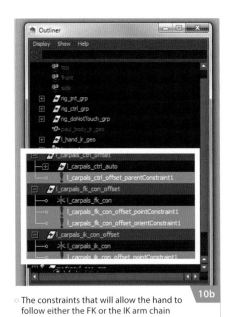

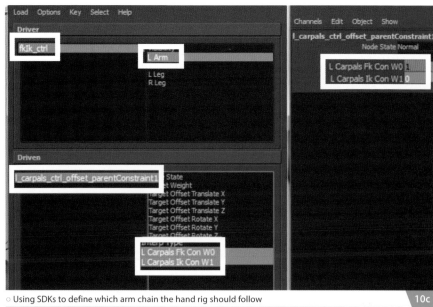

The constraints that will allow the hand to follow either the FK or the IK arm chain **10b**

Using SDKs to define which arm chain the hand rig should follow **10c**

set L Carpals Fk Con W0 to 0 and L Carpals Ik Con W1 to 1. Hit Key on the SDK window once more. The palm should now follow the arm correctly in both FK and IK modes (**Fig.10c**).

11: Adding the forearm twist
We are now going to drive the forearm twist through **l_carpals_ctrl** and by using an expression. To do this, open up the Expression Editor (Window > Animation Editor), and type the following into the Expression box:

l_radUlnaTwist1_jnt.rotateY = l_carpals_ctrl.rotateY *.25;
l_radUlnaTwist2_jnt.rotateY = l_carpals_ctrl.rotateY *.5;
l_radUlnaTwist3_jnt.rotateY = l_carpals1_ctrl.rotateY *.75;

Rename the expression to **l_radiusUlna_twist_expr**. If you are going through the video, you'll notice that I initially set this to be driven by **l_carpals_jnt**. I later found that this caused twisting issues and updated the script so that it was driven by the control instead.

12: Tidying up the rig
Now that the majority of the hand rig is set up, let's round off by tidying up the rig in the Outliner (**Fig.12a**). Start by selecting and deleting l_hand_geo_grp. Then select both **l_carpals_fk_con_offset** and **l_carpals_ik_con_offset**, group them together, and call that new group **l_carpals_con_grp**. Select **l_carpals_con_grp** and **l_carpals_ctrl_offset**, group them together and call that group **l_hand_ctrl_grp**.

Select **l_carpals_jnt**, group it to itself and call that group **l_hand_jnt_grp**. Select **l_hand_ctrl** and parent it under **rig_ctrl_grp**. Lastly, parent **l_hand_jnt_grp** under **rig_jnt_grp**.

With the parenting madness now out of the way, let's now hide a couple of things in order to make them unselectable. Select both **l_carpals_fk_con** and **l_carpals_ik_con** and then hit Ctrl+H to hide them. Later on, we'll also lock the visibility so they can't be revealed by Display > Show All.

The next thing to do is to add a little color to the controls so we can differentiate between the left-hand side controls and the torso controls (**Fig.12b**). Once we have the right-hand side controls, we will want to color them also. Using Drawing Overrides in the Attribute Editor, I make the left arm controls green, the FK torso controls orange, the IK torso controls blue, and the COG control yellow. I also like to color the right-hand controls red (right > red) so that during the animation process, it's easy for the animator to know which side of the character they're working with.

I then color-code the geometry to clearly differentiate between the right and left sides. I select the sliced parts of the right arm geometry (including the clavicle and scapula pieces), then hold down the RMB and go to Assign Favorite Material > Lambert. When the shader pops up in the Attribute Editor, I give it a pale green color and rename it **green_lambert**.

For the torso, I color the geometry pale blue; the neck and head are assigned a deeper blue lambert shader. Remember to rename all the shaders as you go.

13: Mirroring the joints over
Mirroring the joints over is a simple process. To do this, select l_shoulder_jnt and go to Skeleton > Mirror Joint (Options). Set Mirror across to YZ and Mirror function to Behavior. In the "Search for" field, type **l_**, and in the "Replace with" field, type **r_**. Then hit Mirror (**Fig.13a**).

In the Outliner, find the mirrored joints (it will also mirror over the FK and the IK arm chains) and delete all the constraint nodes it will have duplicated. The geometry for the arm

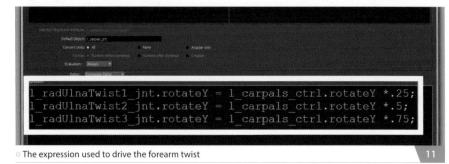

The expression used to drive the forearm twist **11**

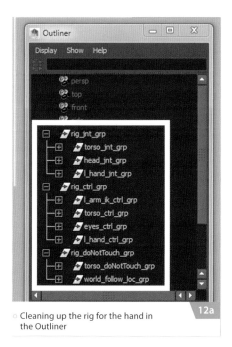

○ Cleaning up the rig for the hand in the Outliner **12a**

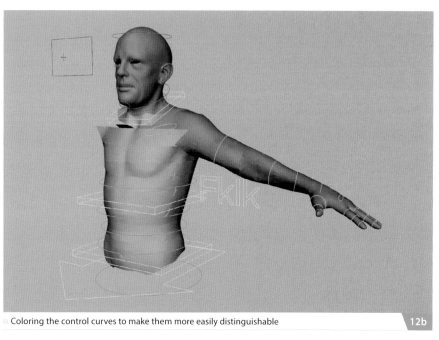

○ Coloring the control curves to make them more easily distinguishable **12b**

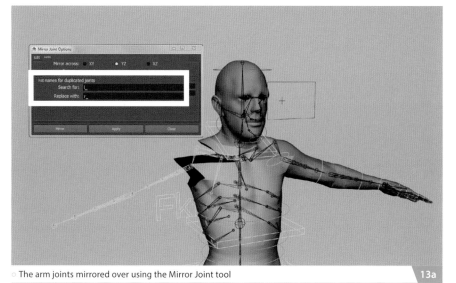

○ The arm joints mirrored over using the Mirror Joint tool **13a**

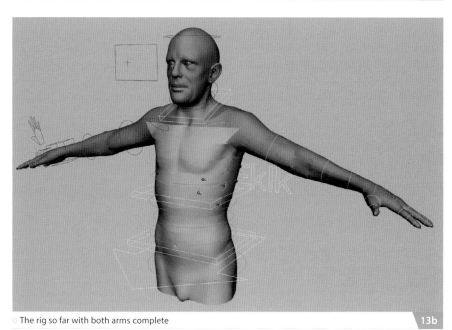

○ The rig so far with both arms complete **13b**

will have also been duplicated and may be randomly placed in your scene, so delete that too. Repeat the step for the joints of the hand.

Now select the geometry of the left arm, duplicate it by hitting Ctrl+D, and then unparent it from the hierarchy using Shift+P. Rename the slices by going to Modify > Search and Replace Names. Search for l_ and replace with **r_**, then hit Replace. Then get rid of the number 1 that exists on any of the ends of the geometry slices.

With all slices selected, hit Ctrl+G to group them together and then pop a -1 into the Scale X attribute of that group. This will flip the geometry over into the correct position. Select all the geometry for the right arm and hit Shift+P to bring them out of the group, then go to Modify > Freeze Transformations to invert the normal, and set Scale X back to 1.

The controls on the other hand are not something you can simply mirror over cleanly in Maya (without the aid of some scripts). For that reason, I tend to rebuild the controls of the right-hand side manually. However, I do copy and mirror the existing controls, drop them into a layer, and then set that layer mode to Reference. This gives me a guide for where to create the new controls.

I'll leave you to rebuild the right arm, and next we will tackle the legs (**Fig.13b**).

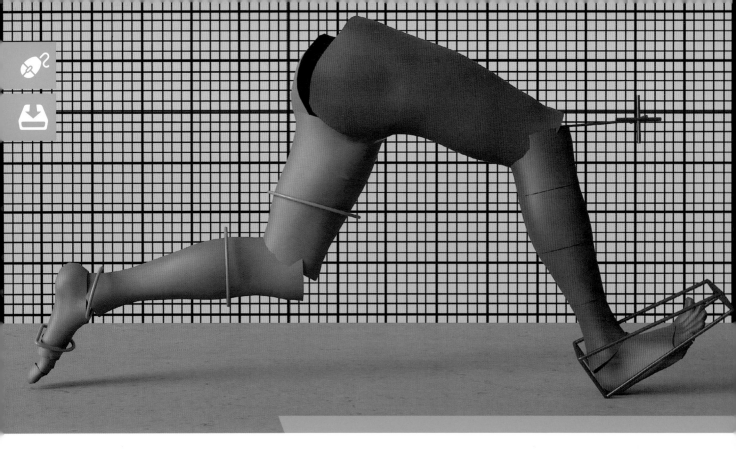

Rigging the legs

Adding joints and controls to the legs

We'll now move on to rigging the lower limb. We'll tackle the legs much in the same way as the arms. We'll create three joint chains, add twist joints, allow for FK/IK blending – the whole shebang.

Before we begin, though, spend a few minutes cleaning up your latest scene, unless you have done so already. I end up deleting a few stray empty group nodes that are hanging around, and also use Layers to partition the joints from the geometry.

01: Creating the leg joints

We'll be creating two main joint chains for the leg: one for the leg itself and one for the foot. This will allow us to create a clean twisting motion from the ankle with just one axis, similar to how we approached the torso.

Jump into the side view, go to Skeleton > Joint Tool, and create a three-joint chain. Place the first joint around the region where the great trochanter of the femur would sit, the next joint at the knee, and the third joint at the ankle.

Add a slight bend to the knee as this makes it easier for the IK to calculate how the leg should flex. Switch to the front view and line the root joint up with the crease that runs from the ASIS to the pubic symphysis (**Fig.01a**).

Select the root joint and go to Skeleton > Orient Joint (Options). Set Primary Axis to Y, Secondary Axis to Z, Secondary Axis World Orientation to Z (-), and hit Apply. Rotate the legs joints to check that the orientations have been set correctly. Rename the joints from root to tip as follows: **l_femur_jnt, l_tibiaFibula_jnt, and l_legEnd_jnt**.

Return to the side view, create a single joint, and name it **l_ankleTwist_jnt**. With this selected, hold the V key and snap its position to the end of the leg chain (**Fig.01b**).

Rotate the joint 180° on the X-axis so Y points downwards like our existing leg chain, then go to Modify > Freeze Transformations to zero out the rotation value. To make it easier to select this joint, increase its radius in the Channel Box. Lastly, we'll create the joints for the foot.

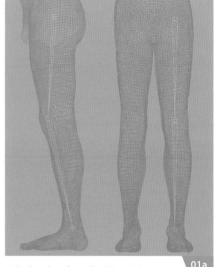

○ The leg chain from the side and the front view

01a

Activate the Joint tool once more, hold down the V key, and create a root joint at the same position as **l_ankleTwist_jnt**. Then create a second joint at the ball of the foot and, finally, add a joint at the end of the toes. I place the joint at the ball of the foot pretty close to the ground, as I find it means I get a more pleasing

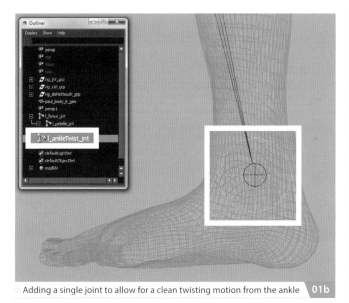

○ Adding a single joint to allow for a clean twisting motion from the ankle **01b**

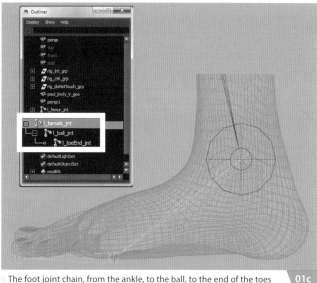

○ The foot joint chain, from the ankle, to the ball, to the end of the toes **01c**

result during deformation. I also hold down the Shift key when creating the final joint in the chain, as this will create a straight joint.

Going from root to tip, you need to rename the joints as follows: **l_tarsals_jnt**, **l_ball_jnt** and **l_toeEnd_jnt** (**Fig.01c**). With **l_tarsals_jnt** selected, go to Skeleton > Orient Joint Tool. The settings should be set from beforehand, so you can simply hit Apply.

Now parent **l_tarsals_jnt** under **l_ankleTwist_jnt**. Then select **l_ankleTwist_jnt** and rotate it on the Y-axis so it sits within the geometry of the foot better. When in place, freeze the transformations. Lastly, parent **l_ankleTwist_jnt** under **l_legEnd_jnt**.

02: The FK, the IK, and the twist joints

To create the FK joint chain, duplicate **l_femur_jnt** and then go to Modify > Search and Replace. Set "Search for" to **_jnt** and "Replace with" to **_fk_jnt**. Delete the 1 that will be present on the end of **l_femur_fk_jnt**. Repeat the same step to create the IK joint chain.

For now, select both the FK and the IK joint chains and hide them (Ctrl+H) so we can create the twist joints. Load up the trusty Joint Splitter tool once more, set **l_femur_jnt** as the Start Joint, set Jnt Qty to 3, and hit Split Joints. Select **l_patella_jnt** and split that joint with the same settings. Parent the twist joints of the upper leg to **l_femur_jnt** and the twist joints of the lower leg to **l_patella_jnt**, like we

did for the arm. Make sure that **l_legEnd_jnt** is parented back under **l_patella_jnt**.

With the twist joints parented correctly, rename the twist joints of the upper leg **l_femurTwist1_jnt**, **l_femurTwist2_jnt**, and **l_femurTwist3_jnt**. For the twist joints of the lower leg, rename them as follows: **l_patellaTwist1_jnt**, **l_**

patellaTwist2_jnt, and **l_patellaTwist3_jnt**. With all the joints created, create the low-resolution mesh and parent each relevant slice to the relevant joint, using the same techniques as for the torso, head, and arms.

Remember to delete the history from the slices and rename the geometry appropriately.

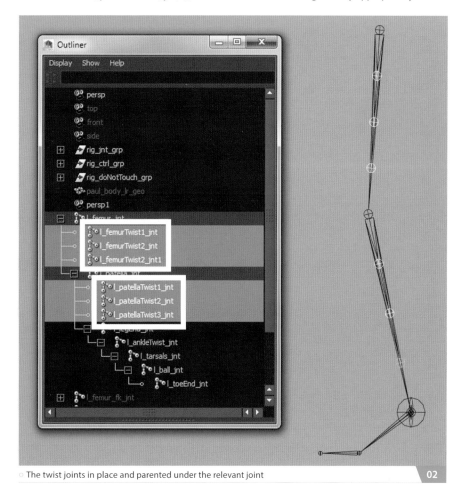

○ The twist joints in place and parented under the relevant joint **02**

"If something pops, then the joints are not aligned correctly and will need to be looked at. If nothing pops, we're good to go"

03: FK/IK blending

Let's now set things up so that our original joint chain will be driven by either the FK or the IK joint chain. Again, we'll do this using constraints and Set Driven Keys. Select, in this order, **l_femur_fk_jnt, l_femur_ik_jnt, l_femur_jnt**, then go to Constrain > Orient (Options). Set the Constrain axes to All and hit Apply. If something pops, then the joints are not aligned correctly and will need to be looked at. If nothing pops, we're good to go.

Select in this order: **l_patella_fk_jnt, l_patella_ik_jnt, l_patella_jnt**, and go to Constrain > Orient. In this order, select **l_ankleTwist_fk_jnt, l_ankleTwist_ik_jnt, l_ankleTwist_jnt**, and again apply the orient constraint. Lastly, select in this order: **l_ball_fk_jnt, l_ball_ik_jnt, l_ball_jnt**, and go to Constrain > Orient.

The original leg chain will now follow both the FK and IK joints with equal weighting (**Fig.03a**). Let's use SDKs to go between the two joint chains. In the Outliner, select the four **orientConstraint** nodes we just created (they're under **l_femur_jnt, l_patella_jnt, l_ankleTwist_jnt**, and **l_ball_jnt**) and go to Animate > Set Driven Key > Set. The constraint nodes should be placed into the Driven box.

Select **fkIk_ctrl** and hit Load Driver. Set the L Leg attribute to 0 (FK enabled) on **fkIk_ctrl**. Select the **l_femur_jnt_OrientConstraint1** node in the Driven box of the SDK window, and in the Channel Box set L Femur Fk Jnt W0 to 1 (FK enabled) and L Femur Ik Jnt W1 to 0 (IK disabled) (**Fig.03b**). Do the same for the remaining three constraint nodes so that all the Fk Jnt W0 attributes are set to 1 and the Ik Jnt W1 attributes are set to 0.

Back in the SDK window, highlight L Leg in the top-right box, highlight **l_femur_jnt_OrientConstraint1** in the bottom-left box and highlight both L Femur Fk Jnt W0 and L Femur Ik Jnt W1 in the bottom-right box. With everything highlighted, hit Key on the SDK window, and then do the same for the remaining three constraint nodes.

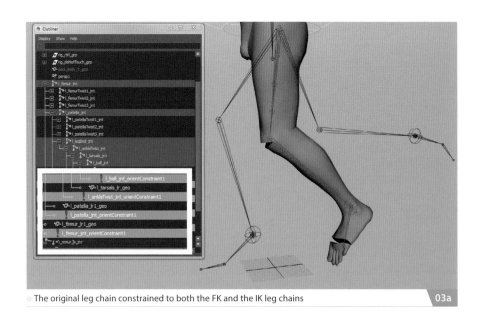
The original leg chain constrained to both the FK and the IK leg chains 03a

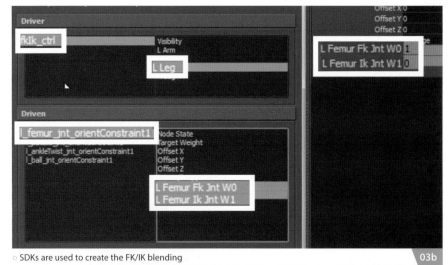
SDKs are used to create the FK/IK blending 03b

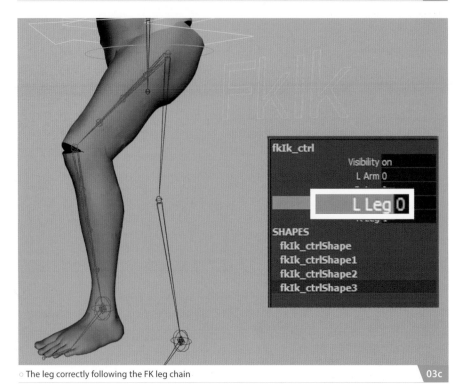
The leg correctly following the FK leg chain 03c

"Make sure you rotate the FK and IK joint chains to see if they're driving the leg correctly"

When you've set the first key for all the constraint nodes, simply set the L Leg attribute to 1 (IK enabled) on **fklk_ctrl**, set all the W0 to 0 (FK disabled) and the W1 to 1 (IK enabled) on all the constraint nodes. Hit Key once more.

Make sure you rotate the FK and IK joint chains to see if they're driving the leg correctly and that you can switch between the modes before moving on (**Fig.03c**).

04: Create the FK controls

We'll now create the controls for the FK leg. We won't need to work with the original leg chain and the IK leg chain, so select them both and hide them. Select **l_femur_fk_jnt**, **l_patella_fk_jnt**, **l_ankleTwist_fk_jnt**, and **l_ball_fk_jnt**. Open up the Script Editor and load the createControls.py script into a Python tab. Make sure the following lines read as below, and then execute the script:

```
16  ctrl = cmds.circle( nr=(0, 1,
        0), r=5, n=ctrlName)[0]

21  cmds.orientConstraint(ctrl, s, mo=0)
```

You can now switch to component mode and edit the shapes and position of the controls.

Next we need to create the FK control hierarchy. Parent **l_ball_fk_ctrl_offset** under **l_ankleTwist_fk_ctrl**. Then parent **l_ankleTwist_fk_ctrl_offset** under **l_patella_fk_ctrl**. Next parent **l_patella_fk_ctrl_offset** under **l_femur_fk_ctrl**. Lastly, parent **l_femur_fk_ctrl_offset** under **hip_fk_ctrl**.

05: Create the IK controls

Now hide the FK joint chain and unhide the IK joint chain by selecting it in the Outliner and hitting Shift+H. Let's now add the IK handle that will drive the IK leg.

Go to Skeleton > IK Handle Tool (Options) and set the Current solver to Rotate-Plane Solver. Then in the Outliner, click on **l_femur_ik_jnt**, hold down the Ctrl key, and LMB-click on **l_legEnd_ik_jnt**. Select the IK handle now and rename it **l_leg_ik** (**Fig.05a**).

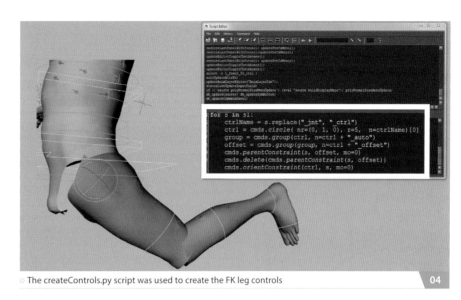

○ The createControls.py script was used to create the FK leg controls   **04**

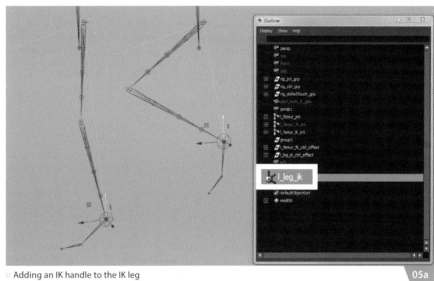

○ Adding an IK handle to the IK leg   **05a**

I'd like two controls for the IK leg: one for the knee; one for the ankle, much like the setup we have for the arm (**Fig.05b**). We could create two new controls for this but instead, I've selected both **l_arm_ik_ctrl_offset** and **l_elbow_ik_ctrl_offset** and hit Ctrl+D to duplicate them. I then used the Search and Replace tool to rename the hierarchy for **l_arm_ik_ctrl** to **l_leg_ik_ctrl**, and **l_elbow_ik_ctrl** to **l_knee_ik_ctrl**.

Next we need to position to controls into the correct place. Let's start with **l_leg_ik_ctrl**. Start

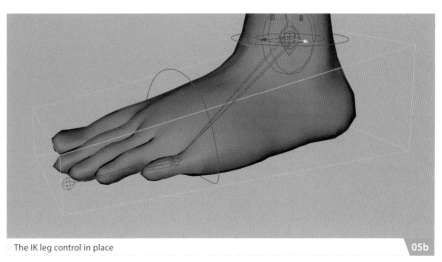

○ The IK leg control in place   **05b**

by selecting **l_leg_ik_ctrl_offset**, hold down the V key and snap it to the same position as **l_leg_ik**. You can now parent **l_leg_ik** under **l_leg_ik_ctrl**. Switch to component mode and then reshape the control around the foot.

"For the knee control, we will tackle it in the same way we did for the elbow"

For the knee control, we will tackle it in the same way we did for the elbow (**Fig.05c**). Select in this order: **l_femur_ik_jnt**, **l_patella_ik_jnt**, **l_legEnd_ik_jnt**, and then **l_knee_ctrl_offset**. Then go to Constrain > Point (Options). Make sure Maintain Offset is disabled and then hit Apply. Now select in this order: **l_patella_ik_jnt**, **l_knee_ik_ctrl_offset**, and go to Constrain > Aim.

Jump into the Outliner now and delete the two constraint nodes living under **l_knee_ik_ctrl_offset**. With the Move tool active, make sure you are in object mode and then translate the **l_knee_ik_ctrl_offset** nodes out in front of the character. Now select **l_knee_ik_ctrl**, Ctrl-select **l_leg_ik** in the Outliner, and go to Constrain > Pole Vector.

Let's now add the ability to twist the knee from **l_leg_ik_ctrl**. Select **l_leg_ik_ctrl** and in the Channel Box, go to Edit > Modify Attribute. Select elbowTwist in the Attributes box and set the new name to **kneeTwist**. With **l_leg_ik_ctrl** selected, go to Window > Connection Editor. This should load the control into the Outputs field.

Select **l_leg_ik** and hit Reload Right to drop it into the Inputs field. Highlight kneeTwist on the left-side column and twist on the right-hand column (**Fig.05d**).

06: A bit of a cleanup

We now want to connect the leg to the rest of the rig. Select all three leg chains: **l_femur_jnt**, **l_femur_fk_jnt**, **l_femur_ik_jnt**, and parent them under **hip_fk_jnt**. Then select **l_femur_fk_ctrl_offset** and parent it under **hip_fk_ctrl**.

Now what I want to do is add an expression that will twist the lower leg, much like the forearm twist. To do this, open up the Expression Editor and create the following expression as shown in **Fig.06**:

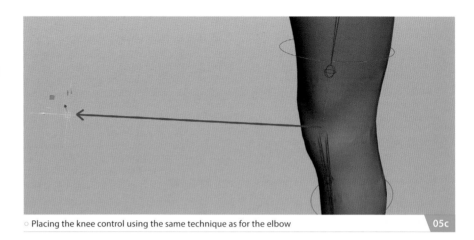

○ Placing the knee control using the same technique as for the elbow   05c

l_patellaTwist1_jnt.rotateY =
l_ankleTwist.rotateY *.15;
l_patellaTwist2_jnt.rotateY =
l_ankleTwist.rotateY *.35;
l_patellaTwist3_jnt.rotateY =
l_ankleTwist.rotateY *.55

Rename the expression **l_tibiaFibula_twist_expr**. In the next step we will be cleaning up and using annotations to create a visual aid to view which direction the knees are pointing.

07: Finishing up and using annotations

Let's clean up the Outliner now (**Fig.07a**). Select both **l_leg_ik_ctrl_offset** and **l_knee_ik_ctrl_offset**, hit Ctrl+G to group them together, and rename that group **l_leg_ik_ctrl**. Then parent **l_leg_ik_ctrl** under **rig_ctrl_grp**.

Now let's create a visual aid between the position of the knee and the knee control. There are many ways to do this but I find that

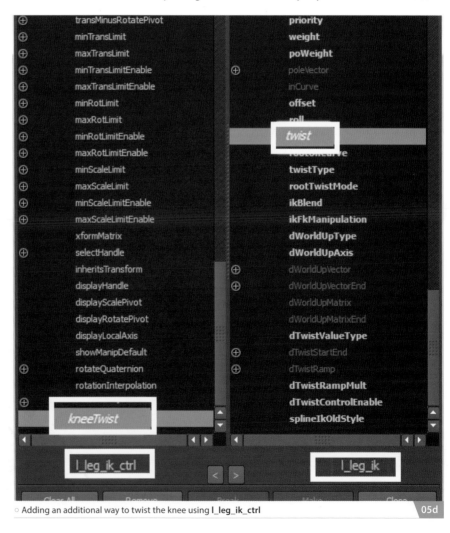

○ Adding an additional way to twist the knee using **l_leg_ik_ctrl**   05d

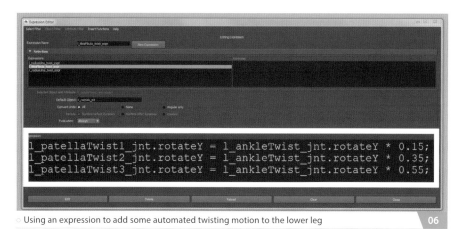

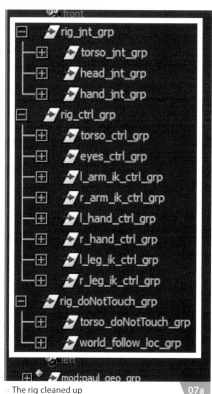

○ Using an expression to add some automated twisting motion to the lower leg **06**

using Annotations works well and is pretty easy to set up (**Fig.07b**). Select **l_knee_ik_ctrl**, go to Create > Annotation, and when the dialog box pops up, call it **l_knee_ctrl**. This will create a locator and an annotation node with a line created between the two.

Select **annotationLocator** from the Outliner and point snap it to **l_patella_ik_jnt**. Parent the annotation node under **l_knee_ik_ctrl** and zero out the Translate and Rotate values to snap it into the correct place. Now take **annotationLocator** and parent it under **l_patella_ik_jnt**. Select the annotation node and rename it **l_knee_annotation**.

In the Attribute Editor, I also decide to delete **l_knee_ctrl** from the Text field. I'll leave it up to you if you'd like to do the same or not. I just don't want it on display in the viewport.

Under the transform node for **l_knee_annotation**, set Display type to Template so it cannot be selected. If you now translate the knee control, the visual line will help to indicate the direction in which the knee is pointing.

Repeat this step for the right leg, elbows, and eyes if you wish, then we will move on to the foot.

○ The rig cleaned up **07a**

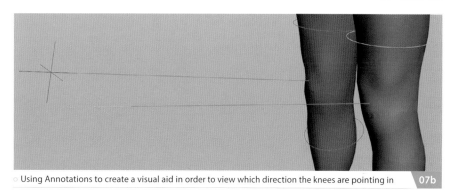

○ Using Annotations to create a visual aid in order to view which direction the knees are pointing in **07b**

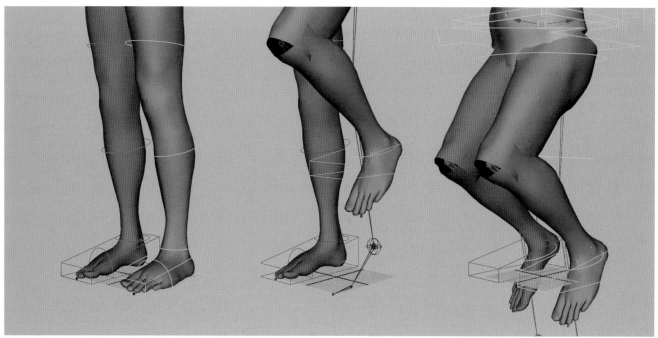

○ Testing the current leg rig in IK mode

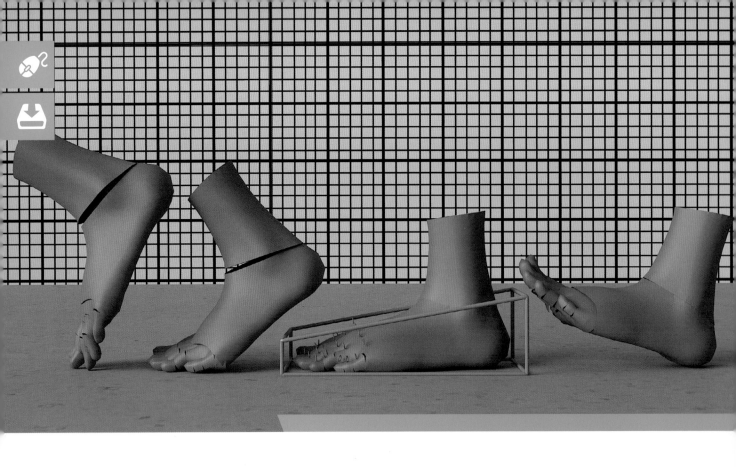

Rigging the feet

Rigging the character's feet and toes

We now come to the foot. We've already created its FK controls, so here we'll mainly focus on creating the reverse foot setup for the IK leg. Without the reverse foot setup, it'll be tricky for the animator to create the necessary poses for the character to make contact with and push off from the ground. We'll also create additional joints and controls for the individual toes so the foot doesn't feel too stiff when animated.

01: Reverse foot locators

To drive the reverse foot, we will need a series of locators. These locators will be organized in a parent-child hierarchy, allowing the IK foot to pivot from different positions. Create the first locator by going to Create > Locator and call it **l_heel_loc**. If it is a bit small, increase Local Scale in the Channel Box, under SHAPES (**Fig.01a**). We want to position this locator at the back of the foot as well as orient the locator to match the angle of the foot.

First, parent **l_heel_loc** under **l_ankleTwist_jnt**, zero out the Translate values and only the value

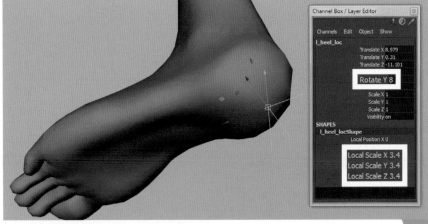

○ Positioning the first locator at the heel of the foot and using Local Scale to increase its size   01a

in Rotate Y to match the position and the angle of the foot. We will be duplicating all the other locators from this one so that their orientations will all match the angle of the foot. Do not zero out the value in Rotate X. We want to leave this as it is so positive Y equals up in world space.

Once you have positioned and oriented the locator correctly, hit Shift+P to unparent it. Translate the locator down slightly and towards

the heel of the foot. To make it easier, activate Snap to Points (hold down the V key) and snap it to one of the vertices on the back of the foot.

With **l_heel_loc selected**, hit Ctrl+D to duplicate it and then rename it **l_ball_loc**. Use Snap to Points to snap it to **l_ball_jnt**. You may want to hide the geometry to do this so it does not snap to any points on the mesh. Duplicate **l_ball_loc** and rename the new

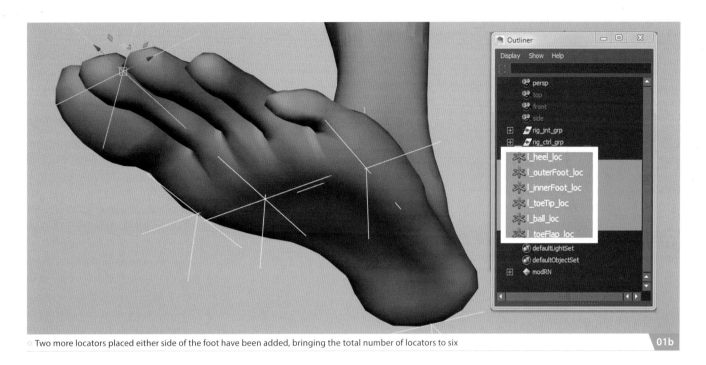

Two more locators placed either side of the foot have been added, bringing the total number of locators to six   01b

locator **l_toeFlap_loc**. Leave this locator in its current position. Now duplicate **l_toeFlap_loc** and rename it **l_toeTip_loc**. Use Snap to Points to snap this locator to **l_toeTip_jnt**.

We now need two more locators for the inside and outside of the foot. Duplicate **l_toeFlap_loc** and rename it **l_innerFoot_loc**. Translate this to the widest part of the inside of the foot, then duplicate **l_innerFoot_loc** and rename it **l_outerFoot_loc**. Position this locator on the widest part of the outside of the foot. We should now have a total of six locators spread around the foot (**Fig.01b**).

02: Reverse foot hierarchy

We'll now create the hierarchy for the reverse foot and also add the additional IK handles that will allow the reverse foot to happen. Start by taking **l_toeFlap** and **l_ball_loc** and parent them under **l_toeTip_loc**. Now take **l_toeTip_loc** and parent it under **l_innerFoot_loc**. Then take **l_innerFoot_loc** and parent it under **l_outerFoot_loc**. Then take **l_outerFoot_loc** and parent it under **l_heel_loc**.

We now need to add some IK handles into the equation. Go to Skeleton > IK Handle Tool (Options) and set Current Solver to Single-Chain Solver. Now click on **l_ankleTwist_ik_jnt** and then on **l_ball_ik_jnt**. Rename this IK handle **l_ball_ik**. Now jump back into the IK Handle tool (press Y to reactivate the last tool), click

on **l_ball_ik_jnt**, and then on **l_toeEnd_ik_jnt**. Rename this new IK handle **l_toeTip_ik**.

Now let's add the IK handles to our hierarchy for the reverse foot. Select both **l_ball_ik** and **l_toeTip_ik**, and parent them under **l_toeFlap_loc**. Then select **l_leg_ik** and parent it under **l_ball_ik**. Rotate the locators to test if the hierarchy has been created

correctly and that you can create all the motion needed for a walk cycle and more.

03: Adding custom attributes

We need to connect the reverse foot to the rest of the leg, as translating **l_leg_ik_ctrl** currently has no effect. I first want to neutralize the Rotate value that currently lives on **l_heel_loc**. To do this, with nothing selected, hit Ctrl+G to

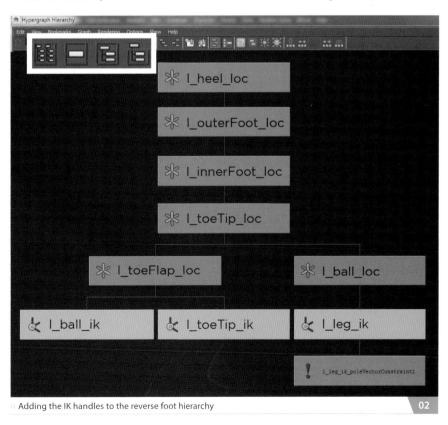

Adding the IK handles to the reverse foot hierarchy   02

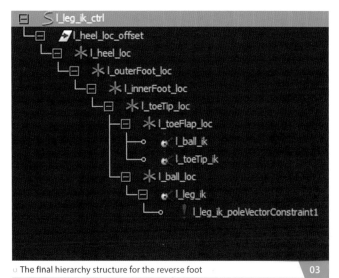

○ The final hierarchy structure for the reverse foot   03

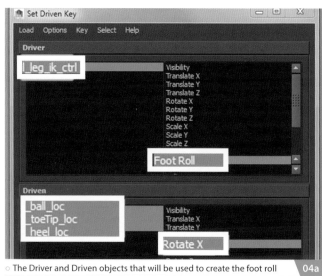

○ The Driver and Driven objects that will be used to create the foot roll   04a

create an empty group node, and rename this to **l_heel_loc_offset**. Parent **l_heel_loc_offset** under **l_heel_loc**, and then zero out the Translate and Rotate values to snap it into place.

Select **l_heel_loc_offset** and hit Shift+P to unparent it. Select **l_heel_loc** and parent it under **l_heel_loc_offset**. **l_heel_loc** should now have no values for the Translate and Rotate attributes. Select **l_heel_loc_offset** and parent it under **l_leg_ik_ctrl**.

The hierarchy should now be complete and the foot should be connected back to the leg.

Next, we want to add some custom attributes to drive the reverse foot. Select **l_leg_ik_ctrl**, go to Modify > Add Attribute and add the following as shown in the table:

Long name	Data type	Min, Max, Default
footRoll	Float	10, 10, 0
heel	Float	10, 10, 0
ball	Float	0, 10, 0
topTip	Float	0, 10, 0
heelTwist	Float	-10, 10, 0
toeTwist	Float	-10, 10, 0
sideToSide	Float	-10, 10, 0
toeFlap	Float	-10, 10, 0

With our custom attributes created, we'll next use SDKs to drive the locators.

04: Driving the foot with SDKs

The footRoll will be the main attribute that we'll use for animating the walk cycle, so we'll start with that. With footRoll, we can roll the foot back onto the heel (for the contact pose), then onto the ball of the foot as the

foot prepares to lift off, and then onto tip-toes as it finally leaves the ground. We could handle all this with multiple controls, but I find having them under one attribute makes it simple for the animator to use, with fewer animation curves to balance and refine.

We will, however, give the animator the choice to use individual attributes to drive the foot, or even to add an offset from the main footRoll attribute. This will be handled by the Heel, Ball and Toe Tip attributes.

Open up the SDK window by going to Animate > Set Driven Key > Set, and load **l_leg_ik_ctrl** as the Driver object (**Fig.04a**). Select **l_heel_loc**, **l_ball_loc**, and **l_toeTip_loc**, and hit Load Driver. Make sure the Foot Roll attribute on **l_leg_ik_ctrl** is at 0 and all the

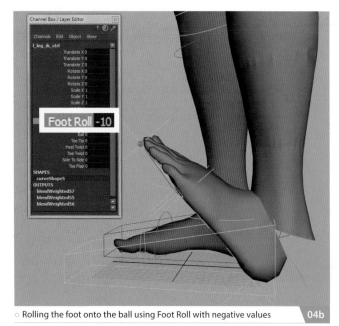

○ Rolling the foot onto the ball using Foot Roll with negative values   04b

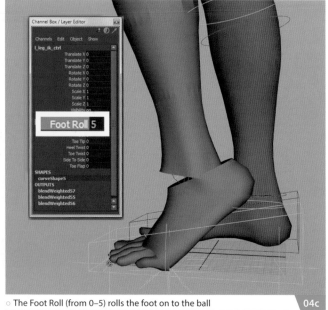

○ The Foot Roll (from 0–5) rolls the foot on to the ball   04c

Rotate channels for the locators are also at 0. Highlight Foot Roll in the top-right box of the SDK window, and in the bottom-left box, highlight all the driven objects. In the bottom-right box, highlight Rotate X. With everything highlighted, hit Key to set the default pose.

Set the Foot Roll attribute to -10 (Fig.04b), then select l_heel_loc and set the Rotate X attribute to around -50. Highlight all three driven objects in the SDK window and hit Key again. Going from 0 to -10 on the Foot Roll attribute should now roll the foot back onto the heel. Now set the Foot Roll attribute to 5 and use Rotate X on l_ball_loc to roll the foot onto the ball (Fig.04c).

I set Rotate X to around 40. Highlight all three driven objects in the SDK window and hit Key. Set the Foot Roll attribute to 10 and zero out the rotations on l_ball_loc. Set Rotate X on l_toeTip_loc to a value of around 70. Highlight all three driven objects again and hit Key on the SDK window. The Foot Roll attribute should now drive the necessary motion needed to plant the foot and for the foot to take off (Fig.04d).

Let's now tackle the Heel, Ball, and Toe Tip attributes (Fig.04e). These attributes will allow the animator to work on top of the Foot Roll, or to use these three independent attributes instead of one. I'll describe the process for the Heel attribute and leave you to handle the Ball and Toe Tip.

First make sure all the attributes on l_leg_ik_ctrl are set to 0. In the SDK window, highlight Heel in the top-right box, highlight l_heel_loc in the bottom-left box, and Rotate X in the bottom-right box. With everything in its original pose, hit Key on the SDK window. Now increase the Heel attribute to 10 and use Rotate X on l_heel_loc to rotate the foot back onto the heel. I set Rotate X to -50, the same amount as we did using the Foot Roll attribute. Hit Key when ready. Using the same method, repeat the process for the Ball and Toe Tip attributes.

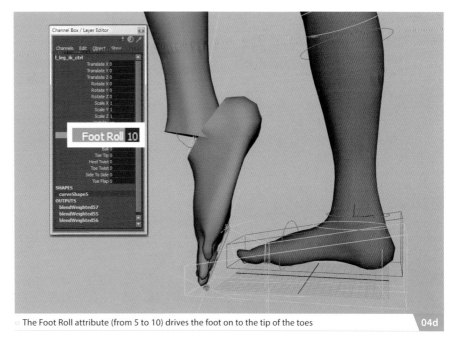

The Foot Roll attribute (from 5 to 10) drives the foot on to the tip of the toes 04d

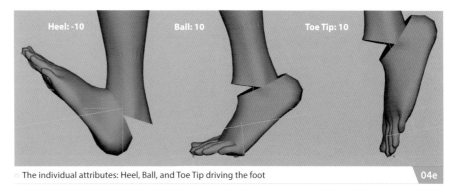

The individual attributes: Heel, Ball, and Toe Tip driving the foot 04e

Let's introduce Heel Twist and Toe Twist (Fig.04f). In the SDK window, highlight Heel Twist in the top-right box, l_heel_loc in the bottom-left box, and Rotate Y in the bottom-right box. With everything in the default pose, hit Key.

"We now want to add the ability to roll the foot from side to side"

Increase the Heel Twist attribute to -10 and rotate l_heel_loc so that the foot rotates inwards. I end up setting the Rotate Y attribute to -40. Hit Key when you're

happy with the pose. Set Heel Twist to 10 and Rotate Y to 40 on l_heel_loc in order to rotate the foot outwards. Hit Key on the SDK window. You'll need to repeat the process for the Toe Twist attribute, this time using l_toeTip_loc as the Driven attribute.

We now want to add the ability to roll the foot from side to side. We'll add that with (surprise, surprise) the Side To Side attribute (Fig.04g). Select l_outerFoot_loc and l_innerFoot_loc, then hit Load Driven on the SDK window.

Highlight Side To Side in the top-left box, both driven objects in the bottom-left box,

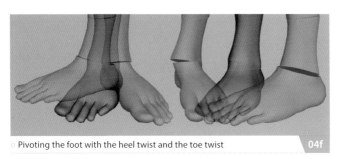

Pivoting the foot with the heel twist and the toe twist 04f

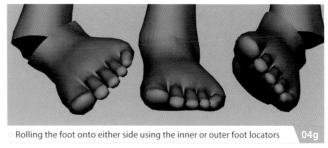

Rolling the foot onto either side using the inner or outer foot locators 04g

209

and the Rotate Z attribute in the bottom-right box. Hit Key to set the default pose.

Set the Side To Side attribute to 10 and Rotate Z on **l_outerFoot_loc** to -45. Make sure both driven objects are highlighted in the SDK window and hit Key. Set the Side To Side attribute to -10 and the Rotate Z on **l_innerFoot_loc** to 45, highlight both driven objects once more in the SDK window, and hit Key.

The last attribute to work with now is the Toe Flap. In the SDK window, highlight Toe Flap in the top-left box, **l_toeFlap_loc** in the bottom-left box, and Rotate X in the bottom-right box. With everything at 0, hit Key on the SDK window. Then increase the Toe Flap attribute to 10 and set Rotate X to -40 for **l_toeFlap_loc**. Hit Key once more in the SDK window (**Fig.04h**).

Now, set the Toe Flap attribute to -10, Rotate X to 40 on **l_toeFlap_loc**, and hit Key one last time on the SDK window. At this stage, all the attributes for **l_foot_ik_ctrl** should now be working. Make sure you test them out.

05: Finishing the knee setup

We are now going to add a feature that will let the animator decide if they would like the knee control to automatically follow the foot control or not. This is one way to reduce knee-popping when the leg is raised quite high.

Start by creating a locator (Create > Locator) and rename it **l_knee_follow_loc**. If you need to increase the size of the locator, remember to use Local Scale in the Channel Box. Then parent **l_kneeFollow_loc** under **l_leg_ik_ctrl**.

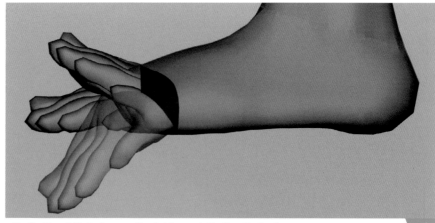

○ The Toe Flap attribute does exactly what it sounds like: flaps the toes!   04h

Zero out the Translate and Rotate attributes in the Channel Box to snap it into place and then unparent the locator (**Fig.05a**).

We want the locator to be driven by the foot, so select in this order: **l_leg_ik_ctrl** and **l_knee_follow_loc**, and go to Constrain > Point. With the same selection, go to Constrain > Orient (Options), set Constrain Axes to only Y, and hit Apply. You can orient-constrain the X and Z axes if you wish, but I find it causes too much movement in the knee control, especially when you twist the foot from side to side.

Now we want **l_knee_follow_loc** to drive the **_offset** node of our knee control. Select in this order, **l_knee_follow_loc** and **l_knee_ik_ctrl_offset**, and go to Constrain > Parent (Options). This time, make sure you have Maintain Offset enabled and hit Apply. Translating the IK foot control now will carry the knee with it. We now want add the ability to turn this feature on and off (**Fig.05b**). Let's add a custom attribute to the knee control to

drive enable this. Select **l_knee_ik_ctrl** and go to Modify > Add Attribute. Give it a Long name of kneeFollow. Set Data Type to Enum and add the following Enum Names: foot and world.

Open up the SDK window now and load **l_knee_ik_ctrl** as the Driver object and the parent constraint that we just added (it should be living under **l_knee_ik_ctrl_offset**) as the Driven object.

Make sure the Knee Follow attribute is set to Foot and L Knee Follow Loc W0 is set to 1 (on the parent constraint). Hit Key. Then set the Knee Follow attribute to World and L Knee Follow Loc W0 to 0. Then hit Key once more. Test out the results and we should be good to go.

06: Rigging the toes

I won't go into so much detail regarding the rigging of the toes, as they're handled in much the same way as the fingers. I'll give you a brief run-down, and more importantly, go over how I connect the toes up to the rest of the foot.

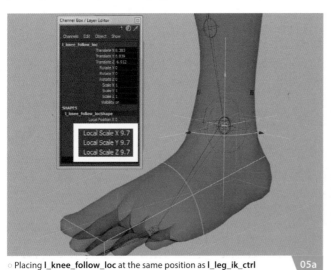

○ Placing **l_knee_follow_loc** at the same position as **l_leg_ik_ctrl**   05a

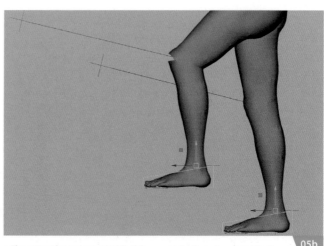

○ The animators can now decide if they want the knee to automatically follow the IK foot control or not   05b

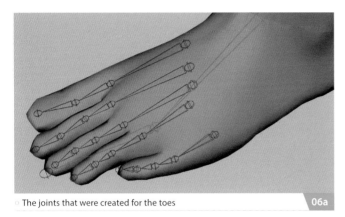

The joints that were created for the toes　　06a

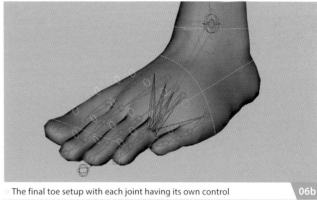

The final toe setup with each joint having its own control　　06b

For each toe, I create a metatarsal joint and then a joint for each phalanx (Fig.06a).

Using the createControls.py script, I create a control for each joint (minus the end joints). The controls are then organized in a parent-child relationship so that they mimic the FK setup of the joints.

Now it's a case of connecting the toes to the foot rig. First, all the root joints for each toe are parented under **l_ball_jnt**. Then it's a case of getting the toes' controls to follow both the FK and the IK foot controls. We could simply parent the top node of each control to **l_ball_jnt**, like we've done for the joints, but I'd like keep the joints separate from the controls.

Instead, I create an empty group node by hitting Ctrl+G with nothing selected. You should call this node **l_toes_ctrl**. With this node selected, hit Ctrl+G to group it to itself and rename it **l_toes_ctrl_offset**. This will be used as an offset node. Now take the **_offset** node, parent it under **l_ball_jnt**, zero out the

Translate and Rotate values to snap it into place, and then hit Shift+P to unparent it.

Take all the top nodes for each of the toes' controls and parent them under **l_toes_ctrl**. With all the control hierarchies for the toes now in a single group, we'll simply parent constrain that group to **l_ball_jnt**. So, select in this order: **l_ball_jnt** and **l_toes_ctrl_offset**, and go to Constrain > Parent.

The toes should now follow the foot correctly, but make sure you test it in both FK and IK mode (Fig.06b). Do this for both legs and then move on to the next stage, which is to do a little spring cleaning.

07: Cleaning up the foot rig

With both legs complete, it's time to tidy up the Outliner. Select **l_knee_follow_loc** and **r_knee_follow_loc**, and hit Ctrl+G to group them together. Rename this group **knees_follow_loc_grp** and parent it under **rig_doNotTouch_grp**. Select **l_toes_ctrl_offset**, group it to itself, and call that group **l_toes_ctrl_grp**.

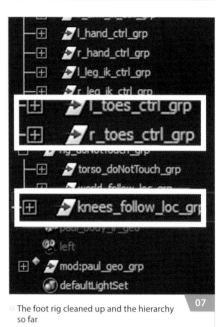

The foot rig cleaned up and the hierarchy so far　　07

Do the same for the right-hand side. Select both **l_toes_ctrl_grp** and **r_toes_ctrl_grp**, and parent them both underneath **rig_ctrl_grp**.

That's it for the leg. Next, we'll do some major tidying up to prepare us for the skinning stage.

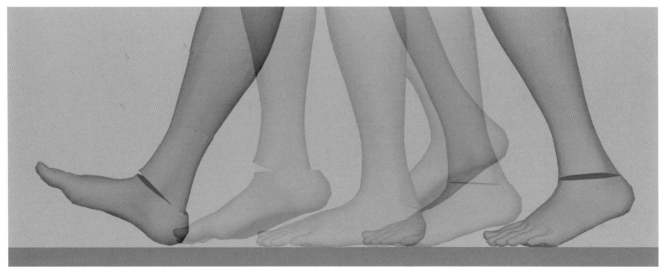

Rigging the feet, including extra toe joints for more natural movement

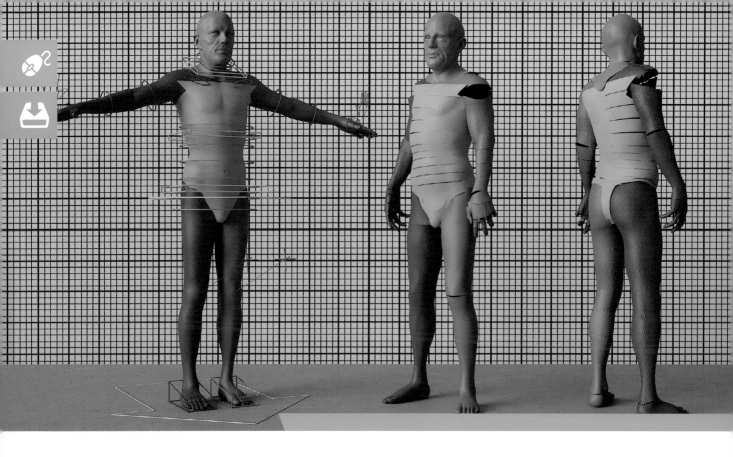

Cleaning up the rig

Getting the rig ready for the skinning process

We're almost ready to begin the skinning process, but before we do, we'll add space-switching for the arms and legs and check the rig carefully for any problems. Check that you're getting the correct behavior in your rotations, ensuring that none of the joints are flipping out of place. Make sure you lock and hide any attributes that are meant for the riggers' eyes only. We'll also set the FK and IK controls so they appear when the relevant mode is enabled.

In addition we will create globalSRT: a main control that allows the animator to place a character in its initial starting position for a shot. We're also going to hide those objects that the animator won't require in the Outliner.

Finally, we'll add some attributes to drive the movement of the chest during breathing. These tasks amount to a stage that's devoted to "dotting the Is and crossing the Ts" – not the most thrilling part, but it's one which makes a real difference.

01: Space-switching

To start things off, I want to add some space-switching functionality to the FK arms and legs. This employs the same technique as for the head and eyes. I'll go into detail on setting up the left arm, then give a breakdown on setting up the leg.

I want the arm to follow the clavicle or chest, the COG, or the world. Create four locators and call them: **l_arm_clavicle_follow_loc, l_arm_chest_follow_loc, l_arm_COG_follow_loc**, and **l_arm_world_follow_loc** (**Fig.01a**). (Please note that in the downloadable video, I miss **l_arm_clavicle_follow_loc** but come back to rectify it later.)

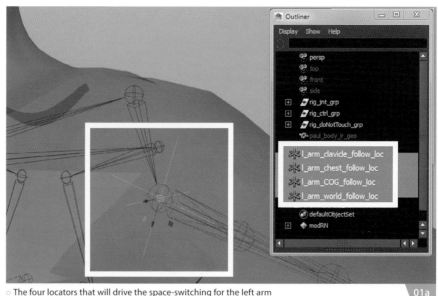

○ The four locators that will drive the space-switching for the left arm   01a

212

Select all four locators, parent them under **l_humerus_fk_ctrl**, zero out the Translate and Rotate values to pop the locators into place, and hit Shift+P to unparent them. If you need to increase the locators' size, use the Local Scale under SHAPES in the Channel Box.

Now we'll drive **l_humerus_fk_ctrl_auto** using the four locators. Select in this order: **l_arm_clavicle_follow_loc**; **l_arm_chest_follow_loc**; **l_arm_COG_follow_loc**; **l_arm_world_follow_loc**; **l_humerus_fk_ctrl_offset**. Then go to Constrain > Orient. We now need to parent the four locators to the areas of the body that they should follow. Parent **l_arm_clavicle_follow_loc** under **l_clavicle_ctrl**. Parent **l_arm_chest_follow_loc** under **spine_chest_ik_ctrl**. Parent **l_arm_COG_follow_loc** under **COG_ctrl**. Finally, parent **l_arm_world_follow_loc** under **world_follow_loc_grp**.

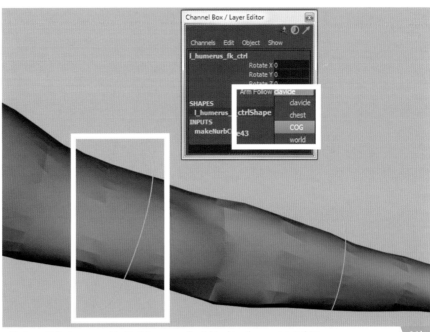

○ Custom attributes were added to **l_humerus_fk_ctrl** to drive the space-switching 　01b

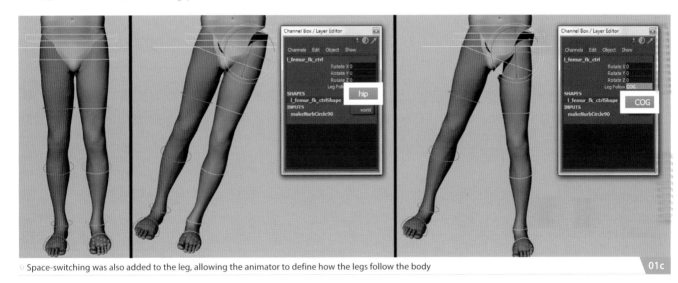

○ Space-switching was also added to the leg, allowing the animator to define how the legs follow the body 　01c

Next we need a custom attribute to allow the animator to control the space-switching. Select **l_humerus_fk_ctrl** and go to Modify > Add Attribute. Give the attribute a Long name of **armFollow**, set the Data Type to Enum, and add the following Enum Names: clavicle, chest, COG, and world (**Fig.01b**).

We now want to use Set Driven Keys (SDKs) to drive the weight values living on the orient constraint that we added earlier. You'll find this constraint under **l_humerus_fk_ctrl_auto**. Select it and go to Animate > Set Driven Key > Set. This should load it as the Driver object.

Then select **l_humerus_fk_ctrl** and hit the Load Driver button on the SDK window.

Select **l_humerus_fk_ctrl** and make sure the Arm Follow attribute is set to clavicle. Then select the constraint node and turn off all the weight values except for that of the clavicle. Hit Key on the SDK window when ready. Then set the Arm Follow attribute to chest, and on the constraint node turn off all the weights except that of the chest.

Repeat the process for the COG and world attributes. Once completed, you should be able to set which part of the body the FK arm should follow.

I tackle the legs in exactly the same way. First, you will only need three locators positioned in the same place as **l_femur_fk_ctrl**.

The three locators should be renamed **l_leg_hip_follow_loc**, **l_leg_COG_follow_loc**, and **l_leg_world_follow_loc**.

Once in place, orient constraint **l_femur_fk_ctrl_auto** to all three locators and then parent the locators under the relevant control. So parent **l_leg_hip_follow_loc** under **hip_fk_ctrl**, parent **l_leg_COG_folllow_loc** under **COG_ctrl**, and then **l_leg_world_follow_loc** under **world_follow_loc_grp**. Now add a custom attribute to the leg and use SDKs to control the space-switching (**Fig.01c**).

02: Lock and hide objects

With the space-switching set up, we now want to run through the rig and lock and hide certain objects. Without doing so, an animator could reveal parts of the rig and possibly set a key or delete something that we don't want them to.

Let's start by revealing everything in the viewport. To do this, go to Display > Show > All. Now we can start to lock and hide the objects. Select the four camera planes and hide them (Ctrl+H). If you have any additional cameras in the scene, feel free to delete them.

Delete all unnecessary geometries from the scene that have been revealed. Then jump to the Layers tab and go to Layers > Delete Unused Layers (Fig.02a). At this stage, I'm looking at everything that I want to keep in the scene.

Under the Viewport menu, go to Show and uncheck Polygons, Joints, and NURBS Curves to hide them. Everything else in the scene needs to be kept away from the animator. Select all the IK handles and set Visibility to 0 in the Channel Box (Fig.02b). Then hold down the RMB over Visibility and go to Lock Selected. Select all the locators in the scene and do the same again, and then repeat the process for the IK effectors. Now go to Display > Show > All to see what objects are revealed. Hopefully nothing (other than the cameras) pops up.

We'll move on to the joints now. First, reveal them by unhiding them from the Viewport display. With the joints on display, we now want to hide all the joints other than those that will be used to bind the character to.

Here's a quick list of the joints and joint chains that I hide and then lock the visibility for. I'll only mention the left-hand side controls

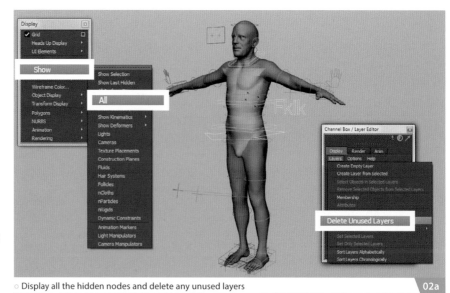

○ Display all the hidden nodes and delete any unused layers　02a

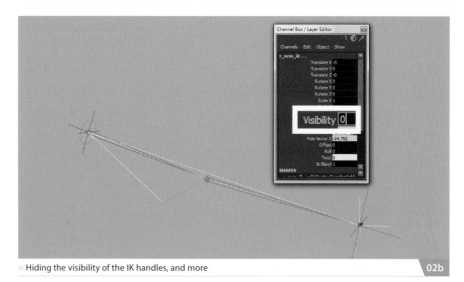

○ Hiding the visibility of the IK handles, and more　02b

here but make sure you do the same for the right-hand side: **spine_hip_ik_jnt**, **spine_mid_ik_jnt**, **spine_chest_ik_jnt**, **spine_fk1_jnt**, **l_humerus_fk_jnt**, **l_humerus_ik_jnt**, and **l_femur_ik_jnt**.

03: Create the global SRT control
The final control to add to the rig is the **global_SRT** control. This will be the parent control of the rig and is used to initially place the character in the correct position in the shot. For

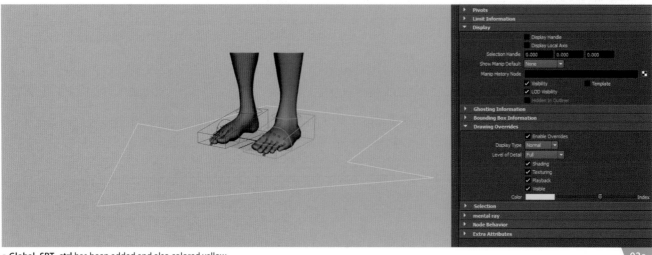

○ **Global_SRT_ctrl** has been added and also colored yellow　03a

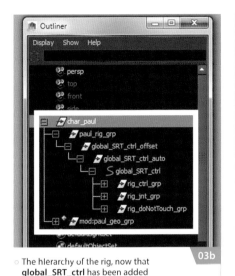

○ The hierarchy of the rig, now that **global_SRT_ctrl** has been added

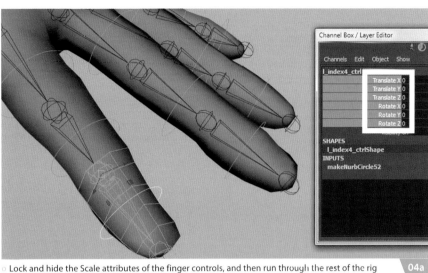

○ Lock and hide the Scale attributes of the finger controls, and then run through the rest of the rig

03b

04a

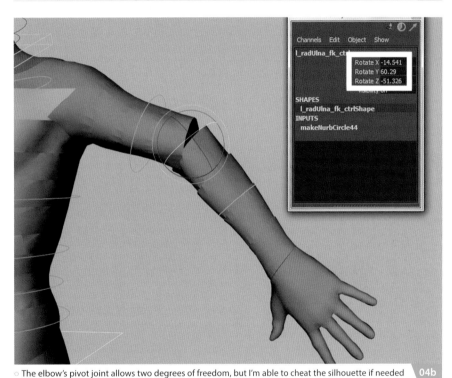

○ The elbow's pivot joint allows two degrees of freedom, but I'm able to cheat the silhouette if needed

04b

this control, I go to the Comet shelf and go to Shapes > Arrow. With the curve in the scene, go to component mode and edit the shape so that it's larger and more easily selectable. Make sure the pivot for the control is in the World center and then go to Modify > Freeze Transformations. If you want, you can add a little color to the new control using the Drawing Overrides (**Fig.03a**).

Rename the curve **global_SRT_ctrl** and, with the control selected, hit Ctrl+G twice to create the control hierarchy. Rename the top node of the hierarchy **global_SRT_ctrl_offset**, and the node below **global_SRT_ctrl_auto**. Take **rig_jnt_grp**, **rig_ctrl_grp**, and **rig_doNotTouch_grp**, and parent them under **global_SRT_ctrl**.

Navigate **global_SRT_ctrl** to check that everything behaves as it should (**Fig.03b**). Do not parent the geometry group under **global_SRT_ctrl**, as this will create double transformation. Instead, select both **mod: paul_geo_grp** and **global_SRT_ctrl_offset**, hit Ctrl+G, and rename the new group **char_paul**. Lastly, select **global_SRT_ctrl_offset**, hit Ctrl+G, and rename this group **paul_rig_grp**.

04: Lock and hide attributes

Now we want to get back to locking and hiding attributes on controls that we don't want the animator to key. Start by selecting all the FK controls of the torso, arms, legs, neck, and head (including the ears and eyelid controls).

Lock and hide the Translate and Scale attributes in the Channel Box. For the jaw control, however, just hide the Scale attributes. For all the finger controls, just lock and hide the

Scale attributes also (**Fig.04a**). The reason I don't lock the Translate attributes here is because I also want to point-constrain the finger joints to their relevant controls. Do this now by selecting a finger control, Shift-selecting its relevant joint, and going to Constrain > Point. Do this for all the fingers.

In the downloadable video guide, I do this towards the end of the clean-up process. It's not anatomically correct, but it'll help the animator pose the fingers more easily. Do the same for the toe controls as well.

Select the IK controls of the arm (including the elbow control) and lock and hide the Rotate and

Scale attributes. Select **l_clavicle_ctrl** now and lock and hide the Translate and Scale attributes. Do the same to **l_scapula_medial_ctrl**. For **l_scapula_spine_ctrl**, just lock and hide the Scale attributes. For the IK foot control, just hide the Scale attributes. For the knee controls, lock and hide the Rotate and the Scale attributes.

I haven't limited the number of axes in which you can orient any of the controls. For example, I have not restricted **l_radUlna_fk_ctrl** to just the X-axis (allowing for flexion and extension). If I was following anatomy to the letter, I should have. As with the fingers, this will allow me to cheat the poses and push the silhouette more easily (**Fig.04b**).

215

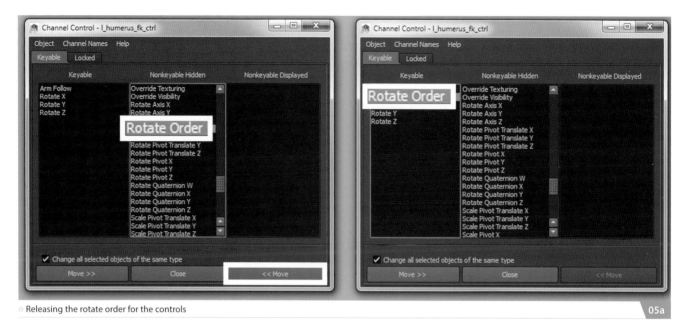

○ Releasing the rotate order for the controls

05a

"The rotate order of the control will now drive the rotate order of the joint"

05: Rotation order controls

I want to give the animator the ability to change the rotation order of the controls and joints. We could let them jump into the Attribute Editor to do this, but I like to set it up so that they can alter the rotate order in the Channel Box. To do this, select all the controls and go to Edit > Channel Control in the Channel Box. In the Nonkeyable Hidden column, look for and highlight Rotate Order and click on the << Move button to make it keyable (**Fig.05a**).

With the rotate order of the controls on display, we can now use this attribute to drive the rotate order of the joints. I'll describe the process for **l_carpals_jnt** and then leave you to handle all the remaining controls.

First open up the Connection Editor (Window > General Editors) and load **l_carpals_ctrl** (the control) into the left Outputs column (**Fig.05b**). Select **l_carpals_jnt** and load it into the right Inputs column. Highlight rotateOrder in both columns and we should be good to go. The rotate order of the control will now drive the rotate order of the joint. Repeat the process for the rest of the controls.

06: Control visibility

I now want to go through the rig and hide any controls that don't need to be on show. For example, when the arms are in IK mode,

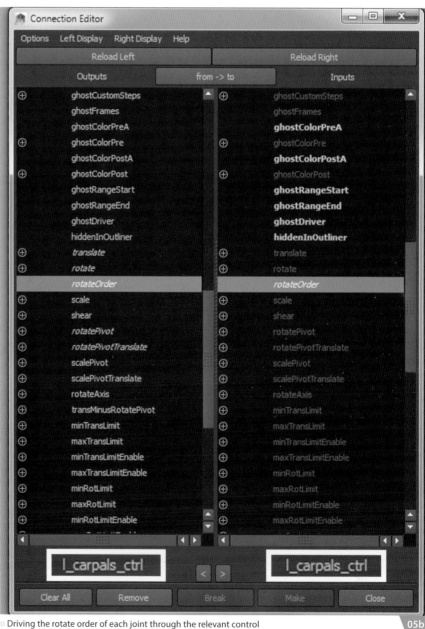

○ Driving the rotate order of each joint through the relevant control

05b

the FK arm controls do not need to be on display. This will help the animator quickly assess which mode he or she is animating in.

Starting with the arm controls, select **l_humerus_fk_ctrl**, **l_arm_ik_ctrl**, and **l_elbow_ik_ctrl**, and go to Animate > Set Driven Key > Set. This will pop them into the Driven box of the SDK window.

"I want the ability to display or hide the finger, toes, rib, and head controls"

Select **fklk_ctrl** and hit Load Driver on the SDK window. On **fklk_ctrl**, set the L Arm attribute to 0 (FK mode) and then hide both **l_arm_ik_ctrl** and **l_elbow_ik_ctrl**. Back in the SDK window, highlight L Arm in the top-right box, highlight all three objects in the bottom-left box, and then highlight Visibility in the bottom-right box. Hit Key on the SDK window when ready.

Now set the L Arm attribute to 1 (IK mode), enable the visibility for the IK controls, hide the FK controls, and then hit Key again in the SDK window. Switching between the two modes should now reveal only the necessary controls. You can lock the Visibility for all three controls. Once you've done the left arm, do the same for the right arm and legs.

07: Additional visibility controls
I want the ability to display or hide the finger, toes, rib, and head controls. This is because they don't need to be shown all the time and it will make the rig less busy.

First, we need a control to house the attributes that will allow us to show and hide the controls. You can make any control shape you like, but I choose the Text tool and create the word "visibility". I parent all the curve shapes under one transform node and then re-arrange the letters.

Rename the new control **visibility_ctrl**, position it close to **fklk_ctrl**, and then parent it under **COG_ctrl**. Then go to Modify > Freeze Transformations on the control and lock and hide all the Translate, Rotate, and Scale attributes.

Add the attributes to **visibility_ctrl** with the settings shown in the table here:

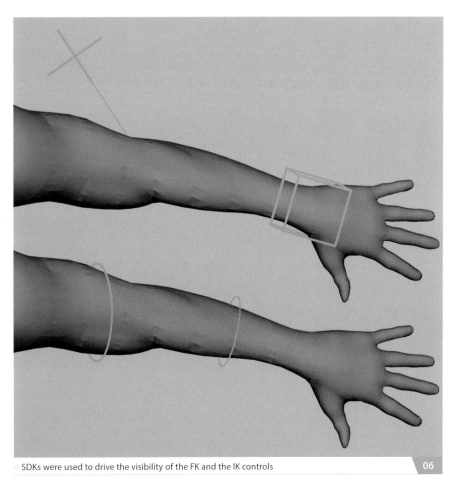

SDKs were used to drive the visibility of the FK and the IK controls   **06**

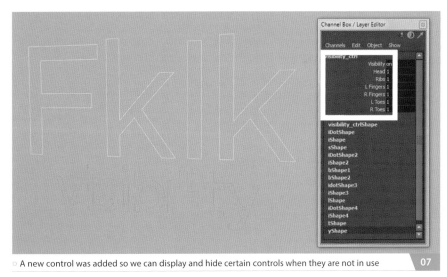

A new control was added so we can display and hide certain controls when they are not in use   **07**

Long name	Data type	Min, Max, Default
Head	Float	0, 1, 0
ribs	Float	0, 1, 0
l_fingers	Float	0, 1, 0
r_fingers	Float	0, 1, 0
l_toes	Float	0, 1, 0
r_toes	Float	0, 1, 0

In the SDK window, set **neck1_ctrl** as the Driven object and **visibility_ctrl** as the Driver object.

Set the Head attribute to 1 on **visibility_ctrl** and, in the SDK window, highlight Head in the top-right box and Visibility in the bottom-right box.

Hit Key on the SDK window. Set the Head attribute to 0, turn the Visibility to 0 on **neck_ctrl**, and hit Key again on the SDK window.

Repeat this process for the ribs, fingers, and toe controls, and then lock and hide the Visibility attribute on all the controls.

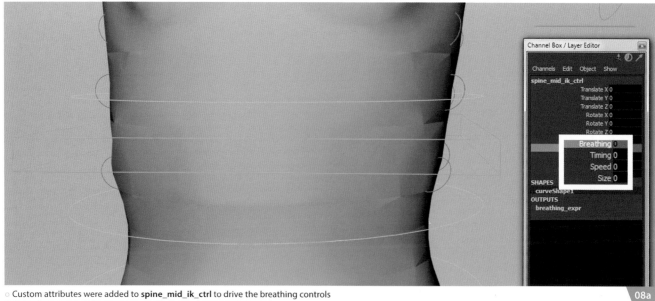

○ Custom attributes were added to **spine_mid_ik_ctrl** to drive the breathing controls

08a

08: Automated breathing controls using expressions

Currently, we have a set of controls that could be used to manually animate the character and create the illusion that he is breathing.

However, manually animating breathing would be a time-consuming job, so let's add some attributes to automate this process, while still giving the animator the choice to work manually or on top of the automated controls.

The first thing we need to do is add a couple of attributes that will drive the automated breathing by a control. For this, I decide to pick **spine_mid_ik_ctrl**. With this control selected, add the attributes as shown in the following table (see also **Fig.08a**):

Long name	Data type	Min, Max, Default
Breathing	Float	leave blank, leave blank, 0
Timing	Float	leave blank, leave blank, 0
Size	Float	leave blank, leave blank, 0
Speed	Float	leave blank, leave blank, 0

In the Channel Box, highlight the Breathing attribute, hold down the RMB, and go to Lock Selected. This attribute is created simply to act as a divider between the attributes above it and the breathing controls.

To allow the animator to still drive the controls, we'll be applying the expression to

the **_auto** nodes for the controls. Let's create that expression now. Open up the Expression Editor (Window > Animation Editors), create the expression as shown in the colored box on the next page, and call it **breathing_expr**.

Here's a quick breakdown of how the expression works. First we have three float variables. These variables will be driven by the custom attributes we added to **spine_mid_ik_ctrl**, allowing the animator to edit the timing, speed, and size of the breathing. Then we have the lines that drive the rotation X attribute of the **_auto** nodes.

A sine wave has been utilized to allow for expansion and contraction of the rib cage. To have finer control over the sine wave, we are using the float variables to drive its

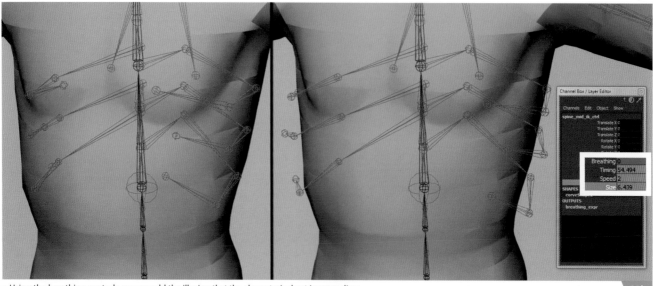

○ Using the breathing controls, we can add the illusion that the character's chest is expanding

08b

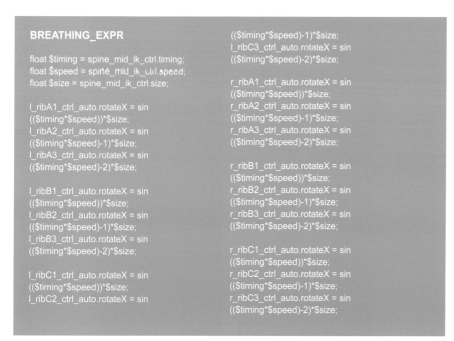

```
BREATHING_EXPR

float $timing = spine_mid_ik_ctrl.timing;
float $speed = spine_mid_ik_ctrl.speed;
float $size = spine_mid_ik_ctrl.size;

l_ribA1_ctrl_auto.rotateX = sin
(($timing*$speed))*$size;
l_ribA2_ctrl_auto.rotateX = sin
(($timing*$speed)-1)*$size;
l_ribA3_ctrl_auto.rotateX = sin
(($timing*$speed)-2)*$size;

l_ribB1_ctrl_auto.rotateX = sin
(($timing*$speed))*$size;
l_ribB2_ctrl_auto.rotateX = sin
(($timing*$speed)-1)*$size;
l_ribB3_ctrl_auto.rotateX = sin
(($timing*$speed)-2)*$size;

l_ribC1_ctrl_auto.rotateX = sin
(($timing*$speed))*$size;
l_ribC2_ctrl_auto.rotateX = sin
```
```
(($timing*$speed)-1)*$size;
l_ribC3_ctrl_auto.rotateX = sin
(($timing*$speed)-2)*$size;

r_ribA1_ctrl_auto.rotateX = sin
(($timing*$speed))*$size;
r_ribA2_ctrl_auto.rotateX = sin
(($timing*$speed)-1)*$size;
r_ribA3_ctrl_auto.rotateX = sin
(($timing*$speed)-2)*$size;

r_ribB1_ctrl_auto.rotateX = sin
(($timing*$speed))*$size;
r_ribB2_ctrl_auto.rotateX = sin
(($timing*$speed)-1)*$size;
r_ribB3_ctrl_auto.rotateX = sin
(($timing*$speed)-2)*$size;

r_ribC1_ctrl_auto.rotateX = sin
(($timing*$speed))*$size;
r_ribC2_ctrl_auto.rotateX = sin
(($timing*$speed)-1)*$size;
r_ribC3_ctrl_auto.rotateX = sin
(($timing*$speed)-2)*$size;
```

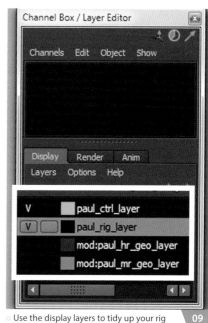

Use the display layers to tidy up your rig — 09

frequency and amplitude. We are also adding an offset to some of the joints so that the breathing motion feels less mechanical.

Once you've created the expression, animate the Timing attribute between one frame and another and use the Speed and Size attributes to test out the expression (Fig.08b). I find that low values work best, otherwise it can get a little extreme.

Once you've had a play around, make sure you set all the attributes back to 0 so that the joints' rotation values are back to their default state.

09: Cleaning up the display layers

The last thing to do is clean up the display layers. This will help to quickly show and hide parts of the rig, which can be useful during animation and creating playblasts (page 250).

The main model is referenced in and already comes with its own display layer, so we don't need to worry about that. Select all the visible joints and create a new display layer for them. Rename this layer **paul_rig_layer**. As the low-resolution geometry is parented to the joints, it will be affected by this layer as well. I also want the ability to keep the joints visible

but hide the low-resolution geometry. This will be extremely useful during the skinning phase. Select all the low-resolution geometry, pop it into a new display layer, and rename this layer **paul_lr_geo_layer**. For now, I've also set both of these layers to Reference mode.

I select all the controls and drop them into their own display layer, called **paul_ctrl_layer**. Popping controls into a layer may kill some of the colors of the controls, so ensure you re-color them. I color the Shape nodes for the controls so they don't clash with the display layer's color. We're now ready to add the volume joints.

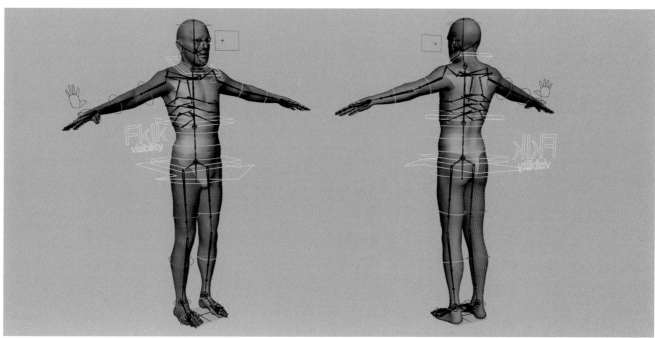

The model complete with color-coded controls!

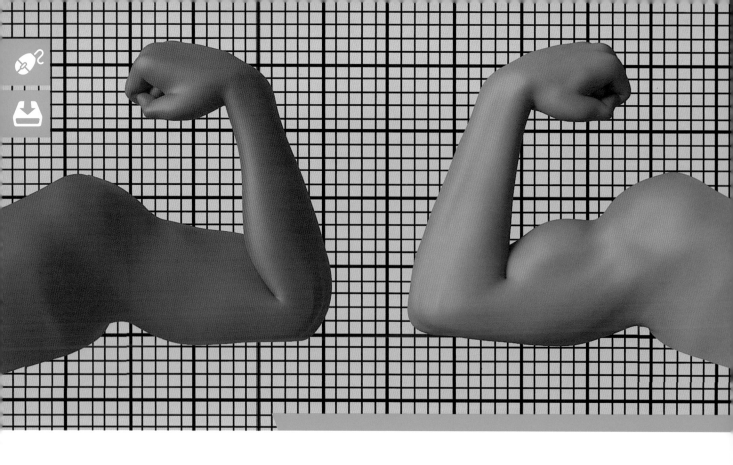

Adding the volume joints

Quick Select Sets and extra volume joints

We'll now create Quick Select Sets (QSS) to make it easier to select the joints that will be used for the skinning process. We will also add some additional volume joints so that we can maintain form as we pose the character.

01: QSS for skin joints

I'd like to start off with a QSS that contains all the initial joints that will be used for the bind. I say initial joints as later we'll be adding additional joints that will be used to add volume and maintain form.

I'll work in the Outliner to select the joints, but feel free to work where you're most comfortable. In the Outliner, I also want to restrict the objects that I can see to just the joints. To do this, go to Show > Objects > Joints.

Now we want to select all the joints that will be used for the bind process. In the table on the right here there is a large list of all the joints I selected. I've only listed joints on the left-hand side and down the center line, but make sure you pick the right-hand joints, too.

Including the right-hand joints, I have a grand total of 156 joints selected. Once we've added the volume joints, this will probably jump closer to 200. (You can find this information by going to Display > Heads Up Display > Object Details.)

With all the joints still selected, I want to rename the suffix of **_jnt** (that sits on the end of all the names) to **_skin_jnt**. This will allow us to use wildcards (see page 223) in the Outliner to search for these joints

should we need to. To rename the suffix, go to Modify > Search and Replace Names. In the "Search for" box, type **_jnt**, and in the "Replace with" box, type **_skin_jnt**.

Now, with all the joints still selected, go to Create > Sets > Quick Select Sets. When the dialog box pops up, call the set **paul_skin_set** and hit OK. If you look in the Outliner now, you will find a QSS that allows you to quickly select all the joints that will be used for skinning.

L_carpals_jnt	l_thumb1, 2, 3_jnt	l_index1, 2, 3, 4_jnt	l_middle1, 2, 3, 4_jnt	l_ring1, 2, 3, 4_jnt
l_pinky1, 2, 3, 4_jnt	spine_ik1, 2, 3, 4, 5, 6, 7, 8, 9, 20, 11, 12_jnt	l_shoulder_jnt	l_clavicle_jnt	l_clavicle_jnt
l_humerus_jnt	l_humerusTwist1, 2, 3_jnt	l_radUlna_jnt	l_radUlna_twist1, 2, 3_jnt	l_scapulaSpine_jnt
l_scapula_me-dial_jnt	hip_fk_jnt	l_femur_jnt	l_femurTwist1, 2, 3_jnt	l_patella_jnt
l_patellaTwist1, 2, 3_jnt	l_ankleTwist_jnt	l_ball_jnt	l_bigToe1, 2, 3_jnt	l_indexToe1, 2, 3, 4_jnt
l_middleToe1, 2, 3, 4_jnt	l_ringToe1, 2, 3, 4_jnt	l_pinkyToe1, 2, 3, 4_jnt	neck1, 2_jnt	head_jnt
upperJaw1, 2_jnt	lowerJaw1, 2_jnt	l_upperLid_end_jnt	L_lowerLid_end_jnt	l_ear_root_jnt
l_ear1, 2_jnt	l_ear_lobe_jnt			

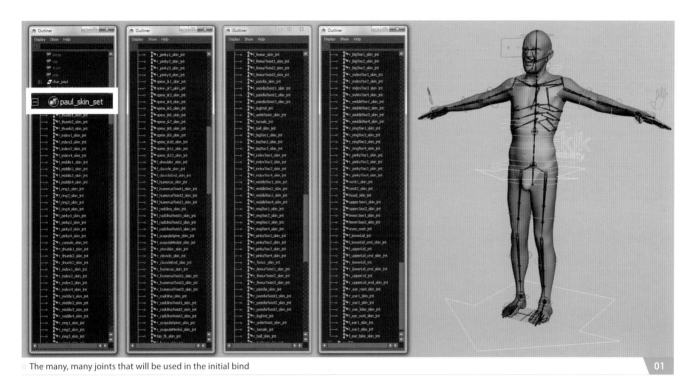

○ The many, many joints that will be used in the initial bind
01

02: Volume joints for the arm

I now want to add additional joints that will help to maintain form, also creating the illusion that muscle and bone exist beneath the polygonal surface. I'll describe the process for the left arm and leave you to tackle the right arm and the legs.

Select **l_humerus_skin_jnt**, hit Ctrl+D to duplicate it, and then Shift+P to bring it out from its current hierarchy. Select all the geometry, locators, and constraint nodes that live under the duplicated arm chain and delete them. Select the first twist joint of the upper arm and duplicate it twice. Translate one of the duplicated joints to the back of the arm, and the other joint forward to the front of the arm (Fig.02a). It will be easier to translate the joints in object mode.

You should now be at **l_radUlna_skin_jnt1**. For this joint, I only duplicate it once and translate it out to sit at the elbow. Select all the child joints that come with this joint and delete them. Leave this joint parented to **l_humerus_skin_jnt1** for now.

On to the forearm (Fig.02b). Repeat the process of duplicating a twist joint twice and translating them out in opposite directions. For the end joint of the upper arm, also duplicate this twice, and position one joint

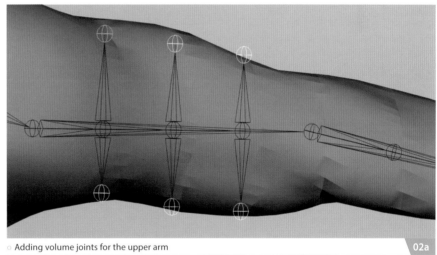

○ Adding volume joints for the upper arm
02a

at the styloid process of the ulna and the other at the styloid process of the radius.

Select all the new volume joints and hit Shift+P to unparent them from the current

hierarchy (Fig.02c). Take the arm chain that we originally duplicated to create the volume joints and delete it. You should be left with 15 individual joints. At this stage, it's a good idea to rename them all.

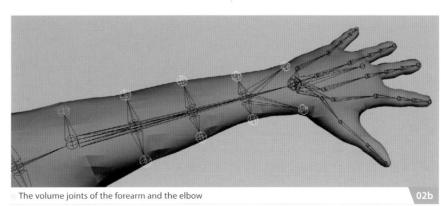

○ The volume joints of the forearm and the elbow
02b

For the volume joints of the upper arm, I name the front set **l_bicep1_vol_jnt**, **l_bicep2_vol_jnt**, and **l_bicep3_vol_jnt**. For the rear set, I follow the same naming convention but replace bicep with tricep. I rename the elbow joint **l_elbow_vol_jnt**.

I rename the forearm joints **l_flexors#_vol_jnt** for the rear set; **l_extensors#_vol_jnt** for the front set. This is clearly not anatomically correct, but I think it's suitable here. Lastly, I rename the two additional wrist joints **l_styloid_ulna_vol_jnt** and **l_styloid_radius_vol_jnt**.

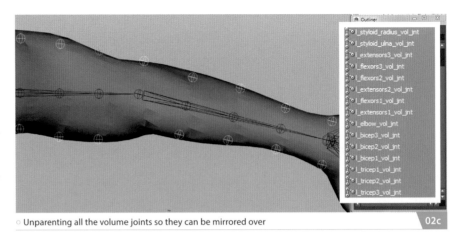

○ Unparenting all the volume joints so they can be mirrored over   02c

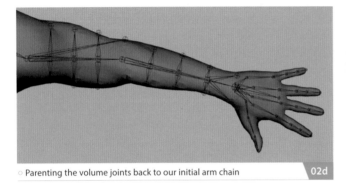

○ Parenting the volume joints back to our initial arm chain   02d

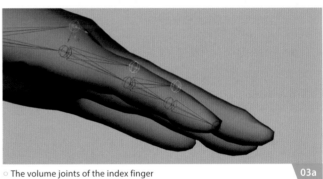

○ The volume joints of the index finger   03a

With all the joints renamed, select one joint at a time and go Skeleton > Mirror Joint (make sure the rename settings are still in place). To speed up the process, once you've mirrored one joint, simply select another and hit G on the keyboard to repeat the last command. We can now take the volume joints and parent them to our original arm chain.

Parent **l_bicep1_vol_jnt** and **l_tricep1_vol_jnt** to **l_humerusTwist1_skin_jnt**. Then select the next two volume joints down the arm and parent them to **l_humerusTwist2_skin** and so on, until all the volume joints are parented to the arm chain (**Fig.02d**). **l_elbow_vol_jnt** is parented under **l_humerus_skin_jnt**. And lastly, both **l_styloid_ulna_vol_jnt**

and **l_styloid_radius_vol_jnt** are parented under **l_radUlnaTwist3_skin_jnt**.

03: Fingers and legs

I now want to add some volume joints to the fingers to help maintain their bony structure. I'll describe the process for the index finger here and let you handle the rest.

Begin by selecting **_l_index2_skin_jnt** and hit Ctrl+D to duplicate it. Translate the joint chain up slightly and then select and delete all the geometry that comes with the joint chain and the end joint itself. Select the

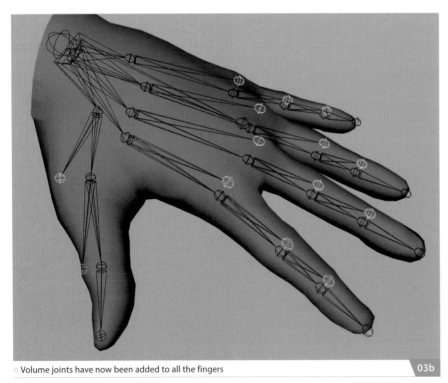

○ Volume joints have now been added to all the fingers   03b

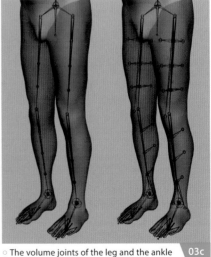

○ The volume joints of the leg and the ankle   03c

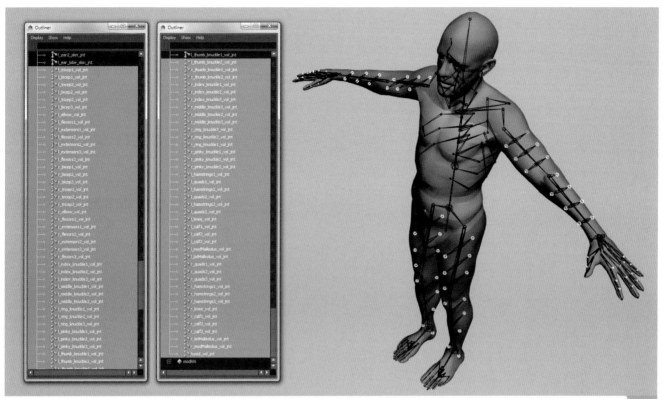

I've added the volume joints to the QSS so that we can quickly find them when required

04

current end joint of the new chain and parent it under **l_index3_skin_jnt**. Now select the end joint again from our duplicated chain and parent it under **l_index2_skin_jnt** (**Fig.03a**).

Repeat the step for the remaining fingers and the thumb (**Fig.03b**). Once you have all your joints for the left fingers, rename them accordingly and mirror them to create the right fingers' volume joints.

Once the arms and hands are done, repeat the process for the legs (excluding the feet). Here's a quick overview of the legs.

For the upper legs, I created additional volume joints at the front and rear (quads and hamstrings) (**Fig.03c**). I create an extra joint for the knee (like for the elbow) and then three volume joints for the calf muscles. I don't create additional joints for the shin, as the existing twist joints in that region will be enough to handle the deformation.

Next I create two additional joints, one for the medial malleolus and one for the lateral malleolus. These are renamed, mirrored over, then parented to the relevant joints, as with the arm. I add one final volume joint in the neck (where you'd find the Adam's

apple). You could also add additional joints along the sternocleidomastoid but, for now, I have decided to leave them out.

So we have all our new volume joints. Before we move on, select all the joints of the rib cage and go to Modify > Search and Replace Names. When the window pops up, set the "Search for" to **_jnt** and the "Replace with" to **_vol_jnt**. Now all the joints that will be used to maintain volume are following the same naming convention.

04: Volume joints Quick Select Set

The last thing we need to do before we start the actual skinning process is to add the volume joints to the current Quick Select Set. To do this, simply select all the volume joints (you can use the wildcard of *_vol_jnt* in the Outliner to make it easier to find them) and then in the Outliner, MMB-drag-and-drop them on top of **paul_skin_set**. Open up the QSS to check that they are in there and we should be good to go. Including the volume joints, I have a grand total of 262 joints.

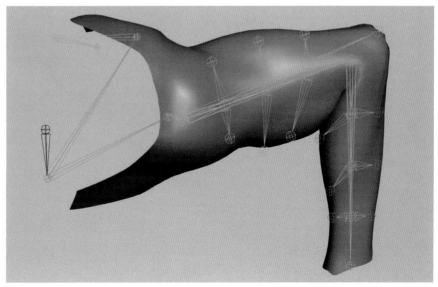

The many joints required to animate our character

223

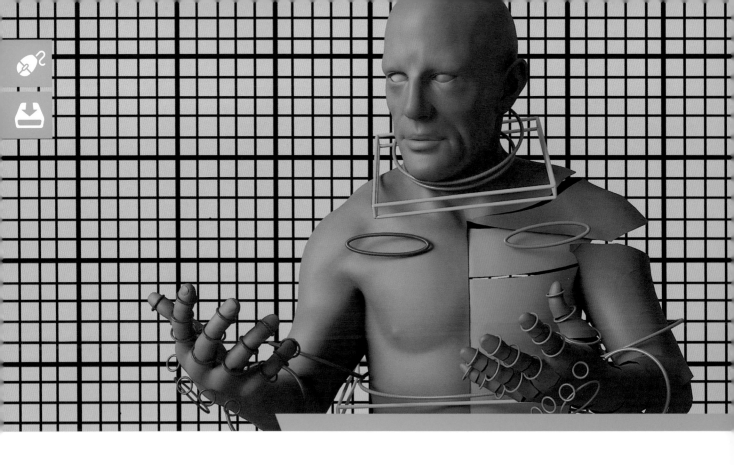

Skinning

Skinning with Smooth Bind and weight painting

We're now ready to begin the process known as "enveloping", "binding", or "skinning". It is the process of assigning how much influence a joint has over a vertex, therefore defining how the skeleton will deform the geometry.

The relationship between the joints and vertices will be established using Smooth Bind, Maya's skinning solution. After this, the initial bind calculation will be reviewed through a process called "weight painting".

Don't be tempted to cut corners during the skinning process, as it's this stage that lays the foundation for most of the deformation. Extra tools such as corrective blend shapes, muscle setups, or volume joints (which we've employed before) can be used to push the believability of the deformation. However, none of these tools will be of much use if the skinning hasn't been done well first.

01: Skinning breakdown

Before we actually start skinning the main model, I just want to give you an overall picture

of the process I follow to skin a character. For this example, I've chopped off a leg and reduced the joints to a five-joint chain.

Following this, I tend to take a similar approach to skinning as I do the majority of CG tasks,

breaking it down into three distinct stages: blocking, smoothing, and refining (Fig.01a). This helps to avoid the "can't see the wood for the trees" syndrome, where too many fine details early on can obscure broader changes that may need to be made.

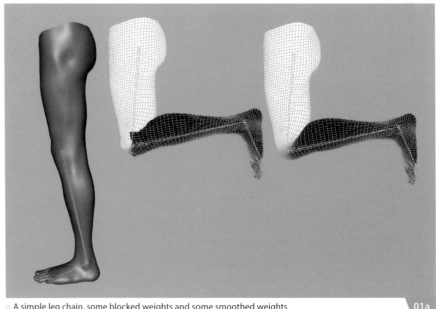

○ A simple leg chain, some blocked weights and some smoothed weights

01a

224

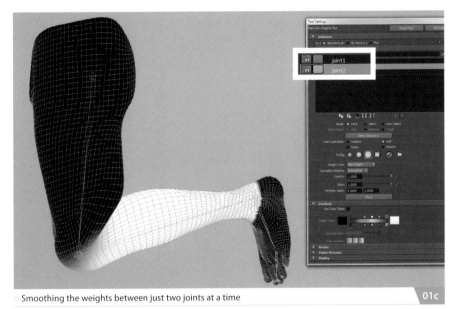

Blocking the weights by giving each joint 100% influence over the surrounding vertices   **01b**

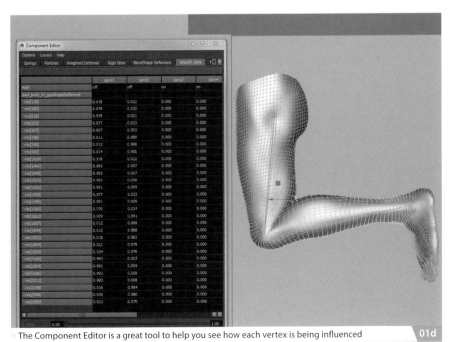

Smoothing the weights between just two joints at a time   **01c**

The Component Editor is a great tool to help you see how each vertex is being influenced   **01d**

"We'll aim to get the skinning to produce 80–90% of the final outcome"

Having created the initial bind, we'll get rid of the default calculation by giving every joint 100% influence over its surrounding vertices (**Fig.01b**). This is the blocking stage, and the reason I do this (rather than simply fixing what needs fixing) is because I want to be fully responsible for the weighting of the character.

With the recently added Geodesic Voxel bind method in Maya 2015, the initial bind you get, especially with simple skeleton rigs, does a fantastic job. But as our rig has twist joints and volume joints galore, I find it quicker to start weight painting from a clean slate, rather than working over Maya's initial bind. Now we've blocked out the initial weights, we have a mesh that's very chunky-looking as it deforms.

After the initial blocking, we can smooth out the weights between two to three joints at a time (**Fig.01c**). During this stage, we'll also set a lot of keyframes on the rig (see page 230), to get a better idea of how the mesh transitions from pose to pose. After all, it's the movement between poses we need to focus on, not just the key poses that we hit.

While we're doing this, it is advisable to maintain the natural creases and bulges that occur as the body articulates. If you're going for a cartoony feel, though, you may find it works better to avoid adding the inclusion of wrinkles and folds.

Lastly, we'll examine the deformation and fix any anomalies, using tools such as the Paint Skin Weights tool, the Component Editor (**Fig.01d**), and the Hammer Skin Weights tool. We'll aim to get the skinning to produce 80–90% (with the volume joints) of the final outcome. Any other fixes can be handled with corrective shapes that we'll add post-animation, where necessary.

After that, we can simply mirror the weights over. I mirror the weights regularly during the skinning process to get a good feel for how the whole character deforms. As our character is not perfectly symmetrical, some areas of the skinning may not mirror perfectly, so we'll have to go in for some manual weight painting.

02: Creating the initial bind

With your latest scene loaded, let's create the initial bind. In your viewport, make sure you can see all the joints and the high-resolution mesh we'll be skinning. In the Outliner, open up **paul_skin_set** and highlight all the **_skin_jnt** joints. Leave out the **_vol_jnt** joints for now – we'll add these later on. With all the joints selected, Shift-select the mesh (**mod:paul_body_hr_geo**) and in the Animation menu set, go to Skin > Smooth Bind (Options).

A few notes on the settings: the bind method is the skinning algorithm used to create the bind. The default bind method is **Closest Distance**, which simply binds the closest vertices to the joints. If you had two legs positioned close together, the joint of one leg could affect the vertices of the other, which is hardly ideal.

The **Geodesic Voxel** method overcomes this problem by voxelizing the mesh (imagine the mesh being filled with small cubes) and searching for the closest vertices to the joints. Voxelizing the mesh essentially works out the boundaries of the geometry, so the joint from one leg won't affect the vertices of the other. We'll be fully recreating the skin weights, but if you wanted a good initial bind, I would recommend you go for the Geodesic Voxel bind method (**Fig.02a**).

We have three skinning methods: Classic Linear, Dual Quaternion, and Weight Blended. **Classic Linear**, or Linear Blend Skinning (LBS), is my preferred method and I use it 90% of the time. However, due to the math behind it, it causes issues when twisting joints (**Fig.02b**). This "candy wrapper" effect can be avoided by adding additional joints to help maintain the structure. Luckily for us, we have twist joints to handle such tasks.

Dual Quaternion performs a different calculation for the bind and is great for reducing the "candy wrapper" effect. However, it tends to cause more trouble than I would like in areas such as the shoulders and hips.

Lastly, **Weight Blended** allows you to mix the two previous methods together. I find that I can get 80–90% of the way there with Classic Linear and can then finish things off to a more than adequate level with volume joints and additional corrective shapes.

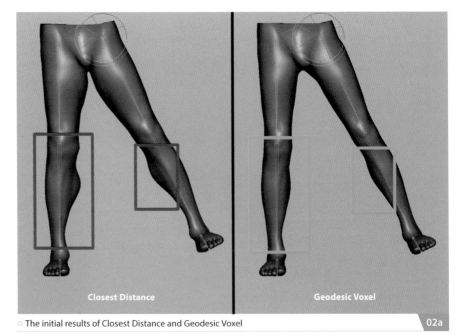

Closest Distance　　　**Geodesic Voxel**

○ The initial results of Closest Distance and Geodesic Voxel　　02a

"Normalize weights" set to Interactive only allows the weight value for each vertex to total 1 (100%). So if you have two joints and try adding influence to a vertex from either of them, when you add influence to one joint, it will take away influence from the other. Set "Normalize weights" to Post and you can go beyond 1 as it presumes you'll fix this later. I get vertices flying around in this setting so I prefer Interactive.

"Max influences" sets the number of joints that can affect a vertex. I tend to have this setting quite high, but if you are rigging for a game engine it may be necessary for you to check if there are limitations that you will be required to follow.

Falloff and Resolution are specific to the Geodesic Voxel bind method. The Falloff controls the stiffness of the bind: the higher the value, the stiffer the bind. The Resolution refers to how the mesh is voxelized: the higher the resolution, the better the initial bind, but the longer it takes to calculate.

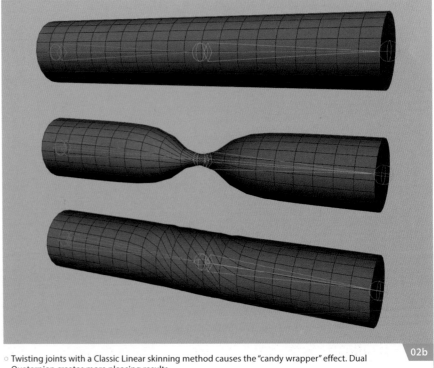

02b

○ Twisting joints with a Classic Linear skinning method causes the "candy wrapper" effect. Dual Quaternion creates more pleasing results

With all this in mind, the settings I used are shown in (Fig.02c).

Hit Bind Skin when ready. If you now select the model, you'll notice a skinCluster and a bindPose node living under OUTPUTS in the Channel Box. The transform attributes of the model will also be grayed out, indicating that the model is now being driven by joints.

The skinCluster itself stores the skinning data (see more in step 08) and the bindPose allows us to go back to the pose that the model was originally skinned in. You can do this by selecting the model and going to Skin > Go To Bind Pose. With the model skinned, have a little play with the control to test out the initial bind.

03: Blocking the weights

Now we've created the initial bind, the next step is to rebuild all the skin weights. Select **mod:paul_body_hr_geo** and go to Skin > Paint Skin Weights Tool (Options). This tool will be used for almost the whole skinning process (Fig.03a).

Click on the Options for this tool to reveal a window housing all the joints that influence the model and a range of tools that allow us to determine how much influence each joint has over the model's vertices. The main mode

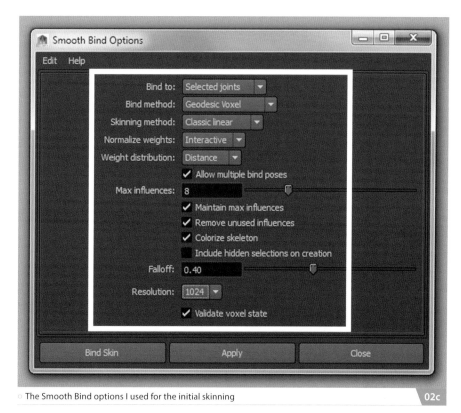

The Smooth Bind options I used for the initial skinning   02c

we'll be using is Paint, and I'll be editing the Radius and Value of the brushes interactively by holding down the B key (Radius) or N key (Value) and LMB-dragging in the viewport.

To select the joint we want to work with, we could pick it from the Influences column,

but another shortcut I often use is to hold down the RMB over the joint in the viewport and go to Select Influence.

In the Paint Skin Weights tool, select **hip_fk_skin_jnt** from the Influences column, set the Paint operation to Replace, Opacity to

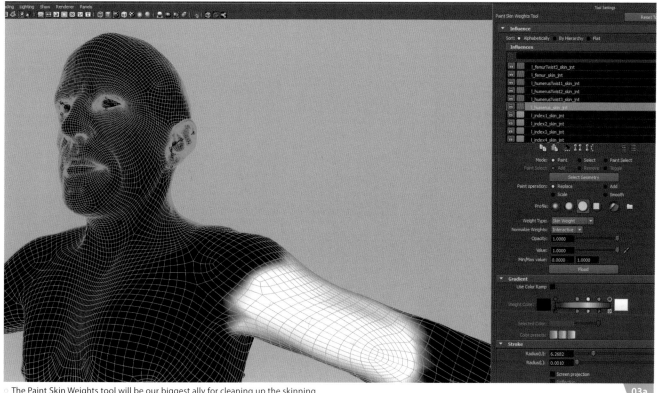

The Paint Skin Weights tool will be our biggest ally for cleaning up the skinning   03a

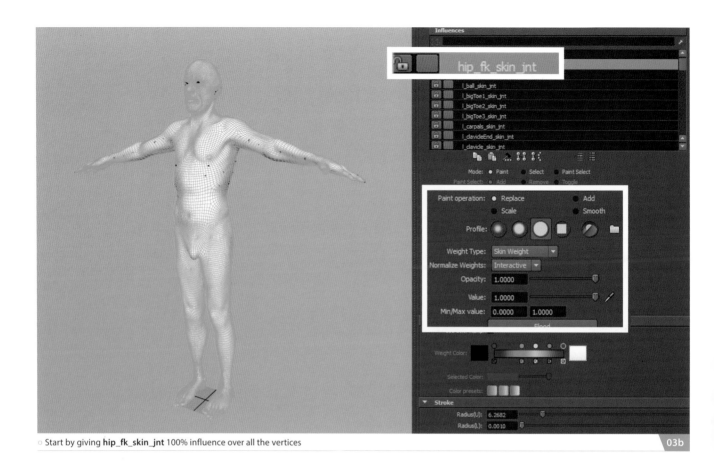

○ Start by giving **hip_fk_skin_jnt** 100% influence over all the vertices

03b

1, and Value to 1. Select the third Profile for the brush (flat and round) and hit Flood.

The **hip_fk_skin_jnt** will now have 100% influence over the entire model (**Fig.03b**). Try rotating any other control to see if it has any effect and you should see that only **hip_fk_skin_jnt** has influence.

We now want to block out the weights by giving each joint 100% influence over the vertices surrounding it. I'll detail the process for the left fingers, but it's the same for the rest of the body (**Fig.03c**). Go back into the Paint Skin Weights tool, highlight all the joints in the Influences box, and then click on any of the padlock icons to lock all the weights for all the joints.

Then unlock the padlocks for only **hip_fk_skin_jnt** and **l_index4_skin_jnt**. With **l_index4_skin_jnt** selected in the Influences box, paint over the vertices that surround that joint.

Next use the padlock icon to lock the weights of **l_index4_skin_jnt** (or hold down the RMB over the joint and go to

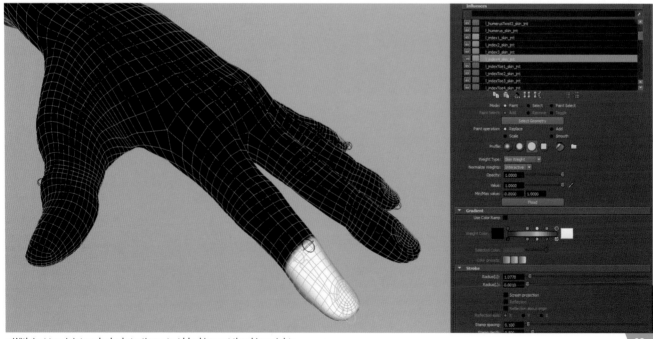

○ With just two joints unlocked at a time, start blocking out the skin weights

03c

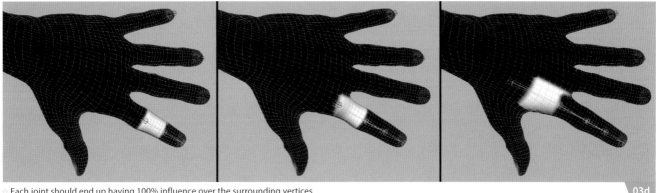

○ Each joint should end up having 100% influence over the surrounding vertices
03d

Lock Influence). Select **l_index3_skin_jnt**, unlock the padlock, paint the vertices around that joint, and again, lock the weights.

As we do this, we are only ever taking influence away from the **hip_fk_skin_jnt**, as it's the only other joint that has its padlock unlocked. Even though we've added influence to **l_index4_skin_jnt** and **l_index3_skin_jnt** now, we cannot take influence away from these joints as we have locked the weights from them.

Continue to block out the weights for the rest of the joints of the index finger. Once the index finger is blocked out, do the same for the remaining fingers and work your way up the arm (**Fig.03d**).

I like to block the skin weights from the fingertips to the shoulder, then from the tips of the toes to the hip, and lastly from the top of the head down to the hip. I used to work from the core outwards, but the method described here works best for me.

Continue this process so all the model's weights are blocked out (**Fig.03e**). Only do the left arm and left leg, as we'll mirror the skin weights after we've blocked them out. I do, however, find it easier to block in the weights for both sides of the torso, neck, and head, as it makes it easier to smooth weights during deformation test poses later.

Now try rotating the joints and see what you get. It might be a very rigid bind, but don't be concerned as this is the desired outcome at this stage.

04: Mirror the blocked weights

With the skin weights blocked out, let's mirror them so we can focus on smoothing

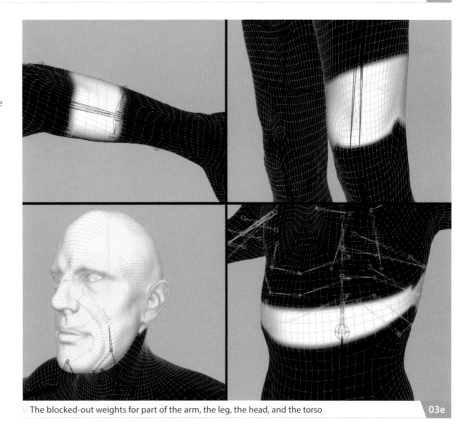

○ The blocked-out weights for part of the arm, the leg, the head, and the torso
03e

the weights out. Select the mesh and go to Skin > Mirror Skin Weights (Options). As I've weight painted the left side of the mesh, I set the Mirror Across attribute to YZ and enable Direction. Now try rotating

the same control for both the left and right sides to see if the weighting has been cleanly mirrored. As the mesh is slightly asymmetrical, there may be a few minor discrepancies, but these can be cleaned up later on.

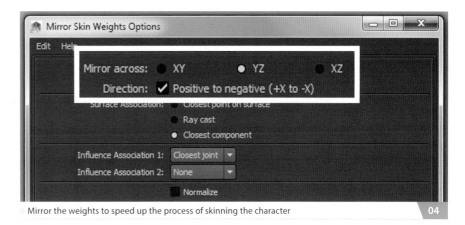

○ Mirror the weights to speed up the process of skinning the character
04

05: Range of motion

We can now start to smooth out the weights. As I do this, I set some keyframes on each control, one by one, so I can examine the skin weights during deformation. A keyframe essentially allows us to record a pose in time. By setting multiple keyframes, we can transition from one pose to another to view how the character deforms.

It's best to work on a deforming character, as rigid poses don't show how the model deforms during articulation. Using the FK controls usually gives me a clearer idea of how the joints are deforming the model, as we can isolate the movement to a single joint. Using IK controls would result in two or three joints being activated, making it harder to determine which joint is influencing the vertices in question.

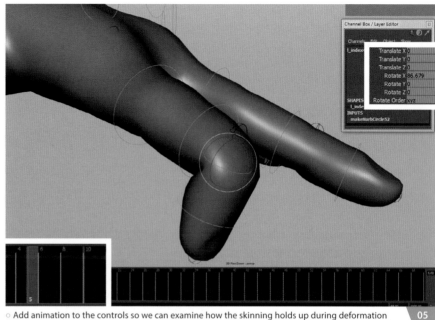

○ Add animation to the controls so we can examine how the skinning holds up during deformation   05

As before, I start with the fingers and work my way towards the shoulder. I set keys every five frames by selecting the controls and hitting S on the keyboard. I also enable Auto Key (the small key icon just beneath the Playback controls) so I don't have to keep pressing S to set keys. For now, set a range of poses for all the finger controls, one at a time.

06: Smoothing out the weights

We can now start to smooth out the blocked weights. Again, I try to focus on painting the weights between just two joints, but sometimes I'll go between three or four joints. Areas such as between the fingers, the shoulders, and the hips are good examples of this. By smoothing the weights between just two joints where possible, we can be certain which joints influence the vertices of that region without confusing the issue.

So let's focus on the procedure for the fingers to provide an example. In the Paint Skin Weights tool, lock the weights for all the influence joints other than **l_index4_skin_jnt** and **l_index3_skin_jnt**. Then set

the Paint operation to Smooth, select the second brush Profile, and paint between the two unlocked joints (**Fig.06a**).

As you smooth out the weights anywhere on the body, try to keep the natural creases that occur, and study your own deforming body as you paint. Keeping creases or adding bulges helps to create the illusion that a character has an underlying skeleton, muscle, and fat.

Once you've smoothed out the weights between **l_index4_skin_jnt** and **l_index3_**

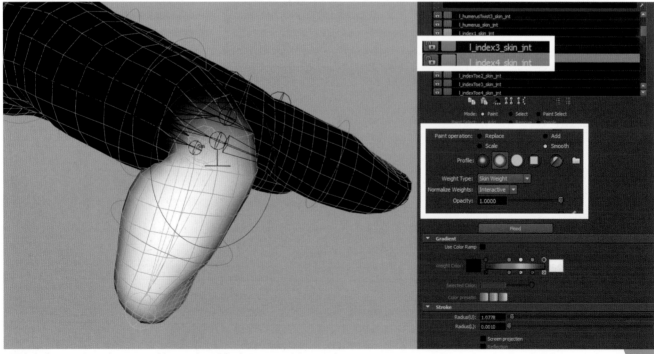

○ With the fingers animated, start smoothing out the weights between two joints at a time   06a

skin_jnt, lock the weights of **I_index4_skin_jnt**.
Unlock the weights for **I_index2_skin_jnt**
and smooth out the weights between the
two unlocked influence joints. Continue to
do this for the entire character (**Fig.06b**).

You may find it's worth doing a second pass
over the character after you've completed
it. Also feel free to mirror the joints over to
test out the deformation; this is especially
useful as you work on the torso.

Smoothing with the Paint Skin Weights tool will
only get you so far. You will, without a doubt,
need to manually direct some vertices to where
you want them to sit between the joints. To do
this, I like to (if possible) lock all but two joints,
set the Paint operation to Add with a very low
value (for example between 0.1 and 0.25), and
start to add very small amounts of influence to a
vertex (**Fig.06c**). If I apply too much, I can simply
select the other unlocked influence object
and paint the influence back to the vertex.

I also like to use the Component Editor as it
clearly describes how much influence the
joints have over a vertex. To use this tool,
select a few vertices and go to Window >
General Editors > Component Editor. Scroll
to the Smooth Skins tab, and on the left you
should see a list of all the selected vertices.

Running horizontally, you should find all the
joints that influence a specific vertex and
by how much. You can punch values into

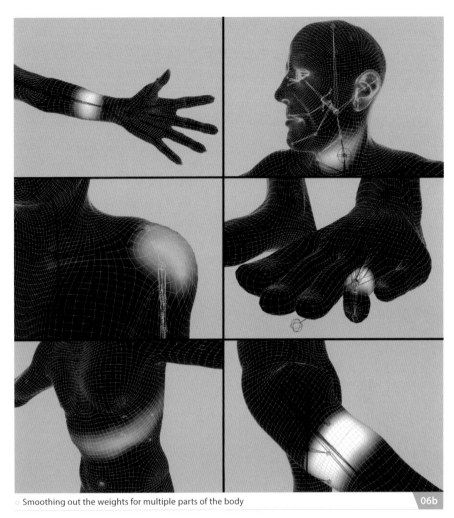

the boxes in order to edit the influence. I
find that this tool comes in very handy with
unruly vertices, of which there are usually
many. Again, this is a very time-consuming
process, but I would like to emphasize that

it's really not worth cutting corners here
if you want a mesh that deforms well.
The last tool I use at this stage is the Hammer
Skin Weights tool. Select a vertex or small
group of vertices and go to Skin > Hammer

Smoothing out the weights for multiple parts of the body　06b

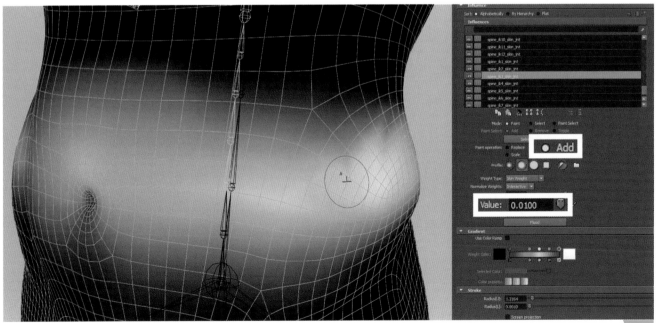

With the Paint operation set to Add, use a very low value to start pushing and pulling the vertices between the joints　06c

231

Skin Weights. I find the results are clearer if you put the mesh into a pose when using this tool. Hammer Skin Weights tries to average out the positions of the vertices, based on their neighboring vertices, and knocks them into shape by assigning a similar weight (**Fig.06d**). It's very useful for adding a final level of polish.

By the way, try not to focus too much on the eyelids, mouth, or ears at this stage. As our character is asymmetrical, we'll rectify them with a final pass of manual weight painting after we've skinned the volume joints.

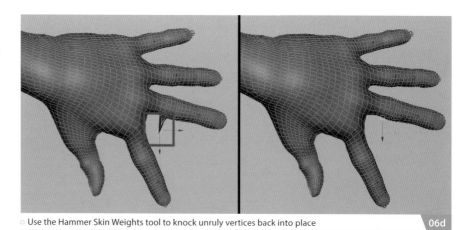

○ Use the Hammer Skin Weights tool to knock unruly vertices back into place   06d

07: Mirror the smoothed weights

With the smoothing complete, mirror the skin weights and test out the deformation of both sides and the torso. The shoulder and hip regions are always tricky to weight paint due to the amount of joints coming together, so ensure you spend a lot of time on those areas. Mirror the weights and test again until you're really certain that you can't push them any further.

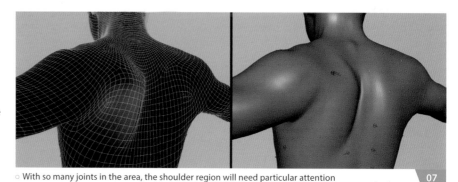

○ With so many joints in the area, the shoulder region will need particular attention   07

08: Skinning the volume joints

Now we want to add the volume joints to our skinCluster. Go into the Outliner, open up **paul_skin_set**, and select all the joints with a suffix of **_vol_jnt**. Add **mod:paul_body_hr_geo** to the selection and go to Skin > Add Influence (Options). When the options box pops up, ensure Weight locking is enabled and hit Add (**Fig.08a**). If you select the model now and open up Paint Skin Weights, you'll see that the volume joints are in the Influences list and that

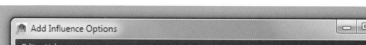
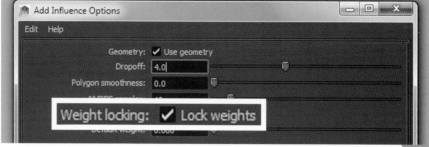

○ Add the volume joints to the current skinCluster but make sure the weights are locked   08a

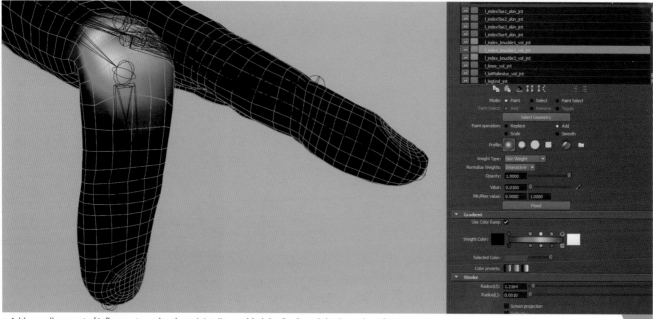

○ Add a small amount of influence to each volume joint; I've enabled the Gradient Color Ramp here for clarity   08b

their weights have been locked. If we hadn't locked their weights to begin with, this would have ruined all the weight painting done so far.

We can start allowing the volume joints to have some effect on the model (**Fig.08b**). Select all the joints in the Influences list and unlock all the weights. This will make it easier to have the volume joints affect the model. Set the Paint operation to Add, Value to 0.0150, and select the softest brush Profile (the first one). As we'll only be using the Add paint operation, we'll only be taking influence away from the neighboring joints. Don't use Smooth with all the joints unlocked; this can cause problems (page 231).

Now select a volume joint and start to give it some influence over the region on which it sits. If you want, you can also animate the volume joints, but remember, we have not created any controls for these joints so we cannot simply zero out the values to get them back to their default position. If you are animating the volume joints, ensure you set an initial default key so that you can get it back to its original position. To test out the joints of the rib cage, simply animate the breathing controls and

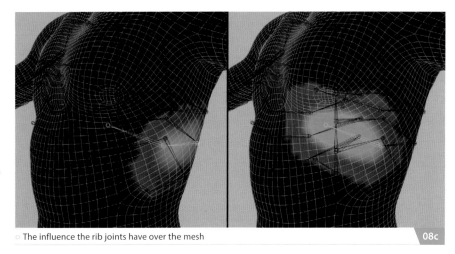

○ The influence the rib joints have over the mesh   08c

then paint the weights (**Fig.08c**). Go through the entire model and give each volume joint some influence over the surrounding vertices.

09: Mirror the weights and clean up

The skinning should now be close to final. Once we've completed the animation, we can come back to update the skinning to improve the deformation if needed. For the final time, mirror the skin weights. If your model is asymmetrical you'll need to manually paint the skin weights to fix the mouth, eyelids, and ears. Now that the

character has been skinned, we need to delete all the keyframes from the controls. To do this, in the Viewport menu, go to Show > None, then Show > NURBS Curves. Select all the animation controls and LMB-double-click in the Timeline to highlight all the keyframes. RMB-click and go to Delete to remove all the keys. Scrub through the Timeline to check that the model isn't animated, then bring back the geometry and joints.

Next, we'll finalize and publish the rig so that it can be picked up for animation.

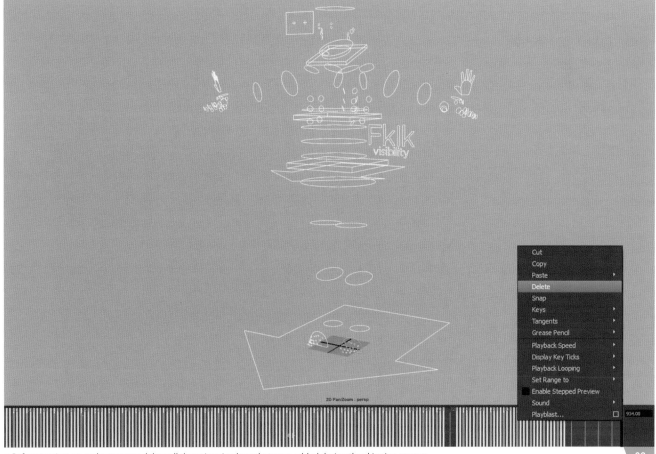

○ Before moving on, make sure you delete all the animation keys that were added during the skinning process   09

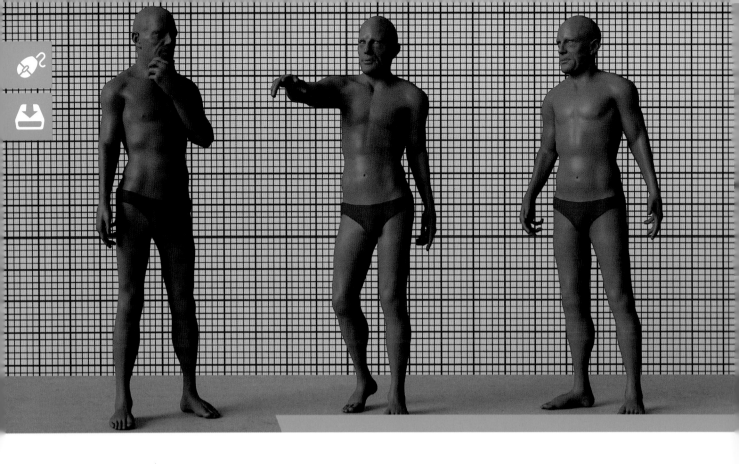

Finalizing the rig

Testing and publishing the final rig

So we have come to the final stage of our rigging marathon. Here we will test the rig and then publish the file so that the animator can begin animating.

There is no reason why we could not have published the rig at an earlier stage, say before pre-skinning, to allow the animator to get started. In a sense there is no such thing as a finished rig, as it can always be improved upon.

However, by the end of this chapter, we will have completed all the necessary checks and balances that will enable us to confidently pass the model to the next stage in the pipeline.

01: Testing the rig

With the skinning complete, go through the model using multiple controls to see how the rig reacts. So far we've mainly rotated one control at a time, but this will only reveal so much; using multiple controls allows you to see the body deforming as a unit.

You'll probably find the odd random vertex being a pain. To knock it back into shape, select it and use the Hammer Skin Weights tool (**Fig.01a** and **01b**). Look for any areas where twisting of the geometry occurs. For example, I have trouble with the forearm twist, which is being driven by **l_carpals_jnt**.

To fix this, I simply update the expression so that **l_carpals_ctrl** drives the motion.

02: Rigging the extra bits

We now want to use a combination of constraints and skinning to hook up the eyes, inner mouth parts, and nails.

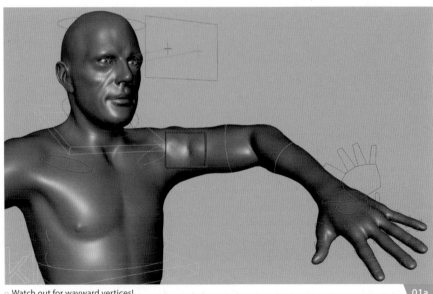

○ Watch out for wayward vertices! 01a

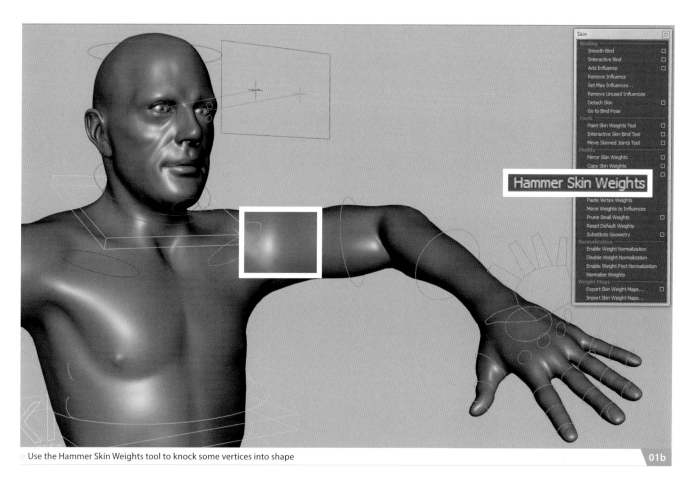

Hammer Skin Weights

○ Use the Hammer Skin Weights tool to knock some vertices into shape **01b**

Feel free to skin the briefs, if you like. If you decide to, duplicate the original briefs geometry first, then hide it. We'll use the hidden version later on and apply a cloth simulation to it.

Let's start with the teeth, gums, and tongue, for which we'll use parent constraints (**Fig.02a**). Select **lowerJaw1_skin_jnt**, then Shift-select **mod:tongue_hr_geo** and go Constrain > Parent Constrain (Options. Enable Maintain Offset and hit Apply. Then parent-constrain the lower

teeth to the same joint and parent-constrain the upper teeth to **upperJaw1_skin_jnt**.

I also use constraints for the eyes. All three geometry parts of the left eye (cornea, iris/sclera, and pupil) are parent-constrained under **l_eye_jnt**, and all three parts of the right eye are parent-constrained under **r_eye_jnt**.

As for the nails, each set of nails has been merged together, so we can't simply parent-

constrain each nail to its relevant joint. Instead, we'll skin the nails so they follow along with the hand. I'll focus on the left hand here, then leave you to handle the right fingernails and the toenails. Select **mod:l_nails_geo** and add the following joints to the selection: **l_thumb3_skin_jnt, l_index4_skin_jnt, l_middle_skin_jnt, l_ring4_skin_jnt,** and **l_pinky4_skin_jnt.** Then go to Skin > Smooth Bind. Rotate the fingers to check that the nails follow along and then repeat the step for the other nails (**Fig.02b**).

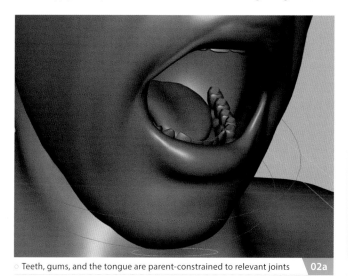

○ Teeth, gums, and the tongue are parent-constrained to relevant joints **02a**

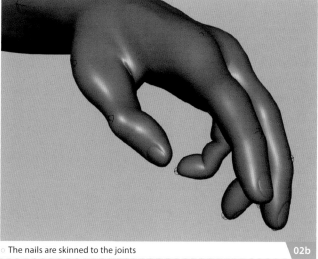

○ The nails are skinned to the joints **02b**

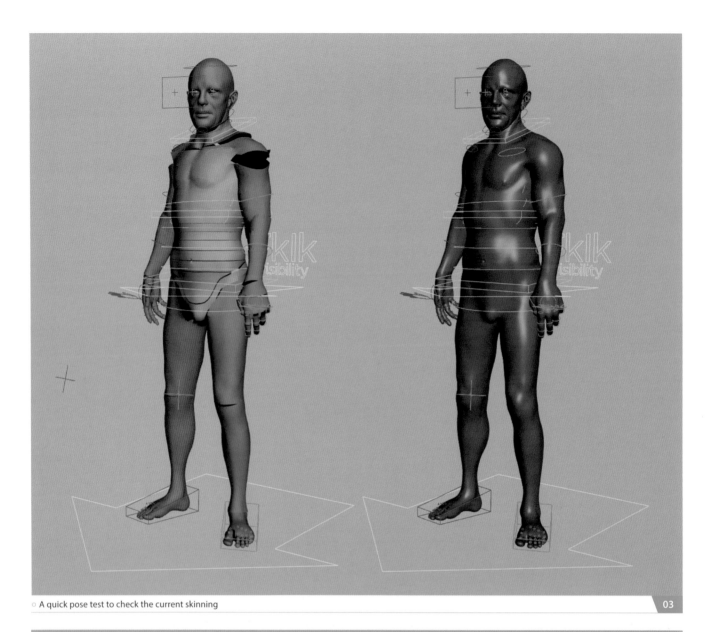

○ A quick pose test to check the current skinning

03

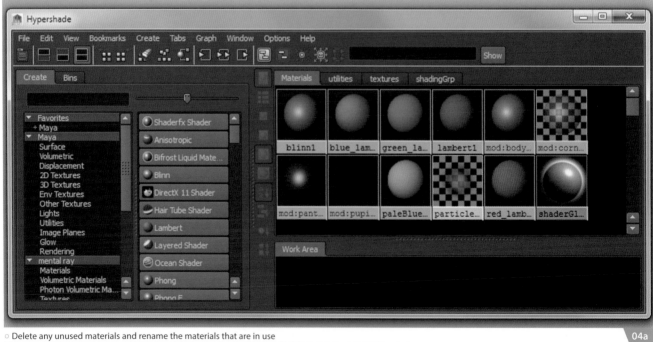

○ Delete any unused materials and rename the materials that are in use

04a

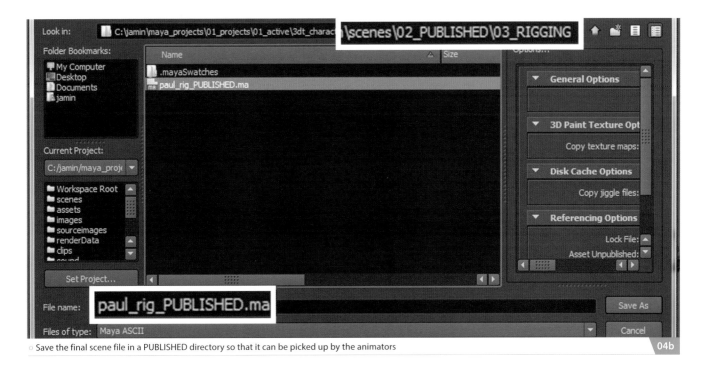

Save the final scene file in a PUBLISHED directory so that it can be picked up by the animators

04b

03: Pose test

Save your latest rig file as a temporary file and use the controls to pose the character. I normally create three or four different poses to give me a good idea of how the character will deform. I've just gone for a standing idle pose and a few poses from a generic walk cycle to see if the rig is fit for purpose.

I don't try to create highly exaggerated poses, as this isn't a cartoony rig and it's not what the rig intended to do. If you spot any areas that look like they need improving, don't worry too much – like I said before, we can always come back and update the rig.

04: Publishing the rig

We are now going to publish the rig. Open up your latest scene file, make sure that all the controls are back in their default position, and ensure all the geometry layers and the **paul_rig_layer** are set to Reference. In the viewport, you should now only be able to select the animation curves.

Next, jump into Hypershade (Window > Rendering Editors) and go to Edit > Delete Unused Nodes to get rid of any unused shaders. Make sure you appropriately rename any shaders that have been left in the scene (**Fig.04a**). Now save this scene

file so you have a local copy that you can come back to and update should you need to. Then go to File > Save As, navigate to \scenes\02_PUBLISHED\03_RIGGING, and save the scene as **paul_rig_PUBLISHED** (**Fig.04b**). We're done and ready to animate (**Fig.04c**)!

A final point on publishing: as this rig will be Referenced in by the animator, we can continue to build on it if we need to. For example, we could add controls to the volume joints and add corrective blend shape fixes. Although the rig is complete, like any work, we should never class it as final and should always be prepared to make updates to better the final outcome.

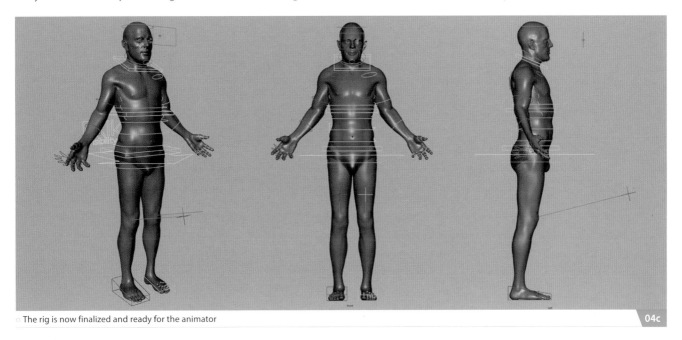

The rig is now finalized and ready for the animator

04c

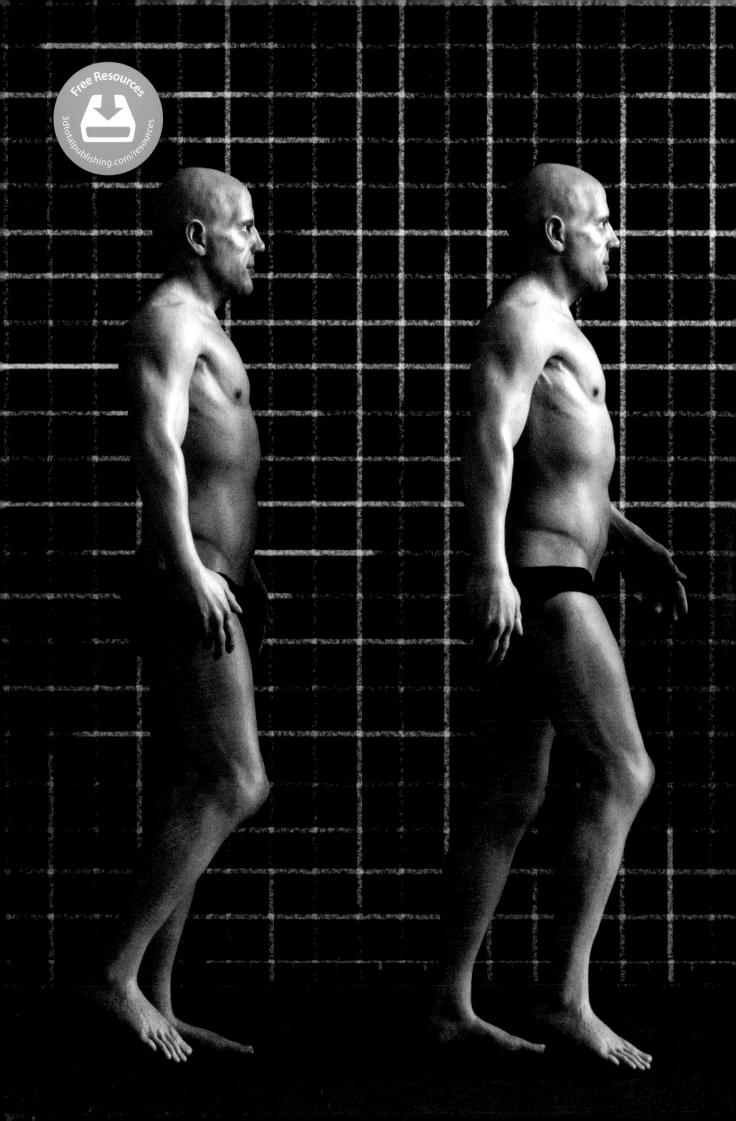

Locomotion and animation in Maya

Putting your rig into action with a walk cycle animation

Now that your model is fully rigged, it's time to make it move. This section will cover the mechanics of movement and motion, showing you how to create a convincing animation with squashing, stretching, and careful timing. We'll start off with the classic exercise of animating a bouncing ball, learning how to create an animation with lifelike impact and momentum, before graduating to making a walk cycle for your model.

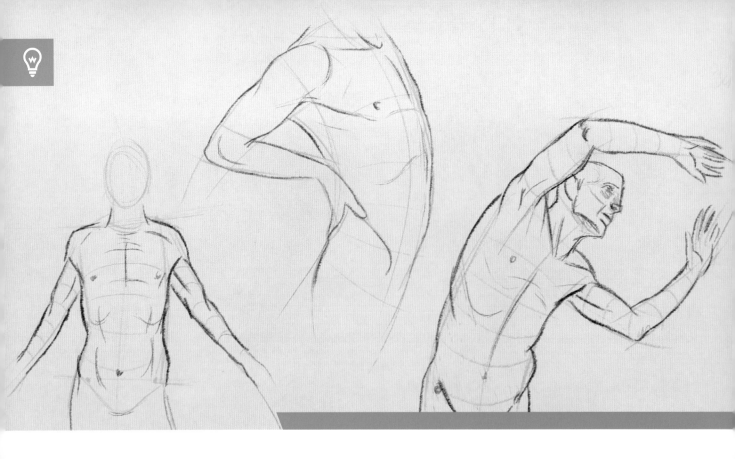

Principles of animation

Understanding movement and motion

By the end of this section focusing on animation, we will have made our character perform a walk cycle. To ready ourselves for this exercise, we will examine two areas of theory to guide us on our way. The first are the principles of animation, which were observed in the 1930s onwards by Disney's leading animators, and which were first expounded in *The Illusion of Life* by Frank Thomas and Ollie Johnston in 1981. These principles are worthy of your very close attention, as they provide a beautifully simple set of guidelines that can stand you in no better stead when beginning to animate.

> "These laws need to be brought from the back to the front of our minds when looking to create movement in CG"

We will then go a little further back in history: to your school days, to the 17th century and the work of Isaac Newton. These laws, while part of our

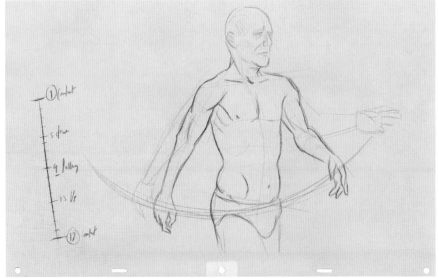

○ It is important to understand different kinds of movement before you begin animating

consciousness, need to be brought from the back to the front of our minds when looking to create movement in CG.

As we enter Maya, we will get to know the animation tools this package has to offer through the old animation chestnut:

the bouncing ball. We will take a look at how the principles of animation and Newton's laws are clearly present in this exercise, and see how the simple bounce of a ball can be related to so many forms of movement. You will have the opportunity to try to bounce a digital ball yourself.

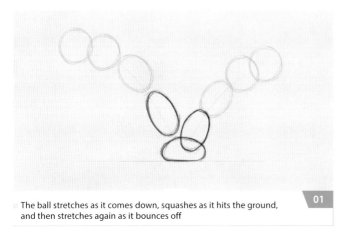

The ball stretches as it comes down, squashes as it hits the ground, and then stretches again as it bounces off **01**

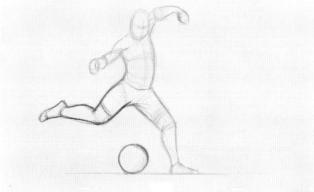

To prepare the audience for what is to come, we need to add anticipation **02**

Finally, we will move on to the walk cycle, which is another perfect way to see Newton's Laws and the principles of animation in action. We will begin by taking some walk cycle reference and breaking it down to analyze core poses, timing, weight, and so on before having a go at a walk cycle ourselves.

01: Squash and stretch

This principle of animation is based on the fact that all matter in motion retains its volume but does not retain its shape. Consider the human form jumping: in preparation for the movement, the body squashes down into a crouch before stretching into the leap. Consider facial expressions: a smile will stretch the lips and squash the cheeks while a look of surprise will widen the eyes but squash the forehead.

When applied to an animation, these changes in shape through the use of squash and stretch will lend characters fluidity, elasticity, and vitality, and therefore believability. The same rules also apply to material forms, and a bouncing ball demonstrates this very clearly: it stretches as it descends, squashes on impact, and then gradually returns to its original shape as it ascends.

Squash and stretch is a perfect illustration of the necessity of grounding CG in real-world examples.

02: Anticipation

To allow an audience to understand and engage fully with an animation, we need to give them a certain amount of information to be able to anticipate what is to come. Many a gag is built on creating an expectation of what is to come, and then turning that expectation on its head.

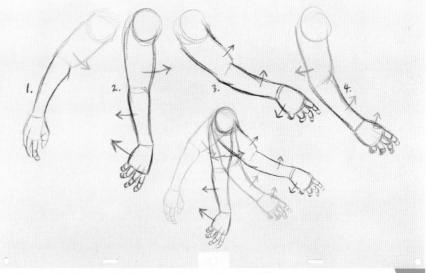

As the arm swings forwards, the forearm and hand are delayed, and likewise as the arm swings back **03**

As with squash and stretch, this principle is grounded in physical law: very few movements are not preceded by preparation, which here we call anticipation. Take the following as an example: before standing up, the head and upper body move downwards and the hands grip the side or arms of the chair. Before kicking a ball, the leg is first pulled behind the body, to then come forwards and make contact with the ball.

It's clear from these examples that the anticipatory action, which often moves in the opposite direction to the main action, serves to generate energy to power the action to come.

03: "Follow through" and "overlapping action"

These terms concern techniques which evolved in order to avoid movement coming to too abrupt a stop. If actions stop dead, then the scene literally dies and the illusion is broken.

Therefore, to soften the stops, animation needs to pay attention to the fact that some parts of the body will become stationary after movement more quickly than others, depending on their mass and on the nature of the action taking place.

In many cases, the pelvis will lead the movement, and the rest of the body will follow behind, and of course, clothes and hair will invariably come to a stop last. For example: as we walk and our arms swing, while the upper arm has already begun to move backwards, the forearm can still be swinging forwards.

04: Timing

This principle concerns the time in frames that a movement will last for. The exact same movement played slowly or quickly (or somewhere in between) will give an audience very different information. Take the example of a woman running her hands

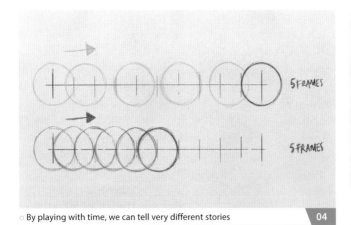

○ By playing with time, we can tell very different stories 04

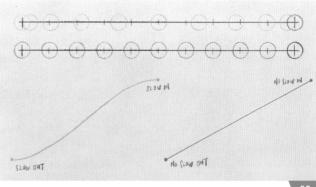

○ By using the principle of "slow in and slow out", we can add a natural rhythm to the movement 05

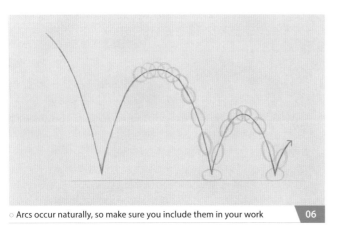

○ Arcs occur naturally, so make sure you include them in your work 06

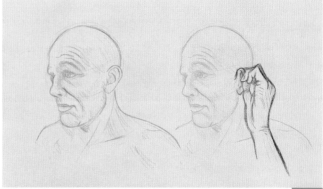

○ Adding secondary motion can give further clues about a character 07

through her hair. Played quickly, the action will transmit to the audience the sense that she is anxious or harried. Played slowly, on the other hand, the same action may give an impression of thoughtfulness or exhaustion.

Timing is also linked to the principles of overlapping and follow through as outlined on the previous page, where we discussed that an action will come to a stop gradually, with some parts of the body returning to a stationary position faster than others.

05: : "Slow in and slow out"

In an animated piece, attention needs to be drawn towards the key poses, or those poses which actually tell the story, so that an audience can follow the narrative unfolding in front of them.

For this reason, the in-between poses that create the transition from one key pose to the next, are mainly clustered around those key poses, and there is a breakdown pose at the halfway point between each key pose. Such an arrangement serves to draw the eye toward the key poses while also adhering to natural rhythm, in the sense that

we move into and out of positions through gradual acceleration and deceleration.

06: Arcs

Most movement in nature, unless it is very short, travels in an arc rather than a straight line. As you are reading this paragraph, take your hand from the page and touch your nose. Unless you are holding the book no more than a few inches from your face, your hand will trace an arc in the air. When

animating, an absence of arcs will result in very stiff, abrupt, and unnatural movement.

07: Secondary action

A secondary action is one which is added to a main action with the intention of supporting and strengthening the narrative or mood of a piece. Picture a scene where two characters are talking (main action). One character gesticulates strongly while talking (secondary action) while the other responds but takes

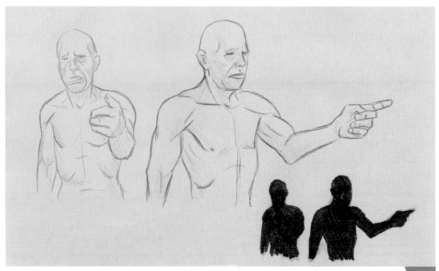

○ It is important that poses are clear and readable for the audience to read the action 08

surreptitious glances at the clock behind the other's head (secondary action). These secondary actions clearly provide additional character information for the audience.

> "An artist needs to lend his or her art a real believability in order for it to work, whether on paper or on screen"

08: Staging

This principle concerns the necessity of presenting concepts in such a way that there is no ambiguity for the audience. A character must be posed in a recognizable way and positioned, with respect to the camera, with perfect visibility. Even the subtlest facial expressions must be staged correctly for the audience to follow the narrative.

09: "Straight ahead action" and "pose to pose"

These are two methods of animating a piece. In "straight ahead action" the animator starts animating from the beginning of the piece and works through to the end, knowing the premise but not exactly where the journey will take him, just as you might write a story. It is a very spontaneous, organic way of working that can produce some very innovative results.

"Pose to pose", in contrast, means that the animator will block out all the principal poses of the piece, and the intervening action will be filled in afterwards. Though there is clearly an absence of spontaneity here, there is opportunity for very strong, very readable poses.

10: Exaggeration

Exaggeration is the idea that animation, though it may try to mimic reality, is not reality, and requires an extra push to achieve believability.

A realistic walk cycle, for example, will need a bit more weight going down with each step, and a little more lift with each rise than you'd normally expect to see on the street, in order for it to look "correct" on screen.

Expressions or movements which are too subtle may be lost entirely. When aiming for a realistic look, exaggeration will be slight; when aiming for a cartoony feel, the forms can really be pushed for great comedic effect.

11: Appeal

Appeal essentially relates to anything that an audience takes pleasure in seeing.

Though it may be said that beauty is in the eye of the beholder, we are all naturally drawn to good, simple designs, and to ideas that are communicated in an unambiguous way.

Appealing work means that a relationship is formed with the audience, and the audience, therefore, continues to watch.

12: Solid drawing

In this book there is an emphasis on the need to understand real-world examples before trying to recreate their counterparts in CG. This principle similarly insists on having strong foundations – here in traditional artistry – before trying to animate.

An artist needs to lend his or her art a real believability in order for it to work, whether on paper or on screen.

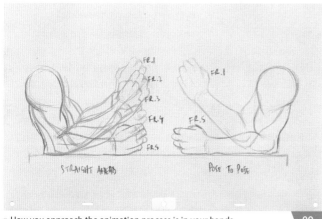
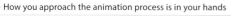

○ How you approach the animation process is in your hands　**09**

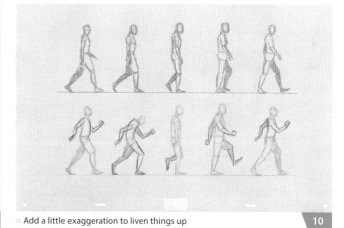

○ Add a little exaggeration to liven things up　**10**

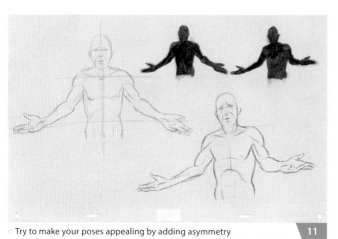

○ Try to make your poses appealing by adding asymmetry　**11**

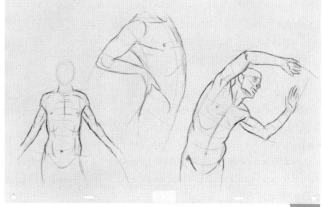

○ Think about volume, mass, and structure as you pose and animate　**12**

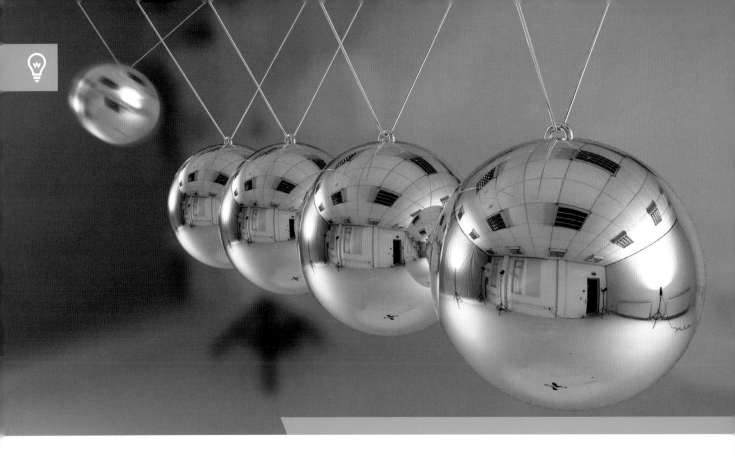

Newton's laws of motion

Isaac Newton's laws and what they mean for an animator

Before attempting to make anything move in CG, it is essential to understand the laws that govern movement: Newton's three laws of motion. Much of what makes up these three laws is already a part of our consciousness; we move and observe movement all day. We understand, for instance, that heavy objects move more slowly than light ones.

However, by actually studying Newton's laws, this implicit understanding is made much more active and can be kept in mind when animating. While we may not be able to recite the three laws spontaneously, when they are absent from an animation, they are very conspicuous by their absence, and the bubble of illusion is burst. Let's look at the three laws in turn.

01: Newton's first law of motion

An object in motion stays in motion at the same speed and in the same direction unless acted on by an unbalanced force. An object will keep on doing what it's doing (that is, either resting or moving) until a force acts on it to change that.

This law is also known as the law of inertia, and it is the reason why wearing a seatbelt while in a car is a very good idea. If you are driving and the car stops very suddenly, wearing a seatbelt will ensure that you and the car share the same motion, and that you will also come to a stop. Without a seatbelt, however, your motion will continue and off you fly through the windscreen and beyond.

The principle of animation called "follow through", which we looked at previously, is based on this law. Let's take the example of a car driver who was wise enough to wear a seatbelt. It's easy to visualize what would happen to his body on impact. His torso, wearing the seatbelt, shares most closely the motion of the car and is brought to a stop equally fast. The head and neck will continue to move for a few

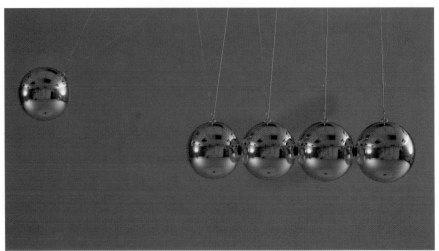

○ Understanding Newton's laws will help your animations look believable

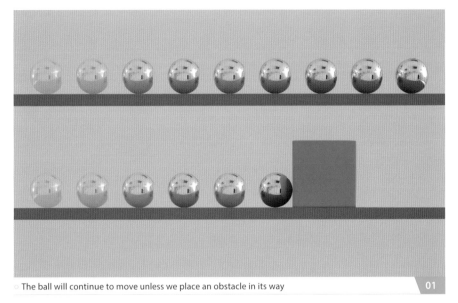

The ball will continue to move unless we place an obstacle in its way   01

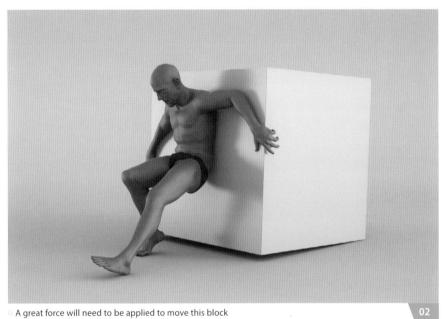

A great force will need to be applied to move this block   02

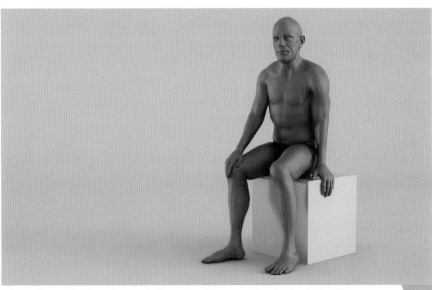

As the sitter applies force downwards, the seat applies an equal force back onto the sitter   03

moments, and the hair, if it is long, will be the last part of the body to become stationary.

02: Newton's second law of motion

When a force acts on a mass, acceleration is produced. The greater the mass, the greater the force required to achieve acceleration. Therefore, the same force acting on two different objects will produce two different accelerations. This is why it is far easier to push your broken-down scooter than your broken-down SUV.

The law provides an equation:

force = mass × acceleration

Let's relate this to anticipation, one of the principles of animation described in the previous paragraphs. Imagine that you're going to animate two characters: one is going to lift a heavy weight, and the other is going to lift something very light. Clearly, the first character is going to need to prepare to lift the heavy object, so the anticipation will be bold moves: he may pull up his sleeves and brace himself to handle the weight.

Anticipation for the second character will need to be far more subtle: the character will turn his eyes to look at the object and his hand will reach for it, with the fingers adopting an appropriate pose.

03: Newton's third law of motion

For every action, there is an equal and opposite reaction. Acting forces meet other forces acting in the opposite direction. As a perfect example of this natural symmetry, when you sit down, you exert a downward force on the chair. At the same time, though we are not conscious of it, the chair is exerting a similar force upwards on you. Were the chair unable to exert this equal upward force, it would collapse.

Let's relate this to a gun being fired. The gunpowder explosion inside the gun pushes the bullet forwards at great speed. The same force is exerted backwards causing the gun to "kick". Naturally the bullet travels much faster and further because its mass is far smaller than that of the gun itself. If this equal and opposite reaction (in this case, the "kick") was not depicted in an animation, the audience would register its absence.

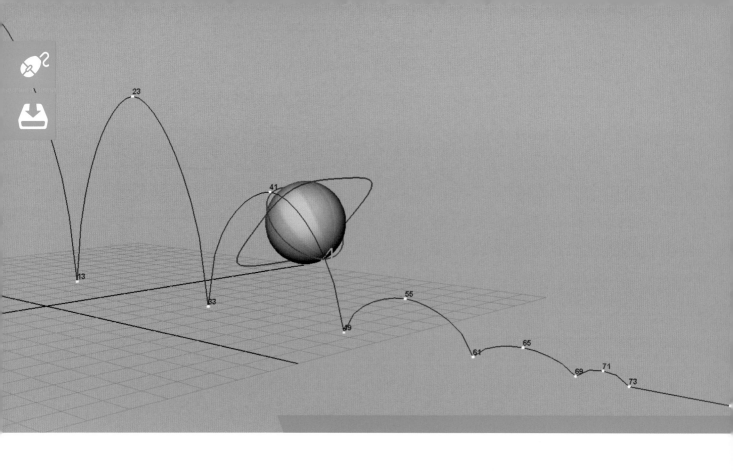

Animating a bouncing ball

Starting off with a classic animation exercise

In this chapter we're going to animate a ball bouncing. This simple exercise is actually a rite of passage for all animators, involving key principles of animation: timing, spacing, weight, and squash and stretch. As you develop your skills and move on to the walk cycle, it'll become clear that a walking figure is basically a bouncing ball with appendages, following the same patterns of movement. In fact, many kinds of movement, when analyzed, lead you right back to the bouncing ball. Let's do our best to crack it.

01: Gathering and examining references

The best starting point is to get your own references. All you need is a half-decent camera, a tripod, and a few balls of varying weight and bounce. If you also have a meter stick to place against the wall to measure the height of the bounces, even better. Film the balls bouncing: first, simply drop them, but next, allow balls to fall from your tilted hand, as if falling from a slope. In each set of filming, vary the height of the drop.

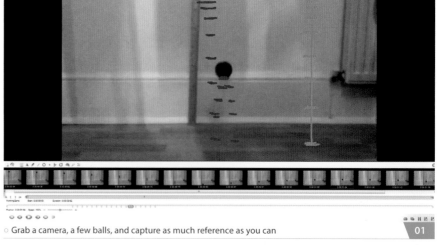

○ Grab a camera, a few balls, and capture as much reference as you can 01

The next step is to break down the reference frame by frame. I strongly recommend the totally free and totally fantastic Kinovea (**www.kinovea.org**), a motion analysis tool allowing you to draw over what you've captured, with tools to measure distances, timing, and arcs, and much more besides.

Be aware that your camera only records a certain number of frames per second; some

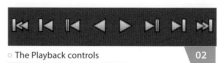

○ The Playback controls 02

information will be lost on camera, and you'll have to fill in the blanks using your understanding of the laws of motion. The intention is not to copy the reference frame by frame, but to achieve an understanding of the arcs, timing, and gradual loss of energy.

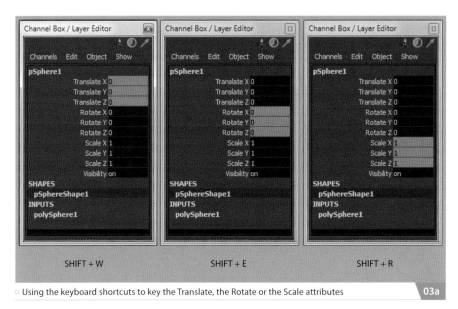

SHIFT + W   SHIFT + E   SHIFT + R

○ Using the keyboard shortcuts to key the Translate, the Rotate or the Scale attributes   03a

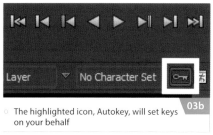

○ The highlighted icon, Autokey, will set keys on your behalf   03b

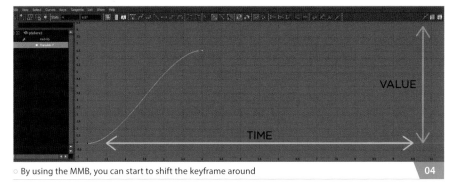

○ By using the MMB, you can start to shift the keyframe around   04

02: Playback controls

Now let's examine the Playback controls in Maya, found on the bottom-left corner of the screen. These are the standard controls you'd find in any package. Working from the outside in, you have the Go to start/ end of playback range, Step back/forward one frame, Step back/forward one key, and the Play backwards/forwards buttons.

It's fine to use the buttons, but I prefer keyboard shortcuts to speed up my workflow. The shortcut for Play forwards is Alt+V. With your cursor in the viewport, you can also scrub through the Timeline by holding down the V key and LMB-dragging in the viewport. You can also do this in the Graph Editor and the Dope Sheet.

Hold down the V key and MMB-drag in the viewport to move backwards and forwards in time, but keep the objects in their place. This is great for copying poses from one frame to another. The shortcuts to go frame by frame are Alt+comma or Alt+full-stop. You can go from one keyframe to the next by pressing

just the comma or full-stop, but this only works if the selected object has keyframes.

03: Setting keys

Let's look at setting keyframes. In a clean Maya scene, create a polygon primitive (I've gone for a sphere). At frame 1, select the sphere, and hit S on the keyboard. If the Channel Box is open, you'll notice that every attribute has now been keyed; I use this a lot when blocking out the animation.

Jump to frame 10, translate the sphere in any direction, and hit S again. If you now scrub through the timeline, between frames 1 and 10, the sphere will transition from one pose to the next.

I'll now explore how to key a set of attributes, or just individual attributes. As our sphere currently has all the attributes keyed, we first need to delete these existing keys. There are many ways to do this, but for now, double-click in the Timeline to highlight everything. You can also hold down Shift and LMB-drag in

the timeline to create a red selection window. Either way, with the keys highlighted, hold down the RMB and press Delete. To key just the Translate attributes, select the sphere (at any frame) and press Shift+W; for just the Rotate attributes, use Shift+E; for the Scale attributes, use Shift+R (Fig.03a).

Let's delete the keys and key an individual attribute. To delete the keys this time, with the sphere selected, go to Edit > Keys > Delete Keys. To key an individual attribute, highlight the attribute in the Channel Box, hold down the RMB and go to Key Selected. Do this to the Translate Y attribute at frame 1, then jump to frame 10, translate the ball upwards, and set another key on Translate Y.

Before we move on, I want to mention the Autokey feature (Fig.03b). We've been manually setting keys, which is all well and good, but on many occasions, as I pose a character from one frame to another, I want to scrub through the timeline to see how the poses hold up. As I do this, I might forget to set a key, and have to go back and re-create the pose. To address this problem, I enable Autokey. With Autokey, once an initial key is set on an attribute, any changes you make to that attribute and at any frame will be keyed.

This is great for my work style, but does have drawbacks. If you forget that it's enabled and just want to experiment with a pose without committing, you can't, but you can enable and disable it at any time. From here on in I will have Autokey enabled.

04: Using the Graph Editor

You should have just two keys for the Translate Y channel for your sphere: one at frame 1 and the other at frame 10. We'll use the Graph Editor now to manipulate the keys and change the way in which the sphere travels from one position to the other.

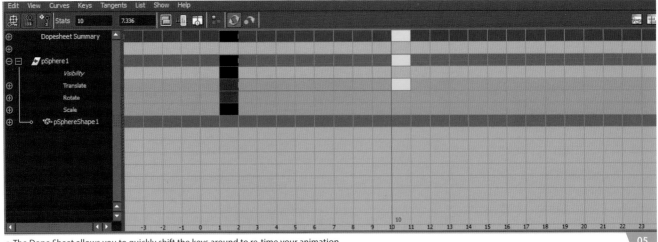

○ The Dope Sheet allows you to quickly shift the keys around to re-time your animation

05

To open up the Graph Editor (GE), simply go to Window > Animation Editors > Graph Editor.

If you have nothing selected, the GE will be empty. With an object selected (one that has keyframes), you should see the animation curves. These curves are a graphical representation of the animated attribute, describing how it gets from one position to the next. As we only have keys on the Translate Y attribute, we'll only see one curve. The small points on the curve are the keys. There's also a left–hand column listing all the attributes that have been keyed for the selected object.

We've spent time in Maya's other 2D editors, such as the Hypershade, so I won't go into detail on navigating the GE or the upcoming Dope Sheet, as they're handled in the same way. Simply use the Alt key with either the MMB (Pan) or RMB (Zoom). Just be aware of where the cursor is: Is it floating in the viewport or in the GE? I mention this because it's easy to delete an object/animation control when you actually intended to delete a keyframe in the GE.

Let's now edit the current animation data. If you switch to the Move tool and select any point (keyframe) on the curve, you can easily use the MMB to drag the keyframe around. Note that translating in the vertical will update its value, while translating in the horizontal will update its position in time. By holding Shift and MMB-dragging in either the vertical or the horizontal, it will restrict movement along the corresponding axis. You can also use the Scale tool to edit the curve and the keyframes but, personally, I prefer to stick with just the Move tool.

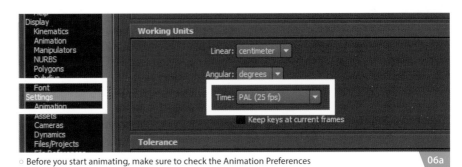

○ Before you start animating, make sure to check the Animation Preferences

06a

If you analyze the curve, you'll notice it gradually curves out and in. Press play and you'll see how this affects the sphere as it transitions from one pose to the next: it eases out, picks up a constant speed, and then eases in. Select the curve and go to Tangents > Linear. Press play again and see the sphere transition from one pose to the next with equal pace. By simply changing the behavior of the curve, we can get dramatically different results. There are multiple ways to edit the shape of a curve, which we'll look at once we start animating our ball.

For now, try adding additional keyframes to the curve. With the curve selected, go to Keys > Insert Key Tool, then hold down the MMB and let go over the curve to add a keyframe at that position and time.

05: The Dope Sheet

We'll move on to the Dope Sheet now, found under Window > Animation Editors > Dope Sheet. The Dope Sheet is used for re-timing the animation; in 2D land, its equivalent is the Exposure Sheet (X-Sheet). On the top line, you'll see the Dope Sheet Summary. By moving keys on this line, you'll affect the keys for all the attributes. With the Move tool activated, you can LMB-click a key on that line and use the MMB to move it in time. If you have

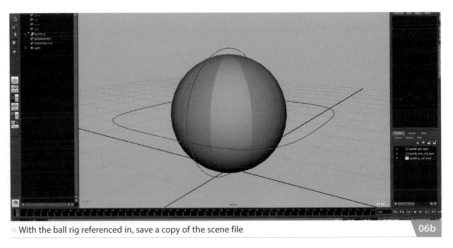

○ With the ball rig referenced in, save a copy of the scene file

06b

multiple attributes keyed, you can individually shift the keys around by revealing the keyed attributes in the left-hand column. In both the Dope Sheet and Graph Editor, you can press the RMB to access an additional set of controls such as Copy, Cut, Paste, and so on.

06: Animation preferences and the ball rig

Now let's animate a bouncing ball. Open up a new scene and start by setting the animation preferences. I tend to do this before starting any animation. You can open up the preferences by clicking on the highlighted icon in Fig.06a, or by going to Window > Settings/Preferences > Preferences. When the window pops up, in the left-hand column, highlight Settings and set the Time to PAL (25 fps). PAL is usually what I use for personal projects, but feel free to edit this to match your region or the format that best suits your project.

Highlight Animation and make sure the Default in and Default out tangents are set to Spline. If we now set a number of keys on an attribute, the interpolation from one key to the other will have a spline tangent by default (which we saw previously). You could also leave this as Auto, which is a combination of Spline and Clamped. This helps to reduce overshoot in the animation curves.

When we block out the walk cycle later, we'll set this to Stepped tangent, so we can animate in a more pose-to-pose method with no interpolation between the keys. Go to Time Slider and set the Playback Speed to Real-Time [25 fps]. Check the Timeline, as switching the Time attribute can result in the Playback Range expanding or compressing. I've set my Playback Range to run from 1 to 100. Once the settings are updated, hit Save (Fig.06b).

You may also want to enable a display setting (the Frame Rate), allowing you to see how close to real-time your playback speed is running on your machine. I'm sure it'll be fine with a ball, but once we're creating a walk cycle with the main mesh, the playback speed will probably be affected. To reveal the Frame Rate, go to Display > Heads up Display > Frame Rate.

Now that the scene is set up, let's call in the bouncing ball rig. Go to File > Create Reference (Options). In the "Use selected namespace

as parent and add new namespace string" field, type **rig** and hit Reference. Navigate to the following Maya directory: scenes/02_PUBLISHED/03_RIGGING and select the **ball_rig_PUBLISHED.ma** file. Save this scene file in the 01_WIP/04_ANIMATION directory.

07: Bouncing ball key poses

We're ready to start bouncing. Hopefully you'll have spent some time capturing and examining references. Although I've broken down my reference, I'll keep these steps quite prescriptive so you can achieve similar results. If you wish to create an animation resembling your own reference material, simply tailor the following steps to your needs.

Before we start, take a bit of time to get familiar with the rig. I recommend running through each control, assessing the attributes available in the Channel Box and observing how one control affects the other. When you're happy with the rig, re-open the scene file and hit the 6 key to see the texture applied to the ball. This makes it easier to see the rotations we'll be applying later.

We'll start by simply getting the ball to move up and down (Fig.07a). Make sure you're at frame 1, raise the ball using the ball_main_ctrl, and then key just the Translate Y attribute. (I raise the ball by around 8.5 units.) Let's presume it takes 12 frames for this ball to hit the ground from this height. Jump to frame 13, set the value of the Translate Y attribute to 0, then set another key.

The ball will lose some energy (or technically, transfer the energy) as it hits the ground, so its second bounce won't be as high. I jump to frame 23 and set the Translate Y attribute to 5.6. We now want gravity to do its magic and bring

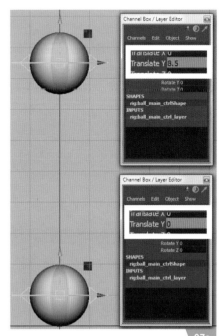

Setting the first two poses for our ball: the start position and the contact position
07a

the ball back down again. As it takes 10 frames for the ball to reach its apex, it surely takes the same number for it to come back down to the ground. Therefore, jump to frame 33, set the Translate Y attribute to 0, and set another key.

As we hit the ground, we'll transfer some energy again, creating a smaller bounce. Jump to frame 41, translate the ball up by 3.2 units and set another key. Then go back down to 0 at frame 49.

Hopefully you get the idea here, so continue to create two or three more bounces. With each bounce, try to make it seem like the same amount of energy is transferred, e.g. each time, the ball may reach 70% of the height of the bounce before it. By doing this, the animation should feel natural (Fig.07b).

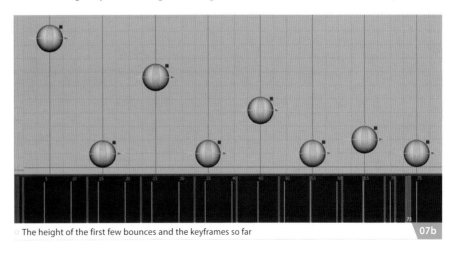

The height of the first few bounces and the keyframes so far
07b

08: Playblasting

Now that we have some animation, hit Play to see the results. It's probably not the most exciting bouncing ball you've ever seen, and without a doubt lacks weight and impact on the floor. If you open up the Graph Editor, you'll see a lot of easing out and easing in on the animation curve for the Translate Y attribute, and this is reflected in the animation.

It's fine to play back the animation by simply pressing play, with the Frame Count indicating that it's playing in real time, but I recommend you create a playblast. This records the animation and plays it back to you, independently from the viewport. To do this, RMB-click over the Timeline and go to Playblast (Options). I use the following settings: Format: Image, Encoding: jpg, Display size: From window, Scale: 1. When ready, hit Playblast. During the animation process, I'll assess the animation by creating regular playblasts, so make sure you do the same.

09: Use the Graph Editor to add Weight

Now let's add some weight. Additional keys would help create the illusion of weight, but instead, let's manipulate the existing animation curve. Open up the Graph Editor, and with the Move tool active, select any keyframe. You'll notice two small tangent handles appear either side of the selected keyframe. You can RMB-drag left and right to change the angle of the tangent handles, which in turn affect the behavior of the curve. This essentially controls the spacing of our animation without affecting the timing.

At the moment, if we manipulate one half of the tangent handles, the other half is also affected, which isn't to our advantage here. For what we want, select all the keyframes that have a value of 0 (the contact poses where the ball hits the ground) and go to Keys > Break Tangents. For those keys, we can now affect one half of the tangents without affecting the other.

We can make the ball feel like it's making contact with the ground. To do this, edit the curve so that a sharp V-shape is present for all the contact poses. (The curve should start to mimic a parabolic arc.) The ball should descend more quickly, hit the ground hard, go up more quickly, and slow down slightly at the apex of its bounce.

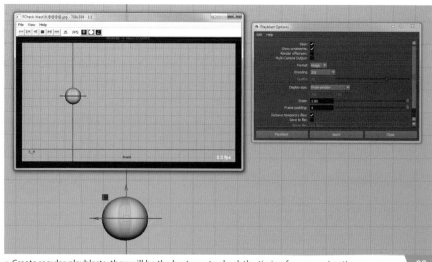

○ Create regular playblasts; they will be the best way to check the timing for your animations **08**

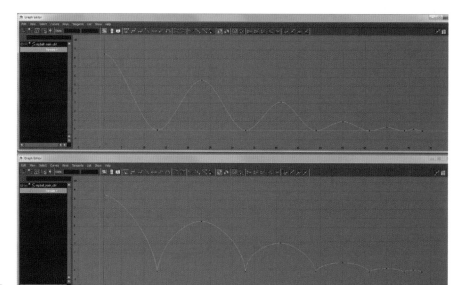

○ By manipulating the curve, we can give the ball a feeling of weight and mass **09**

Remember to do a playblast to assess the results. If the timing feels off or odd, I'd move the keyframes around using either the Graph Editor or the Dope Sheet. You can also do this in the Timeline.

10: Moving from left to right

Now let's get our ball moving across the screen. I'm working in the Front view as I do

this, so I'll be using the Translate X attribute to get it from one side to the other. Jump back to frame 1 and set a key on the Translate X attribute. Then go to the final frame of your current animation, translate the ball using the Translate X attribute, and set another key (Fig.10a). In the Graph Editor, select the curve for Translate X, and go to Tangents > Linear. Press Play to see what you get.

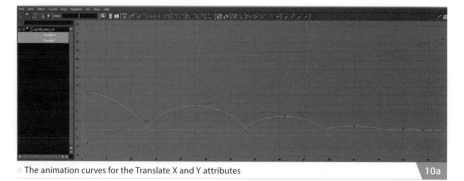

○ The animation curves for the Translate X and Y attributes **10a**

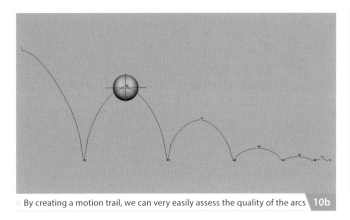

○ By creating a motion trail, we can very easily assess the quality of the arcs **10b**

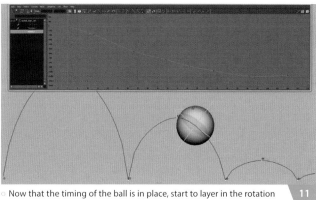

○ Now that the timing of the ball is in place, start to layer in the rotation **11**

To get a better idea of how it moves in our viewport, select the **ball_main_ctrl** and go to Animate > Create Editable Motion Trail. This is pretty much the Graph Editor in 3D space, and a great way of updating the animation. Using this, you can move keys around in time and edit the tangents to affect an object's trajectory. I use this often to assess the arcs. For now, try to get the balance right for the ball as it bounces across the screen (Fig.10b).

You may want to add additional keyframes on the Translate X attribute as it hits the ground, to create the idea of some friction between the ball and the ground. Again, as the ball moves across the screen, it should create a number of parabolic arcs.

I also like to use the Ghost Selected tool. With the **ball_main_ctrl** selected, go to Animate > Ghost Selected. This is like a 3D version of onion skinning and is a fantastic tool to monitor the spacing. I find it works fine for simple objects, but for more complicated characters – and if you would like to ghost the geometry – it's not great.

For that reason, when we start creating a walk cycle, I'll introduce you to the fantastic bhGhost tool by Brian Horgan, but more on that later.

11: Adding Rotation

Now let's add some rotation. Use the Rotate Z attribute on the **ball_main_ctrl**. I've made sure that for the initial three bounces, the ball rotates onto one of its poles as it makes contact with the ground, so that when I add the squash and stretch in the next step, the texture won't distort too much.

As a general rule, we shouldn't allow a thing like texture distortion to restrict how we animate, but I'll let myself bend the rules slightly for this simple rig. Once you've added rotation, you may also want to add the ball rolling back slightly as it comes to a stop. A subtle touch like this can make the animation feel more natural and organic.

12: Adding squash and stretch

To add squash and stretch, I'll use the **ball_top_ss_ctrl** and **ball_bottom_ss_ctrl**. I

add squash poses by pushing down on the controls (Fig.12a). Don't go too mad here unless you want a very exaggerated piece. Add less squash each time the ball makes contact with the ground, and little-to-no squash for the final few bounces. Add some stretch as the ball comes down to make contact with the ground, and also as the ball bounces off again. Like we did for the contact poses, every time the ball comes down and goes up again, add less and less stretch, and then none at all for the final few bounces.

You'll also want to ensure that as the ball stretches, it does so into the arc in which it's moving, adding fluidity to the animation. You can use the **ball_ss_rotate_ctrl** to orient the squash and stretch controls to allow for this. Lastly, when the ball is at the apex of each bounce, it slows down, so make sure that no squash or stretch is happening. At this stage, it's a case of continuously refining the animation until you're happy (Fig.12b). Once you've animated your ball, try playing with timing and spacing to create balls of different weights.

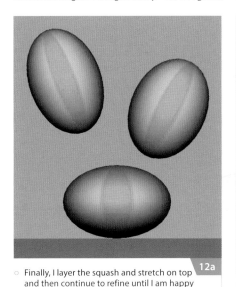

○ Finally, I layer the squash and stretch on top and then continue to refine until I am happy **12a**

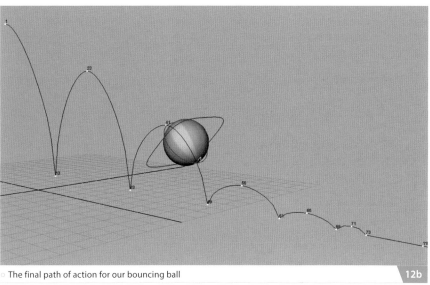

○ The final path of action for our bouncing ball **12b**

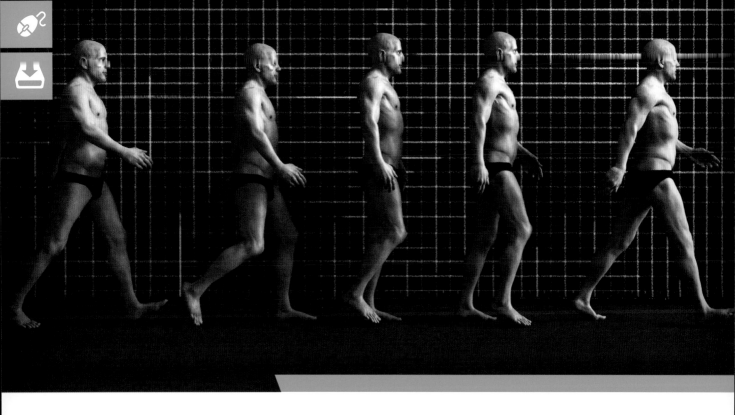

Animating a walk cycle

Creating a realistic walking animation for the model

In this second animation exercise, we'll make the character we've created walk. A walk cycle involves more principles of animation such as timing, spacing, weight, drag, and overlap. In a sense, we'll take the bouncing ball and complicate our lives by giving it a head and limbs.

As with the bouncing ball, the walk cycle may appear simple. However, perhaps because we see people walking every day, a badly executed walk cycle screams out from the screen. With the bouncing ball, the computer initially interpolated how the ball transitions from one keyframe to the next, but with a walk cycle those techniques would produce a very "floaty" result, and we could end up focusing too much on the frame-to-frame movement. Instead we'll work with a "pose-to-pose" style, focusing on getting the key poses readable before thinking about how we transition between them.

So each pose needs to be clearly readable by the audience and should be set from the

hips, with the movement spreading down to the legs and up the spine to the head and neck, and then to the arms and hands.

Once the poses are set, the keys can be splined, and the refining process can begin. You may prefer to go straight to splining; find what works best for you. Either way, make

sure you're the one making the decisions on how the character is moving, and not your computer. There's no substitute for getting your hands dirty and manually refining the curves, sometimes even frame by frame.

First, a quick update on some changes I've made to the published model and

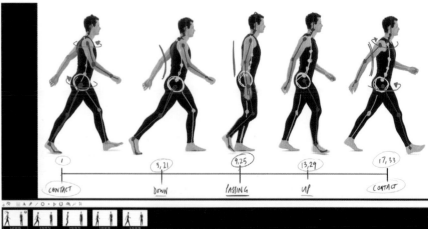

○ Breaking down the reference will prepare you for what's ahead

01

rig files. In the published model file, I've duplicated pants_hr_geo and named the duplicate pants_cloth_hr_geo. We'll add cloth dynamics to this geometry later on.

For the published rig file, I've skinned pants_hr_geo to the existing skeleton, but I haven't done any weight painting as the dynamic briefs will be included in the final render. I skinned the briefs so we can constrain our dynamic briefs to them, and because it feels a little risqué to do a walk cycle with the character in the buff.

01: Gathering reference

Like the bouncing ball exercise, the first step is to gather good references. There's reference aplenty online, but no substitute for getting out there and watching people move with your own eyes and their own legs. Try to get a feeling for when and how the weight shifts from one leg to the other. Get an understanding of which body parts lead and which follow: the arms follow the swing of the torso, for instance. Observe subtle details such as the slight bob of the head; subtleties, like a pinch of salt added to soup, make all the difference.

For this exercise, we've been given permission to use the Athletic Male Standard Walk from Endless Reference (**www.endlessreference.com**). Do have a look at the other references they have on offer if you want to animate a different style of walk.

As with the bouncing ball, I recommend taking the reference into Kinovea (**www.kinovea.org**) to break it down. Try to identify the key poses which provide the building blocks of your walk cycle. Notice contrasting lines from the hips and shoulders as the torso twists. Observe the angle of the feet, which are not perfectly straight.

Be aware that reference material will only ever be a guide: you'll need your animator's eye to push and pull these key poses into something that looks believable in CG. Think back to the rigging section, in which we sometimes deliberately decided to not to copy nature, so as to create a rig that would actually produce natural-looking movement. It's the same concept here: sometimes the reality you find in reference needs to be pushed or pulled further to recreate that reality digitally.

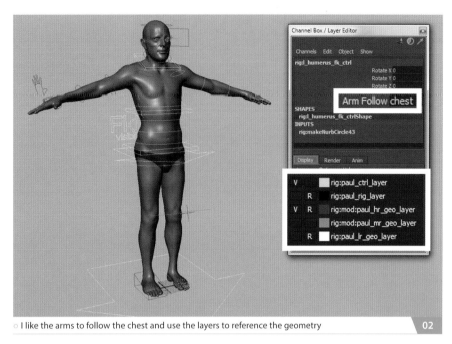

○ I like the arms to follow the chest and use the layers to reference the geometry   02

02: Referencing the rig

The first thing we want to do is open a new Maya scene and set the animation preferences. This time, however, change the Default Out Tangents to Stepped, allowing you to animate pose to pose. Once you've checked the preferences and updated the tangents, set the Frame Range to go from frame 1 to frame 33. Each step we create will take 16 frames, with the full cycle totaling 32 frames. The first and last frames (1 and 33) will be identical to ensure that the animation cycles without any hiccups.

With the scene set, Reference in the rig by going to File > Create Reference (Options). In the "Use selected namespace as parent and add new namespace string" field, type "rig" and hit Reference. Navigate to the scenes/02_PUBLISHED/03_RIGGING directory, select **paul_rig_PUBLISHED.ma**, and save this scene file in the 01_WIP/04_ANIMATION directory.

Make sure that the rig's arms are set to FK mode and the legs to IK mode. I've also set the Arm Follow attribute of both upper arm controls to chest, so I can reposition each shoulder without affecting the arms. This is a personal preference of mine, so test out the results and do what best suits your style.

Now make sure the joints are hidden in the viewport and set the geometry layer to Reference so you can only select the animation curves. Lastly, save the scene file locally.

03: Create the contact poses

We now need to create the contact pose. This is where the heel of the front leg makes contact with the ground, and the hips are centralized between the legs to maintain balance. To translate the hips, use **COG_ctrl**; to rotate the hips, I'll be using **hip_ik_ctrl**, but you could use **hip_fk_ctrl** to get purely independent movement from the hip without affecting the spine. I don't recommend using both, as it can complicate things when cleaning up the animation curves later.

For the front leg, use the Foot Roll attribute on **leg_ik_ctrl** to roll the front foot onto the heel. Use the same attribute on the back leg to rotate the foot onto the ball. A slight rotation of both feet outwards (using the Heel Twist attribute) should help to avoid creating a waddle. Bring some rotation to the hips with the forward leg. Work your way up the spine to achieve a contrasting angle between shoulder and hip, which should create a subtle C-shape running up the spine.

The arms and legs will need a similar contrast, as the opposite arm will swing as each leg comes forward. Finally, make sure you bring some drag and overlap to the hands. As you can probably see from my pose, I haven't created a totally straight contact leg; I find this helps to reduce knee-popping later on. Create this pose at frames 1 and 33 (to complete the loop) and then position its opposite at frame 17.

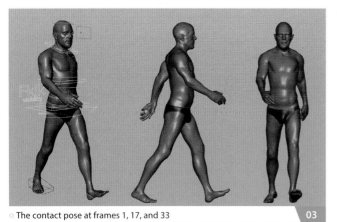
○ The contact pose at frames 1, 17, and 33   03

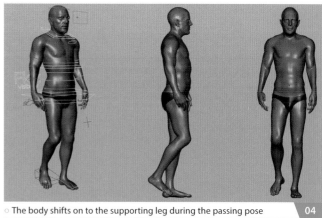
○ The body shifts on to the supporting leg during the passing pose   04

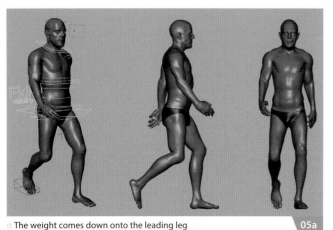
○ The weight comes down onto the leading leg   05a

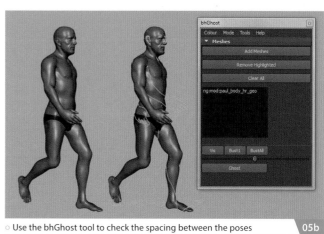
○ Use the bhGhost tool to check the spacing between the poses   05b

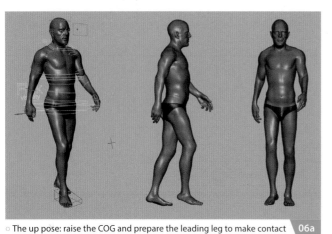
○ The up pose: raise the COG and prepare the leading leg to make contact   06a

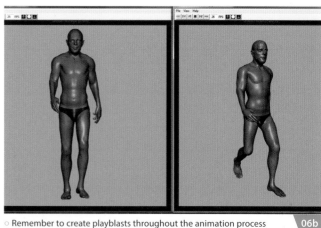
○ Remember to create playblasts throughout the animation process   06b

04: The passing pose

The first passing pose will be placed at frame 9. In this pose, the now straightened front leg should be directly beneath the torso, the body's weight should pass to the side of the supporting leg, and the torso should move up slightly. The back leg needs to come through. Give some drag to the toes using the Toe Flap attribute on the foot control.

Straighten the spine, hips, and shoulders to contrast with the C-shaped spine in the contact poses. Rotate the arms down to the side, moving from the shoulder towards the hands. When you've made a pose you're content with, create its mirror image at frame 25.

05: The down pose

The down position needs to be placed at frame 5. Making sure the front foot is flat on the floor, make the hips go down as the weight is taken onto the leg. The back foot needs to be on its toes before it comes off the ground, using the Foot Roll attribute (Fig.05a). Bring drag to the hands as they begin to follow the rest of the arm, then mirror this pose at frame 21.

As you start to lay in these poses, make sure you constantly view the poses that come before and after. I'm using the bhGhost tool for this, which allows you to select an object and create an outline of that object at a frame of your choosing (Fig.05b). It's great for seeing the spacing and getting the desired poses. Simply load the tool, select the model, and hit Add Meshed in the bhGhost window. Then go to the frame where you'd like to ghost the geometry and hit the Ghost button. Use the slider to increase and decrease the thickness of the outline.

06: The up pose

Move to frame 13 for the up pose. Translate the root up a little and add some roll to the back foot. I don't like to push the root up too much here, as it can look quite forced and unnatural. The forward-moving leg requires some rotation to the corresponding hip and the contrasting rotation in the shoulders (Fig.06a).

Add some drag to the toes of the forward moving foot, and when you're content with your results, create the opposite pose at frame 29. Set Frame Range to 32 frames (since 1 and 33 are identical, we don't want to view the same frame twice in playback) and do a playblast (Fig.06b).

Make sure the poses are readable from all angles, and check that the character feels balanced and that the stride isn't too small or too wide (Fig.06c). Create some playblasts to see if the timing is working for you. If you want a slower or faster walk, I'd make those changes now; it's possible to do it later on, but once we spline the animation curves it'll make it a more laborious process.

07: Splining our stepped curves

Now that we have the key poses, let's convert the animation curves from Stepped to Spline. For any additional keys that I add now, I want their Default out tangents set to Spline – as opposed to Stepped – so jump into Animation Preferences and update the Tangent settings.

Select all the animation controls now and open up the Graph Editor. Select all the curves and go to Tangents > Spline. Press play and see what happens. Everything suddenly feels "floaty" and weightless. This is why I like to start off in Stepped mode; I don't want to see what's happening between poses or I may get too focused on fixing them rather than making the key poses readable. I'm now content with main poses, so it's just a case of refining and adding the weight back in.

The first thing to do before cleaning up is set the animation curves so that they loop and so we can see how the curve comes in and goes out at frames 1 and 33. To do this, go to View > Infinity. Select all the animation curves again, and go to Curves > Pre Infinity > Cycle, and Curves > Post Infinity > Cycle. Remove any keys on any attributes that aren't doing anything by going through each attribute in the Graph Editor and

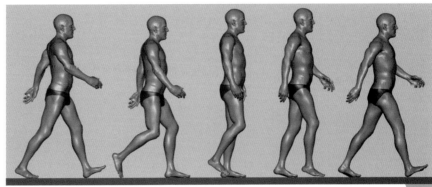
The key poses of our animation from the side view
06c

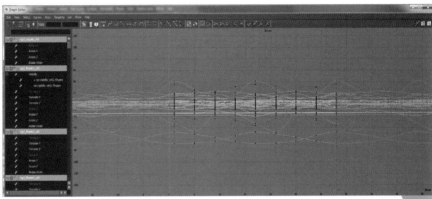
Make sure you are viewing how the curves come in and lead out
07a

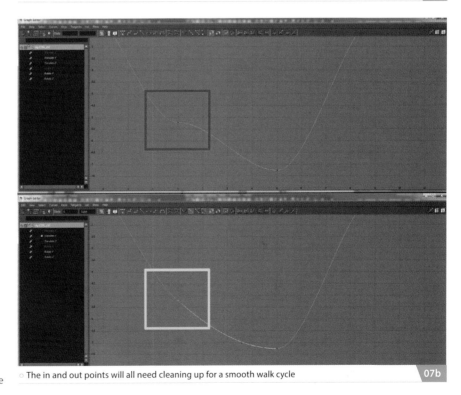
The in and out points will all need cleaning up for a smooth walk cycle
07b

looking for any straight curves. When you find any, select the keys on them and delete them.

If you take a look at the remaining curves, at frames 1 and 33, you will now observe that they are sharp in places. It is important to make sure that the curves here are

clean and smooth so that no popping occurs in the loop cycle (Fig.07a, 07b).

08: Cleaning up from the root

Now that the curves are splined, let's clean them up. With walk cycles, I like to work from the core outwards. First I like to get the hips

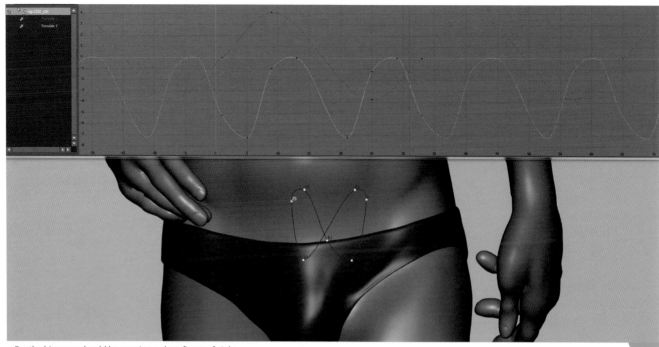

○ For the hips, you should be creating a clean figure of eight
08

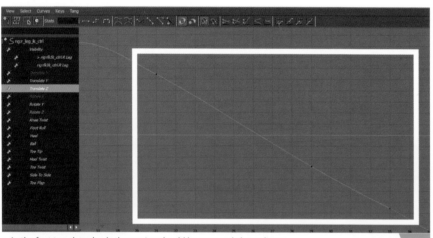

○ As the foot translates back, the motion should be even and almost linear
09a

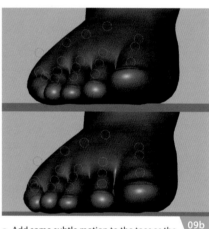

○ Add some subtle motion to the toes as the weight comes down
09b

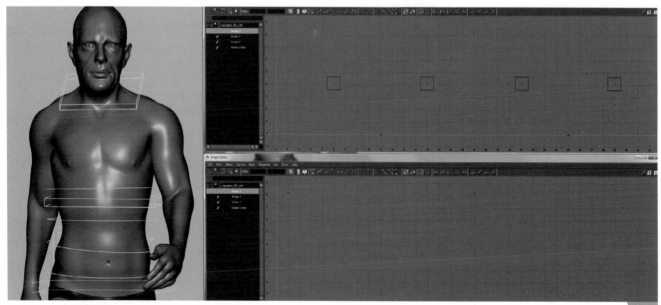

○ Remove any keys that are causing noise in the motion of the spine
10

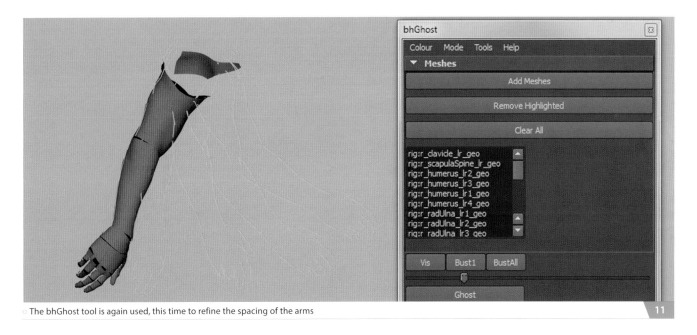

bhGhost

Colour Mode Tools Help

▼ Meshes

Add Meshes

Remove Highlighted

Clear All

rig:r_clavicle_lr_geo
rig:r_scapulaSpine_lr_geo
rig:r_humerus_lr2_geo
rig:r_humerus_lr3_geo
rig:r_humerus_lr1_geo
rig:r_humerus_lr4_geo
rig:r_radUlna_lr1_geo
rig:r_radUlna_lr2_geo
rig:r_radUlna_lr3_geo

Vis   Bust1   BustAll

Ghost

○ The bhGhost tool is again used, this time to refine the spacing of the arms   11

working well; then I work with the legs in conjunction with the hips; then I work up the spine, down through to the arms, and back up to finish the head. So starting with the hip, go into the Graph Editor and remove any noise from the animation curves. Do this one curve at a time and delete any keys that aren't adding anything to the animation.

What you're aiming for is hips that create a subtle figure of eight as the weight shifts from one leg to the other. To see the figure of eight of the hips more clearly, use Editable Motion Trail. If you want to exaggerate the walk, playing with the behavior of the hips is the place to start.

09: Refining the legs

Once you're happy with the hips, move on to the feet and knees. Here you'll also need to balance out the rotation of the hips so that the knees don't "pop". Getting the legs to work with the hips well is probably the trickiest part of a walk cycle, so do spend some time here. You can enable the low-resolution mesh and hide the upper torso geometry, so you can focus on the lower body without distractions.

I would start off with the timing of the foot coming down. At the moment, it currently becomes flat on the ground at frame 5, but I'd rather have it come down around frame 3 to help add weight and impact. As this is a walk cycle, we also need the front foot to transition back at a constant speed, as if the character is on a treadmill. You can do this in the Graph Editor by making sure that the curve for the

attribute translating the foot back is linear during this stage of the walk (Fig.09a).

As well as getting weight back into the legs, play with the toe controls to break up the rigid mass of the foot. Add drag and animate the toes individually. A nice touch is to spread the toes slightly as weight is applied to the foot, like adding squash to the bouncing ball as it impacts the ground (Fig.09b).

For the knees, I'm using the Knee Twist attribute that lives on the IK foot controls, rather than the locator l/ r_knee_ik_ctrl controls. This is a personal preference, as I find it easier to deal with a curve for one attribute in the Graph Editor than with three different translation attributes. Once again, motion trails, ghosting, and continuous playblasting will be your friends here, so make the most of them.

10: Cleaning up the spine

Now that the hard work's out of the way, we can start to layer in the spine. The focus here is balancing the twist of the spine and angle of the shoulders. Reduce any jerking movements by massaging the animation curves so that they're clean and smooth.

I like to set the tangent handles to Flatten for the spine to achieve this. The twist and the angle of the shoulders should oppose the hips. To break up the way the body twists and to help loosen things up, try to offset the keyframes of each control by two frames or so. Remember the presence of the rib cage as you

work. It's a solid mass. Respect its structure as you pose and refine the character's animation. If the spine doesn't feel right, rather than tinkering with it till you're blue in the face and fingertips, it can pay to delete all the animation from it and rework it again, as daunting as that may sound.

11: Working on the arms and hands

With the spine in place, the arms can come next. Start the clean-up process from the shoulder controls and work your way down the arms. As the arms are set to follow the chest rather than the shoulder, we can luckily reposition the shoulder controls without upsetting the position of the arms too much.

With the arms, we should try to create a natural swing with smooth arcs. I like to bear in mind the motion created by Newton's cradle as I animate the swing of the arms. The arms' spacing should be quite bunched either side of the swing and then spaced apart in the middle. Use the bhGhost tool to really review the spacing of the arm swing.

Once the main arm is working, offset the forearm from the upper arm and the hand from the forearm. This should create drag and overlap and keep the entire arm feeling organic and fluid, rather than mechanical and robotic. Then we come to the fingers, to which some subtle animation should help add further life. As a whole, we want to make sure that we're animating every part of the character, even if the motion is small. With a walk cycle, every part of the body is being driven in some way.

12: The neck and the head

Animating the neck and head should feel like a continuation of the spine. If the poses are too extreme, the head will bob up and down too much. I add delay to these parts by shifting the frames back slightly, offsetting them so that their motion comes just after that of the spine.

You may also want to change the head's space-switching behavior to make it easier to manage. Setting the head to follow the COG, for example, can help to reduce the mad bobbing effect. Feel free to add jaw movement and blinking if you want, but as we're only doing a single instance of the walk cycle, having the character blink too often can be a bit much. I'll leave that to your discretion.

Now that most of the animation is in place, do another pass of each control, working from the root outwards. Check everything in both the viewport and Graph Editor, making sure there are no pops in the animation. Check that the transition from the start to the end of the loop is smooth and use all the tools at your disposal to check the spacing, arcs (**Fig.12**), and so on.

13: Breathing and volume joints

With the walk close to complete, you can add some subtle breathing into the equation and use the volume joints to maintain form and add the illusion of muscle acting on the body.

As we've not created controls for these joints, you'll need to unhide the joints to animate them. Areas such as the elbow and knee need attention to create the appearance of bone beneath the skin, and you may also want to animate the volume joints of the upper arm to simulate the bicep and tricep muscles in action. I wouldn't go too wild

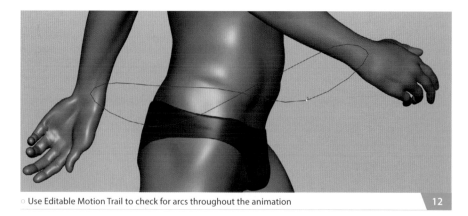
○ Use Editable Motion Trail to check for arcs throughout the animation   12

when adding breathing, as this can be a little distracting. Keep it light and subtle.

14: Simulating the briefs

Now we want to simulate the briefs. I won't go into great detail about cloth simulation but by the end of this step we should have the dynamic briefs successfully following the animation of the walk. First we need to set our playback speed to run every frame, as any simulation will require this. To do this, RMB-click in the Timeline and go to Playback Speed > Play Every Frame, Max Real-time.

We need a few extra frames to allow the cloth simulation to settle, or else it can get a little erratic, so set Frame Range to run from -50. Make sure you disable Autokey if you've been using it, then jump to frame -20 and copy the exact pose that you have at frame 1.

To do this, I select all the animation curves, and, in the Timeline, I go to frame 1. Still in the Timeline, I MMB-drag the cursor over to frame -20, then hit the S key to key the exact same pose. (Once the dynamic briefs are done, we'll delete these extra keyframes.) Go to frame -50 and set the character back to

the default pose by zeroing out all the controls. Then key the pose. Also key this pose at frame 35. Between frames 50 and 35, we'll allow the cloth to settle before any motion takes place. Then, from frames -20 to 1, we'll allow the briefs to settle into the first pose of the walk.

Unhide the briefs (**pants_cloth_hr_geo**) that will be simulated (**under clothes_hr_grp**). With the briefs selected, in the nDynamics menu, go to nMesh > Create nCloth. In the Attribute Editor, go to the nucleus1 tab and open the Time Attributes. As we're starting from frame -40, we need to update the Start Frame attribute to match this. If you press play now, the briefs will simply fall down and reveal too much for our innocent eyes. Select the main model, go to nMesh > Create Passive Collider, then play again. The briefs will interact with our character, but still fall down eventually. To stop this, we need to use nConstraints (**Fig.14a**).

As we have the skinned briefs to hand, I simply constrain the dynamic briefs to them so that they follow the body as closely as possible. To do this, select in this order, **pants_cloth_hr_geo** and **pants_hr_geo** and go to nConstraint > Attract to Matching Mesh. Save your scene file

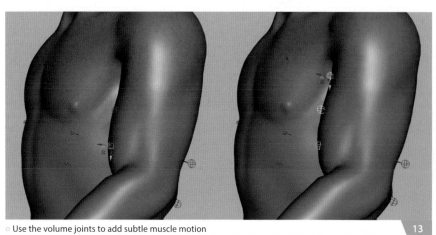
○ Use the volume joints to add subtle muscle motion   13

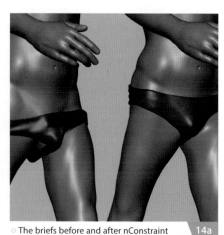
○ The briefs before and after nConstraint   14a

○ Edit the properties of the briefs for the desired results and Substeps for a cleaner simulation   14b

and press play to see the results. If everything's going as planned, we can adjust the cloth settings to get the desired behavior, then increase the Solver Attributes to get a less jittery simulation. With the dynamic briefs selected, jump into the Attribute Editor and go to the nClothShape1 tab. In here go to Presets > tshirt > Replace. The only other thing I do in this tab is increase Damp to 2 (under Dynamic Properties), to reduce stretchiness. Jump to the nucleus1 tab and increase Substeps to 15 under the Solver Attributes section (**Fig.14b**). You can go higher, but it'll affect how long it takes for the simulation to run.

When you're happy with the briefs, bake the simulation down into the geometry. To do this, select the dynamic briefs and go to nCache > Create New Cache (Options). Now create a new folder in the nCache Maya directory. Set File Distribution to One file, and Cache Time Range to Time Slider, and hit Create. Once this has cached out, you'll be able to scrub through the timeline and see the simulation

in action. Delete the extra poses that we created for our character, and set the Frame Range to run from 1 to 32 once more.

15: Caching the animation

The animation is complete, but I don't want to publish this scene file and call it in for lighting as it is. It'd be fine to do, but the lighting scene would be heavier than necessary. Instead, we'll cache out the geometry, essentially baking the animation down onto the models, so we don't need to have the rig in the scene. To do this, we could use Maya's Geometry Cache tool, but with Alembic being implemented into Maya, let's go for that option as it gives us better speed and memory performance.

Select all the geometry that needs to be cached out then, in the Main Menu bar, go to Pipeline Cache > Alembic Cache > Export Selection to Alembic (Options). In the options window, scroll down to Advanced Options and make sure UV Write is enabled. Hit Export Selection and call the file **paul_anim_PUBLISHED.abc**.

I'm actually saving this file in the following two places: /cache/alembic and /scenes/02_PUBLISHED/04_ANIMATION. With the cache files created, test them out in a new scene file. Make sure you set the animation preferences correctly and then, in the new scene file, go to Pipeline Cache > Alembic Cache > Import Alembic and select the file from the 04_ANIMATION directory. You should be able to press play and have the animation play back.

You can also pipe the Alembic cache onto the graphics processing unit (GPU), which gives amazing performance results and is a great way to add large amounts of data to a scene. If your graphics card supports this, go to Pipeline Cache > GPU Cache > Import and load in the Alembic file. Then duplicate the cached asset and check the performance. I was able to duplicate the asset over 150 times – that's over 12,750,000 faces in the scene – and still have it play back in real time. At this stage, we should be ready to take all our elements into the lighting scene for final rendering.

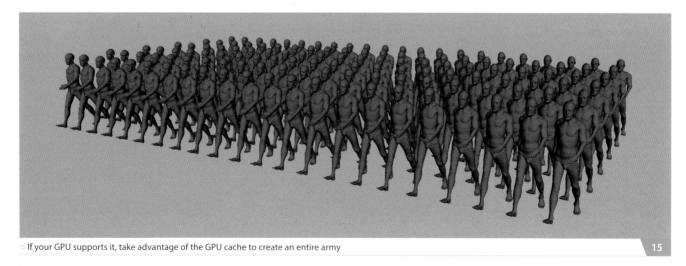

○ If your GPU supports it, take advantage of the GPU cache to create an entire army   15

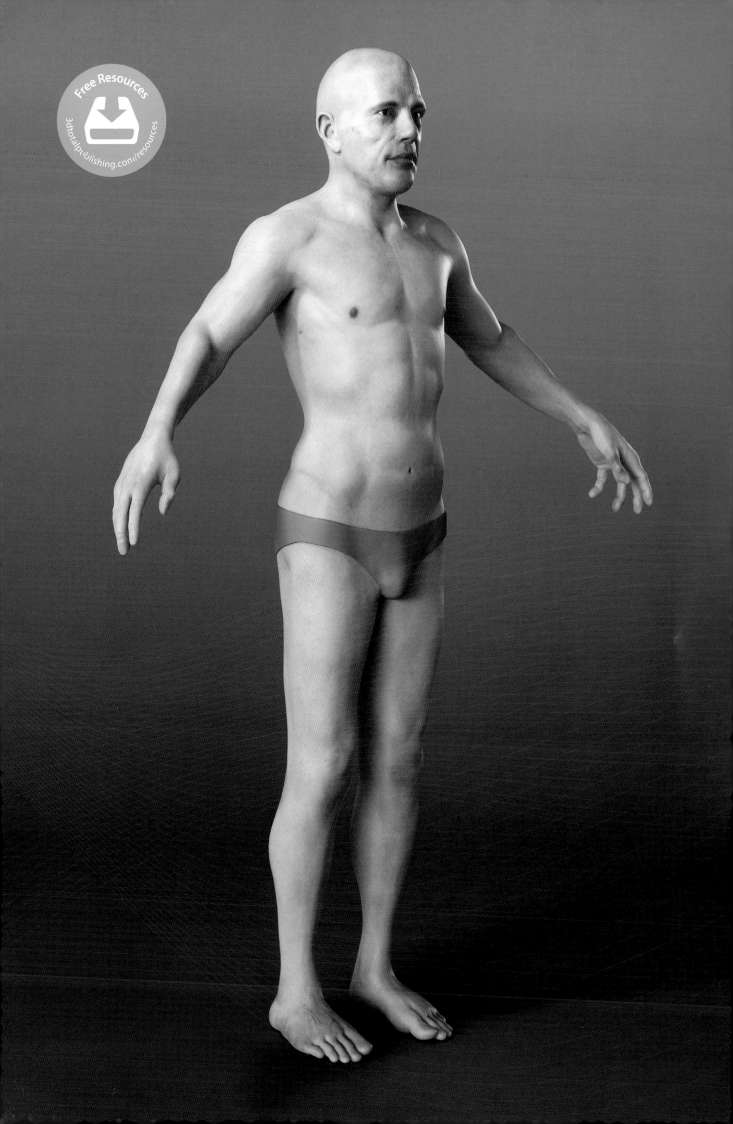

Lighting and rendering in Maya

Understanding light and gamma, and finishing your project

This last section of the book will show you how to finish and present your project. First we'll explore the theories of light and color, how they affect surfaces, and what this means for our lighting setup. Then we'll look at gamma and why it's important to our CG processes. We'll set up a realistic studio-style lighting scene to showcase the animated character, make some adjustments in NUKE, and produce a short final video worthy of your portfolio.

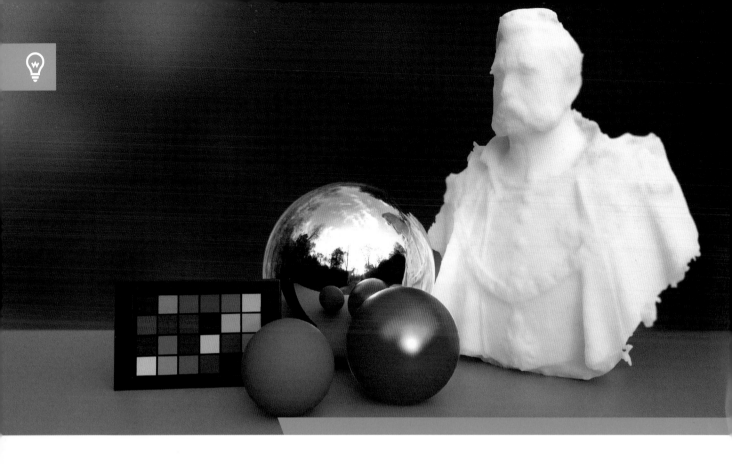

Light and color

How light works and creates color

We now come to the sixth and last section, which will open with an overview of light theory and end with the creation of a final render. Once we've got a grounding in the way light works, we'll bring matters back to the CG pipeline and develop an understanding of the importance of working with linear workflow. Taking this understanding, we'll return to Maya and create the basis of the look development environment that we used in section 03, and push that environment further to provide the final lighting scene. Following that, we'll see how the lighting setup can be enhanced through using Maya's Area

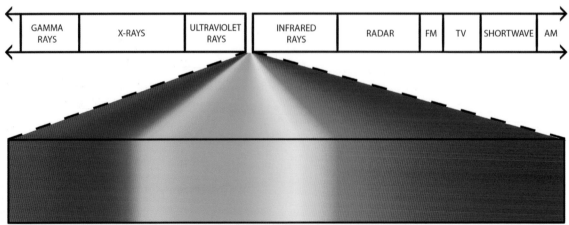

ELECTROMAGNETIC SPECTRUM

GAMMA RAYS	X-RAYS	ULTRAVIOLET RAYS	INFRARED RAYS	RADAR	FM	TV	SHORTWAVE	AM

VISIBLE LIGHT

○ The electromagnetic spectrum

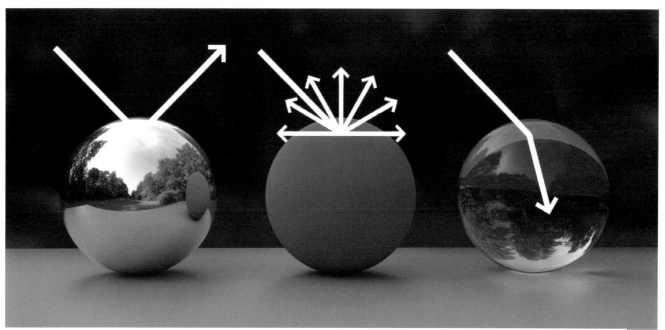

○ If light hits a flat surface, the outward angle is equal to the input angle; a rough surface scatters light. Light rays bend as they pass through different mediums **02**

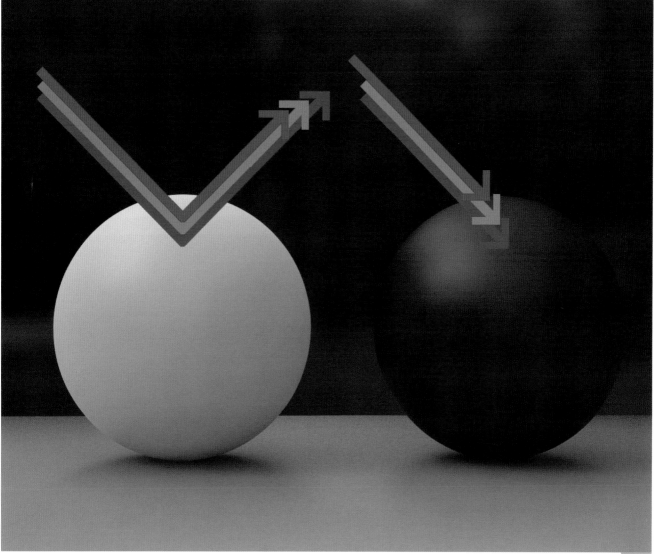

○ A white object will reflect all colors, while a black object will absorb all colors **03**

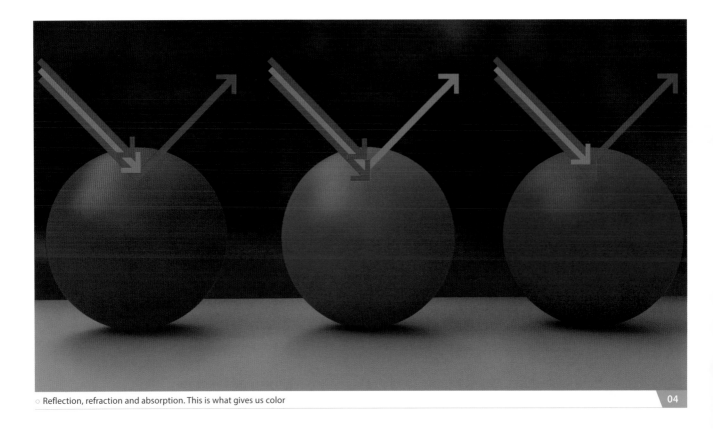

○ Reflection, refraction and absorption. This is what gives us color

04

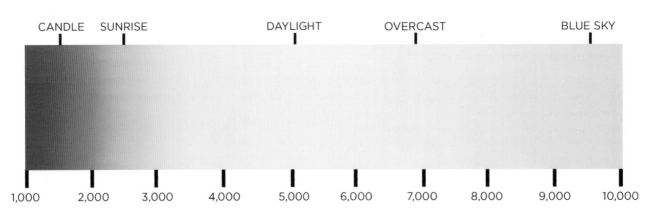

CANDLE   SUNRISE   DAYLIGHT   OVERCAST   BLUE SKY

1,000   2,000   3,000   4,000   5,000   6,000   7,000   8,000   9,000   10,000

○ The Kelvin meter describes the temperature for light

05

Lights, after which we'll render out an image sequence to be polished in comp, then given a final edit in Adobe Premiere Pro.

By the end of these steps, you will have in your grateful – if slightly sweaty – palms, a final animated walk cycle. So, let's get cracking and open with an overview of light theory.

Light and color

In recent years there has been a movement towards Physically Based Rendering (PBR), where lighting setups mimic real-life light situations. Both realistic and cartoony work

require believable lighting, so it's very much in your interests to get an appreciation of how light behaves in the real world.

So what is light exactly? Essentially, light is a type of wave; one that is composed of electric and magnetic fields. Hence it is referred to as electromagnetic radiation.

From the electromagnetic spectrum, which consists of radio, microwave, infrared, ultraviolet, X-ray and gamma rays, the human eye is only able to see a small portion, known as visible light (**Fig.01**). As light is emitted, small packets of energy called photons

are produced, and it's these photons that allow us to view the world around us.

"Essentially, light is a type of wave; one that is composed of electric and magnetic fields"

Our first stop is to take you back to your physics classroom and re-acquaint you with the phenomena of reflection, refraction, and absorption. In reflection, when light rays hit a smooth surface such as a mirror, they bounce off at an angle equal to the angle at which the rays hit the surface. The majority of surfaces are

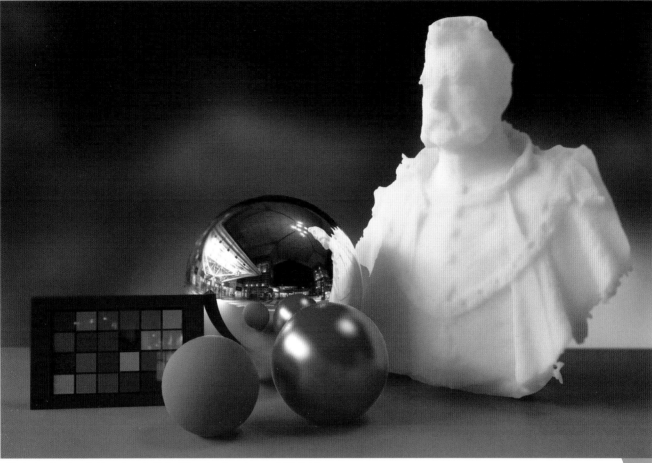

○ Understanding how light works and affects different surfaces is essential to lighting a scene

not smooth, however, which brings us to the concept of scattering, whereby light rays hit a rough surface and bounce off at multiple angles.

"Refraction occurs when light rays pass from one transparent medium to another : for example, from air to water"

Refraction occurs when light rays pass from one transparent medium to another: for example, from air to water. As this happens, the speed of the light changes and the ray bends either towards or away from the normal line, which is an imaginary line running perpendicular to the surface of an object.

The degree to which the light bends is known as the angle of refraction, and its size depends on the degree to which the object has slowed the light rays down.

The higher a material's index of refraction, the more it slows down incoming light. Diamonds have a high index of refraction, and sparkle so very famously by effectively trapping light. Lenses work by refracting light and can serve to improve a person's vision by making distant objects seem nearer, or vice versa.

Staying in the physics classroom, you may remember splitting light using a prism and seeing light is made up of the colors of the rainbow. The fact that the world around us does not have color in itself – that objects simply reflect, refract, or absorb color and therefore appear colorful – is pretty mind-bending!

The color of an object is the color of the light it reflects. Your red Ferrari parked outside is not red, it just reflects red wavelengths; the grass of your croquet lawn is green because it reflects green wavelengths. Objects appear white because they reflect all color; conversely, objects appear black because they absorb all color, and in that absorption, heat is created.

Which brings us neatly to the topic of color temperature. Each light source, be it a candle, the Sun, or a headlamp, has its own individual color, or color temperature. This varies on a scale from red (warm) to blue (cool).

Color temperature is recorded in Kelvin. Cool colors such as blue will have a Kelvin of over 7000, while warmer colors such as orange or red will measure around 2000. Daylight, with a Kelvin of about 5000, comes around the middle of this scale.

"Cool colors such as blue will have a Kelvin of over 7000, while warmer colors will measure around 2000"

In CG, though we can use parameters such as hues, or give light color, a black body node can be employed to control the color of the lights. This node governs the color temperature using a Kelvin value.

By doing this, we breathe further real-world life into the CG work we create, enhancing its believability.

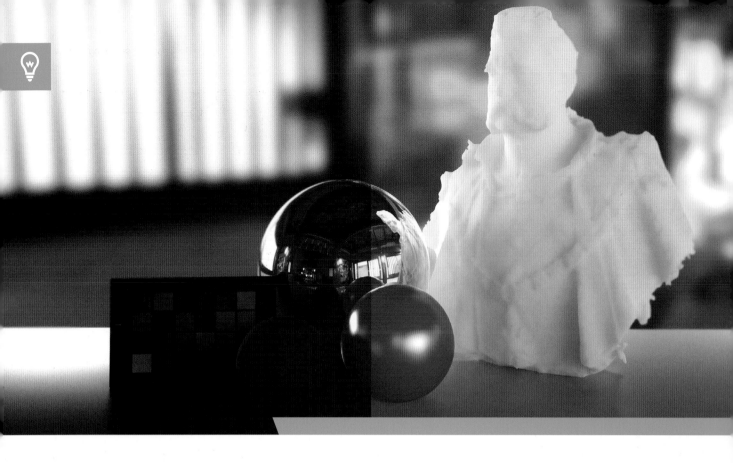

Gamma and linear workflow

The importance of gamma in our lighting setup

I now want to cover the topics of gamma and linear workflow. It's important to understand both in order for lighting calculations to be properly computed, and so the textures and color swatches that we use in a 3D package are displayed and rendered correctly.

After this, we will be ready to proceed with creating our final lighting setup.

What is gamma?

So, why do we need to talk about gamma? This takes us back to when ye olde CRT (Cathode Ray Tubes) monitors were all the rage. A problem arose where, by default, the images displayed on the screens were too dark.

This was due to the fact that the input voltage going into the computer was not

equal to the output of the light intensity being displayed on the screen. Therefore, the monitor's response curve was not linear. This curve is called gamma and it is a power function. Take note of how the minimum and maximum intensities are unaffected (**Fig.01**).

In order for the images to be displayed correctly, it was discovered that an inverse gamma would

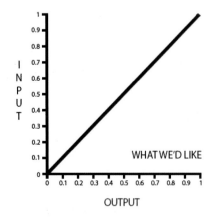

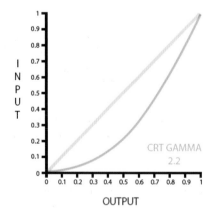

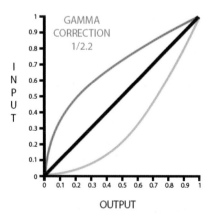

○ To display our images correctly, we must understand how gamma works

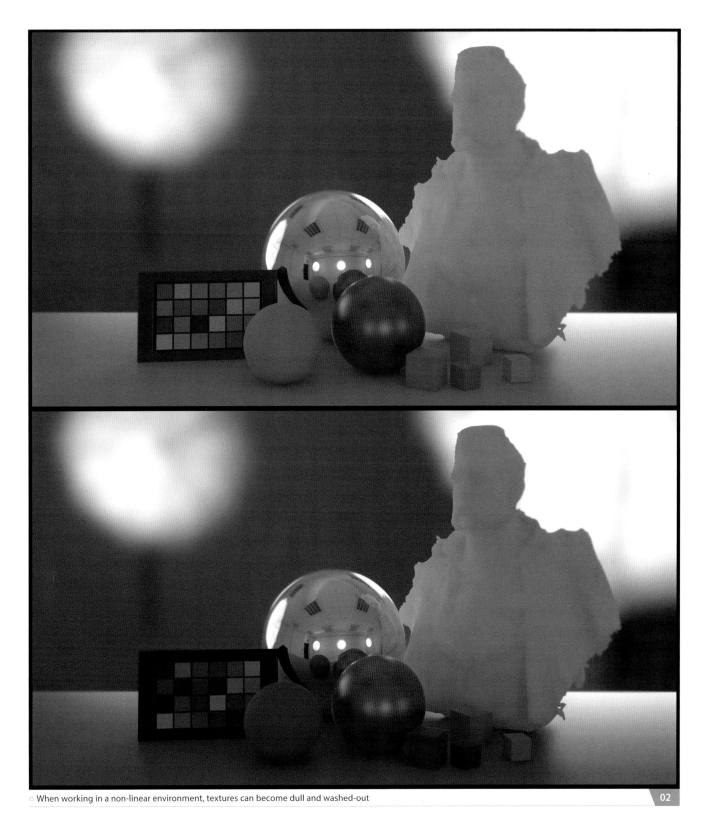

○ When working in a non-linear environment, textures can become dull and washed-out

02

need to be applied to make the response curve linear once more. Although this is why gamma encoding was developed, it also does more than just correct the display of images.

Gamma also helps to mimic the human eye's response to luminance: to light and color. Because the human eye does not perceive light

in a linear way, using gamma makes it easier and more efficient for us to encode 8-bit images.

Almost all off-the-shelf monitors now, from your computer screen to your mobile device, will have a gamma applied to them (usually sRGB). This has a gamma of around 2.2. I say "around" because it's ever so slightly off.

"Gamma also helps to mimic the human eye's response to luminance: to light and color"

As we're using a monitor while working, everything that we see on screen – texture images (8-bit/16-bit), color swatches,

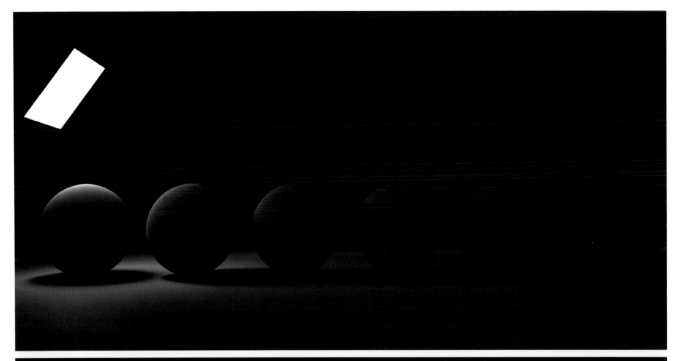

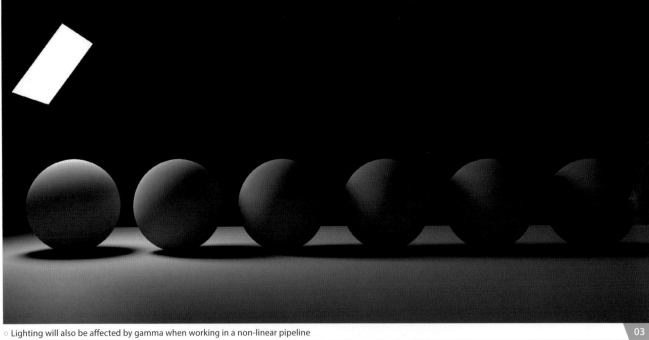

○ Lighting will also be affected by gamma when working in a non-linear pipeline   03

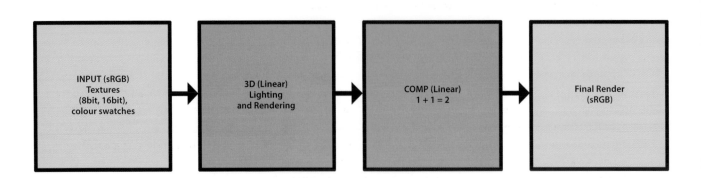

○ This is a breakdown of how we will treat the data going into the 3D package and then coming out   04

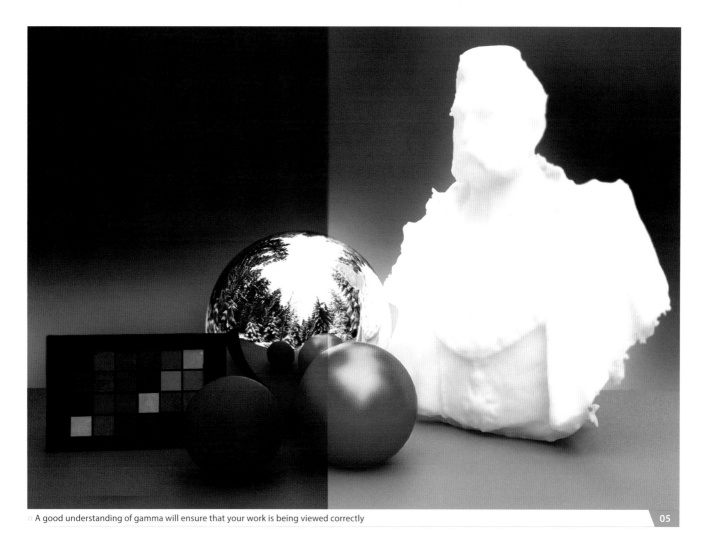

○ A good understanding of gamma will ensure that your work is being viewed correctly   **05**

and so on – has a gamma applied to it so that it can be viewed correctly.

The trouble with this, when working in a 3D package such as Maya, is that all the lighting calculations and rendering magic happens in linear color space so that the math works correctly in both 3D software and 2D compositing software. By working with elements that are already gamma-corrected, final rendered images from 3D will have elements that are in both linear and sRGB color spaces.

These renders are then taken into a compositing package, which works in linear color space but applies an sRGB gamma so that we are correctly viewing what will be the final output. Therefore, the final images will end up having elements (textures and so on) that will have been double gamma-corrected and will consequently appear washed out (**Fig.02**).

Other problems related to lighting can also arise from working with a non-linear

> "This can force you as an artist to think that you need additional lights to brighten up the scene, when all that actually needs to be done is to make sure you're working in the correct color space"

workflow, such as unrealistic falloffs from lights, highlights being blown out, and shadows appearing to get too dark too soon (**Fig.03**).

This can force you as an artist to think that you need additional lights to brighten up the scene, when all that actually needs to be done is to make sure you're working in the correct color space.

So here's a quick breakdown of the linear workflow that we'll be employing. Firstly, all 8-bit/16-bit images and color swatches will need to have the gamma removed from them in the 3D package in order to make them linear. This includes diffuse colors, reflection and

refraction elements with color information, and specular elements with color information. You will not need to gamma-correct Open EXR, HDRI, 32-bit TIF, bump, normal, displacement, or transparency maps.

We'll then work in the linear 3D environment, making sure we're viewing the renders with an sRGB gamma. The renders will then be outputted from our 3D package as linear images to be edited in comp (compositing) (**Fig.04**).

In comp, as mentioned above, we will again work in a linear color space, but view the images with an sRGB gamma applied. Lastly, we'll render the images out from the compositing package with an sRGB gamma applied to them. Through this process, we'll ensure that the elements going into our 3D pipeline come out as they should (**Fig.05**).

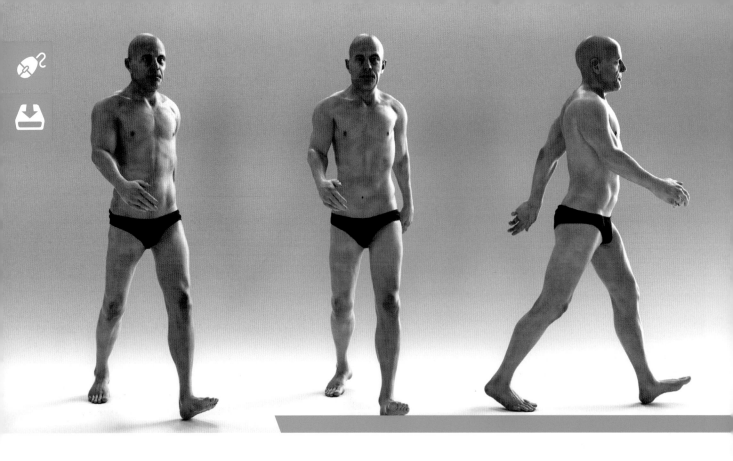

Creating a look development environment and lighting

Look development and rendering final images

Now we have reached the final steps of our digital journey. We're going to set up the lighting scene, which we'll base on the look development scene used in section 03.

We'll bring in the cached animation and the shaders, then set up the linear workflow environment. Next we'll create additional light sources using area lights, then look at how we can add additional nodes to the mix to create a more realistic lighting setup.

We'll then look at using 32-bit images and surface shaders to help illuminate the scene. Once we're happy with the lighting setup, we'll render out an image sequence to be manipulated in NUKE. Finally, we'll cut the images together before turning them into a short video clip.

As these are the final steps, we're allowed a little cheese: lights, camera, render!

01: Importing the animation cache and shaders

Open up a new Maya scene and set the animation preferences to what we used in section 05. This ensures that our cached animation doesn't skip any frames. Now we'll bring in the cached animation so we can get an idea of the scene's scale. Go to Pipeline Cache > Alembic Cache > Import Alembic, and select the .abc file that we exported from section 05. The file I'm using is in the following directory: /scenes/02_PUBLISHED/04_ ANIMATION/. Once the animated cache file is in the scene, hit Play to make sure that everything is at is should be. Then jump into the Outliner and select all the different parts of the model, group them together and call this group **paul_animCache_grp**.

Now we need to bring the shaders in. Go to File > Create Reference (Options), set "Use selected namespace as parent and add new

namespace string" to shader and hit Reference. Navigate to the following directory: /scenes/02_ PUBLISHED/02_TEXTURING_SHADING. Then select **paul_shaders_PUBLISHED.ma**.

Unfortunately, unless you have a fancy script to automatically hook the shaders up to the geometry based on a name or unique attribute, you'll need to manually reassign the shaders. For now, I don't do this, since I want to get the lighting right first, and shaders would slow the renders down. Instead, I simply apply a MILA material with a Gamma Correct node plugged into the Color input. I set the Value of the gamma node to 0.5 and Gamma to 0.455, 0.455, 0.455.

02: Create a background

Next I'll create a background plane for the character to sit against. Do this by first creating a polygon plane and naming it **bg_geo**. Increase the scale of the plane so that it's

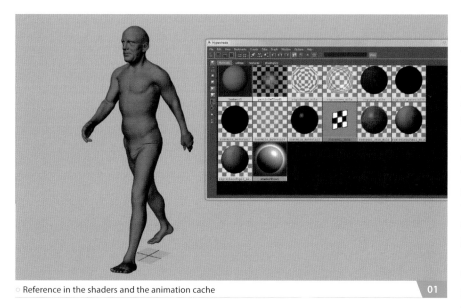

○ Reference in the shaders and the animation cache **01**

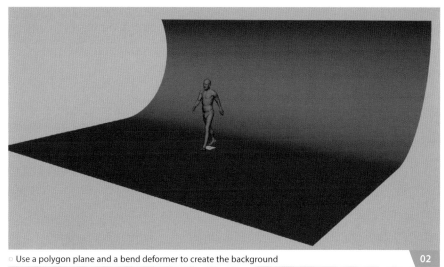

○ Use a polygon plane and a bend deformer to create the background **02**

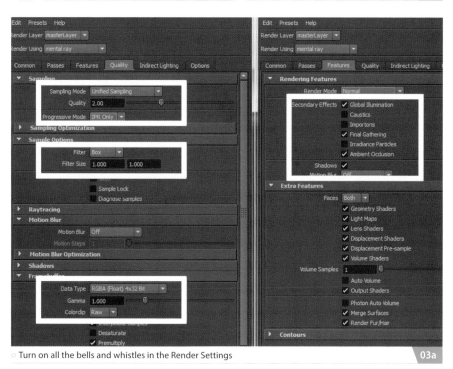

○ Turn on all the bells and whistles in the Render Settings **03a**

pretty large, and set Subdivision's Width and Height to 50. I want to curl the plane slightly to mimic a background sheet, like you'd find in a studio lighting environment, so select **bg_geo** and in the Animation menu, go to Create Deformers > Nonlinear > Bend. Select **bend1Handle** now and set Rotate X and Z to 90. Under the **bend1** node in the INPUTS stack, set Curvature to around 115, Low Bound to -1, and High Bound to 0. With **bg_geo** selected, go to Edit > Delete By Type > History. You can now continue to scale and translate the plane into the desired position. For the background, apply a new MILA material.

03: Render settings and linear workflow

Now we need to set up the render settings to work with a linear workflow. Go to Window > Rendering Editors > Render Settings (**Fig.03a**). At the top of the Render Settings window is the renderer that we will be using. Make sure this is set to mental ray. If mental ray isn't on the drop-down menu, you may need to load the plug-in by going to Window > Settings/ Preferences > Plug-in Manager, searching for **Mayatomr.mll**, and enabling it. Back in Render Settings, in the Common tab under File Output, set the File name prefix to walkCycle_anim, Image format to OpenEXR (exr), Image compression to none, Frame/Animation ext to name_#.ext, and Frame padding to 2.

Scroll down to Frame Range and set it to start from frame 1 and end on frame 32. Under Image Size, set the presets to HD 1080. The last thing to do in this tab is to open up Render Options and ensure that Enable Default Light is disabled.

In the Features tab now, make sure Global Illumination, Final Gathering, and Ambient Occlusion are enabled. These settings enable the light to bounce around the environment, creating a more believable lighting result.

Now Jump to Quality and set Sampling Mode to Unified Sampling. This reduces the settings we need to play with to one slider: the Quality slider. For now, set this to 2. I've also set the Filter option to Box as it creates a slightly sharper render. Jump down to Framebuffer and set Data Type to RGBA (Float) 4x32 Bit. As we're using OpenEXR, this will ensure that our images are not clamped to [0, 1].

271

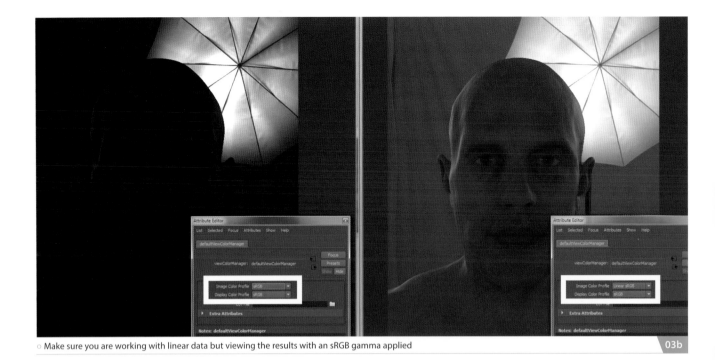

○ Make sure you are working with linear data but viewing the results with an sRGB gamma applied ·························· 03b

Last of all, open up Render View (Window > Rendering Editors > Render View) and go to Display > Color Management. To view our images correctly, we need to set Image Color Profile to Linear sRGB and Display Color Profile to sRGB. Later on, when we start rendering, I encourage you to pop Image Color Profile back to sRGB and see what happens (**Fig.03b**).

04: Adding a HDRI
Now we need to add some light into the scene, starting with the HDRI. Jump back into the Render Settings window, open the Indirect Lighting tab, make sure Global Illumination and Final Gathering are enabled, and then take Accuracy of Final Gathering down to around 20. This is pretty low but fine for our initial setup.

Click on the Create button for Image Based Lighting to create a **mentalRaylbl** node. Jump into the Attribute Editor, click on the folder icon next to Image Name and select a .hdr image of your choice. Again, I'll kick things off with **ScanRoom_06.hdr** from Panocapture (**www. panocapture.com**). Still in the Attribute Editor, drop down to Light Emission, enable Emit Light, and set the Quality to 1. Lastly, scale the **mentalraylbl** environment down slightly.

05: Create a render camera
Let's add a camera to render the shot from. We could use the current perspective camera, but I like to leave it as it is and use it to navigate the scene. Instead, go to Cameras > Camera.

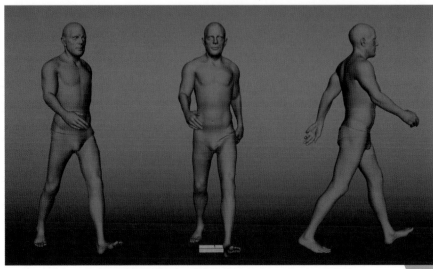

○ Add a **mentalraylbl** node to create the environment lighting ·························· 04

○ Add a couple extra caches and frame the shot accordingly ·························· 05

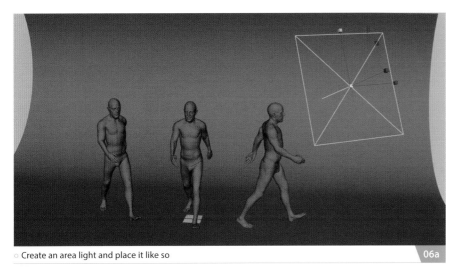

○ Create an area light and place it like so `06a`

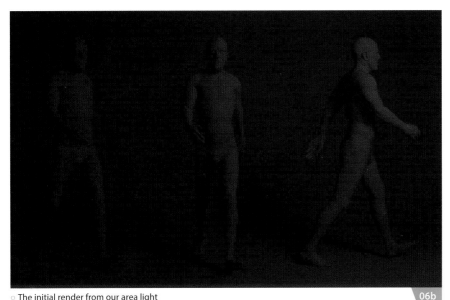

○ The initial render from our area light `06b`

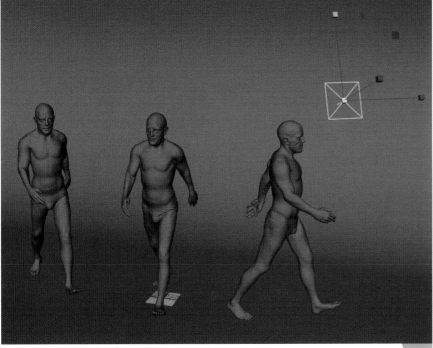

○ Scale the area light and see how it affects your lighting `07`

Rename the camera **render_cam**. Open up the Attribute Editor and set Focal Length to 50 (or a value of your choice). With the new camera selected, on the Viewport menu, go to Panels > Look Through Selected, then View > Camera Settings, and enable Resolution Gate.

Now you can frame just one character walking from one angle. I find that a little boring though, so I've imported two more Alembic caches of the walk cycle and positioned them to show the walk from the front, side, and a three-quarter view. Once you're happy with the camera's position and framing, lock all the attributes in the Channel Box. Go into the Render Settings and make sure Renderable Camera is set to **render_cam**. We now have a scene that's close enough to the look development environment.

06: Adding area lights

Now that the scene's ready, let's take a closer look at area lights. If you're attempting to create realistic lighting in Maya, area lights are the way to go. For now, select and delete the **mentalraylbl** node so we can focus on just the area lights. Go to Create > Lights > Area Light and rename this light **key_light**. Select **key_light**, scale it up, then position it to come down from above and to the screen's right (or wherever you like) (**Fig.06a** and **06b**).

If you open up the Attribute Editor, you'll see that this light's Decay Rate is set to No Decay. We need to change this to Quadratic to give the light a realistic falloff. In order to see any light, however, we will need to crank up the intensity, so set it to 10000 or so and then do a render.

07: Resizing an area light

Hopefully the scene was illuminated pretty well. If it feels dark, you can crank up the Intensity, or do the opposite if it's too bright. You might see that there's some noise in the image too, which we can remove by increasing the Final Gathering Accuracy. For now, just leave it as it is.

Now I'd like you to scale the area light so that's much smaller and then do a render; then scale so that it's huge and do another render. Hopefully this will help you get the idea that the scale of an area light plays a huge part in illuminating the scene. When it's small, the shadows are sharper; when it's large, they're softer. Highlights, details, and so on are all affected by the size of an area light.

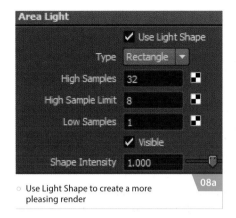

Area Light

	✔ Use Light Shape
Type	Rectangle ▾
High Samples	32
High Sample Limit	8
Low Samples	1
	✔ Visible
Shape Intensity	1.000

○ Use Light Shape to create a more pleasing render

08a

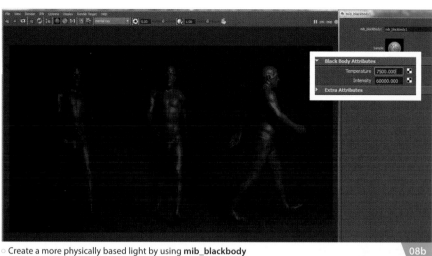

○ Create a more physically based light by using **mib_blackbody**   08b

08: Light shapes and physical lights

Let's push this light further. First, add a weighted glossy reflection layer to the gray MILA material so that we can get a better shape to the models. Set the weight of the glossy reflection layer to something very small, such as 0.1, and increase Roughness to 0.7 or so. Select the area light and, in the Attribute Editor, open up the mental ray tab. Then open up the Area Light tab, enable Use Light Shape, set High Samples to 32 and High Sample Limit to 8 (these two will help remove noise), and then enable Visible (Fig.08a). The area light will now appear in the render (if it's in the camera view) and also in the reflections.

This is all moving in the right direction, but I want to make this light more plausible and realistic. With the area light selected, scroll down to Custom Shaders in the Attribute Editor and click on the input icon next to Light Shader. When the Create Render Node window pops up, go to MentalRay Lights and select **physical_light**. The color and strength of the light is no longer controlled by the previous attributes, but is driven by this new node.

Click on the Color swatch of **physical_light** and you'll see it has a default Value setting of 1000. We could play with this, but I want to take this light even further. Click on the input icon beside Color and select **mib_blackbody** from the Mental Ray Lights section. The **mib_blackbody** node allows us to use both temperature (in Kelvin) to drive the color of the light and an intensity value to drive its strength (Fig.08b). Experiment with the temperature to see what results you get. You'll also need to crank up the intensity to increase the overall illumination.

So that's pretty much how I set up area lights. In a final scene, I'd then have a key light (as we

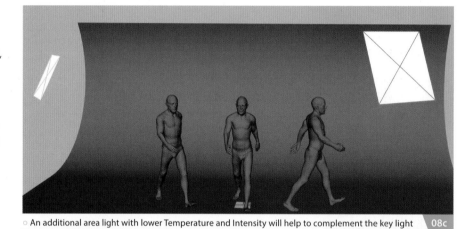

○ An additional area light with lower Temperature and Intensity will help to complement the key light   08c

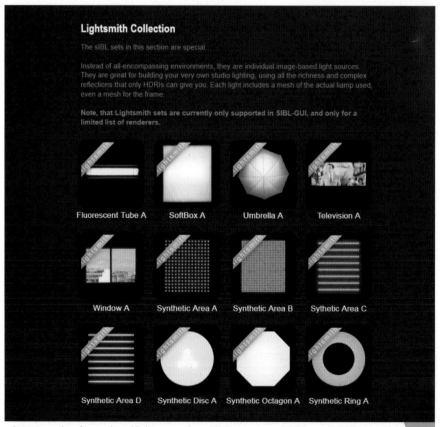

○ Some examples of image-based light sources from sIBL Archive (**www.hdrlabs.com/sibl/archive.html**)   09a

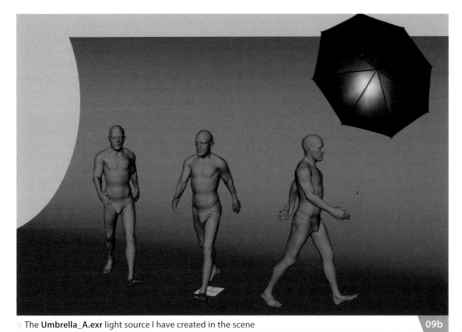

○ The **Umbrella_A.exr** light source I have created in the scene `09b`

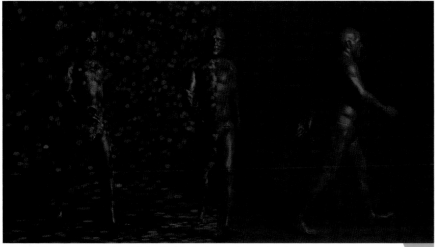

○ To edit the exposure of the 32-bit texture, use the value on the Color Gain attribute `09c`

have) on one side, emitting a bluish color, and then a smaller area light on the other side (**fill_light**), emitting a complementary color (in this case, orange) with a lower intensity (**Fig.08c**).

09: Light cards and surface shaders

One final thing I want to show you is what happens when you mix 32-bit textures of lights with surface shaders. Start by hiding the current area lights. Create a polygon primitive plane and scale it up. This will act as the light source. Rename the plane **light_card** then, with the plane selected, hold down the RMB and go to Assign Favorite Shader > Surface Shader.

Click on the input icon next to Out Color to, and select File. Then plug a 32-bit image-based light source into the file node. I've downloaded the Lightsmith Collection from sIBL Archive (**www.hdrlabs.com/sibl/archive.html**) (**Fig.09a**). They're free and amazing, so do grab a few to test out. Once you've plugged your 32-bit texture into the shader (I'm using **Umbrella_A.exr**), position the plane in the desired spot and hit 6 on the keyboard to see the light in the viewport (**Fig.09b**).

"A combination of area lights and light cards works a treat, especially for reflections"

You'll also want to apply the mask image into the Out Transparency of the surface shader, again through a file node. Do a render, and if things are a little dark, increase the value of the Color Gain attribute (**Fig.09c**), found under the file node that has **Umbrella_A.exr** plugged into it.

The initial render may look like a dodgy disco is taking place. To get rid of the noise, increase Accuracy of the Final Gathering to around 200 and increase Point Interpolation to 80 (**Fig.09d**). This acts almost like Photoshop's Gaussian Blur. While you're there, increase Secondary Bounces to 2. This will create a better render, but some noise may still exist. To help remove this, pop an area light in front of it and use the Type attribute to match the shape of **light_card**.

A combination of area lights and light cards works a treat, especially for reflections. When you add the image-based lighting back on top, it can really work wonders for your scenes.

○ An initial render and a render with the Final Gathering settings updated `09d`

"As the character is in full frame, a lot of the detail won't be seen from this distance"

At this stage, take everything we've done with the lights and create a lighting setup that you are happy with. Once you're done, pop all the shaders back onto the models and pop the **mentalraySubdivApprox** node back onto the models to subdivide the mesh at render time. You may want to reduce the Subdivisions on the **mentalraySubdivApprox** node to get things rendered out in a decent time. Plus, as the character is in full frame, a lot of the detail won't be seen from this distance.

10: Rendering out the image sequence

Once you're happy with your lighting setup and the shaders have been applied, it's time to render out the image sequence. The render settings have already been set, so let's get these images over to NUKE (**www. thefoundry.co.uk/products/nuke**) or the compositing package of your choice, by switching to the Rendering menu (F6) and going to Render > Batch Render. The images will be rendered out and saved in the /images folder of your Maya project directory.

11: Editing the images in NUKE

With the images rendered out, we can load them into NUKE. I'm not going to go into NUKE in detail, other than to say I use a Sharpen node, Grade node, and Grain node.

As I've only rendered out a single pass (known as the "beauty" pass), we can't really deconstruct the image and edit each of the components (diffuse, reflection, spec, and so on), which would give us more control over the final outcome. If you're interested in going down that road, do have a look at Render Passes and Contribution Maps in Maya.

Once you're happy with how your image sequence appears, we need to write the images out of NUKE so we can drop them into the editing package. Create a Write node and plug the final node of the current network into this node. Click on the folder icon next to **file** and name the file: **walkCycle_comp_##. tif**. This will allow us to render out the entire image sequence. Save these images to a folder

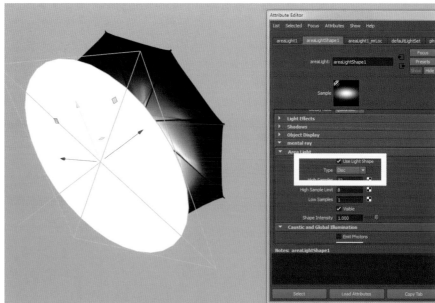
○ Mix a 32-bit texture with an area light to remove noise   09e

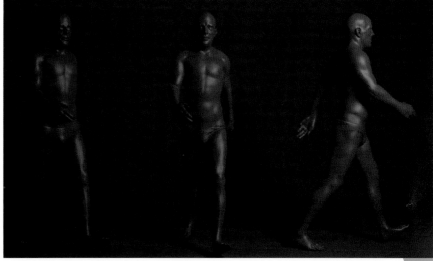
○ The render of the area light with the 32-bit texture   09f

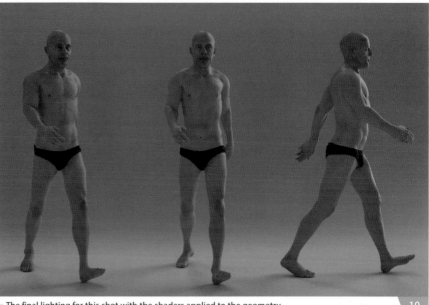
○ The final lighting for this shot with the shaders applied to the geometry   10

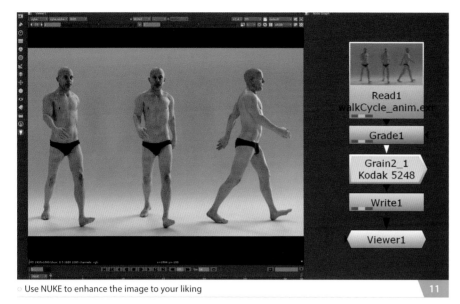

○ Use NUKE to enhance the image to your liking   11

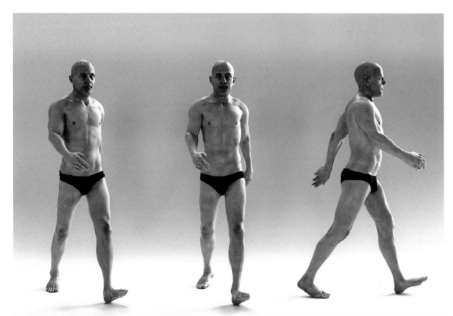

○ Use Adobe Premiere Pro to create a 15 second looped video   12a

○ The final rendered animation   12b

of your choice. I save mine to a folder called nuke_renders. Make sure compression is set to None on the Write node and then hit Render.

12: Editing and creating the final movie

We now hit the editing stage. We only have a loop cycle to cut together, so this shouldn't take very long. I'm using Adobe Premiere Pro (**www.adobe.com/uk/products/premiere. html**), but you should be able to do exactly the same (albeit by pressing different buttons) in any other editing package.

Once Premiere Pro kicks off, the first thing we need to do is click the New Project button. Give the project a name (I've gone for walk_animation), make sure Capture Format is set to HDV, and hit OK. When the New Sequence window pops up, under 1080p, select AVCHD 1080p25 and hit OK. This brings us to the main GUI, where we can string clips together and edit them using Video Effects and Transitions.

To bring in the animation frames, go to the Project tab, RMB-click in that window and go to Import. Navigate to the directory housing your images, select the first frame from the sequence, and make sure you enable the Numbered Stills box at the bottom of the screen. With the sequence in the Project tab, LMB-drag it onto the Timeline. As the animation is a cycle, feel free to drop the sequence into the Timeline multiple times to create a longer animation. I've gone for an animation of around 15 seconds.

Once you're happy with the length, we can create the movie. Go to File > Export > Media. The following settings are the ones I usually use to create a video, but feel free to experiment with other formats and codecs.

I set Format to Quicktime and Video Codec to Sorenson Video 3. Under Basic Settings, I make sure Frame Rate is set to 25, Field Type is Progressive, the aspect is set to Square Pixels (1.0), and Render at Maximum Bit Depth is enabled. Fill in Output Name and then hit Export when ready.

And that's it! You should have an animated video of your own digital walk cycle. Don't forget to visit **www.3dtotalpublishing. com/resources** for over 30 hours of video tuition that accompanies the book!

Closing words...

So, that's almost all folks. Thank you for getting this far. I really hope you feel like you now have a solid grounding in all stages of the CG pipeline and are able to take an asset through from modeling to the final render.

I also hope that I've succeeded in engendering a spirit of experimentation, based on the understanding that there is never only one way to get results in CG. Additionally, I by no means underestimate the importance of knowing how to get what you want from your software. However, I would like to think that the skills you've picked up from this book, because they are rooted in fundamentals, can be transferred from one package to another. More than all of this, I hope you've enjoyed the process and feel eager for more; I love working in CG and I want to pass the bug on.

If you've enjoyed the ride, then you'll be happy to know that this is just the beginning and that the CG world truly is your oyster. The next step could be to rig the face and bring a smile, frown, or even a gurn to your character's face. Perhaps you could give him some clothes and hair, as the poor guy must be freezing. You may also want to look at blend shapes, muscle systems, and other deformers, as they can really help bring a character to life.

Whichever way you turn, if you keep in mind that all digital work has its basis in reality and proceed from there, you'll be starting strong. Good luck, and as the worst thing that can happen is your computer crashing, just keep on experimenting!

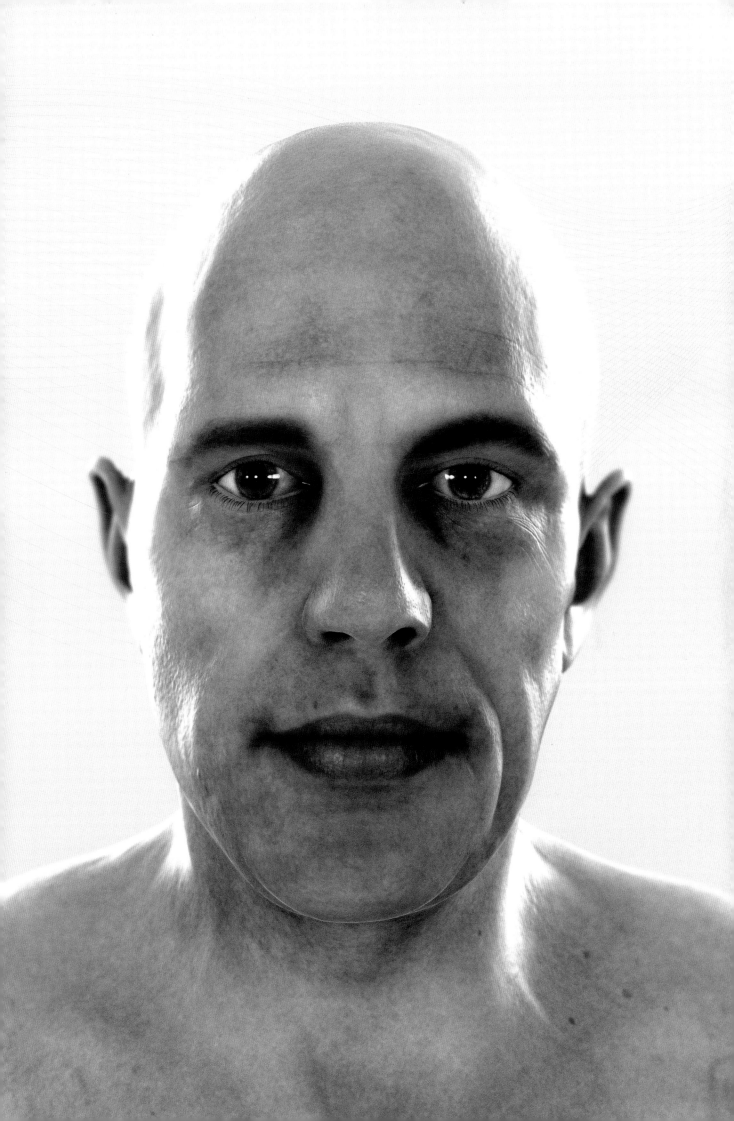

Acknowledgments

Like any project, the end result is usually the sum of many parts and the help of many hands. This is true of the creation of this book. From start to finish, this book has been a constant group effort and I would like to thank all of those who played their part.

First and foremost, I would like to thank my amazing wife, Nicola, without whom this book would not have happened. This book is as much hers as it is mine.

Along with my wife, I would like to thank my beautiful daughters, Mya, Jasmine, Amelia, and Evangeline. You made me smile, laugh, and keep going through the writing process.

Next, I'd like to thank Ann Milliam, for enabling me to jump out of the frying pan and into the CG fire.

I'd then like to thank the fantastic staff at 3dtotal.com. Lynette Clee – a huge thank you for having faith in me and giving me so many great opportunities. My thanks also to Tom Greenway for allowing me the freedom to teach in my own way. Finally, I'd like to thank Marisa Lewis for her patience and support throughout the creation of this book.

Further thanks go to Neil Goridge (**www.neilgoridgephotography.com**) without whose help I could not have captured the reference material. Thank you, Neil, for giving me your time.

This project could not have happened without a model. Thank you Paul Stillwell (**www.Autograph-Art.com**) for your patience, forbearance, and your body!

I am grateful to the following people and organizations for their very valuable contributions towards the making of this book and to the CG community in general:

To AMD, for their fantastic FirePro W8000 graphics card (**www.fireprographics.com**).

To Paul Callender of Surface Mimic (**www.surfacemimic.com**) for permission to use your excellent scans.

To Image Trends (**www.imagetrendsinc.com**) for the very effective ShineOff.

To Michael Comet (**www.comet-cartoons.com**) for his amazing Comet Tools.

To Brian Escribano (**www.meljunky.com**) for your very handy Joint Splitter tool.

To Melinda Troughton of Endless Reference (**www.endlessreference.com**) for providing such useful and abundant animation reference.

To Brian Horgan (**www.graphite9.com**) for your tremendous bhGhost tool.

To Andy Turner and James Busby of PanoCapture (**www.panocapture.com**), Andreas Reimer of HDRI Hub (**www.hdri-hub.com**), and Christian Bloch of HDR Labs (**hdrlabs.com**) who have all captured such great lighting material.

Once again, without the help and support of those mentioned above, this book would still be a bunch of ideas in a notebook.

Jahirul Amin

Bibliography

Beverley Hale, Robert. *Drawing Lessons from the Great Masters*. New York: Watson-Guptill Publications, 1964.

Goldberg, Eric. *Character Animation Crash Course!* Los Angeles: Silman-James Press, 2008.

Goldfinger, Eliot. *Human Anatomy for Artists*. Oxford: Oxford University Press, 1991.

Richer, Dr. Paul. *Artistic Anatomy*. New York: Watson-Guptill Publications, 1986.

Rogers Peck, Stephen. *Atlas of Human Anatomy for the Artist*. Oxford: Oxford University Press, 1951

Thibodeau, Gary A. *Anatomy and Physiology*. St Louis: Times Mirror/Mosby College Publishing, 1987.

Thomas, Frank, and Johnston, Ollie. *The Illusion of Life*. New York: Disney Editions, 1981.

Tortora, Gerard J., and Anagnostakos, Nicholas P. *Principles of Anatomy and Physiology*. New York: Harper and Row, 1990.

Unay, Jeff, Miller, Erick, Grossman, Rudy, and Thuriot, Paul. *More Hyper-Realistic Creature Creation*. Sybex, 2009.

Williams, Richard. *The Animator's Survival Kit*. London: Faber and Faber, 2001.

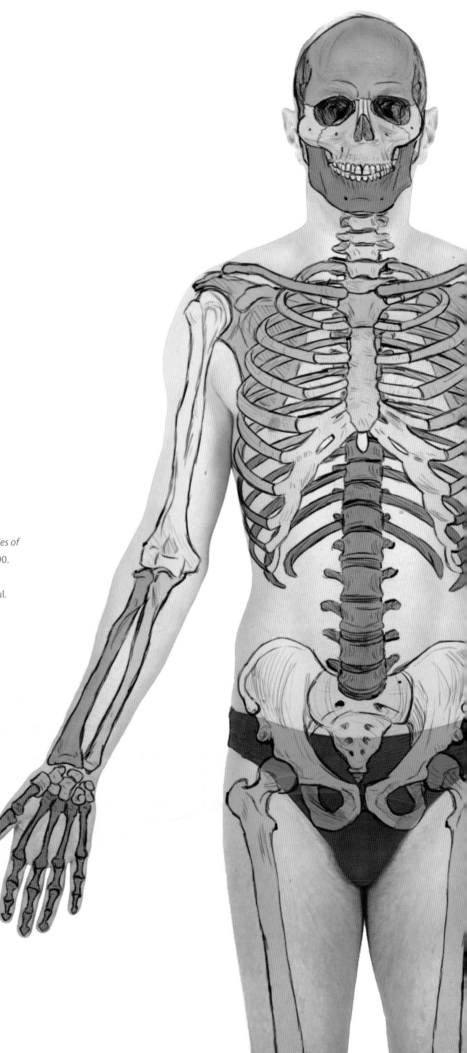

Index

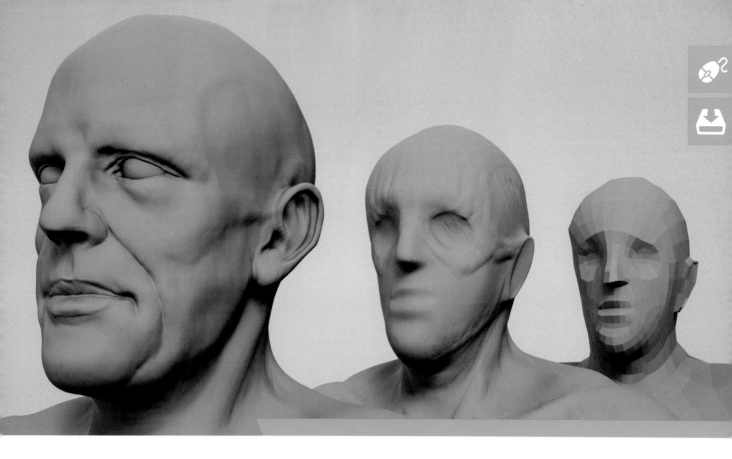

Sculpting the forms

Adding realistic surface anatomy with Mudbox

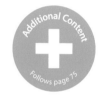

Additional Content

Follows page 75

**We are now ready to push the forms of
the base mesh through sculpting. During
the entire process, always think about the
bony landmarks. If you sculpt over them,
remember to bring them back into play,
even if it's only subtly. This will enforce
this digital asset's sense of anatomy.**

01: Updates to the base mesh

Before we jump into Mudbox or your preferred
sculpting package, I just want to describe a
couple of updates I've made to the base mesh.
First I spent a bit more time pushing the base
geometry to bring it closer to the reference by
simply translating the components. I introduced
an extra edge loop around the phalanges of
each finger and toe, which will allow me to
easily sculpt the webbing between them.

02: Exporting for sculpting

Once you are happy with the base mesh, select
all the geometry in the scene and go to Edit
> Delete By Type > History, followed by Edit >
Modify Transforms > Freeze Transformations.
Next, make sure everything is clearly named

(**paul_geo**, **turntable_geo**, and so on), select
everything in the scene from the Outliner
(including the camera groups), and go to File
> Export Selection. In the dialog box, change
"Files of type" to FBX export and save the
scene file as **01_baseMesh_cameras.fbx**.

03: Setting up the Mudbox cameras

In Mudbox now, go to File > Open and bring
in **01_baseMesh_cameras.fbx**. An error dialog
box will pop up regarding the turntable, but
just hit Keep this Mesh (**Fig.03a**). You can also
go to Display and disable Mesh Errors to hide
the highlighted trouble spots. In the Object

List, lock (or hide) the turntable for now. If you
hold the RMB over one of the cameras that
we created while you're in the Object List,
you can select Look Through to do just that.
Unfortunately, the cameras are not locked
down, so you can also throw off their positions.

To lock a camera down, select it, go to the
Transform tab, and enable Lock Pan, Lock
Rotate, and Lock Zoom (**Fig.03b**). Do this for
all the cameras that we created in Maya. To
get closer to our reference, we can still use
the 2D pan and zoom feature in Mudbox by
holding down the Ctrl+Alt+LMB/MMB or RMB.

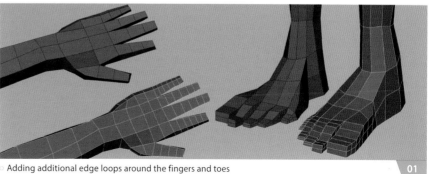

Adding additional edge loops around the fingers and toes

01

04: Setting up camera bookmarks

Rather than holding the RMB over a camera and using Look Through, I'll be using camera bookmarks to switch between the cameras more efficiently. Let's start by creating a bookmark for the Perspective camera. In the Object List, select the Perspective camera. Look through it and position it in a sensible place from which to view the model. Now go to the Camera Bookmarks tab, click on the options icon, and go to Add Camera Bookmark (**Fig.04a**). Call it **persp** and hit OK. Now select **fullBody_camera_0** and repeat the step, ensuring you give it an easily identifiable name.

Repeat the process for all the cameras. You should now be able to switch between the cameras easily with the Camera Bookmarks tab.

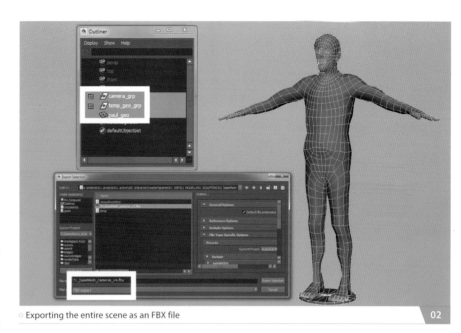

○ Exporting the entire scene as an FBX file   02

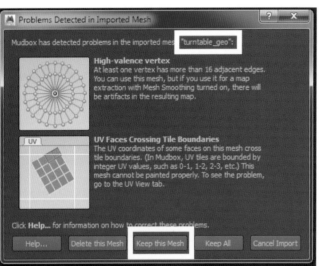

○ The turntable geometry won't agree with Mudbox, but it's not a problem   03a

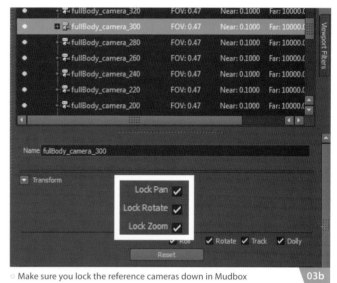

○ Make sure you lock the reference cameras down in Mudbox   03b

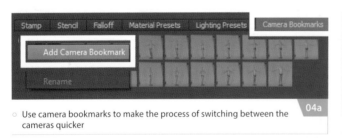

○ Use camera bookmarks to make the process of switching between the cameras quicker   04a

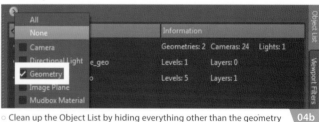

○ Clean up the Object List by hiding everything other than the geometry   04b

🔍 PRO TIP
Send to Maya, Send to Mudbox

I tend to use the File > Export method of transferring data between Maya and Mudbox. It's just my old habits, I guess; plus it allows me to easily store versions and backups. If you'd like to speed up the process slightly, try using the Send to Maya feature in Mudbox and the Send to Mudbox feature in Maya. You'll find both under File. As long as you are using the same version, that is, Maya 2015 with Mudbox 2015, you should be able to transfer and update models very simply.

Go to the options for the Object List and enable None to hide everything in the Object List. Then go back in and only enable Geometry (**Fig.04b**). This just makes the Object List tidier to work with. Save this scene for now as we'll be re-opening it once we've done a couple of tests.

05: Test out the mesh

To test if the base mesh is suitable for sculpting, subdivide the mesh three or four times by hitting Shift+D. Use the Wax brush to lay down a few strokes to see how the mesh reacts. Paint around the chest, face, fingers, and so on, to get an impression of whether it will withstand the pressures of sculpting.

06: Maya to Mudbox workflow

I now want to run through how I work with both Maya and Mudbox simultaneously to create an asset. Start by taking the sculpt back down to its lowest level by hitting the Page Down key on your keyboard, or going to Mesh > Step Level Down. Hold down the spacebar over the mesh (like the hotbox in Maya), hover over the head icon, and go to Select Mesh. Now go to File > Export Selection and save this mesh as an .OBJ file called **paul_modified_lv1.obj**.

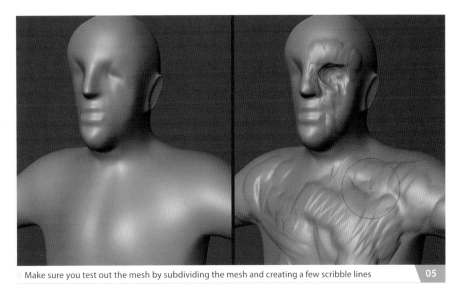

○ Make sure you test out the mesh by subdividing the mesh and creating a few scribble lines   05

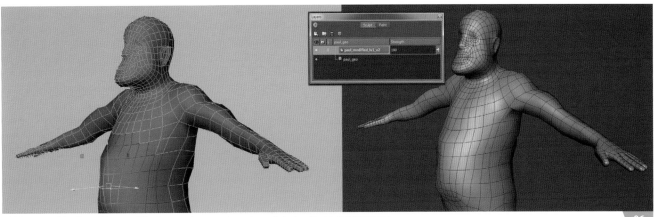

○ Using a combination of Maya and Mudbox can be a great way to work during the sculpting process   06

Jump into Maya, go to File > Export, and bring in **paul_modified_lv1.obj**. Switch to component mode now and move some of the vertices, edges, or faces around. Once you are happy with the changes you have made (anything you feel beneficial will do), export the . model and call it **paul_modified_lv1_v2.obj**.

Back in Mudbox, click on the Options icon for the Sculpt window, go to Import layer, and call in **paul_modified_lv1_v2.obj**. Hit OK when the dialog window pops up and you should see the changes applied to the mesh. You can also use the Sculpt window's Strength slider to decrease, go into the

negative, or over-crank the effects (you have to enter values manually to do this). I find this a pretty useful workflow as some things, such as posing, I prefer to handle in Maya.

07: Reference materials

Before we start laying into the sculpt, I want to share a few of the additional reference images, videos, books, figures, and apps I will be looking at to flesh out the forms.

As mentioned earlier, one of the biggest references will be myself, just as you should be yours. For artistic purposes, I examine myself to get a good feeling for the bones, muscles, tendons, and the fat that makes us who we are.

I have the images of the model, Paul, which I've also turned into videos that I can play on loop to keep me working around the forms and trying to build everything up together. I then have the 3dtotal male anatomical reference figure in front of me as a sanity check (**https://shop.3dtotal.com/figures.html**).

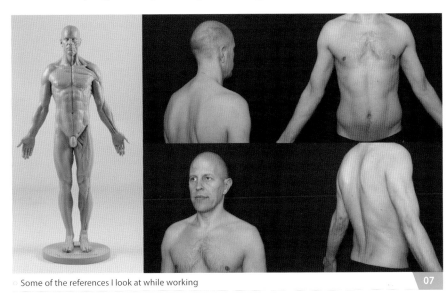

○ Some of the references I look at while working   07

In terms of books, I use *Artistic Anatomy* by Dr. Paul Richer, *Atlas of Human Anatomy for the Artist* by Stephen Rogers Peck, and *Human Anatomy for Artists: The Elements of Form* by Eliot Goldfinger. All of these are amazing and have been indispensable in understanding anatomy.

I also have a couple of medical apps that I refer to here and there: Muscle System Pro III and Skeletal System Pro III. As you can probably guess, I surround myself with references, so that if I'm not sure about anything I can quickly find my way.

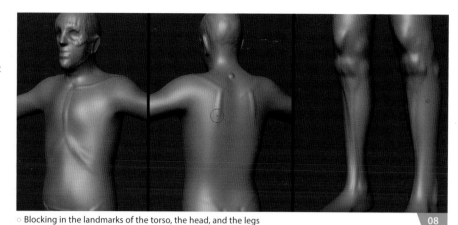

○ Blocking in the landmarks of the torso, the head, and the legs   08

08: Laying down the landmarks

To begin with, I'll be working with symmetry turned on by setting the Mirror attribute to X. This is primarily for the body. Once I get to the face, I'll be turning the Mirror attribute to Off. Now we're all prepped up to start sculpting.

Make sure you're working with the untampered scene that we saved after we set the cameras up. Start by subdividing the mesh to level 4 and then create a new sculpt layer and rename it **landmarks**. Using the Wax brush with the bw_strip alpha stamp and falloff preset 6, begin to block in the bony landmarks. You can use the camera bookmarks and sculpt through the images to guide you on where to lay your marks.

Some areas (such as the pit of the neck or the sacral triangle) will be best created by cutting into the mesh. To do this, hold down the Ctrl key to invert the brushstrokes. Try not to worry about being perfect at

this stage; working loosely will ensure that changes can be easily made.

> "Don't worry about getting every measurement to match the captured data 100% – some inaccuracies are inevitable"

09: Checking the proportions

Create a new sculpt layer and rename it **proportions**. Then switch to the Select/Move Tools tab and select the Caliper tool. Use it to take measurements by LMB-clicking in one position and dragging to another. For example, click from the top of the head to the bottom of the chin.

Compare your findings with the data captured during the photoshoot and make any adjustments using the Grab brush (with Grab Silhouette enabled).

Don't worry about getting every measurement to match the captured data 100% – some inaccuracies are inevitable. Using your eye and your artistic judgment to figure out what "feels" right and what looks good to you is preferable to striving for absolute accuracy.

If you are having trouble pushing the forms, you can always take the lowest resolution of the mesh into Maya, make the changes, and bring it back into Mudbox as a sculpt layer. However, when sending assets between the two packages, it's worth flattening all the sculpt layers in Mudbox before you send the mesh out, otherwise you may get some unexpected results.

10: Using paint layers to create a guide for muscles

The next stage is to start building up the muscle mass. This can be a little overwhelming if it's your first sculpt, so let's create a paint layer

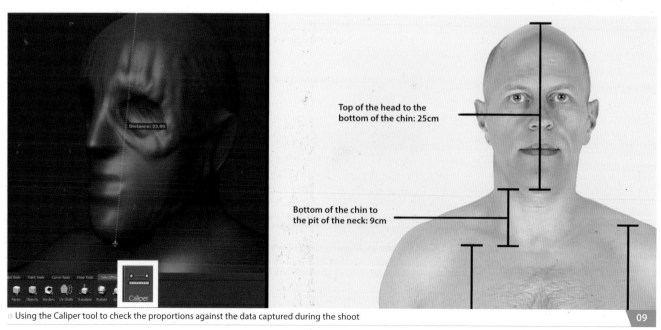

Top of the head to the bottom of the chin: 25cm

Bottom of the chin to the pit of the neck: 9cm

Distance: 23.90

○ Using the Caliper tool to check the proportions against the data captured during the shoot   09

to help guide us along the way. First, use the Page Down key to drop down to level 1 and switch to the UV View. We need to rebuild the current UVs (you've probably noticed they're pretty poor at the minute), so go to UVs & Maps and click Create UVs (Fig.10a). When the dialog window pops up, hit Replace Existing UVs and then leave the number of tiles as 1. You should now get some UVs that you can paint over, but by no means would you use this new UV set in production.

Jump over to the Paint tab and select the Paint Brush from the Paint Tools tab. Click on the mesh now, which should prompt you to

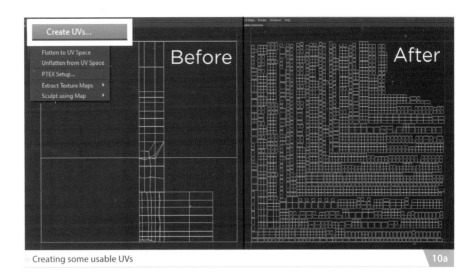

○ Creating some usable UVs 10a

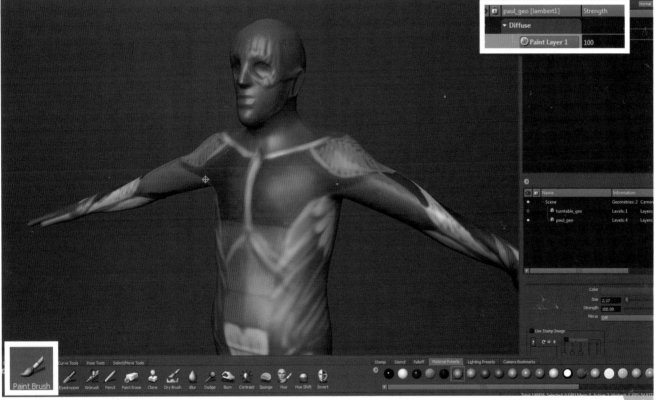

○ A quick paint-over to help lay down the muscles 10b

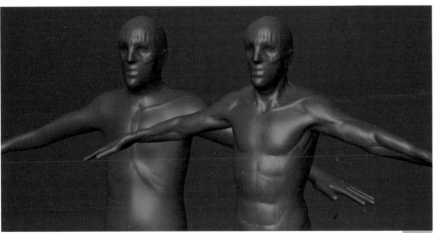

○ Building up the forms of the torso and the arms. Note how the presence of the landmarks stay intact 11a

create a new paint layer. Leave the settings in their default state (Size = 2048, Channel = Diffuse) and click OK. You can now paint over the mesh to block out where the muscle masses will go. I like to switch colors to help differentiate one muscle mass from another (Fig.10b). When you have painted in your guides, lower the Strength of the paint layer slightly so it does not become too distracting.

11: Building up forms with the Wax brush

Using the Wax brush once more, run strokes from the origin points to the insertion point

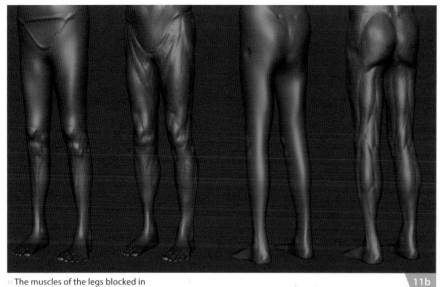

○ The muscles of the legs blocked in   11b

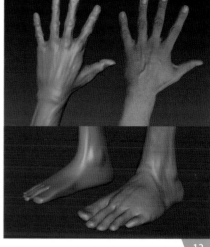

○ Using images as Mudbox Stencils to help block in the hands; the original and current foot   12

to add volume to the form and build up the muscle masses (**Fig.11a**). Focus on the torso, arms, and legs for now (we'll cover the hands and head later) and remember to treat the majority of the muscles as groups (quadriceps, adductors, and so on) (**Fig.11b**).

"Step back from the monitor now and then to get a fresh perspective"

Compare your sculpt's silhouette to the reference images and push any forms back into play with the Grab brush. If something isn't working, flatten out the troubled region by inverting the Wax brush or using the Flatten brush and rework it. Step back from the monitor now and then to get a fresh perspective.

12: Working on the hands and feet

For the hands and feet, I again rely on the Wax brush to build up forms, focusing on the relationship between bones and fat. I also separate the fingers slightly by taking the mesh (at level 1) into Maya, moving the vertices around, and returning that mesh to Mudbox as a sculpt layer. I also add a reference image of the hands (via the Stencil tab) in Mudbox to help line the fingers up more accurately. I tackle the feet the same way, making an effort to create distinction between the bony forms and the fleshy forms.

13: Working on the face

To prepare for the face, I jump back into Maya, set up some cameras (in the same way we did for the full body), and export them

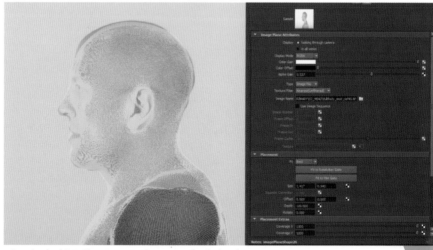

○ Jumping back into Maya to create the cameras for the head   13a

into Mudbox with the reference images attached. I make sure all the cameras line up with the model (or as closely as can be) and then create some camera bookmarks to switch between the new cameras (**Fig.13a**).

Again, I rely on the Wax brush to develop most of the forms, but also use the Grab brush here and there to push the silhouette. For instance, parts of the lips need pushing back in the lateral aspect and the Grab brush handles this just fine.

At this stage, I also start to develop the fat that lies on the face and the natural folds such as the nasolabial fold (**Fig.13b**). Remember: top half = bony, bottom half = fleshy. I also disable Symmetry during this stage so I can create a better likeness of Paul.

14: Working on the ears

To build up the ears, I drop the mesh down to the lowest subdivisions, use the Grab brush to pull the ears slightly away from the main

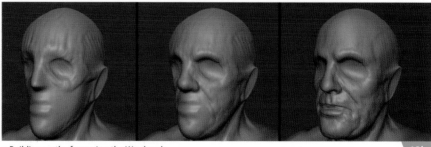

○ Building up the face using the Wax brush   13b

mesh, and finally reshape them to better match the reference. I use the Wax brush and sculpt through the reference cameras to block in the core forms of the ear, such as the helix, antihelix, tragus, and lobe. I then invert the Wax brush to cut into the mesh and around the ear to make it look less "stuck on". I handle the ears individually, as you'll notice that one of Paul's ears is slightly larger than the other, and I want to incorporate this into the sculpt.

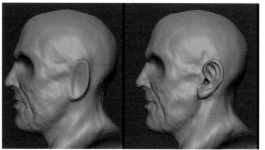
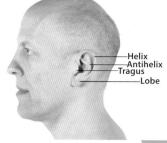

Helix
Antihelix
Tragus
Lobe

○ Blocking in the ear by paying attention to its major anatomical structures 14

15: Working on the eyes

For the eyes, I create a couple of spheres in Maya and position them accordingly, then export them back into Mudbox so I can sculpt around them. Using the camera bookmark that looks directly at the front of the face, I use the Wax brush to very roughly draw the outlines of the upper and lower eyelids. I continue to build up the forms and then switch to the Move tool to pull out the forms so they wrap around the eyeball geometry (**Fig.15a**).

Moving back to the Wax brush, I invert its behavior to cut into the mesh and create a rough cavity for the eyeball to sit in (**Fig.15b**). This allows me to create a tighter "ledge" around the eye and add the detail of the caruncula and the plica semilunaris (the vestigial third eyelid).

As I continue to push the forms around the eyes and brows, I find that I begin to get some tearing, mainly around the crease of the upper lid. For this reason, and also because the eyes are already at a good stage, I decide to leave them for the moment. Later down the track, once the mesh is retopologized, we can always come back and improve things if need be.

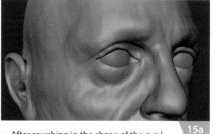

○ After roughing in the shape of the eye I sculpt the region around a sphere 15a

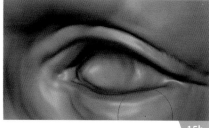

○ Using the Wax brush to create a cavity for the eyeball to sit into 15b

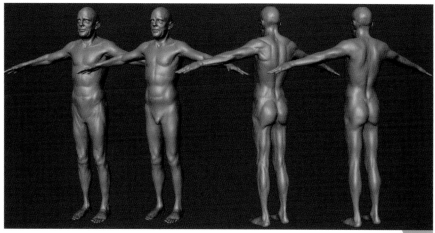

○ Once you've sculpted in the forms of the muscles, add evidence of fat 16

16: Adding the fat and finishing up

At this stage, you should hopefully have a mesh that captures a likeness of the reference images, but lacks a bit of fat. Let's add that fat now. I use the trusty Wax brush and work around the entire form, adding the effects of skin draping over the underlying structure. I blend the muscles together to create groups, rather than leaving them as individual muscles. Make sure the bony landmarks remain intact and present in some shape or form.

By sculpting very lightly with the Wax brush, I start to add some softness without losing all the roughness. The Smooth brush can be used for this, but I find it makes things feel too soft. With the fat added on top, make sure you check the model against numerous reference cameras to make sure it still matches as much

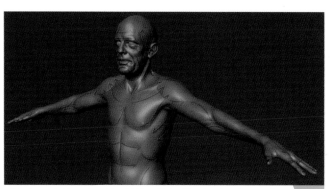

○ Create a paint layer to add guidelines that will make retopology easier 17a

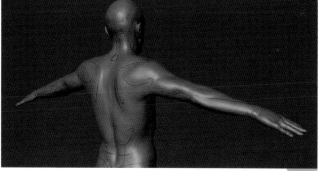

○ Blocking in the proposed major edge loops of the back 17b

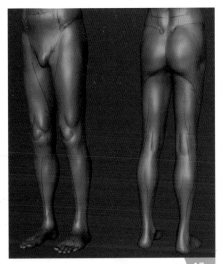

o Blocking in the proposed major edge loops of the legs

17c

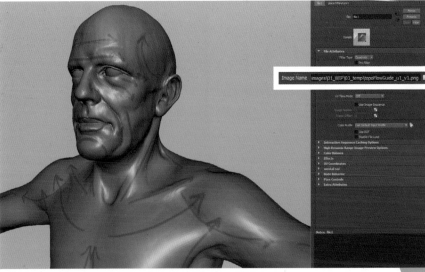

o Apply the topology guide as a texture map to the shader in Maya

18

as possible. If needed, use the Grab brush to get the sculpt back in line with the reference.

17: Painting a topology map

We could export this model into Maya now and begin retopologizing the mesh, but first let's paint a map to guide us during the process. Switch to the Paint tab and create a new Diffuse channel. Change the color to a mid-gray and flood the paint layer by clicking on the Paint Brush tool, sliding down the Attributes window for the tool, and clicking on the Flood Paint Layer button.

Switch colors and paint some guidelines that follow the muscle and skin flow (**Fig.17a**). Using wrinkle lines as a guide is also good to do, as it allows you to create the natural lines that occur

on the body during articulation. The closer you plan your model to flow with edge loops that mimic muscle, skin, and wrinkles, the better the deformation should be (**Fig.17b**, **17c**).

Once you're happy with the topology draw-over, hold down the RMB over the paint layer, go to Export Selected, and save this map into the sourceImages/01_ WIP directory (I pop it into a new folder in here called **03_temp**). Call the map **topoFlowGuide** and save it as a .PNG file.

18: Export and import

We now want to send the mesh over to Maya. First, make sure the mesh is a level 4, then hold the RMB over the mesh and go to Select Model. Then go to File > Export Selection and save him in the 01_MODELLING_SCULPTING/03_sculpt/

objFbxMa_files directory. Save the sculpt as an .OBJ file and rename it **paul_lv4_latest**.

In a new Maya scene, go to File > Import and bring in the **paul_lv4_latest.obj** file. Bring in the eyes that were previously created and rename all the geometry appropriately. Hold the RMB over the sculpt and go to Assign Favorite Material > Blinn. In the Attribute Editor (Ctrl+A), find the blinn1 tab and click on the checkered (input) icon to the right of the Color attribute.

When the dialog window pops up, select File. This should take you to a file1 tab. In here, click on the folder icon next to Image Name and select the **topoFlowGuide.png** file. If you now hit the 6 key on the keyboard, you'll see the painted map in the viewport.

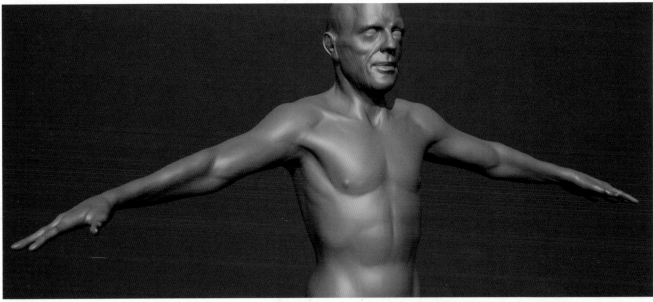

o The model after defining the anatomical forms and fat

Now return to page 76 to retopologize the model »

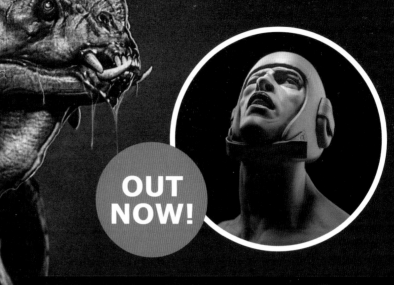
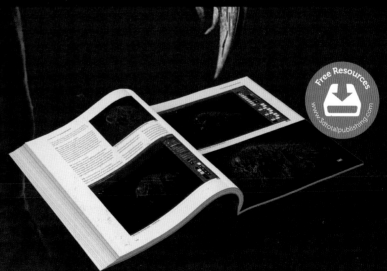

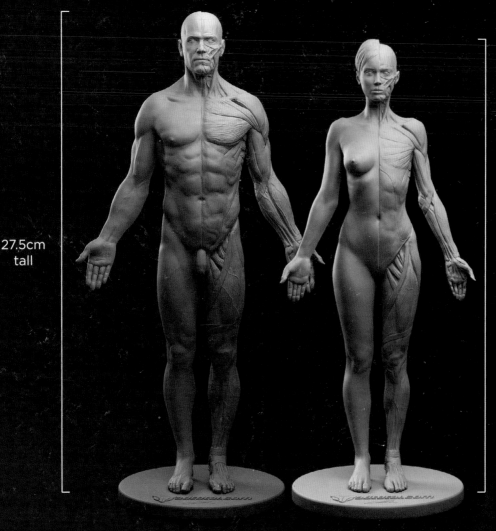

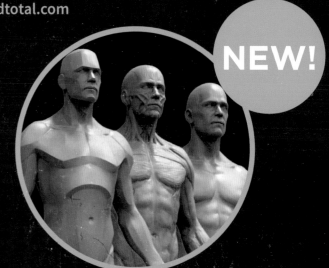